MADRID

MADRID
A NEW BIOGRAPHY

LUKE STEGEMANN

YALE UNIVERSITY PRESS
NEW HAVEN AND LONDON

For information about this and other Yale University Press publications, please contact:
U.S. Office: sales.press@yale.edu yalebooks.com
Europe Office: sales@yaleup.co.uk yalebooks.co.uk

Set in Adobe Caslon Pro by IDSUK (DataConnection) Ltd
Printed in Great Britain by Clays Ltd, Elcograf S.p.A

Library of Congress Control Number: 2024938783

ISBN 978-0-300-27633-6

A catalogue record for this book is available from the British Library.

10 9 8 7 6 5 4 3 2 1

To my beloved daughter Eva

Contents

Illustrations

1 & 2. *Plano de Madrid* (*Map of Madrid*), by Pedro Teixeira, 1656.

3. Emir Mohamed I Park, photo by Maya Balanya, 2015. Album / Alamy.

4. El Escorial, photo by Michael Runkel, 2022. robertharding / Alamy.

5. *Calle de Alcalá*, by Antonio Joli, 1750. Jimlop collection / Alamy.

6. Aerial view of the Plaza Mayor, 2019. Roy Johnson / Alamy.

7. *La Cometa* (*The Kite*), by Francisco de Goya y Lucientes, 1777–8. © Museo Nacional del Prado.

8. *Vista de Madrid desde la pradera de San Isidro* (*View of Madrid from the Meadow of San Isidro*), by Aureliano de Beruete, 1909. © Museo Nacional del Prado.

9. Royal Palace of Madrid, 2009. JLImages / Alamy.

10. Cibeles Fountain, photo by Figurniy Sergey, 2016. Zoonar GmbH / Alamy.

11. *Proclamación de la II República Española, 14 de abril de 1931* (*Proclamation of the Second Spanish Republic, April 14, 1931*), photo by Alfonso Sánchez Portela, 1931. © DACS 2024 / Photographic Archives Museo Nacional Centro de Arte Reina Sofia.

12. Victims of street fighting in Madrid during the Spanish Civil War. World History Archive / Alamy.

13. Noviciado Metro station, Calle de San Bernardo, 1955. Album / Alamy.
14. *Celia y May en la sala Rock-Ola, Madrid* (*Celia and May at Rock-Ola, Madrid*), photo by Miguel Trillo, 1983. © DACS 2024 / Photographic Archives Museo Nacional Centro de Arte Reina Sofia.
15. Plaza Santa Ana at night, photo by Rene Mattes, 2010. mauritius images GmbH / Alamy.
16. Skyline of Madrid with the Sierra de Guadarrama, photo by Fernando Astasio, 2023. Fernando Astasio / Alamy.

Maps

Acknowledgements

My heartfelt thanks to all those who have provided research assistance, advice or personal support throughout the writing of this book: Antonio Jiménez Barca, Juan Manuel Molina, Ignacio Peyró, Ana Bustelo, Pedro Calvo-Sotelo, Montserrat Ginés Gibert, Ana Palacio, David Jiménez Torres, Alejandro Castellote, Arturo Lezcano, Carmen Pérez Romero, Juan Claudio de Ramón, Adolfo García Ortega, Daniel Gascón, Carol Álvarez, Bárbara Ruiz Parra, Vega Yubero, Nicolas Rothwell and Elspeth Menzies. I am grateful for the extraordinary professionalism of the editorial and production teams at both Yale University Press in London and Espasa in Madrid.

As always, to Encarna and Eva.

The research for this book was delayed by international shutdowns between 2020 and 2022. During this time, access to the virtual library of the Instituto Cervantes in Sydney, courtesy of director Coral Martínez and librarian María Magariños Casal, proved invaluable.

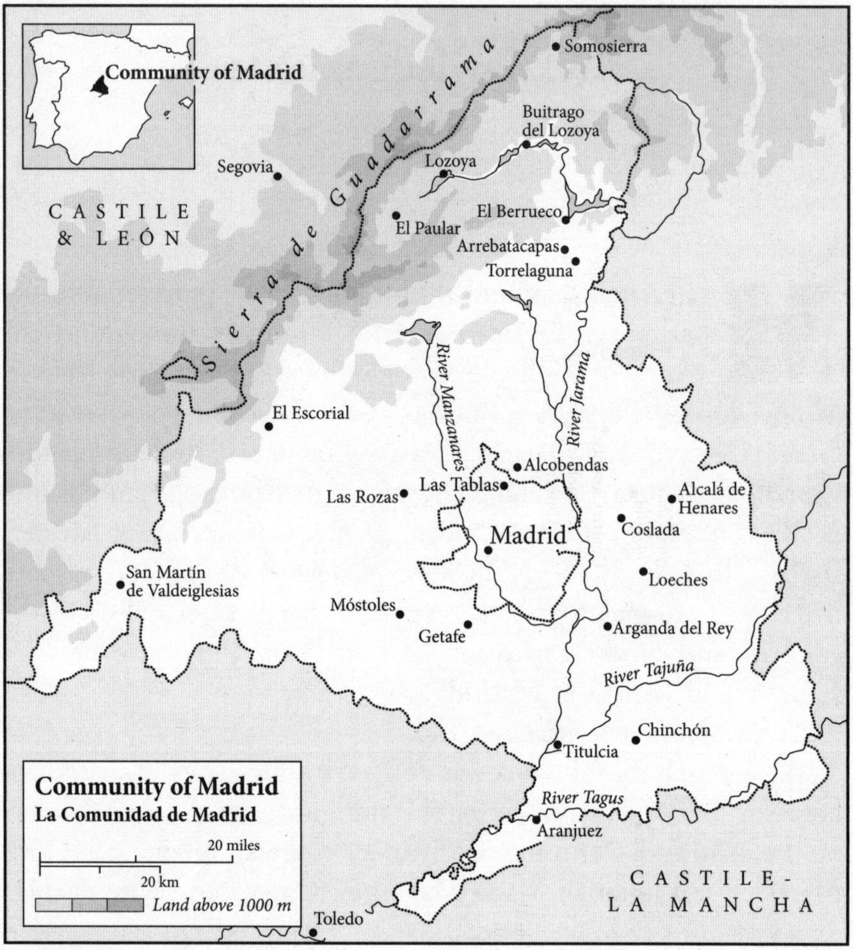
Community of Madrid
Somosierra
Buitrago del Lozoya
Lozoya
Segovia
Sierra de Guadarrama
CASTILE & LEÓN
El Paular
El Berrueco
Arrebatacapas
Torrelaguna
River Manzanares
River Jarama
El Escorial
Alcobendas
Las Tablas
Las Rozas
Alcalá de Henares
Coslada
Madrid
San Martín de Valdeiglesias
Loeches
Móstoles
Getafe
Arganda del Rey
River Tajuña
Chinchón
Titulcia
River Tagus
Aranjuez
Community of Madrid
La Comunidad de Madrid
20 miles
20 km
Land above 1000 m
CASTILE-LA MANCHA
Toledo

1. The Community of Madrid.

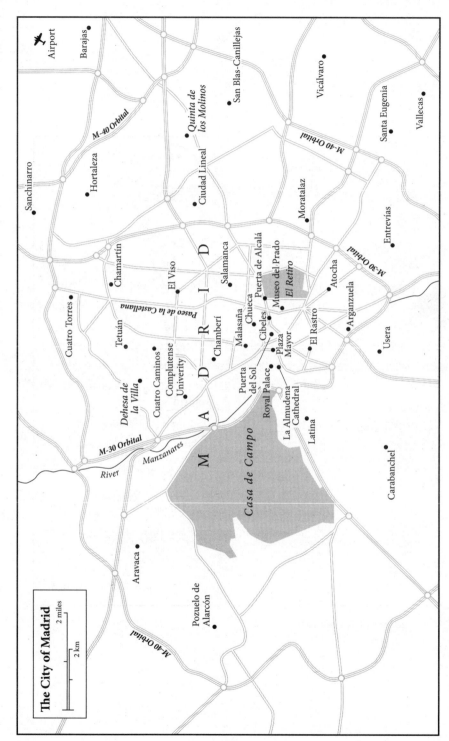

2. The City of Madrid.

A note on usage

Spanish personal names are preferred (Felipe, Juana, Enrique) as are the names of towns (Cádiz,Córdoba, Alcalá de Henares), with the exceptions of Lisbon and Seville. Spanish names are preferred for geographical features such as rivers or mountains, with the exception of the River Tagus. English names are used for regions and provinces (Navarre, Castile, Leon, Aragon, Catalonia).

Unless otherwise indicated, all translations from Spanish sources are the author's own.

A city remembered, a city imagined

Built on the high central plains of the Iberian Peninsula, Madrid – dynamic and thrilling, steeped in over a thousand years of culture and history – remains largely unknown. One of the great cities of the world, and the most important metropolis in southern Europe, Madrid has been a neglected and undervalued European capital. Despite its remarkable social and political history, its monumental architecture, its magnificent landscapes and sunlit vistas, and all the cultural treasures contained within both the city and eponymous province of Madrid, for hundreds of years foreign travellers as well as native Spaniards found endless fault with the unlikely capital: dirty, ugly, barren, shambolic. Neither Spain nor Madrid were part of the nineteenth century Grand Tour; only a limited selection of travellers took on the apparent hazards of the Iberian Peninsula. Madrid lacks, the legend goes, the grace of Moorish forms or the clever lines of modernism; it is without a beach or port or substantial river. Dry, bulldozed, concreted. In addition, Madrid is a city constantly tearing down and being remade. Its truly old buildings are in rare supply, albeit the path of its medieval walls can still be traced along certain narrow, sinuous streets of the old centre, and here and there remnants of its ninth- and tenth-century Islamic walls break through the modern crust of the city like a scattering of dinosaur bones.

To the dismissive disdain, combined with opportunistic folk-lorism, of French, British and North American observers from the seventeenth to the nineteenth centuries, one might add the friendly fire of national authors such as Pío Baroja, Manuel Azaña or Camilo José Cela. Madrid was an inhospitable city, boring, sterile and chaotic. At around the same time as the mother of writer and broadcaster Arturo Barea was working as a laundress, washing clothes in the Manzanares, Baroja described it as an 'unsightly, tragic and sinister river; foul-smelling, black with the refuse of the city's sewers, a river that carried along foetuses and dead cats . . .' Much the same may have been said of the Seine or the Thames in those earlier years, when rivers carried the bulk of human waste to the sea. Yet those rivers are cloaked in myth and literary legend, a fortune that has always escaped the ill-treated Manzanares.

How everything changes. The stereotype of Madrid as a graceless city of reactionary generals and slow-moving civil servants has been replaced by a splendid, thriving and cosmopolitan city with centuries of cultural heritage and outstanding artistic achievement as its bedrock. Twenty-first-century Madrid, untroubled by the neglect to which it has often been subject, has cast off its apparently dull clothing to become a place of beauty. Madrid now takes maximal advantage of its extraordinary cultural vitality and wealth – the city boasts over 1,800 monuments, 200 historic buildings and 70 museums, among them a superb new Gallery of Royal Collections and the finest art museum in the world, the Museo del Prado. Meanwhile, other elements, such as global finance and digital technologies, have come to the fore to assist in the reinvention of the Spanish capital, attracting strong inflows of both capital and population. Madrid's natural setting of clean air and usually clear skies, 650 metres above sea level at the base of the Sierra de Guadarrama, has always been privileged, and the backdrop of that spectacular mountain range looms large in the visual reframing of the capital. The shiny algorithms of social media have turned a loving face to Madrid, more confident than ever in its status as one of the world's great cities: vistas now open out that have never been available, from the rugged walls of the Islamic fortress to the freshly imagined streets of baroque Madrid at the zenith of Habsburg rule, through the legacies of its French and Italianate eighteenth-century, splendid nineteenth- and early twentieth-century architecture, to the glassy, twenty-first-century skyscrapers, manifestations of the contemporary power of finance, technology and invention. These stand as cut-outs against the brazen orange of the western sky; beyond, the snow-capped Guadarrama mountains. A full moon favours the photographers who gather to celebrate this remarkable new vision of Madrid for social media: a soaring capital, reinventing itself and embracing digital futures while still framed by ancient mountains and the eternal sky. Or seen from now ubiquitous drones, hovering with guile above the city: Madrid as a triumph of human creativity, a zigzagging accumulation of centuries of cultural endeavour. Here are the epic landscapes of war and politics, of social experiment and upheaval.

These visions contain all the doubt supposed by glossy appearances: they flatter and bend reality and yet, under all the narcissistic embroidery of a new media lens, they contain a fundamental truth. For Madrid is indeed remarkable, endlessly alive and beautiful. Centuries of imperial and analogue dust have been washed away and a different Madrid has emerged: as crowded and urgent as ever, while also scrubbed, polished, splendid. No longer forlorn or neglected, twenty-first-century Madrid is cosmopolitan in a way it has never been before, not even when, in the sixteenth and seventeenth centuries, it was the capital of a transcontinental empire.

One of the countless pleasures of living in Madrid is to be steeped in legend: to walk daily in the footsteps of majesties, murderers and the infinite anonymous; to shadow a disreputable bishop, a duchess, a lady in waiting; to wander the same streets as novelists and painters, revolutionaries and utter bastards. Along a street of broad footpaths lined with graceful shops, a street tight with trees reaching their freshly sprung crowns up to second- and third-storey balconies, I recall a morning in late March, a sense of newness and *primavera* in the air. A lovely street in the middle-class district of Chamberí, full of sunshine, blossom and beauty. The Madrid sky, as so often, bluely splendid. Passing cars purred; buses chuckled rather than growled. At that moment I was contemplating an upcoming summer which would involve work trips to New York and Berlin, which was then still riven by the Wall. The world and I were young, and it was very heaven. It was 1989 – a year both formidable and unforgettable anywhere in Europe. Years later, the memory of this apparently innocent street scene, on that particular day and at that particular time of life, became mixed up with a different image, that of a sickly gentleman being beaten up along the same stretch of road. Drawn from the most famous of Madrid novels, Benito Pérez Galdós's *Fortunata y Jacinta*,[1] it was a scene age and distance had rendered more squalid, and reduced to sepia tones. This vision, full of shadow and threat, emerged not from personal experience but from a literary memory combining the menace of a street thug with a contradictory feeling towards the fallen man: both compassion and disdain. This was late nineteenth-century Madrid, and the assaulted man was the vaguely ridiculous Maximiliano Rubín, a weakling husband being thrashed in the street by his wife's lover. Such were those vanished days when a gentleman's honour was held in high esteem: fought over, easily lost, rarely recovered. Ignominy was a fate from which few might return.

Even allowing for the treacherous fondness with which we look back upon moments of our youth, the memory has largely held good: that sun-drenched street in central Madrid remains as lovely as my youth supposed, albeit the commercial profile has changed and its dimensions have shrunk with the perspective of time. Impossible not to recall the words scrawled on a scrap of paper found in the wretched gabardine pocket of poet Antonio Machado[2] – with whom fate had been equally wretched – upon his death in exile: 'Estos días azules y este sol de la infancia.' *These blue days, this childhood sunshine*. Elemental things from our earlier, surely happier days, bathed in the warm light of nostalgia: deceitful yet comforting.

Insignificant and insubstantial, one nevertheless adds one's own weight to the history of the city, to its periods of apparent coma and those of great bloodshed; of wretchedness and conspiracy; of darkness and bright reform. I remember vividly how happy I had been under those spring-green trees and in that clean light of a

Madrid morning, along the very section of road – Santa Engracia, leading to Ríos Rosas and Cuatro Caminos – where Maximiliano Rubín had been assaulted in the latter part of the nineteenth century, at a time of horse-drawn carriages and dingy street lamps. Where I had glowed with health and youth, under a blue sky, full of the future, Maxi had been as feeble as the lamplight under which he fell, groaning and humiliated in the close evening, his chest crushed by an insolent boot before being tossed, semi-conscious, into a vacant lot.[3]

'Things may have turned out any other way, and yet they happened just like this.' So runs the famous opening line of Miguel Delibes's *El camino*, one of the most beloved of twentieth-century Spanish novels. As things transpired, my great expectations came to naught. That summer, I reached neither New York nor Berlin, but remained in Madrid. In hindsight, it was the best possible outcome. As a citizen from the furthest antipodean reaches of the European imperial adventure, and with no ancestral connection whatsoever to the country, Madrid has always been the principal lens through which I have observed the rich, bewildering and infinitely generous universe of Spain. Three years before taking up residence in the city, I had made a brief visit, arriving one morning in 1984 at Atocha station on an overnight train from Lisbon. In the full light of morning and putting Atocha behind me, I walked past an ugly and rowdy concrete overpass, popularly known as the Scalextric,[4] and up into the heart of the old city. I was not, like many travellers in literature, seeking meaning, enlightenment, justice, love, revenge, wealth or pleasure. I was sleepy and, like countless others before me and countless others since, entered Madrid by ascending the Calle Atocha with all its din and flux, its clutter of cheap restaurants and rooming houses, its family businesses, bars, churches and traffic. It was a plain introduction as far as these things go, entering the unkempt capital anonymously, and without any moment of epiphany.

'Madrid, of all capital cities in the world, is the most difficult to understand,' wrote one of her famous native sons, the literary modernist Ramón Gómez de la Serna.[5] Why might this be? The city is deceptive: Madrid's treasures are broader and deeper, its history more abundant, its culture more nuanced and sophisticated, than might first appear. Few people, for example, recognise Madrid as the only European capital with an Islamic foundation. The city is magnificent without being *obviously* so; from never bothering too much about its reputation – Madrid has often paradoxically combined enormous pride with a lack of self-esteem – it has held its secrets close to its chest. 'In its layout, its monuments and the imperial grandeur of much of its official architecture,' wrote Deborah Parsons in her brief cultural history of the city, 'Madrid bears testimony to a succession of more or less autocratic rulers and regimes.'[6] This, she suggested, left Madrid beyond the righteous and mostly democratic paths of European modernity, which were politically progressive, forward-looking and comfortable with plurality. Madrid's modern evolution has not followed that of the 'paradigmatic' cities of Paris, London and New York; the city has developed in its own way, outside the conventional parameters of 'urban modernity' as demanded by the examples of more famous western capitals.

Therein lies one of its greatest strengths. What for some is proof of waywardness, is for others proof of originality. Gómez de la Serna's observation confirms the long puzzle of Madrid: it has indeed been resistant to interpretation. Despite being the centre of a Hispanic mandala whose arms are flung and gyred around the globe, Madrid has remained somewhat obscure, even cryptic; a city flooded with beautiful light has remained dark, an essentially *untranslatable* phenomenon. It is extraordinary how many accounts of the European twentieth century largely ignore the city; even a tome as brilliant and comprehensive as Tony Judt's *Postwar* has next to nothing to say about Madrid. On home soil, historically there have been the occasional nostalgic social and intellectual currents in Madrid opposed to any 'foreign' influences that might affect the cultural purity of the city: a pre-industrial *castizo*[7] wonderland both imagined and remembered, untroubled by modernity or global forces. Years of relative international disdain originated in the sixteenth century with northern European rivalry and hostility to generations of Spanish monarchs and their armies. There has likewise been a predictable domestic hostility: while local residents often display a weary cynicism about their city, elsewhere in Spain expressing contempt for Madrid and its *madrileños* is a national pastime, especially common among nationalists of the peninsular peripheries. No greatness without attendant jealousy.

'Baroque, festive, sleepless, ferocious, friendly and cruel: Madrid is a city built by those who arrived to heal wounds, to rise and prosper.'[8] Madrid is the most generous of lovers, but it is a love that requires the patience that precedes all rich rewards; a love that must be earned. The city was not only a summery text, blue-skied, hot and benevolent, full of life for a young man from the other end of the world, a city bursting with history, art and music, boasting the twin treasures of a beautiful language and an overwhelmingly generous people; it was equally a winter parchment whose folds contained the grind of hard work, loneliness, heartbreak and despair. There is no romance involved in standing in the winter morning dark, breathing the diesel fumes of buses, heading exhausted – sleepless – and crumpled for a day's work; there is no romance in chronic traffic jams, the choke and press of overheated Metro carriages. It can be a city with which one does not immediately fall in love: 'In Madrid there is nothing to do, nowhere to go, nothing to see,' wrote former prime minister Manuel Azaña as far back as 1920. 'Madrid is a town without history. In Madrid nothing has happened because in two centuries almost nothing has happened in Spain, and the little that has occurred has done so elsewhere.'[9] Azaña was writing at a time of political upheaval and soul-searching for many Spanish intellectuals,[10] and his comments must be placed in this context, not least as he was someone who avidly sought Madrid and its literary-political circles. As well as being a tragic figure lost in the black hole of a civil war that dragged so many names from public life, Azaña was wrong: Madrid was packed with adventure and incident during those two centuries he dismisses as so dull. The nineteenth century might have been chaotic, and opportunities for social progress missed, even wilfully overlooked, but the city was never boring.

Azaña's complaint was part of a centuries-long tradition. The charge of plainness, a way of overlooking the extraordinary nuances and beauties of Madrid, has been constant: 'Madrid may not grab you at first', wrote Elizabeth Nash in her cultural history of the capital; it has 'few splendid buildings or views'.[11] This is completely untrue, but the point stands that this is how many first perceive Madrid. The city 'isn't easy to know' despite the extraordinary openness of its people. 'The unquestionable ugliness of Madrid is part of its beauty,' asserted Andrés Trapiello, a writer from northern Spain who long since made the capital his home.[12] 'Madrid ... comes in a poor second to other majestically sophisticated cities,' wrote Michael Ugarte in *Madrid 1900*, his study of late nineteenth- and early twentieth-century literature in the Spanish capital.[13] In similar vein, 'Madrid is a strange place ... I do not believe anyone likes it much when he first goes there. It has none of the look that you expect of Spain,' wrote Ernest Hemingway in *Death in the Afternoon*, a book both deeply flawed and anthropologically fascinating.[14] Hemingway may have been responsible for any number of dreadful clichés about the country, while at the same time being critical of other writers – pretentious mystics, apparently – who set down their impressions of Spain. Yet amid the storm of chaff there are grains of worth. After whining that in its functional modernity Madrid lacks the touristic colour one seeks in other Spanish towns, Hemingway admits: '... when you get to know it, it is the most Spanish of all cities, the best to live in, the finest people, month in and month out the finest climate ...'[15] Papa then adds fuel to a long-burning and apparently never-to-be-quenched fire by remarking that while other Spanish provincial cities are representative of their regions, the essence of the country as a whole is only to be found in Madrid. This always controversial statement remains to a large extent true: for centuries, Madrid has attracted and retained citizens from around the peninsula, their multiple backgrounds and traditions all finding a home in the capital. Putting aside Hemingway's dubious and intangible notion of a 'national essence', like all major contemporary cities Madrid has had elements of its character dissolved by the uniformity of global capital with its ubiquitous brands, conforming social trends and apparently unstoppable gentrification.

The national capital makes for perfect target practice. A capital city by royal decree, many have argued – wrongly – that the city lacks historical merit, that its rise was fortuitous rather than virtuous. Madrid has been seen as a Castilian upstart, variously cast as a bullying, centralising and reactionary thug among Spanish cities. Once the centre of a global empire – in the sixteenth century, the largest the world had ever known – it later hosted the twentieth century's first major fight against fascism and then one of its most enduring dictatorships. Madrid is inevitably a metonym, a target for grievance against perceived Castilian oppression and greed, and against the Spanish state more broadly. Viewed as ground zero for Spanish nationalist arrogance, it additionally faces the charge of being the nation's home of political and social conservatism, despite the city's reputation as the site of many of the nation's social revolts and its leading role in the resistance to fascism in the 1930s. Curiously, much of the charge of conservative incorrigibility emerges from regional strongholds such as Catalonia or the Basque region where ruling hierarchies do everything to ensure their anachronistic privileges live on into the contemporary world.

Madrid has also experienced the suspicious fear of Castilian reactionaries: in the 1930s, conservatives of the rural Catholic and urban fascist stripe saw in the city's modernity, industrialisation and capitalism a range of evils, from moral corruption to Marxism: the decadence of luxury and the danger of a politicised working class. Thus, paradoxes abound: Madrid is a bastion of political conservatism and libertarian freedom, *and* one of southern Europe's most progressive and demographically diverse cities. Politically capacious, it is home to conservative local governments and radical social movements; it is part of the greatness of Madrid that the city embraces them both equally.

A significant component of the story of Madrid is the story of power: royal, military, religious and secular, cultural and economic. Indomitable kings, weakling princes, irresolute queens, unscrupulous politicians and demagogues, clerics both cruel and generous, dictators, pretenders and generals all pass across its stage, as do many artists of universal influence. Political and cultural power work side by side with economic and demographic power: Madrid is the seat of the royal court and the national parliament, of the most significant cultural institutions, of national and multinational corporations, and is by some margin the most populous city in Spain.[16] Its power is everywhere, and obvious, yet the story of power is never the whole story; forms and relations of power reveal only a part of any individual, institutional or national reality.

Madrid is both heart and head, as per the custom of medieval manuscripts – before the world was fully scoped and compassed, before the birth of the modern nation – where countries were sometimes drawn fancifully as bodies, with heads and hearts and limbs. These strange maps drew on representations of the City of God where the divine was anthropomorphised, with Christ as the mystic head and citizens as the secular and often corruptible body. Rivers might be sacred arteries, the great circulating system of blood and life; the cramped centres of the city a beating heart, both source of life and site of possible disease. In early visual metaphors of the holy nation of Spain and its God-instructed empire, the most likely candidate for the head, the crown of the mystic body, was the granite symmetry of El Escorial, from which Felipe II directed an empire.[17] Madrid, where most of the administrative apparatus was based, and where much of the scheming and jockeying of lesser mortals was carried out, was the beating heart. 'It was right', wrote chronicler Luis Cabrera de Córdoba, a contemporary of Felipe II, 'that so great a Monarchy should have a city which could function as its heart – a vital centre in the midst of the body, which ministered equally to every State in time of peace and war.'[18] In 1656 Pedro Teixeira, a Portuguese cartographer in the service of Felipe IV, produced a legendary map of Madrid in which the crown stands as the locus of imperial, political power, reaching out to the circumference of the world.

This sentiment caused jealousy in the sixteenth and seventeenth centuries, and little has changed since, given Madrid's historic tendency to attract a significant percentage of internal migration, concentrate national administrative capacities and to be the epicentre of cultural and political institutions, along with modern transport, logistics and finance hubs. Later Spanish rulers may have chosen elsewhere to locate the national capital: Toledo (just as central) and Valladolid had enjoyed short periods as the capital; Córdoba had been the splendid capital of Islamic Spain; Barcelona the major city of a medieval Mediterranean trading empire under the crown of Aragon; and Seville the most important trading centre of the transoceanic empire of the Americas. While many capital cities sit at the geographic edge of their nations, Madrid is placed squarely at the heart, a placement both literal and metaphoric. Opinion is divided as to whether the almost mathematical precision of its centredness played a part in Felipe II's sixteenth-century decision to locate the capital in what was, many considered, an unassuming place. What is certain is that Toledo's missing out on the royal appointment has meant large areas of that marvellous city have been preserved that would otherwise have been attacked, burnt or bulldozed over the intervening five centuries.

Despite being at the epicentre of the Iberian Peninsula, the history of Madrid is not the history of Spain. The relationship between the capital city and its nation is inevitably symbiotic, enduring, deeply complex, webbed and braided across the centuries. Love and antagonism abound in this necessary coupling. Yet for all their closeness, the two entities do not always map onto each other. During the earliest periods of *Spanish* history, Madrid is absent, for it had not yet come into being, other than an anonymous grouping of shepherds and traders dwelling on the central Iberian tableland. The city that grew and the nation that came into being with it are in a constant dialogue, a dialogue that at times resembles a slanging match, a push and pull of mutual loathing and admiration, of repulsion and desire.

In its diverse geography, Spain is a world; in both the national imagination and the national reality things often lead to, or emerge from, Madrid. The city and province have grown from a centuries-long process of mixing of peoples from all over the peninsula, whether resettling agricultural territory in the centuries following the defeat of Islamic forces, or flooding into the capital in search of employment and opportunity, a process that continues unabated in the twenty-first century. The tendency to centralise is nothing new: in Part I of *Don Quixote* the priest, in conversation with the canon from Toledo, wonders, 'if there were some intelligent and sensible person in the capital to scrutinize all plays before they're performed, not only there but anywhere in Spain, and if no local authorities could permit the production of any play without his approval, seal and signature'.[19] Madrid is proposed here not just as a centre of political power, but also as a site of aesthetic quality control, Cervantes's priest preferring stylistic and ideological purity to be sanctioned from the centre as a means to control the wayward peripheries – geographic, conceptual and cultural.

Centuries later, literary and academic narratives of 'the city' emerged with western modernism. The urban, industrial human was a political subject with new homes, lifestyles, webs of community and meaning, systems of order and knowledge, ideas of productivity and forms of alienation; even an array of new Gods. And with the metropolis of the nineteenth and twentieth centuries came new ways of telling: a melody of politics, literature, sociology, urban studies, feminism, class theory and economics. From the marginal to the most embedded relationships of privilege, new ways of telling abandoned faith or religion as explanatory tools, and the city became an analysable patient, full of moods, crises, triumph and despair. The city is catalyst for the deliberate breakage of the old and the birthing of the new; the city is the built, industrial, aesthetic, affective and psychic space – and the site where all may blend, if not collide. There were reactions against the newly forming city in the nineteenth century – the generic city, as well as Madrid specifically – as a breeding ground for multiple sins and spiritual treasons, yet against those who praised the apparently noble and unsullied peasant lifestyle which had been a source, among much else, of cheap labour and cannon fodder, the city presented an unstoppable momentum. For vast numbers of people, the city was now the world, and every idea or mood, technique or desire, found its home among these centres of human invention, of belonging and of solitude.

Madrid's rich history and the path to its present vitality remain poorly known, especially outside the Spanish-speaking world, albeit contemporary tourism is fast changing this historic ignorance of the city. This new enthusiasm for Madrid focuses, understandably, on only a small part of the city; for the foreign visitor, the Madrid that lies beyond the inner city of fabled art collections, palaces, stylish homes, historic parks and gentrified old quarters, spectacular night-life and gastronomy is invisible. Greater metropolitan Madrid is rarely considered an appropriate subject for history, much less the ubiquitous travel guides. A number of towns in the province of Madrid are heavy with legend: Torrelaguna, Chinchón, Buitrago de Lozoya, Aranjuez, San Lorenzo de El Escorial. Others are mostly ignored, true to the division between Madrid the city – royal, governmental, administrative and cultural – and Madrid the prov-ince, a later invention that drew a series of smaller Castilian towns into the larger galaxy of the Spanish capital. Some double as dormi-tory towns, boosting the labour force of the capital; others are known for their summer or winter retreats, their leisure sites, their beautiful natural landscapes, their mausolea.

Such divisions are not only conceptual, but follow historic phys-ical markers. For a thousand years after the Islamic walling of the town in the ninth century, the centre of Madrid was encircled by one form or another of military protection or tariff and customs barrier. In the early 1970s an orbital motorway became the latest iteration of this encirclement. Upon its construction the M-30 wrapped the central area of Madrid and baptised the city as a conventional mid-twentieth-century metropolis. Demarcating the dormitory zones, reinforcing the concept of *extrarradial* (outlying) Madrid, the M-30 quickly became a part of folk history, symbolising the 'bubble' within which live, according to conventional wisdom, the ruling political and financial elites of Spain, ignorant of and oblivious to the realities of the rest of the nation. Once so innova-tive, so wide, so modern, the M-30 is now ageing, superseded by a proliferating web of ring roads and connectors which have served to confirm its status as cultural and historic artefact. Unavoidably, the M-30 played an important role in my first experiences of the city. Navigating its wild flow was part of an initiation: three times a week, over the course of an academic year, I travelled the motorway, a passenger in a red, matchbox-sized car, a chain-smoking Englishwoman with sharp, crooked teeth at the wheel. A relentless talker – much like her Spanish husband – and occasionally perilous driver, she had found in Madrid the ideal environment for an unceasing dialogue. We would enter the traffic flow from the bottom reaches of the Puente de Toledo or Santa María de la Cabeza – historically one of the lowest and most flood-prone areas of the city – and there we swung anti-clockwise, above the now-buried channel of the Abroñigal River, and followed the M-30 in its dense stream all the way to the northern suburb of Alcobendas. There we worked in an industrial estate, teaching English to factory workers whose company imported obscure items from around the world, and boasted significant trading connections with the rest of Europe.

Those factory classes were one of the places where my own education into the city of Madrid began, exposed to the tremendous generosity and humour of those men and women. The trips out to Alcobendas, and similarly to industrial zones in Coslada and Canillejas, were the first lesson that Madrid was a city to be lived in intimate communication with its citizens.[20] While it has always been a city with a rich and often undiscovered history, replete with art collections both glittering and brooding, and relentlessly fascinating politics, a city of brilliant bars, clubs, galleries, markets, architecture and gastronomy, Madrid was above all a city to be enjoyed in the friendship and humour of salons, offices, terrace roofs, living rooms, kitchens and bedrooms; equally in the city centre as among the outlying suburbs and the dull industrial polygons of stunted trees and concrete walls topped with shards of glass and enlivened, at that time, with anti-US and anti-NATO graffiti. Madrid, for all its spectacular offerings for weekend escapees from northern Europe, was also to be found beyond the guidebooks, in those places where people forge their lives without artifice or recognition. On the old No. 9 bus, I travelled for months to and from the (then) outer district of Hortaleza to visit a Galician girlfriend; beyond her apartment stretched yellowing paddocks, a train line, the odd flock of goats. The city, compliant to global capital, is now sprawling and endless, and Hortaleza no longer a distant calling.

These once remote zones where the city fell off into barren fields of grass rising away to nearby mountains – snow-crested, dark blue, dark green – have now been enclosed within a mesh of orbital motorways and business towers – Sanchinarro and Las Tablas – field after field of apartment complexes, shopping malls and a sea of warehousing that stores the infinite exchange of goods which pass through Madrid, in and out of Europe, in and out of Asia, in and out of the Americas, and Africa.

This biography is not only an expression of love; it is also an act of recovery. Nationalist historians may suggest the neglect of Madrid in the literature of the English-speaking world has been deliberate: one cultural dimension of empire wars whose military outcomes were decided long ago. There is an element of truth in this. Other major cities, from colonial outposts to engines of empire, have been more brightly sketched, more broadly drawn: countless volumes extol the thrill and virtue of the great metropolises that cast spells, delight and dazzle, steeped in history or design. Madrid, meanwhile, has tended to be at one remove from dominant narratives or changing fashions: a city seemingly dressed in awkward clothing that nevertheless has always retained the brashness of a capital. For Spanish writers, the city has been absolutely central: extensively explored and appraised, not always flatteringly, by her native sons and daughters, and used as backdrop to countless works of art, literature and cinema. Yet until recently, foreigners have for the most part stayed away from declaring their love for this odd, perhaps unclassifiable jewel upon the high plains of central Iberia.

There is an ongoing political and cultural struggle for the *definition* of Madrid, for the opportunity to guide its present and craft its future, to create the narrative of the city. Always an object of desire, political control of Madrid – no small prize indeed – is the subject of constant debate and sometimes aggressive confrontation. Huge amounts of money, pride and cultural esteem are at stake, as are major infrastructure projects, housing developments and the rolling out of new digital and business environments within one of the most important Hispanic cities in the world. Disputes over ecology, sustainability, political accountability and social justice are often fierce in a city accustomed to strategic and continuous attempts to create 'our' Madrid in the multiple and often conflicting images of those who love the city and call it home. 'Our' Madrid, however, will never be a singular or uniform affair: the city belongs simultaneously to everyone and no one.

'Even the most complete biography', wrote Javier Marías – despite his deserved international reach, a quintessentially Madrid writer – 'is made up of odd fragments and faded scraps' and our lives, or those of whom we write, even as abstract an entity as a city, are replete with 'shadowed zones, episodes both unexplained and inexplicable'.[21] While accepting this simple truth, this biography of Madrid seeks to build a narrative from those odd fragments: the teeming historical, cultural, physical, emotional, political city, with its layered centuries and constant contradictions. This sometimes confounding metropolis, full of great beauty and scattered ugliness, of compassion and deep corruption, of high style and vulgar ordinariness, flows mercurial from the long past into the ever-shifting present. Madrid is an intense concentration of history, ambition, desire, politics, art, style and hedonism; simultaneously generous, ruthless and relentless, it moves to an unstopping and unstoppable pulsebeat. Beyond the 7 million residents of greater metropolitan Madrid, meanwhile, its provincial hinterland boasts wildlife and medieval villages, splendid castles and royal palaces, battle trenches, orchards and forests, clear streams and snow-topped mountains. A city of conflict and triumph, of literary genius, of war and social rebellion, of wonder, agony and pleasure; a city deserving of close description and, above all, of celebration.

Madrid is, in short, a magnificent story waiting to be told.

I

VILLAGE

From the Iron Age to 1516

In Carpetania

By the time of the late Iron Age, some five centuries before the Common Era, a diverse range of peoples were permanently settled on the plains, slopes and sharp ranges of the central Iberian Peninsula. Celts who had crossed the Pyrenees around 1000 BCE merged over time with local Iberian tribes, inhabiting parts of the Duero and Tagus River valleys. In neighbouring Carpetania were the *Carpetani*, the name believed to be of Phoenician origin, 'people of the escarpment'. Like other central Iberian tribes, such as the Vettones or the Oretani, their names have mostly come to us from ancient geographers: Strabo, Pliny the Elder or Ptolemy.

Over time the Carpetani developed small towns such as Toletum (the Roman name given to Toledo) or otherwise simple collections of mud brick and limestone dwellings inside basic protective walls, gathering herds of livestock, always close to reliable sources of water. These were self-contained populations within a confederation, tribes engaged in agriculture and hunting, minor acts of trade or occasional pillage. Their culture moved quickly towards complexity. Adorned with skins and wool, they developed agriculture, jewellery, ceramics and woven cloth; the grinding and storage of grain; simple urban settlement; husbandry of cattle, sheep and goats; from stone to copper, bronze and iron; oxen and the plough; hierarchy, social structure and the symbolic universe; systems of burial; coinage, ownership, property, gods and the rite of seasons.

Early societies thrived in the region of Madrid for the simple reason that life and shelter abound. The centre of the peninsula is a naturally beautiful location, rich with flora and fauna. A series of rivers and streams flowed through the richly watered region: some emerge from distant ranges to the east, others from the close, imposing mountains to the north. They did not yet bear names we know or recognise, but musical names await them all: the Manzanares, Jarama, Henares, Lozoya, Guadarrama, Guadalix, Tajo and Tajuña. Smaller streams flowed through central Madrid with future names every bit as lovely: Abroñigal, Fuente Castellana, Arenal, Butarque, Meaques, Cantarranas, San Pedro and Leganitos. Water – above ground and below – will play a vital role in the development of both the medieval town and modern city.

History is recorded through worked flint and etched remnants, bone needles for sewing, ceramics, simple metals – copper bracelets – or other snatches of jewellery. The relative emptiness of these stretches of the past meets the modern impulse to order and classify, to counter ignorance and impose a set of ideas. 'The structure of pre-Roman "Spain" is almost unknown,' wrote philosopher Julián Marías, and 'far from being an authentic reality, is a hypothesis or a construction of intellectual guesswork, mostly imaginary.'[1] Madrid's Archaeological Museum begs to tell a different story to one of blank invisibility: what Marías – father of novelist Javier – claimed nearly half a century ago has been steadily altered as more and more evidence is dragged from the darkness, polished and examined with sophisticated tools of analysis. For archaeologists and prehistorians there are clues that abound, and the peoples of the Neolithic, Bronze and Iron ages on the Iberian Peninsula are increasingly understood better through deciphered artefacts and artworks. There remain large gaps; for long periods of time there are only occasional glimmers of evidence, even as technology transforms our understanding of nature and culture in those distant times.

In the case of Madrid, a major city has been built over one of the richest archaeological zones of the peninsula. While digs and investigations are carried out in more accessible areas beyond the centre, at sites such as Getafe, Coslada, Parla or Mejorada del

Campo, much of central Madrid's ancient past only emerges by accident. Significant infrastructure projects, such as excavations over recent decades to modernise and bury the M-30 orbital motorway, have revealed great quantities of archaeological evidence adding to the growing knowledge of Neolithic Madrid; clues speak softly through stone tools and pottery of a complex life along the banks of the Manzanares, from the city centre downstream to Villaverde and Butarque. Science always ran behind urban development: the tools for sophisticated diagnosis were only designed long after the city had concreted, sewered and laid bitumen over its fragile prehistory. Elsewhere, human endeavour has silted up or buried many of the musically named waterways. They are still there, only invisible, while the mountains that guard Madrid to the north, fundamental to the droving trails of pre-Roman transhumance, remain impervious, their ecosystems cradled in their heights, skirted by forests and rich pastures.

The shadow of all that was, or has been, exists in quiet but uneven partnership with now. The relics of the earliest settled populations on the site of Madrid lie buried beneath 1,500 years of development. Below the broad avenues and parks, deep below the graceful apartment buildings and the juggernauts of modern capital, below the Metro tunnels, bomb shelters, old wine cellars and bank vaults, below the veiny map of secret passages, below the networks of pipes and channels, the sludge of waste, the centuries of human skeletons, is an immense layering. Under the modern map of Madrid lie worlds that were before: mammoth, wolves, lynx, foxes, deer, a troop of bears; humans attired in skin and fur, with simple ornaments for burial; ceramics decaying back to particulate that speak to old trade routes on the peninsula. The streams that once fed the settlement and its orchards exist now in lightless, cavernous flow. The long, tall drift of generation after generation: the fraying cloth of princes, the stacks of rats' and nuns' bones, the humble awaiting resurrection and the flimsy paper of their prayer books; the dried blood of the murdered; the winding sheets of traitors; dead horses and broken mules; jars of wine or Moorish honey, hand guns, shrapnel, lost coinage, empire silver and a thousand years of masonry all in compacted stillness, the millennia pressed down towards the centre of the earth.

From its snow-capped peaks in the north to the semi-desert plains in the south, the province of Madrid contains much of the geographic diversity to be found across the Iberian Peninsula. To the modern eye, much of this natural beauty has been marred by intense urban-isation, industrialisation and the creation of the vast acreage of warehousing necessary for the distributive networks of global commerce. Yet despite all the complex logistics of modern transport and trade, and the need to house close to 7 million people, Madrid continues to enjoy a spectacular natural setting, with all the untamed zones that loom over the province from the north and north-west. And heading south from the capital it is still possible, barely twenty minutes into a train journey, to be surrounded by the long, dry silence of the plains.

Two diagonals – the furrow of a major river and the risen brow of a mountain range – slant across the misshapen triangle that is the province of Madrid, framing its northern and southern limits. The river is the Tagus (Tajo), the longest of Iberian rivers, on its way from the mountains of Albarracín to its eventual passage through Portugal and into the Atlantic where, Cervantes tells us in the Prologue to Don Quixote, it 'kisses the walls of the famous city of Lisbon'.[2] The Tagus passes peacefully and somewhat lazily through the flatlands at the southern margin of the province, edged with poplar trees and agriculture, before being joined by the Jarama as they head towards Toledo. Two rivers heavy with history, bordered by human societies for thousands of years.

The mountain range that closes the province to the north – a natural barrier that served, even well into the twentieth century, as a strategic stronghold for the defence and protection of the city – is the Guadarrama, a striking range in a peninsula gridded with striking mountains. Its caves have sheltered humans for at least 20,000 years, a home and base camp above the lovely valleys, streams, forests and pastures. In spring and summer the Guadarrama presents beautiful walks for hikers over carpets of wild flower, heath and rocky outcrops, through lovely oaks and pines, chestnuts and juniper, birch and poplar trees. Clear streams, ruined bridges and stone shelters add to the bucolic scenes. Beloved by *madrileños* for generations – since the Romantic turn of the nineteenth century when wild landscapes developed an aesthetic and restorative value – these mountains wear an apparent kindness that can be deceptive: a gentle environment may turn hostile and unforgiving, jagged, snow-bound, icy and treacherous. Pristine lakes sit in high cradles of stone and snow; vultures, eagles, hawks, falcons and kites, sharp-eyed and tilting, look out across the *meseta* – the high central plains – through the capital to the distant south and west, where Madrid gives way to La Mancha. Depending on wind direction and contamination levels the city, its buildings rising like a crown from the plains, may be delineated and clear, or smudged with yellow-brown. The centuries have strewn the Guadarrama with richly descriptive names: Peñalara, La Maliciosa, Risco de los Claveles, la Mujer Muerta, Morcuera or Siete Picos. On the northern face of La Bola del Mundo are mountainsides of grey-green scree, whole sheets of granite; to the south a density of pines, their trunks changing from dark umber to caramel-yellow as they rise into the sky.

Down in the lee of the range, on the outskirts of towns such as Manzanares el Real, Cerceda or Moralzarzal, one witnesses the enormous variety of the province: in the deep calm of late afternoon, amid the dark green of pasture and brighter meadow, horses graze by cold streams and poplar trees, between low fences of stacked granite. Along quiet paths, cattle chew cud beyond time. Cyclists ride their looping way below the famous profile of La Pedriza, amid almond blossom and mossy walls; hikers in orange outfits negotiate a scrubby rise of rockrose; above the great monoliths of granite, the crags, slabs, pillars and deformed boulders – the Tower of Vultures, the Devil's Car – birds of prey draw long curves and tight circles in their pitiless hunt.

While the Iberian Peninsula has always been a geographic fact, it has a specific history as a political or cultural entity. Initially, the only human unity, again according to Julián Marías, 'was that

23

supplied by a few common traits that Strabo, Trogus or Livy thought they saw'.[3] To the extent that our understanding of categories in the pre-modern world depends on relatively recent systems of naming and classification – often products of the nineteenth-century European mind – this is largely true. For centuries the region that would become Madrid was distant from the commercial currents and cultural innovations taking place along the Mediterranean coasts of the peninsula. 'Lonely, melancholy Castile is beyond sight of the sea,' wrote author José Martínez Ruiz, conventionally known by his pseudonym 'Azorín'.[4] As a result of this remove, Madrid has been accused not of lacking *history* but of lacking *antiquity*. While close details of social structure and organisation on the peninsula may be hard to ascertain, there is ample evidence, from around 900 BCE, first of Phoenicians, then Greeks and Carthaginians successively trading and bringing with them new techniques of metallurgy and agriculture, new gifts of ceramics and technology. Coming from the Mediterranean east and African south – the beginnings of a modern history of colonisation – for the traders the peninsula was a rich source of tin, gold and silver. From the east, too, would eventually come a radically new language, an alphabet and a religion.

The plains, mountains and obscure valleys of the interior remained mostly unvisited by the trade that flourished along the coasts. Events moved slowly: change over decades and centuries rather than days, weeks or months. Between the Phoenicians sailing into the bays of southern Spain to found the ancient city of Cádiz, and the Romans setting down an infrastructure of towns, roads and bridges across the interior of the peninsula, there passed nearly a thousand years of comparative silence in which we must suppose the fundamentals of a pre-modern life: the seasons turned with the local economies; animals were shepherded, slaughtered; simple textiles woven; marriage alliances fixed, children raised; tools and ceramics shaped. Rituals followed the course of the sun. A life that appears to us as static pastoral, yet which contained all the complexities of kinship, agriculture and worship; of strategy, skirmish and warfare.

The Mediterranean trading routes stirred waves of influence that rolled inland, up valleys and old paths, their influence weakening with distance yet reaching, eventually, the deep interior. In those pre-Roman centuries, on the fertile coastal plains and river valleys running inland from the sea, vibrant communities began to grow as fruit and cereal production thrived with animal husbandry. These valleys were principally the Ebro, in the north-east, and the Guadalquivir and Guadiana, in the south-west, albeit neither southern river yet wore its Arabic name. The population of the peninsula grew, subject to continuous historic patterns of migration. Trade flourished as travellers came from nearby North Africa and the scattered islands of the Mediterranean, even from the distant shores of Greece and Lebanon, from Syria and Egypt, to examine what Iberia might contain. The native and the foreign were blended, as ever, until 'native' itself became a densely patterned identity with multiple origins. From its very earliest times, the Iberian Peninsula was a mosaic of settlements, peoples, traditions, alliances, lifestyles, technologies, cults and rituals, and its capital city continues to bear witness to this magnificent diversity.

One framing of this early history suggests the peoples of the interior 'preferred tradition over the magic and promiscuity of outside influences'.[5] The notion of wilful provincialism ignores the influence geography played in limiting the opportunities for contact between the tribes of the interior and the coastal, pan-Mediterranean trade. A variant of this idea of hermeticism runs through certain inter-pretations of Spanish history: the peninsula 'sealed off' from Europe and its cultural influence by the great wall of the Pyrenees – a faulty argument that ignores the constant exchange both ways across the mountains, and the substantial, but often unrecognised, contribution of Spain to European cultural development. Within Spain, a jealous topography kept some regions separated from each other until the nineteenth century, yet one need only observe the network of Roman roads that webbed Iberia to understand the extensive peninsular traffic.

Control over sea trading networks from Lebanon to Gibraltar passed from one power to another as part of the natural rise and fall of ancient states. The Phoenicians had established Cádiz nearly a thousand years before the arrival of the Romans, using southern

Spain as a base to exploit and replenish mineral supplies. In turn, they brought ivory and jewellery, perfumes, cloth and worked glass from the Persian east, Crete and the African south: a whole emotional freight of tastes, scents and images. The Greeks came after them, establishing trading ports from southern France and modern Catalonia, south along the Mediterranean into the regions of Valencia and Alicante. Later, the Carthaginians came, in their colonial drive from North Africa, Malta, Sicily and Sardinia through to Andalusia. Across these centuries new coinage arrived; the olive tree was domesticated; navigation mastered; and new gods worshipped.

The cultural and technological impact of these trading networks moved inland over a matter of centuries; local tribes slowly opened the way to the riches of the interior in exchange for gifts and new skills. Slaves were sought, metals and ceramics, jewellery and brides. When their empire was at its height, and taking on the growing rival of Rome, the Carthaginians under the Barca family penetrated as far as the site of present-day Madrid, searching Carpetania not for sites to settle, but in a speculative, mercenary exploration for soldiers and slaves. The historian Livy first mentions the province of Carpetania when he describes 'the sudden departure of Hannibal [from Saguntum] on an expedition against the Oretani[6] and Carpetani [a rough confederation with its capital at Toletum]. These two peoples, surprised and endangered by the severity of Hannibal's demand for troops, had seized and retained the officers in charge of recruitment . . .'[7] The native peoples of the future Madrid are thus documented: scrapping with the Carthaginians, resisting the taking of their men to serve in Hannibal's attempt to overthrow Rome in 218 BCE. There is a suggestion that around 206 BCE the general Hasdrubal passed through central Spain on his way to provide support to his brother Hannibal, most likely walking the plains, gullies and river valleys where Madrid would later grow. Among the ash and oak trees, across the scrubby hills, watched by broad-winged vultures and deer and wary native peoples, among the dust and conscripts of Celtiberia, Hasdrubal sought mercenaries and slaves for the long assault on Rome. Divide, manipulate and conquer: the Carthaginians employed an ancient strategy of control, 'intending to employ African troops in Spain and Spanish troops in Africa in the belief that service by each in a foreign country would provide a sort of mutual guarantee of good behaviour'.[8] Across the future centuries, armies would come again and again into Spain from northern Africa: not just the waves of Arab and Berber peoples from the eighth century but also, more than 2,000 years after Hannibal, the so-called Army of Africa under General Franco would head the assault on the Second Spanish Republic.

Hispania

Stories must begin somewhere; eventually the recording eye and hand arrive. Events are no longer trapped only in stone or plaster, bone-shard, glass or mosaic. Written documents increase, commencing the long path towards modern administration and with it the ever-shifting and contested nature of the historical record. An account begins to take shape: by the time Carthage had been soundly destroyed the whole Mediterranean, including the resource-rich jewel of Iberia at its western edge, lay open to the Romans.

As ever across the European continent and around the *mare nostrum*, the Romans came not just to trade, but to colonise. Hispania would be a Roman province for the next 600 years, bringing infrastructure, urbanism, art and architecture, technology, language, systems of governance, law and justice, taxation, trade and administration. Likewise, the colony had its own profound effect on the coloniser. The ruling classes of the native tribes of the peninsula integrated with a small Roman elite, creating in time 'a profound impression on government, the arts, literature, and the Christian religion in the Roman world'.[1] These are not yet *Spaniards*: to suggest the people of the Iberian Peninsula under Roman rule were 'Spanish' is to invoke a largely sterile nineteenth- and twentieth-century academic debate over the historic cultural origins of the Spanish people. As historian José Álvarez Junco has argued, even during

Roman times Hispania referred to a *geographic* rather than *ethnic* identity;[2] the latter only emerging with the Visigothic period, as exemplified in the paeans of Isidore of Seville who extolled the many virtues of 'sacred Hispania'. Influences on the Roman empire certainly flowed from the Iberian Peninsula, but the Spanish language did not yet exist, few people had any geographic consciousness of the whole peninsula, and the concept of national identity would not become significant until the fifteenth and sixteenth centuries with the dominance of Castile.

Albeit the colonised and colonisers were not yet any meaningful ethnic entity, the history of Spain as a consolidated political and cultural entity begins with the centuries of Roman occupation during which, even if they had nothing else in common, the tribes of the peninsula began to adopt Roman ways of being. There is ample evidence at multiple archaeological sites of Roman settlements around Madrid, on the then richly fertile banks of the Manzanares, at Carabanchel and Villaverde, and to the east at Complutum. This scattered Roman presence does not suggest anything that might be called a city, much less a capital. Other than Toletum, the most significant town was Complutum – later the Muslim Qal'at Abd-al-Salam, now modern-day Alcalá de Henares – mentioned in the first century BCE in the writings of Pliny. Its Roman days were to be perhaps its finest; it fell away into obscurity for centuries until the early modern period when it thrived as a university town that attracted a host of legendary names, among them Catherine of Aragon, Cardinal Cisneros, Miguel de Cervantes and Francisco de Quevedo.

Roman Spain was both rural and intensely urban. Striking provincial cities such as Mérida, Itálica, Lugo, Segovia or Tarragona were like nothing that had been seen before on the peninsula. Five or six hundred years on from the height of Roman influence, however, by which time the Visigoths had come and gone, and the peninsula was largely under the control of the Umayyad caliphate, many Roman towns had either decayed or were deliberately abandoned as being of no strategic interest to the new Islamic rulers. For a thousand years they served as ruins, and their stones as building supplies for future administrations.

The Roman colonisation of Hispania began with two centuries of constant local challenge and pacification. Following Augustus' redrafting of provincial borders, the peninsula was divided into Hispania Tarraconensis (with the future site of Madrid at its south-western edge), Hispania Baetica and Hispania Lusitania. These collected Hispanias provided Rome with intellectual, cultural, mineral, military and agricultural wealth. In short: soldiers, slaves, silver and gold, horses, cereals and taxes, along with philosophers, poets and emperors. Figures such as Martial, Lucan, Seneca, Trajan and Hadrian were all from the peninsula as were, towards the end of the unified empire, Theodosius and Magnus Maximus. Many figures from Hispania enjoyed patronage and influence within the empire; likewise, Rome helped supply the exquisite goods the aristocracy of a successful province could acquire to garland their homes and temples: the finest Italian marble, mosaics, wines, bronzes, perfumes and glassware.

In seeking sources of wealth, or simply military manpower, the Romans scoured the entire peninsula, undeterred by the difficult access presented by often awkward mountain ranges. Sharp cliffs and snow-bound passes, to which could be added the occasional hostility of local tribes, made transport an arduous concern, but never an insurmountable problem. The advent of the Roman system of roads – the *calzada romana* – meant there was, for the first time, a physical and administrative template laid down for a common project across the greater part of the peninsula. Occupation, colonisation and subsequent development established a complex system of transport and government: within 200 years the Romans had all Hispania covered, webbed with roads and monuments, marked with boundaries, statutes and administration. Half an hour south of Madrid, two key Roman roads intersected near the town of Titulcia, crossing from west to east – the Via Augusta from Mérida to Caesaraugusta (Zaragoza), a road that followed the valley of the Tagus – and from south to north. Linking what would later be the two Castiles, a Roman road, parts of which have been preserved to this day along with its stumpy milestones, led across the mountain pass of Fuenfría, towards the uplands of Segovia. From Seville to

Cartagena, Sagunto and Barcelona, or from Cádiz to Salamanca, Lugo and Finisterre, for the modern observer there is a remarkable similarity between the extensive Roman network of roads and the contemporary highway system in Spain: there truly is nothing new under the sun.

Once the Romans understood the peninsula in its entirety, the simple fact of geographic centrality began to increase the strategic importance of the Madrid region. It could not help but be a crossroads. The province was well populated, above all to the south, where thriving *villae* were established around Móstoles, Pinto, Ciempozuelos or Titulcia, along with the aforementioned Carabanchel and Villaverde. These *villae* consisted of a central manor house on elevated ground, close to hunting and fishing sites, to forests as a source of wood for heating and construction, and were surrounded by gardens, orchards and worked fields. The *villa* complex was home to labourers, servants and slaves, and prefigured the *latifundio* or *hacienda* of later centuries; likewise the ranch, homestead or landed estate common to other countries.

As always in Iberian history, populations blended; Hispania became a place to settle veterans of imperial wars, and Roman influences 'could permeate outwards into the countryside and local indigenous settlements, attracting emulation and ultimately assimilation'.[3] The indigenous elite, especially in southern and eastern Spain, could see the upside of Roman culture and citizenship; the two worlds commonly intermarried. There was another obvious reason to accept the new imperium: the 'indisputable hegemony of Roman arms meant that the best way for local elites to maintain the power that they were accustomed to wielding locally was to become Roman'.[4] In a scenario that would be repeated time after time in the centuries to come, native peoples found ways to accommodate an imperial presence if collaboration meant the reinforcement of their own power over neighbours or rivals.

Unlike previous colonisers, the Romans incorporated the full geography of Hispania into the machinery of empire.[5] This meant connecting and, where possible, smoothing out differences between very different communities and peoples. The attempt to forge a common identity across the geographic and cultural variety of the peninsula would create both enormous strength and terrible weakness and conflict over the centuries, according to the historic period and the discretion of political actors. This was also the prelude to new forms of mapping and measuring distances, to a more formally cartographic view of the world. Roman maps of the time show a town in the heart of the peninsula that was to be central to the political and cultural future of the whole region for close to 2,000 years. It was not Madrid, however, but Toletum, built on a privileged site above the Tagus some 50 kilometres south of where the capital now stands. For the moment, the future Madrid remained a collection of dwellings amid a cross-hatching of streams and rivers, mostly silent, influenced principally by the surrounding *villae* culture, in the aspiration of local elites to Roman lifestyles, and the eventual expurgation of pre-Roman ritual and habits as older, native forms of social organisation and economy were superseded by more advanced, more powerful Roman models.

Centuries later, as Madrid came into being, the vestiges of Rome were always present. Eventually, the city would be adorned with elements of classical antiquity in its arches, columns and fountains, even down to the great circus of the bull ring – the first was built by the Puerta de Alcalá – the church creed, the Latin roots of names and the foundations of the judicial system. This cultural inheritance underlay the Christian and later secular development of the city and its laws after the centuries of Islamic occupation. It was an act of memory: here and elsewhere, European cities reached back into the classical past in order to state imperial ambitions, to beautify their streets and palaces, to impose order and authority. Its physical presence mostly vanished, Rome nevertheless continued to haunt city planning and administration for centuries to come.

The Roman towns in the vicinity of Madrid – Complutum, Toletum and Segovia – all experienced the splendour and decay of their parent empire. By the fourth century, Roman power had begun to splinter, its vast borders inadequately defended, its mercenaries turning to ransackery and plunder, its distant provinces increasingly separated from the law, administration and culture of the imperial capital. The first, and premonitory, barbarian invasions from the north had begun, while there were incursions into the peninsula from the south: African tribes such as the Mauri descended from the mountains behind Tangier and crossed the narrow strait, snatching at the decaying Roman world. These incursions were brief and for the time being unsuccessful, but they provided a taste of the future, prefiguring the incursions that would later be made under the banner of Islam.

The Roman period had lasted around 600 years, of which 400 had been years of flourishing Latin culture. It was as thorough a conquest as can be imagined; Hispania was now part of a broader cultural continuity with shared bonds beyond the Pyrenees. The Romans entirely changed not only how the world of Hispania was constructed, with their brilliant roads, theatres and aqueducts, but also how the world was ordered, with their legal system and advanced administration. Finally they changed how the world was conceived, with the introduction of Christianity, albeit in those last years of Roman Spain, before the arrival of the Visigoths, the Word emerging from Judea was still a fledgling set of beliefs, imported from the other end of the Mediterranean, unrecognisable from the overwhelming force into which it would transform across the coming centuries.

By the early 1950s the United States government, in anticipation of the later 'He may be a bastard, but he's *our* bastard' doctrine, had established close relations with the Franco regime as a bulwark against communism in southern Europe. The thaw allowed the first post-civil war inflows of investment and tourism into Spain, and in these years a series of Roman epics was filmed in the countryside around Madrid. Art would create a distorted version of the past, and what had never quite been, now was: in 1960 the battle scenes from Stanley Kubrick's *Spartacus* were filmed on the hills around the town of Colmenar Viejo, with other scenes being shot in the country around Alcalá de Henares. In 1964 an entire Roman forum and temple of Jupiter were constructed at Las Matas, on the northern outskirts of Madrid, for Anthony Mann's epic *The Fall of the Roman Empire*. Mann, who had only a few years before directed *El Cid*, thus jumped from emergent medieval Spain to collapsing Rome, and Madrid became the focus for a level of Roman intensity it had not known 2,000 years before. These films, lurid and absurd like many productions of that era, nevertheless served in their tangential way to bring Spain and Madrid back to international audiences, not least as Hollywood brought a line of stars in its wake: Ava Gardner, Orson Welles, Grace Kelly, Audrey Hepburn, Cary Grant and Elizabeth Taylor all found the energy to turn their heads away from a dictatorship and focused instead on Madrid and the folkloric, Potemkin village version of Spain offered up for broader consumption. One can hardly blame them: given the cushioning effect of money, fame and glamour, and the ability not to look at things too closely, Madrid must have been for them part of an innocent paradise, a strange wonderland being discovered anew.

The first heretics

Traditionally but unfairly sidelined in Spanish history, three centuries of Visigoth kings have their place in central Madrid, celebrated in a series of limestone sculptures atop the Royal Palace, in the gardens of the Plaza de Oriente facing the palace, and in the Retiro Park. From these multiple locations they gaze out over the capital they never knew, over its inconceivable buildings and gardens, its inconceivable residents and the tourists who wander by, mostly oblivious to this unusual period of history.

In the early fifth century the Visigoths were simply the next wave of intruders that broke, in a long historic line, over the Iberian Peninsula. Having expanded their influence over the course of the previous century from their lands beyond the Rhine and Danube rivers, the Visigoths fell southwards into France and crossed the Pyrenees, assuming control of the provinces of Hispania. Following the great Roman roads, the Visigoths entered the peninsula in 409 and had completed their occupation by 475, overcoming other contenders such as the Vandals, Alans and Sueves.[1] The fractured Roman presence meant much of the peninsula was for the taking. Hispania no longer needed to be built from the ground up, with six centuries of infrastructure and coded law in place to serve the new rulers. In comparison to the Romans who came before them, and the nearly 800 years of Islamic culture that would follow, the Visigoth period was a strange interregnum. The years between 409 and 711 have been somewhat submerged by subsequent centuries of invasion and conquest and the survival, from both the Roman and Islamic eras, of a significantly greater number of cultural artefacts. And language, always so critical to cultural transmission: foundational veins of Latin and Arabic run through the Spanish language, while the extinguished Gothic has left barely any trace.

The limestone monarchs by the Royal Palace can appear sleepy: a strong westering sun bakes the white stone, features slowly blurring with time; in one a bird's nest has taken shape in the crook of an ancient arm. Their florid and peculiar names, such as Leovigild, Reccared, Witteric, Sisebut, Chindasuinth, Wamba, Ervig and Wittiza, once terrorised Spanish school students before they disappeared from the curriculum.

As the western Roman empire collapsed, many of the urban centres in Hispania decayed. Seeing political and economic trouble ahead, aristocrats and wealthy landholders had for some time been taking refuge in their estates. Great private holdings of land became their own *latifundio* quasi-states with their own private armies; in rich *villae*, the spirit of Rome lived on even as it was under siege in Rome itself.[2] The majority of the simple settlements built from the fifth to eighth centuries on the fertile river plains and in the mountains around Madrid have vanished. The province contains scattered Visigoth burial sites and diverse archaeological remains, but the contribution is not significant. The ruins of the tiny hermitage of Santa María de Valcamino, near the northern town of El Berrueco, and on the plains to the south, the necropolises of El Jardinillo and La Torrecilla, near Getafe, reveal something of the cultural presence around Madrid. Hispania did not switch from 'Roman' to 'Visigoth' overnight; there was a considerable period of overlap, and archaeological sites show the new arrivals built on or around already existing and convenient infrastructure. Of their own, however, the Visigoths left little behind beyond some beautiful churches – exemplary masterpieces of clean and simple stonework – religious doctrine and spectacular jewellery.

For all they languish in relative silence between the extensive legacy of Rome and the substantial cultural inheritance of Islamic

Spain, those three Visigoth centuries constitute one of those fulcrums indispensable to the movement of history. They contained a number of apparently minor but critical changes that would affect the future development of the nation and its capital. One of these was the decision, after a brief sojourn in the early sixth century in Barcelona, to make the Roman town of Toletum the Visigoth capital from the year 542. Thus was established for the first time the idea of a centrally located geographic point of administrative and, importantly, religious control of the peninsula. Intentionally or not, the centre would increasingly become a locus of power, albeit this would fluctuate during the centuries of Al-Andalus.

The influence of Toletum reached out across the nearby Castilian plains, including to a small Visigoth settlement built around the spring of San Pedro – the present-day Plaza de Puerta Cerrada in central Madrid – possibly known by the Roman name of 'Matrice'. Any such village a day's ride north of the Visigoth capital has been lost for 1,500 years below subsequent development, yet the name is significant, 'Matrice' deriving from *matriz* meaning source, origin, womb, and referring to the region as the source of waters. Those who lived in the basic settlement there would have been aware of the gravitational pull of Toletum as a site of religious and political authority. In the sixth century the challenge was faced, for the first time, of establishing a central power base for the whole peninsula in all its geographic and cultural diversity.[3] Here, foreshadowed, is one of the most vexatious and intractable issues faced by Spanish governments today: what was difficult for Romans, Visigoths and Umayyads has become no easier with the years.[4] One thousand years apart, governments in the years 1000 and 2000 faced much the same conundrum – the balance between 'the demands of the central government and a resistant provincialism'.[5] Toledo was the first capital confronted by this Gordian knot; its younger neighbour Madrid would take on that thankless task in centuries to come. In the late sixteenth century, after the election of Madrid as the capital and the subsequent predominance of Castilian power at the heart of the regime, the Aragonese, Catalans and Valencians felt abandoned and 'looked upon this neglect as part of a Castilian plot to deprive them first of their King and then of their liberties'.[6] Nothing generates resentment so much as the practical distribution of power.

The peninsula and its capital city have much in common: constantly redrawn, remade, re-signified. Early religious doctrine was also subject to this law, as the extinguishment of the heretical Visigoth Arian tradition in favour of orthodox Catholicism from 589 was to prove. In their attempts to unify the peninsula, politically and in faith, the Visigoth rulers had to overcome twin heresies in the shape of Arians and Jews; both groups, in different ways, called into question the divinity of the figure of Jesus Christ.

The Visigoths had first embraced the version of Christianity that emerged from the teachings of Arius in Egypt in the third century. Belief in Arianism is now something of a footnote in Spanish and Christian theological history, yet at the time the belief that all members of the Holy Trinity were not equal, and that God the Father was distinct from His Son – that they were neither equal nor co-eternal, and the son was lesser to Him – was widespread among the Visigoths. Arianism was declared a heresy after the Third Council of Toledo in 589; in the ensuing controversy lives were lost, reputations ruined, martyrs created, dogma enforced. Catholicism, the alternative strand of Christianity in Spain during those centuries, followed the Nicene Creed that Father and Son were of the same essence, and thus co-eternal. The Holy Trinity emerged triumphant.

Religious doctrine, like political authority, was best settled. Theologians such as Isidore of Seville (d. 636), Braulio of Zaragoza (d. 651), Ildefonsus of Toledo (d. 667) and Julian of Toledo (d. 690) helped to establish, through chronicles, councils, codes and codices, the orthodoxy necessary to set the Catholic Church on a singular path. And while Christians fought out their doctrinal differences, the Jews of Hispania, another group of significant presence and influence, were to feel the full weight of Visigoth legislation brought to bear against them. By the end of the sixth century, with the Arian heresy outlawed and the political upheaval of the previous century and a half mostly resolved, a mood of religious conformity spread across the peninsula, coupled with the ongoing project of political unification, including specific anti-Semitic laws designed to either convert practitioners or simply prohibit Judaism.[7] Scholars have attempted to source Visigoth anti-Semitism in the wealth, power, number and influence of the Jewish community. Such an influential group holding heretical views led to harsh legislation, yet that same legislation seems to have been somewhat ineffective, for Jewish communities remained relatively strong (within the context of their historical status as a minority people) even as the first Muslims arrived in Hispania.

By the seventh century, the settlement by the spring of San Pedro was in danger of disappearing. Lacking any specific role, the rural hamlet may have simply merged again with the earth and grasses, as happened to countless Iberian villages over the centuries. For any family involved in trade or crafts, it would have made sense to wander south across the plain, no more than a day or two's walk, to the unfolding treasure that was Toletum, nestled into its bend of the Tagus, to seek a future there rather than stay behind in the anonymity of 'Matrice'. Even the erstwhile Roman town of Complutum could not compete. Thus, the village that would become Madrid remains for another two centuries trapped in historic ice, and Visigoth Spain a weird jigsaw of shifting alliances, ascension by assassination, occasional civil war, unreliable source material and religious heresy across three troubled centuries. By the early eighth century the next great attempt to compass the peninsula had begun, and in spectacular fashion. Brand new masters came wielding a brand new religion: Islamic Spain was on its way, and also was Madrid.

A strange, forgotten and shameful episode took place in Madrid in 1940: in an attempt to 'prove' the Aryan origins of the Spanish people and link them to the ancient tribes of Germania, archaeologist Julio Martínez, an aide to Franco, gifted a series of priceless Visigoth bronze and gold treasures to Heinrich Himmler during a visit by the SS leader to the capital. With the recently conquered Madrid dressed in ruins, this act of 'generosity' formed part of the general toadying up to the Nazi regime that was a hallmark of those awful days. Human bones – that which is most sacred is often that which is most profaned – formed part of this cache, transported to the Third Reich for 'forensic testing' to prove what were clearly spurious links. This Aryan nonsense ran contrary to every historical indicator: if one thing can truly be said of the peoples of the Iberian Peninsula, it is that the bloodlines have been mixed for millennia: native tribes, Celts, Syrians and Phoenicians, Greeks, Romans, Carthaginians, Jews, Berbers, Arabs, Moors, Franks and Goths, to say nothing of later Italian, Irish, Scandinavian, Slavic, Filipino, sub-Saharan African, and the whole universe of the American continent: all have come together to create the hybrid splendour that is the Spanish people today. Distressing as it may be for various nationalist formations, there is no 'pure blood' on the Iberian Peninsula, nor can there be; such claims are bigoted and ahistorical.

The Visigoth artefacts, meanwhile, were distributed by the Nazis to various museums throughout Germany and Austria and from there disappeared, lost to history and future Spanish collections, lost to researchers and art lovers and lost, like so much else, from the patchy narrative of those years of late antiquity.

Heaven and earth

At Arrebatacapas, an hour north of Madrid, stands a thousand-year-old circular stone tower. The site – despite a nearby water treatment plant – is saturated with the quiet melancholy of places whose strategic usefulness has long passed, yet whose construction condemns them to remain. This *atalaya* – from the Arabic for sentinel or watchtower – has been forgotten other than by local hikers and history enthusiasts. There is an enormous simplicity here: stone, heath, sky and earth. The tower stands lonely, solemn, without gentleness or pleasure, looking magnificently both ways: up into the jagged sierra, down into what once were richly forested hills and plains, lakes and pastures, to willow streams and holly oak and ash and juniper. It stands amid a windswept vastness where eagles arc and float above the folded earth; in the distance, hugging the ridges, lowering clouds bring rain or snow.

Madrid is the only European capital with an Islamic origin and, notwithstanding the tenuous claims for 'Matrice', the only European capital with an Arabic name.

Even 1,300 years on, the expansion of Islam in the seventh and eighth centuries remains an explosive and astonishing feat, one without historical precedence until the rapid spread of European colonialism some eight centuries later. Barely eighty years after the death of the Prophet Muhammad, armies had swept across North

Africa, mostly absorbing the Berber peoples into their campaign, and thence into the Visigoth lands of Hispania where they initially entered upon invitation to assist one party in a factional power struggle. Having found easy pickings among a squabbling populace they stayed, as had the Romans and Visigoths before them. Weakened by internal disputes, the Visigoth presence melted before a more ferocious and disciplined force. Local elites once again found cooperation an easier path to follow than resistance; in exchange for tributes and taxes, certain privileges could be maintained. It was often a matter of simple convenience for the largely rural Visigoth population to convert to Islam. Christianity, despite three centuries of Visigoth rule, was not anything like as deeply encultured in the eighth century as it would be some hundreds of years later. Most of the peninsula, barring a northern pocket where Islam would not succeed, began a process of cultural and political adaptation.

As they settled into their occupation of the centre of the peninsula, the new Umayyad rulers set about establishing a series of defences to bolster the frontier regions that separated Islam and Christendom. *Atalayas* were built on high ground, as close as a few kilometres apart, ensuring direct visual communication. Dated to around 950, at Arrebatacapas the rough-hewn ruins befit a rough-hewn site. No one would want to live here, much less in more hostile times; it was a place of emergency warning, of anticipation, but not of settlement. It was simply too exposed, too harsh. A symmetry has been forced onto chunks of stone in all their misshapen variety. Hacked and blunted, they form a cylindrical tower that reaches 13 metres into the sky. Within this structure various internal levels functioned as sleeping quarters, storerooms and warning posts. Fire played an important role, with messages relayed or received via systems of smoke and mirrors, delivered down into the valleys of the Manzanares and Jarama, or to the mountain passes that give access to the uplands of Castile. In this way, messages travelled swiftly between the watch-towers immediately north of Madrid, from El Berrueco to Arrebatacapas to Venturada to El Vellón to Talamanca and beyond.

From Arrebatacapas today, the view is long, sharp and still towards the serrated skyline and always evolving urban developments of the metropolis. Madrid, however, was not the town the watchtower of Arrebatacapas was built to protect; it was Tulaytulah (previously known as Roman Toletum), along with the highways that connected the major towns of Qurtuba (Córdoba) and Saraqusta (Zaragoza). Soldiers would have stood guard here with their burnished weapons, overlooking the raw land; an outpost filled equally with threat and days of boredom. Whether summer-blue or winter-dark, Arrebatacapas constituted one of the limits of the world.

In the very first years of the Islamic occupation, around 713, Arab and Berber troops swept up from southern Spain towards Mérida, thence north-east to Toledo and finally to Zaragoza, captured in 714. These forces and the religion they brought were newly minted and revolutionary; living off the land as they moved and conquered, they avoided a dependence on long logistical or supply lines and thus ensured the rapidity of their progress. As ever, the physical constructions of the past guided and facilitated the construction of the present: the paths and roads were already laid out for them, a Roman network based on the logic of terrain and efficiency. Captained by the Yemeni Musa ibn Nusair in the service of the Damascene caliphate of the Umayyads and the Berber general Tariq ibn Ziyad, these troops may not have noticed, while crossing the land between Toledo and Zaragoza on one of their scouting journeys, a humble settlement built on land rising above the stream of San Pedro[1] in a small ravine between two hills, a stream flowing down into what would become known as the Guadarrama, and then eventually the Manzanares River. It would have made no impression on these brilliant warriors whose eyes were on bigger prizes and greater glories; in common with other settlements of the time 'Matrice' most likely boasted a simple wall erected around a collection of dwellings, animal shelters and garden plots. There was little to suggest it was a place of any importance.

Over the course of the eighth and ninth centuries, the quiet isolation of this settlement ended, never to return. The new Islamic state of Al-Andalus, as part of the broader Umayyad emirate, quickly reached the northern limit of its expansion.[2] From the sandy beaches of southern Iberia, armies had travelled as far as central France at lightning speed, only to find overreach brings a halt to the greatest of enterprises. The long north of Al-Andalus was long indeed, but it was a claim too far; defeated in 732 at the Battle of Poitiers, the invaders under Abd al-Rahman were forced to withdraw. Nor did they make inroads into selected northern strongholds such as the Atlantic kingdom of Asturias; by the late eighth century Islam began to recede from its high-water mark and settled on the substantial prize that was, with minor geographic exceptions, all of the Iberian Peninsula below the Ebro and Duero River basins.

At the instructions of the emir Muhammad I of Córdoba a line of fortifications – effectively an intermittent great wall – was drawn across the peninsula and constructed over the following century, into the reign of Abd al-Rahman III.[3] The hills and mountains north of Madrid were dotted with watchtowers such as Arrebatacapas. Some have disappeared in the thousand years since they were built; others have been beautifully restored and can still be seen in their magnificent locations at Venturada, overlooking the Guadalix River, at El Berrueco, Torrelodones, El Vellón, El Molar or in Talamanca de Jarama. Three marches, or sections, constituted the northern Islamic military frontier. The area including and surrounding Mayrit – some argue this is the Arabised form of Matrice, while coincidentally 'Mayrit' was an Arabic term for 'abundance of water' or, once again, 'source' – fell into the central or Middle March (*al-Thagr al-Awsat*) whose capital was Tulaytulah. Mayrit oversaw the Manzanares Valley, while its companion settlements Talamankah (Talamanca) oversaw the Jarama Valley and Qal'at Abd-al-Salam oversaw the Henares. Along this disputed border stood captured Christian castles that could be repurposed, such as Madinat-Salim (Medinaceli), Atienza or Sigüenza; where not, stone watchtowers were built, visible either to each other or to major fortifications. Either side of this chain of forts and watchtowers became a no-man's-land, demographically depleted and agriculturally less productive. Such territory was subject to constant dispute shifting regional alliances, increasing in strategic value as the frontier between the Christian north and the Islamic centre and south changed with the years, with fortune, with the skill of generals or the luck of seasons.

Rapid though their advance was, not everything was plain sailing for the Islamic forces. A Mozarabic[4] rebellion in Tulaytulah in 854 led to the Battle of Guadalecete, where the troops of Asturian King Ordoño I, initially in the ascendant, fell into an ambush and were routed; a bloody massacre ensued. Prompted by the need to better secure the centre of the peninsula from this type of aggression, or possible usurpation, not long after the middle of the ninth century – historians suggest between 856 and 865 – the emir's eyes had turned to a fertile area atop one of the escarpments rising above the left bank of the Manzanares River. The location was of obvious strategic value, offered generous opportunities for self-sustaining agriculture and boasted an abundance of local waters. The emir ordered a military garrison built as part of the cross-peninsular defensive system. The fortress complex (the *almudaina* or *alcazaba*) consisted of the citadel (the *alcázar*) and a small, separate walled urban settlement (the *medina*) beyond which were a few acres of agricultural plots and extramural houses (the *arrabales*). The citadel and the *medina* were separated by a parade ground, not unlike the Plaza de la Armería that stands today between the Almudena Cathedral and the Royal Palace. Three gates allowed access to the military-civilian complex: the Puerta de la Almudena (later Santa María) faced roughly east, the Puerta de la Vega faced south-west and led down the escarpment to the fields and orchards along the Manzanares, while to the north the Puerta de la Xagra (from the Arabic *shaqra*, or cultivated land) opened onto fields around what is now the Plaza de Oriente.

Standing in the gardens of Las Vistillas, or at the western edge of the Plaza de la Armería, one can appreciate the superb defensive location of Madrid in a time of medieval warfare; as early as the middle of the tenth century, Mayrit was mentioned in chronicles as *Madinat al-Farach* – City of Splendid Views.[5] The views remain splendid to this day, albeit strategic military value long gave way to gentler aesthetics in judging a lovely horizon. A clear line of sight leads out to the west and north, over the contemporary forests of brick apartment buildings to densely wooded ranges and beyond to the snowline of the Guadarrama range. Here, where the original fortifications stood, was perfect for reconnaissance, connecting to other fortresses that watched over the routes down into central Spain from Somosierra or the valley of Fuenfría. Islamic Mayrit was tasked with not only detecting and sounding the alert against attacks from the Christian north but also, along with Talamankah and Qal'at Jalifa (Calatalifa), safeguarding lines of communication between Tulaytulah, Madinat-Salim and Saraqusta. Like many defensive positions, Mayrit could also serve as a point of attack, a citadel from which the emir's or caliph's troops might ride out into the regions of Castile and Leon in expeditions of punishment and looting: stealing, burning, capturing. Given its dual role as both offensive and defensive along the contested boundaries of Al-Andalus, the clifftop military outpost of Mayrit became a place of permanent settlement; emerging from the deep shadows of the past, it would never look back. During the roughly 200 years of its Islamic history, from the late ninth to the late eleventh centuries, Mayrit enters the written historical record. The town had effectively been born into geographic and military fact.

Historians Ángel Bahamonde Magro and Luis Enrique Otero Carvajal write that Madrid came into being principally as a *ribat*, that is, 'a community both religious and military, where small groups of Muslims prepared themselves for seasonal *jihad*, or holy war'.[6] In this, it was mirrored, in a battle that would last for centuries, by Christian knights to the north, preparing themselves for much the same task: like tectonic plates Christianity and Islam often met, in grind and skirmish, in the centre of the peninsula. The two plates, however, were far from monolithic; change and nuance were constant. There were desertions from one camp to the other; treasons; wilfully swapped allegiances; shifts occurred without villagers' awareness or approval. Sometimes – and this was to be the case again, most famously, in the twentieth-century civil war – it was simply a matter of chance that one village or group of farmers, even members of the same family, were found on one side or the other of a permeable dividing line. There are acts that in hindsight might appear to have been made with courage or cowardice that owed all, at the time, to fortune and circumstance.

Central Spain can seem a parched landscape, a thirsty patchwork of fields and stony towns whose palette of dry browns is relieved by the various greens of river valleys and irrigation schemes. It was not always so: evidence points to the fertility of the land around Madrid being one of the attractions to its earliest settlers, a place rich in pasture, abundant in hunting and fishing, and suitable for a wide variety of crops. If there was one element especially in plenty it was water, essential for agriculture as much as for purity and cleanliness; for fertility, therapy and as an energy source harnessed to systems of production.[7]

The military fortress would not have survived without an abundant water supply. It would have been unable to maintain hygiene and an adequately fed population, much less host an increasingly substantial outpost surrounded by seasonal crops and orchards. Far from the popularly imagined sensual perfumes and lazy palm gardens of southern Al-Andalus – essentially a nineteenth-century invention – from around 860 until its definitive capture by Christian forces in 1083 Mayrit had many of the characteristics of a raw outpost: luxuries were few, the enemy was ever-present, prayer and training went hand in hand, an annual crop failure (or sabotage by enemies) could be devastating. By the tenth century, simultaneously at the heart of the peninsula and on the edge of the caliphate of Córdoba, fortified Mayrit was surviving and expanding, living its freezing winters and baking summers, protected by mountains and fed by healthy streams.

Permanent settlements require dedicated infrastructure, and in Mayrit this centred around the construction of defensive walls, streets, markets and a mosque, and the harnessing of local water sources into a rational system of supply. Where the Visigoths had primarily been hunters, the new Muslim population were farmers, gardeners and orchardists, as well as warriors. They knew, from extensive cultural and practical experience in drier lands, how to use water with maximum efficiency, regulating its flow, storing its excesses, directing its place and purpose. In addition to the local springs, streams and wells, from the ninth century Islamic Mayrit began to construct a sophisticated system of water storage and underground channels known as *qanats*. The network of underground galleries, and the method of raising water supplies from the aquifers that fed them, drew on knowledge of ancient Persian technology. From its origins in the ninth century the system, progressively updated, remained in use until the eighteenth century, thus helping provide Madrid for 700 years after the fall of the Islamic regime, contributing to Madrid's long reputation for having an excellent water supply. Public fountains, drinking water, medieval sewerage, local industries (such as tanning), irrigation and troop supplies all relied on the abundant water below the town or from nearby streams. Many have been choked by progress; others still flow like ghost currents, wrapped and channelled in baroque brickwork below the streets, no longer necessary to the demands of the modern metropolis. Some survive, remnant catacombs: in the Ópera Metro station, in the heart of old Madrid, a small museum reveals the original location and workings of the Caños del Peral, a fountain and supply network that provided water from the Amaniel and Arenal streams to central Madrid, including to the Royal Palace, from the fifteenth until the nineteenth centuries.

A new society under the Umayyad rulers began to flourish. Islamic Spain was the most advanced agricultural society in Europe at the time, thriving on domestic consumption and exports such as wheat, olive oil, sorghum, grapes and rice. Technological improvements in irrigation were key; their mark on the evolution of the Spanish diet is indisputable, blooming with figs and apricots, lemons, oranges and grapefruit; with carrots, aubergines, artichokes and parsnips. In the meantime, ancient staples – chickpeas, lentils, beans – carried on their sturdy work of sustaining a populace[8] as they went about their lives, farming in the *arrabales* outside the walled complex, in tanneries and silversmithing, tending to domestic animals or provision of military supplies to a warrior class.

The social classes in early Mayrit consisted of Arabs or Berbers (by origin); of *muladíes* – generally Christians and others converted to Islam; of *mozárabes* – those who remained Christian, and thus adapted to a life more marginalised and with fewer economic possibilities; Jews, who were likewise separate; and members of an unspecified slave class.[9] As people of the Book, Christians and Jews were tolerated, not least given their manual and intellectual skills. Many of the blended Iberian-Roman-Visigoth population had converted to avoid complications and live quietly under their new rulers. Specific quarters were set aside for minorities: during the two centuries of Islamic Mayrit, Christians lived in the Mozarab quarter; it later switched to being a Muslim quarter under Christian rule. This *arrabal* was located around the area that is now La Latina, in the vicinity of the original church of San Andrés. Not permitted to wall their quarter, in the eleventh century the area settled by Christians grew to include Las Vistillas and Puerta Cerrada, as far as the beginning of the ancient road to Toledo. Layers add to layers: the primitive temple of San Andrés was subsequently replaced by a twelfth-century church, frequented by the farm labourer San Isidro, and later replaced in the seventeenth century by the baroque temple of San Andrés that stands today, opposite the museum of San Isidro dedicated to the history of Madrid.

The society was complex and heterogenous;[10] faith strongly determined identity. Unfortunately, we know nothing of those anonymous labourers who built the castle and defences of Mayrit, or stood patrol along its walls, cresting the sharp escarpment, and down to the alluvial river flats. Like so many medieval towns built atop Spanish hillsides, the settlement was a place of tight lanes and constricted space. Within the walls lived military personnel and those who serviced the garrison and their families. Others worked plots of land: the *alquería* was a small rural community, generally established close to the protection of a fort or town, occupied by families dedicated to farming and animal husbandry. Despite Islamic Spain's urban sophistication, a large proportion of the population, including relocated Berbers, lived in these rural settings. Trade flourished at this peninsular crossroads, even in centuries beset by wars or plague. Within the walls of Mayrit, or in the extramural *arrabales*, the military presence brought its own generative economy[11] typical of a medieval town: stores, bakers and butchers, leatherwork and tanning, metalwork and jewellery in ivory, gold and silver, cloth production from cotton, silk and flax; ceramics and pottery, cabinetry and raw timber, abundant in the surrounding forests.

By the eleventh century the heavily walled *alcazaba*, its accompanying walled *medina* and the various extramural quarters with all their religious and ethnic diversity – perhaps the origin of the colloquial term 'los Madriles'[12] that refers to the plurality of Madrid and its citizens – had become a permanent, strategically vital settlement. As historian Cristina Segura has pointed out, its military governors – *alcaides* – were almost exclusively drawn from influential families loyal to Córdoba, underlining the importance of Mayrit to the caliphate.[13] The Spanish countryside may be dotted with apparently impregnable strongholds that history has worn down to stumpy uselessness – the ghosts of Ozymandias are everywhere – yet as the centuries turned, the very geographic centrality of Madrid, its invigorating climate, its extraordinary fortifications and its proximity to fertile land, forests and waterways allowed it to escape that fate.

The pinnacle of *Madrid árabe* or *Madrid islámico* coincided, inevitably, with the high point of cultural brilliance and military strength of Al-Andalus. One of the town's most famous sons was Hispano-Arabic polymath Maslama ibn Ahmad al-Mayriti. Born around 950 in the caliphate's golden years, al-Mayriti became one of the first intellectual giants to emerge from Al-Andalus. Working mostly at the seat of the caliphate in Córdoba, al-Mayriti was a major scientist, mathematician, philosopher, translator and astronomer. All the finest intellectual attributes of Al-Andalus came together in this remarkable figure, including the critical confluence of mathematics and geometry with astronomy and astrology. The latter was held in high regard by the caliphs, who looked to the movements of heavenly bodies to calculate seasonal fluctuations, such as droughts, or the most propitious moments to engage in military expeditions. To a modern mind this seems arbitrary, yet it served the purposes of legendary warrior-general al-Mansur 'the Victorious' (d. 1002), known in Spanish as Almanzor, to whom al-Mayriti served as personal astrologer.

The science and mathematics of Al-Andalus were essential in laying the groundwork for future generations of experimentation across Europe, drawing the thread connecting ancient Persian and Indian observers to modern practitioners; the scientific works emerging from Al-Andalus were a knowledge supply line to the later Renaissance. Al-Mayriti's work on calculations for the astrolabe – aligning for the meridian of Córdoba – connect the astronomical charts of the second-century Egyptian Ptolemy, the eighth-century Persian Jewish mathematician Mashallah, the ninth-century Persian polymath Al-Khwarizmi, his Hispano-Arab contemporary Ibn al-Saffar, and lead ultimately to English poet Geoffrey Chaucer's 1391 *A Treatise on the Astrolabe* and thence to the work of Johannes Kepler. Al-Mayriti founded a school of Astronomy and Mathematics in Córdoba and, far ahead of his time, encouraged research networks and intellectual exchange between centres of learning. The boundaries of the known world being paradoxically both more limited and more expansive than today, his intellectual skills maintained intimate ties to alchemy and magic. This, along with astrology, was playing a dangerous game: one of al-Mayriti's horoscopes, related to the conjunction of Jupiter and Saturn, predicted 'a change of dynasty, general ruin, killings and starvation'.[14] Not the type of future any caliph would like to hear; however, barely one generation after the death of al-Mayriti in 1007, the caliphate of Córdoba did indeed come to an end, though its final days were nothing like the catastrophe of al-Mayriti's horoscope. Al-Mayriti's output over the course of his career was prodigious; unfortunately, many of his books are known only by name, referenced by others, or through Latin translations, while the original content has been lost.

From around 1031, under pressure from political infighting, internal jealousies, tribal rivalries and an increasingly powerful Christian presence to the north, the caliphate of Córdoba began to weaken, splitting into independent *taifas* – essentially mini-kingdoms, regional factions rather than centralised states – often at cross-purposes with each other.[15] From this point, and despite the jewels left scattered across the peninsula, Islamic Spain would never again equal the splendour it had achieved at its tenth-century zenith. Its presence was far from over – it is still obvious today – but political disunity was the beginning of a centuries-long drift towards the end. Political disunity had spelled the end for the Visigoths, and Islamic Spain was repeating the same pattern, though its dissolution would take much longer. Regional ambitions, peninsular disunity and devilish pacts of convenience to maintain local power bases: these will all reverberate down the centuries.

Mayrit fell under the *taifa* of Tulaytulah/Toledo, which occupied much of central Spain. As a town central to the defence of Toledo, Mayrit remained very much in the shadow of its more illustrious neighbour which, in the following two centuries, would assume Córdoba's role as a hub for the translation and transmission of classical knowledge, turning the inheritance of centuries of learning to the benefit of the burgeoning European Renaissance.

The warring among the *taifas* would prove fatal against the Christian armies from the north, given the regional power bases' independence from Córdoba came at the cost of military strength. Due to the increasing power of Christian Spain to the north, and the fragmentation of Islamic Spain to the south, the Muslim leaders of Toledo had no choice but to ensure peace by paying an annual tribute, often in the form of gold, to the kings of Castile and Leon who in turn guaranteed the territorial integrity of the *taifa*. In this way, Mayrit began 'a progressively closer relationship with the crown of Castile' from the middle of the eleventh century.[16] This was a critical shift, historically, from the tutelage of Al-Andalus to the umbrella of the Castilian centre and north. These years were a splendid time for the town, as another important change was taking place: the population outside the defensive walls began to exceed, for the first time, the population within. Islamic Mayrit, while still predominantly a military town, was now thriving as a market, a crossroads for commercial activity.[17] It was driving its roots deep into the soil of Castile. Beyond the walls, old *villae* dwellings and their clustered dependencies from late Roman or Visigoth times were still used as rural estates, or *alquerías*, housing groups of families as space within the garrison was limited by its unassailable defences.[18]

By the late eleventh century, Mayrit boasted a population of some 5,000; not only defence, commerce and agriculture, it was also a centre of teaching and culture, with mathematicians, astronomers and jurists among its citizens. While Mayrit could not yet compete with Toledo, it was quickly surpassing other frontier defensive towns in the region, such as Talamankah and Qal'at Abd-al-Salam, in terms of development, location and opportunity for secular advancement. One of its greatest rivalries, with a rejuvenated Segovia, was soon to come.

In the Parque del Emir Mohamed I, a beautifully reconstructed site below the Almudena Cathedral, tourists now cluster around their guides as they relate the story of the ancient walls of the fortress of Mayrit. There is ambiguity here: as remnants of the walls loom up behind the visitors, they are reminded of the lasting nature of Islamic engineering; at the same time, the limited remains speak to the sheer loss of patrimony in Madrid. The ancient walls appear and disappear in a strange curvature through the old city: traces of this ancient defensive system form the walls of taverns, restaurants; are hidden in private dwellings; emerge again to line one side of a carefully designed and polished park. The city has grown in a coralline crust of centuries around these stones, thousands of which, over the years, have been repurposed and now lie under churches or palaces, in cemeteries, foundations. For centuries it was common practice to reuse the materials of conquered sites and destroyed monuments as part of the construction of the new: from ruin to foundation. While the Islamic walls still maintain a presence in contemporary Madrid, it is an atomised presence: a disassemblage that appears throughout other constructions – a foundation, a sunken pathway, a stable, a church tower. Over the course of a thousand years these stones have served as Islamic, medieval, baroque, neoclassical, modern and post-modern, an ongoing testament to the origins of Madrid.

The period and legacy of Islamic Spain has been subject to a wide array of responses, including centuries of forgetting. As we will see, sixteenth- and seventeenth-century chronicles sought to gild the history of Madrid and thus downplay, when not entirely erase, the Muslim heritage of the city. This was a time of a more prominent role for Christianity in the formation of a Spanish identity, coinciding with a series of historic battles between Spanish forces and the Ottoman Turks, most famously at Lepanto or Halq al-Wadi (La Goulette) in Tunisia. Erased for a time by the ideological priorities of the Habsburg regime, the Islamic origins of Madrid are nevertheless impossible to deny, not only as a matter of historical fact, but also from the way Arabic lives on in the music of words, making Spanish such an extraordinarily rich and beautiful tongue. The Arabic language and Islamic presence were as foundational to Madrid as its cultural and military history, and remain an essential part of the city's oldest quarters: the once impregnable walls run through and below the western edge of the old city centre, the brick *qanats* lace their blind way below the city, the oldest church towers are of Mudéjar[19] design, and Madrid's very cathedral and its virgin, Almudena, take their names from the walled citadel, the *al-mudayna*. It may have been necessary to overcome years of neglect and periodic hostility, but contemporary Madrid is now rightly proud of this inheritance that distinguishes it from any other European capital.

Butcher, soldier, pastor, lord

In the year 1083 forces under Alfonso VI 'the Brave', king of Castile and Leon, laid what was to be the final, successful Christian siege to Mayrit, a siege accompanied by a miracle that would give rise to the legend of the Virgin of Almudena, destined to be one of the patron saints, along with San Isidro, of the city.

Desirous of establishing a Christian past prior to the arrival of Islam, the tale was told that in the late eighth century, observing the rapid Islamic domination of southern and central Spain, the Visigoths of 'Matrice' hid a statue of the Virgin Mary in the walls that surrounded their humble village. As she was sealed up, a pair of candles was placed beside the Virgin. Historian María Cristina Tarrero Alcón recounts what happened some 250 years later, when Alfonso entered Mayrit: 'On November 9, in the year 1083, after various public prayers had been offered, king Alfonso VI, in the company of devout *madrileños*, was witness to the collapse of part of the wall, inside of which was revealed the wooden image of the Virgin, both candles still aflame.'[1] The Virgin, her light alive, released immaculate and uncorrupted from her stony tomb, immediately became a patron saint for the town, providing the newly triumphant Christians not only the comfort of a miracle, but also the assurance that this had been *their* town and inheritance all along. For the Christian forces, taking Mayrit was a restitution of the order of things, and a statue commemorating the signal event – or myth – of the apparition stands in a cornice even today, above the remains of the Arab walls.

The church of Santa María de la Almudena was founded at the start of the central Calle Mayor. It remains in dispute if there had been an original temple dedicated to Santa María on this site prior to the Islamic presence; in itself this would not have been unusual given the Virgin Mary had been the subject of devotion in the Iberian Peninsula since the sixth century.[2] If it did exist, that primitive temple would have been built over and converted into a mosque in the ninth century, and that mosque, in turn, built over and converted back into a church in the late eleventh century, a constant palimpsest of faith and construction. By 1868 any remnant of the medieval period was demolished, and construction of the contemporary cathedral, Santa María la Real de la Almudena, was begun in 1883 very close to where, a thousand years earlier, the first switch of religious faiths had taken place.

Always a target for Christian forces descending from the north, Mayrit had suffered sporadic attacks prior to being definitively taken by troops under Alfonso VI. As early as 932, in the reign of the immensely powerful Abd al-Rahman III, an attempt had been made to conquer Mayrit under the king of Asturias and Leon, Ramiro II. Curiously, having razed the outer walls and looted the surrounding farms and settlements, Ramiro retired before making a final, unsuccessful assault on the *alcázar*, which kept intact its reputation as impregnable. He had come, and seen, but had not been able to conquer: the Islamic keep was beyond his capacity, or patience. Raids of looting and conquest were seasonal; the changing weather may have forced him to abandon the assault. In an early twelfth-century chronicle, a monk of Silos records Ramiro as 'marching to the city they called Mayrit with his troops, dismantling its walls, creating much destruction and returning to his kingdom at peace with his victory'.[3]

Mayrit fell into a period of relative silence; very little is documented between the failed raid of Ramiro and the successful siege of the town by Alfonso 150 years later. This long absence in the historical record speaks well of the town and suggests its mostly peaceful development, and its dedication to agriculture, trade, science and philosophy, beyond the turbulent back and forth of the frontier skirmishes conducted further north, closer to the Duero River basin.

In the mid-eleventh century Fernando I, King of Leon, had carried out an aggressive policy against Al-Andalus with mixed results. To his son and heir, Alfonso VI, fell the opportunity to take both Tulaytulah and Mayrit. The alliances, rivalries and betrayals between various Christian and Islamic leaders at this time makes for bewildering reading. To simplify, around 1080 the Muslim king of the *taifa* of Badajoz, al-Mutawakkil, attacked the neighbouring *taifa* of Toledo, occupying the city. Its king, al-Qadir, sought refuge in the Castilian town of Cuenca, and in a cross-faith collaboration to preserve his power, requested assistance from Alfonso. The Muslims of Toledo were divided: some wanted to collaborate with the Christian forces to recover their city, albeit at the cost of losing independence, while others called for support from the *taifa* kings of southern Al-Andalus, including the famous king of Seville, the poet and chess master al-Mutamid, to whom is attributed the line, 'I would rather be a camel-driver in Africa than a swineherd in Castile'. Bravura aside, after four years Toledo was taken, and the dragnet of conquest inevitably included the nearby hilltop town of Mayrit.

Once in the possession of Alfonso, Toledo was not a jewel to be relinquished; rather than return the town to its former ruler, al-Qadir was packed off to run the kingdom of Valencia by way of a consolation prize. Christian forces now controlled a series of fortifications through the middle of the peninsula. The mountain ranges that separated the Duero region from the central plains had been overcome; over the following century the nominal dividing line between the two faith regimes moved progressively further south towards the Sierra Morena.[4] The long decline for Islam on the peninsula continued; as for al-Mutamid, in 1091 he was arrested by the Almoravids, hardened warriors from the desert lands of North Africa, and taken to Morocco where he died in 1095 in the medieval Berber town of Aghmat, not far from the Almoravid capital of Marrakech.

The year 1085 was a turning point in the history of both the peninsula and the town of Mayrit. For the first time in over 300 years, the balance of forces showed a marked superiority of the Christians over the splintered Islam. With the dissolution of the caliphate of Córdoba and the squabbling of the local *taifas*, it was only a matter of time before another Islamic regime sought to impose order on Al-Andalus and exploit its extraordinary wealth. In the late eleventh century the Almoravids had centred their power in Morocco, extending their influence as far south as Mauritania, and occupying large sections of the Sahara and the Mediterranean coast to Algeria. Their interpretation of Islam was more radical than the caliphs of Córdoba; they did not look kindly on the Iberian *convivencia* whereby Muslims, Jews and Christians lived in harmony, albeit not in equality: hierarchies had always to be observed.

The Almoravids entered Spain in 1086, the year after the fall of Toledo, invited by a collection of Muslim *taifas* to assist in their battles with Alfonso. As they moved through the valley of the Tagus on raids over subsequent decades, reoccupying much of the territory around Mayrit that had been won by Alfonso, they found time and opportunity to lay siege to the town in 1109, and in so doing bestowed the name of one of the city's most famous and beautiful sites. The Campo del Moro, or Moor's Field, is now a sumptuous garden-park, a wave of green that rolls down below the Royal Palace towards the Manzanares River, featuring fountains, shady paths, oaks, pines and acacias, beech groves and the sweet aroma of jasmine. In 1109 this site was the base camp for Almoravid king Ali ibn Yusuf, who sought to take advantage of the death of Alfonso in that same year, believing it the perfect time to retake Mayrit. His army attempted the insurmountable *alcázar* from the lower levels of the river plains. The outer town, the artisans and farmers beyond the walled centre, and much of the broader territory around Mayrit fell to the raiding and sacking Almoravids; only the central *alcázar* held. In a case of history repeating but in reverse, this time it was the Islamic forces who found it impossible to take the fortress their ancestors had built; they were repulsed just as Ramiro had been nearly two centuries before. Mangonels were wheeled into place to facilitate the helter-skelter hurl of rocks and stones, the catapulting of balls of fire; siege engines and battering rams, grappling ladders, bows and arrows, prayer: everything was thrown at the walls and soldiers of Mayrit. Access was cut off completely; perhaps the Christians could eventually be starved out. Yet the plan faced a fatal enemy: Ali's troops were hit by a plague that decimated their strength, and they found the fortress inaccessible. It also became increasingly difficult to feed a large troop of soldiers as the fertile lands around Mayrit were ravaged; unfulfilled, they were forced to withdraw. Despite a number of military victories over the decades, the Almoravids fell back just as quickly as they had arrived. For all their ferocity, control of the peninsula was too much for a kingdom based in southern Morocco. Domestic political strife obliged them to return to their capital Marrakech, which fell to the next great Islamic dynasty, the Almohads, in 1147.

From the twelfth century comes one of the earliest documented references to Mayrit. With the town freshly in Christian hands, it fell under the survey of legendary geographer and quite possibly, for his time, the best-travelled citizen in the world, Muhammad al-Idrisi, who wrote that 'among the towns at the base of those mountains [the Guadarrama] lies the fortress of Mayrit, well defended and prosperous'. Al-Idrisi, from the Almoravid-controlled North African town of Ceuta, makes mention of the mosque that had been sited where, at the end of the eleventh century, the church of Santa María had been built on the instructions of the victorious Christian king. As he penned his observations, al-Idrisi could scarcely have imagined that a thousand years later the Islamic Cultural Centre of Madrid would include one of the biggest mosques in Europe, a construction that looms up over the M-30 in the Barrio de la Concepción neighbourhood, looking out over the traffic that flows, in twenty-four-hour intensity, above the forgotten stream of the Abroñigal.

If Almoravid rule in Al-Andalus had lasted little more than two generations, the same fate awaited the Almohads, occupying southern Spain around 1160 and enjoying the briefest of summers before being soundly defeated in 1212 by an army of combined

Christian forces, including Alfonso VIII 'the Noble' of Castile, Sancho VII 'the Strong' of Navarre and Pedro II 'the Catholic' of Aragon, at one of the most famous battles of Spanish history, Las Navas de Tolosa. With troops from Portugal, France and Occitania joining those of the various Christian kingdoms of the peninsula, combat was engaged across the sloping fields, the sharp cliffs and close, shaded ravines of the pass of Despeñaperros – the gateway that separates Andalusia from Castile. Las Navas de Tolosa was to be a bloody and ruinous killing field for the Almohads where, reportedly for the first time, a company of Christian troops fought under the flag of 'Madrid' – in this case, a bear at pasture with its shoulders and rump featuring the seven stars of the Ursa Major constellation, one of the most clearly visible of the heavenly formations in the skies above Madrid. Heavenly symbols did not stop there; the troops were assisted by no less a figure than San Isidro who, despite having been dead for forty years, appeared to King Alfonso VIII in the guise of a shabbily dressed shepherd, guiding the Christian troops along the most hidden and advantageous mountain paths the better to ambush the numerically superior Almohad troops of Muhammad al-Nasir.

This rout was a further step towards the end for Al-Andalus. The troops from Madrid, with the singular assistance of one of their patron saints, would not be forgotten over the coming years. Throughout the thirteenth century, towns of former splendour fell one after another; soon only Granada, under the control of the Nasrid dynasty, remained in Muslim hands. In one of history's many ironies, the emirate of Granada is remembered as perhaps the most famous element of Islamic Spain, yet it was just the smallest pocket of what had once been a glorious and sophisticated caliphate.

The Madrid of 1212 that so distinguished itself at Las Navas de Tolosa was a significantly more important entity, within the context of the developing Christian control of the peninsula, than the frontier post of 1085. From that year Mayrit begins its transition to Madrid. It is not only a Christian town; importantly, it is now a Castilian town. Madrid was by no means safe, however: Alfonso's victory was still fresh, lines were not hardened, people and armies were still in flux, roaming the peninsula. The mid-twelfth century saw three medieval military and religious orders come into being, all in swift succession in the decade between 1160 and 1170: the Orders of Santiago, Calatrava and Alcántara. These orders operated as a kind of state, or independent authority, and their influence was to last until the late fifteenth century, by which time the Catholic monarchs brought them under the direct control of the crown. Most active around Madrid was the Order of Santiago, to which Diego Velázquez aspired with inordinate longing in the last years of his life.

There was no religious persecution in the wake of Alfonso's victory; large numbers of *mudéjares* remained in the *arrabales* of Madrid, while those who had resided within the walls moved out to the *morería*, the quarter around Las Vistillas and San Andrés, formerly occupied by the Mozarabs, where they continued their trades. Yet again, civilian populations faced the disruptions of war by doing their best to maintain a semblance of continuity. Those who could not live under Christian rule, or who had held military posts, fled south where there were still battles to be fought. The role of Madrid as a military garrison remained vital, albeit its focus was reversed: rather than look north to defend itself from Christian troops, it now looked south to the prospect of sporadic revenge attacks by the Almoravid and later Almohad armies. It remained a battle-ready outpost, brilliantly situated but still not sure of its final destination: the pendulum of Christian and Islamic victories swung back and forth. Yet as the twelfth and early thirteenth centuries passed, Madrid grew with its diverse range of peoples: settlers from Castile and Leon, Mozarabs, Jews and Muslims, some of whom had come up from the south, unable to live under the harsher regime of the Almoravids. Three small extramural settlements developed around the convents of San Martín, San Ginés and Santo Domingo el Real, each home to their sundry artisanal guilds.[5]

Meanwhile, the *transierra*, the fertile territories along the skirts of the Guadarrama, were the source of an ongoing dispute between Segovia and Madrid. This is one of the most naturally beautiful parts of Castile with its clear streams, oak fields, all the birds and beasts we see in medieval codices, the steep pines, the stony outcrops and tender woodlands, for centuries thinly populated and of uncertain title. An intermediate zone that might turn hostile at any time, it was now an object of desire. Further helping to cement its role in the re-established Christian lands, in 1152 Alfonso VII 'the Emperor' had granted Madrid the status of *villa*, removing the town from under the administrative control of Segovia[6] and granting it the right to extensive lands to the north, such as the Dehesa de la Villa, or the more distant pastures and forests of Berrueco, the Lozoya Valley and, most ferociously disputed with Segovia, the rich terrains of Manzanares el Real. This quarrel over land rights would drag on until the sixteenth century.

The interplay of allegiances on the peninsula was not always a matter of ostensible faith, or God. Regions might change from Muslim to Christian and back again in a continuous give and take; allegiances could change over issues of taxation, religion, trade or concessions to nobility. The 'frontier' was an incoming and receding tide; in such circumstances, there was profound cultural intermingling and borrowing among peoples, as they swapped from one faith to another across the years, or generations, as circumstances best demanded for their own survival, or ease of life. Such matters were fluid, often contingent upon the interests or strategies of local nobility. Multiple sources attest to the general cooperation among peoples and the shifting skins they wore. This is not the starry-eyed view of inter-religious harmony some have wished to project backwards upon the various regions of the peninsula, but it is testament to an important cultural mixing, and this mixing was evident in Mayrit, or Madrid, as much as anywhere else: an early indicator of the absolute blendedness of bloodlines and personal histories of all who have come to make the city their home; a space where minorities were tolerated until the late fifteenth century, contributing in different ways to community prosperity through trades, commerce, administration and labour. Minorities were 'unequal in rights, but not marginalised'.[7]

The fight between Christianity and Islam had now shifted well to the south; the tide had receded from Mayrit and the middle frontier. This arm-wrestle of centuries was interspersed with instances of regional and strategic cooperation; it had its drawn-out truces and its years of quiet; in parts of the peninsula, regions might stand undisturbed for decades or even centuries before being dragged back into war. The term 'reconquest' is a difficult one, used and abused by essentialists of different stripes, all pushing their barrows through the ideological mazes of the past two centuries: 'moralizing following hard on the heels of simplifying'.[8] The idea of a 'reconquest' is mother's milk to some conservative and nationalist Catholics who interpret Spain as an eternally Christian nation which found itself needing to win back from godless Moors the lands they had selfishly conquered. Inversely, and just as predictably, the term provokes modern secularists who see anything resembling a 'crusade' as a stick with which to beat Christianity for its overthrow of an apparently golden and convivial age of interfaith harmony, ignoring the fact that the greatest threat to Umayyad Al-Andalus came not from Christians, but from internal dissent and rivalries, and from the far more radical Islamic Almoravid sect who, among other things, could not tolerate the Umayyads' decadent accommodation of Jews and Christians within their caliphate. The Almohads, who succeeded the Almoravids in Al-Andalus in the twelfth century, were, if anything, even more intolerant.

When Al-Andalus emerged into broader western historiography in the nineteenth century, it was subject to an intense degree of romanticisation. A tendency to orientalise and polish the exotic held sway – Al-Andalus wrapped in imaginary perfumes – while in more recent times, there has been an emphasis on the apparent harmony between faith traditions as part of a contemporary project of cultural and political tolerance. For centuries knowledge exchange was fruitful between the learned class of both faiths; both could boast sophisticated thinkers, and both had more than their fair share of the brutish and illiterate. Spain was not a society of zealots; in the Mediterranean 'the confrontation of cultures was more constant than in northern Europe, but so also was the consciousness of living together in a multiple society'.[9] Paradoxically then, both more friction and more tolerance.

Relations between Muslims and Christians were circumscribed by specific limits, and much as the philosophers and translators may have exchanged notes in cultural centres such as Córdoba or Toledo, foot soldiers, well beyond the ken of love poetry and mathematics, had the less glamorous task of conquest, punishment and killing in the name of their respective crusades. Lest we forget: enlightened and civilised discourse and the amiable commercial trade between peoples went hand in hand with the brutal realities of early medieval warfare.

By the time the formal structures, if not the cultural inheritance, of Islamic rule had gone from the peninsula in the late fifteenth century, it had left behind a more fertile place, in both the agricultural and intellectual sense. The eight centuries of Al-Andalus will always be viewed through a contemporary, and thereby ever-shifting, lens, reflecting the concerns or prejudices of the present moment. What is beyond doubt is the vital contribution of Islamic society and culture to the early foundations of Madrid: its fortification, its water supply, its fields and orchards, its narrow streets, elements of its language, many of its names and its intellectual heritage.

The fall of Mayrit, however, was not written into history as an epic, in the manner of Toledo (1085), Valencia (1238), Seville (1248) or Granada (1492): moments that have been interpreted over the centuries as pivotal in the political and social transformation of the peninsula. The taking of Mayrit was in some respects a side effect of the taking of Toledo, and the national narrative did not consider there was any element of grandeur in the way the frontier town shifted from Muslim to Christian hands.

For an event considered largely incidental, over the longer term its repercussions were to prove foundational for the modern nation.

After Las Navas de Tolosa, Madrid began to receive an inflow of population from across the peninsula. The town now enjoyed a life mostly free of onerous military obligations, at liberty to develop laws, industries, social and urban structures that were not conditioned by the threat of a nearby enemy.[10] A major step towards this transformation into a significant urban centre had come just prior to Las

Navas de Tolosa, with the concession in 1202, under Alfonso VIII of Castile, of the right granted to the *concejo*, or administrative body that ruled Madrid, to draw up their own *fuero*. The *fuero* was a species of medieval constitution, a local *magna carta* or set of municipal privileges that gave the town a greater level of control over a wide range of laws. It allowed for the election of city officials, conferred the ability to coin money, set out the rules relating to the taxing of citizens and contained its own penal code. As a legal and administrative framework for the town, the *fuero* established a tribunal to settle the disputes arising from the frictions of medieval life.

The *fuero* gives an extraordinary insight into the daily lives of the citizens of Madrid, and the political and legal development of the medieval town. It begins simply:

> This is the charter the Council of Madrid has prepared in honour of our Lord, King Alfonso, that rich and poor may live together in peace and safety.[11]

Released from the threats of frontier attacks, Madrid maintained a reduced military presence, albeit military service excluded all those who might not be considered reliable for reasons of physical stamina or dubious faith: the clergy, women, children, the aged, Jews and converted Moors.[12] Soldiers were convened for occasional rural pacification or seasonal raiding; they were not knights errant like Quixote, who three or four centuries later would seek distributive justice to protect the vulnerable, unshackle the wrongly held, supply the needy and defend the honour of ladies of rank and the virtue of maidens. Nevertheless, the underlying violence of a thirteenth-century town is clear: the first laws of the *fuero* lay down the penalties for striking a man 'with lance, sword, knife, club, stick or stone'. Murder is swiftly dealt with, as are the punishments for stealing, committing sexual violence, assaulting, breaking and entering with violence, beating servants, participating in gangs or banditry, or simply dishonouring one's word.

There follow prescriptions for dealing with the ownership, control, sale or theft of cattle, sheep and pigs; prohibitions against betting;

laws pertaining to butchers and bakers; for the correct and legal use of weights; for tanneries and vineyards; the correct use of common grazing land; where one must and must not wash offal in the local stream, and where one must not throw human waste; the difference between rabbits skinned and unskinned; restrictions on dogs and travelling salespeople; and how to responsibly carry arms and knives. Specific words were also on the list of prohibited items: no man must call his female neighbour, or her daughter, or any woman a whore, bitch or leper; nor his neighbour, or his neighbour's son, or any male a sodomite, son of a sodomite, a cuckold, liar, perjurer or leper. Given the Spanish propensity for richly inventive forms of swearing, it is doubtful much heed was paid to these linguistic guidelines. The *fuero* concludes with a 'chrismon' – a medieval device to draw attention to important parts of a text. There follows a substantial list of crimes that carry the death penalty: the first, and most categorical, is for any found guilty of sexual violence against women.

The *fuero* lists the town's ten original Christian temples; although some have disappeared, and others been substantially rebuilt, the sites of devotion and their patron saints remain to this day: Santa María, San Nicolás, San Andrés and San Juan among them. Others such as San Miguel de la Sagra or San Miguel de los Octoes have been lost. The latter, the baptismal church of Golden Age poet and playwright Lope de Vega, was ravaged by fire in 1790 and is now the site of the gourmet food market of San Miguel.

Enforcing these laws was a new Town Council. Until the thirteenth century governance decisions in Madrid had been made in an informal and remarkably democratic fashion, with citizens invited to participate regularly, along with a council of worthy patricians, in discussion of local affairs and to help solve any litigious disputes. Tradition suggests these meetings were held by the church of San Salvador. With the *fuero* came a new council, meeting two or three times a week, composed of a chief magistrate, aldermen, solicitors, sheriffs, investigators and juries: a whole municipal administrative complex which, while hinting at the Spanish love for unnecessary layers of bureaucracy, also suggests the increasingly important profile of Madrid in the thirteenth century.

The *fuero* was far from perfect in terms of administering the bustle and strife of medieval Madrid, nor was it as comprehensive as other *fueros* of the time in medieval Castile. Further, these laws applied only to Christians, while the Muslim and Jewish communities followed their own laws, applied by their own judges.[13] Importantly, however, the Christian *fuero* took precedence: in the circumstance of any conflict between community members of different faiths, both Muslims and Jews were subject to the town council's principal code.[14]

Pre-dating King John of England's *Magna Carta* by a decade, this compendium of laws – along with Alfonso IX of Leon holding the first parliament in Europe in the twelfth century, and some of the most powerful and successful medieval monarchs being young Iberian women – helps to demolish popular impressions of Spain as an inherently backward nation. Such notions should have died long ago, but too often they persist in the public imagination: the novelist Pío Baroja was reported to have said that 'half the idiocies about the Spanish soul have been invented by foreigners, the other half by Spaniards themselves'.[15] Recent decades of research have peeled back centuries of neglect and lazy bias to reveal a far more sophisticated medieval society than had been popularly thought, or as would be represented in different versions by Spain's powerful rivals in coming centuries: the French, the Dutch and the English, most especially.

Madrid was moving to the heart of this increasingly rich and complex society, now classified as *villa y tierra* – a small town with surrounding lands that belonged to it and lay under its jurisdiction, known as an *alfoz*. In medieval Castile the *alfoz* – from the Arabic *al-hawz*, rural district – was an important part of the administration and control of territory, composed in turn of a series of *sexmos*, or departments. The *fuero* of Madrid established three *sexmos* in the surrounds of the town: Aravaca, Vallecas and Villaverde; the town council's apparatus of government included administrators to look after the affairs of the *alfoz* and *sexmos*. These agricultural hamlets served the larger population of Madrid; with the establishment of the *sexmos*, Madrid's reach now extended from the Tagus in the south to the Sierra de Guadarrama in the north, much as its geography remains to this day. Thus, a map begins to take shape: a misshapen rectangle in central Spain being the first appearance, fledgling and uncertain, of what would become the province of Madrid.

During the twelfth century the walls of Madrid were significantly expanded. From the original Puerta de la Vega, fortifications now ran through las Vistillas, took in the *arrabal* of San Andrés and ran along Cava Baja and Cava de San Miguel – these narrow contemporary streets still trace the line of the old fortifications – then via the Puerta de Guadalajara (by the Plaza Mayor), down Calle Escalinata, along Arenal and Ópera to the Puerta de Valnadú, and back towards the site of the ancient *alcázar*. Only Santo Domingo el Real and San Martín to the north, and the primitive hermitage of San Francisco to the south – reputedly founded in 1217 by Saint Francis of Assisi himself – remained outside the walls. Significantly, the smaller original walled circuit containing the *alcázar* complex and the ninth-century *medina* remained, with its own gardens and workshops, becoming a separate zone to service nobility and royalty: Madrid had already begun to evolve its later dual designation as *villa y corte* – town and court. Features one can recognise in the modern city were taking shape, such as the Plazas de San Nicolás and Santiago, the Plaza de la Paja – one of the loveliest of the many small squares in central Madrid, it features memorably in Javier Marías's final novel, *Tomás Nevinson* – or the Plaza de San Salvador, later to be the Plaza de la Villa, one of the best preserved in Madrid. Access to open fields and orchards was marked by the appropriately named Camino de las Huertas;[16] roads led out to Hortaleza, Alcalá, Atocha and Vallecas. The banks of the Manzanares, site of the Moorish assault on the town 100 years before, were now flourishing market gardens, accessed by the again appropriately named Puerta de la Vega.[17] The simple limit on the growth of Madrid to the west imposed by topography – the steep escarpment and the Manzanares itself – meant the town initially expanded to the east, from the old *alcázar* out towards the Puerta del Sol, Cibeles, the Prado, Atocha and south towards La Latina.

There was as yet no hint of the grander days that lay in store, but this consolidation of the town, both institutionally and physically, was of vital importance. It meant Madrid would not share the fate of so many other sites, across the centuries, that served a specific purpose for a specific people at a specific historic juncture, only to vanish from history when that set of circumstances – in this case, the defence of the middle frontier – had passed.

Unfortunately, the people themselves are difficult, if not impossible, to trace. Their trades are known to us, but the inner lives of citizens – mostly illiterate – are invisible; it would be centuries before any historical interest would be taken in the 'common people'. The small disputes that knit together to form a life, the loves and cares, fears, desires and ambitions, are all absent. The pre-modern human subject is mostly an absence; the living being occupied a home, a field, a cultural and political space without leaving any other trace. Even their bones are now long gone, ploughed into the earth, sunk beneath future centuries. The usual suspects come into view: kings and bishops; warriors; queens; saints and philosophers; the occasional rebel or traitor – those who had the capacity to leave a written record, or inspired others to leave one of them. The large base of the medieval social pyramid remains mostly speculation; the soldier, shepherd, cook, mother, blacksmith, jeweller, tanner, wool spinner or weaver, or the whole universe of children. Likewise, the histories of certain noble families of Madrid remain: the Vargas or Luján families, to name just two, have documented, archived histories; both contributed substantially to the reconquest or later defence of medieval Madrid as did, somewhat later, the illustrious Mendoza family. They have left voices, no matter how initially faint or distant; they have built, marked the sand, etched the stone, inscribed the parchment. The other families – of peasants, soldiers, artisans, even the great majority of the clergy – are defined by silence.

In the busy commercial activity of twelfth- and thirteenth-century Madrid, weekly markets in several *arrabales* dealt in bread and wine, meat and fish – fresh from local rivers or dried from the ports of Cantabria – fruit and vegetables, along with other essentials such as salt, herbs, oil, honey and cheese, supplying the townsfolk, the militia still stationed there and the nobility.[18] All the artisanal goods typical of the day – metal, wood, leather, wool, wax, cloth, stone, ceramics or jewels – were essential to Madrid's economy. Workers drew on skills drawing on inherited Christian, Islamic and even old Iberian knowledge, ancient crafts carried along the generations, changing with improvements in technology or local variations in primary materials or availability. An abattoir[19] operated on the stream of San Pedro close to the Puerta Cerrada; formerly extramural, it was now within the expanded walls, with its waste products, and that from associated tanneries, tightly controlled. Prices for all the essential products traded through the medieval markets were determined by royal decree; as the 1202 *fuero* showed, there was a tight control on weights and measures to ensure flour was honestly and equitably bought and sold; the scope for cheating, given the unreliable nature of measurement, was enormous. Whereas prior to the late eleventh century the Duero Valley had been the bread basket of Castile, now the ample fields south of Madrid were sown with staple grains; flour mills were built on the Jarama and later, from the thirteenth century, on the Manzanares. Vineyards prospered in times of peace; like all plantings of grains, fruit and vegetables, they were closely guarded in an era when failure meant extreme hunger, poverty or both.

Contrary to the idea that the end of Muslim rule in central Spain ushered in a period of narrow-minded, anti-intellectual darkness, the role of Christian Toledo continued to be critical to advancing the European intellectual heritage, and the town played an important role in the broader continental twelfth-century renaissance. The exceptional Toledo School of Translators was committed to continuing a legacy of the caliphate of Córdoba: the transmission of other knowledge traditions – philosophy, medicine, mathematics and science – from Persian, Greek, Hebrew and Arabic into Latin or, by the thirteenth century, medieval Spanish. The school, under the auspices of the cathedral of Toledo, attracted some of the finest scholars from across Europe; often their paths led through Madrid.

This work, unparalleled in the Europe of the time, laid the foundations for a renewed understanding of the state and the individual.

Madrid had settled into a period of relative peace, growing stronger as a commercial centre. The church was intimately involved in the growth of the town, and historic *arrabales* grew up around parish churches: San Ginés, San Martín, San Andrés, Santa Cruz and the religious community of Santo Domingo el Real. A group of Benedictine monks had been granted land to the north of the town walls in the early twelfth century, and in roughly 1126 San Martín came into being, initially under the tutelage of the monastery of Silos. As the *arrabal* grew, the monks were charged with attending to the spiritual needs of the new settlers, arriving from the Castilian lands north of the Guadarrama. This internal migration was strongly encouraged by the new Christian sovereigns, deemed necessary to counterweigh the immediate post-conquest prevalence of Muslim citizens of Madrid, the *mudéjares*.[20] The mendicant orders flourished: in the early thirteenth century, the convent of Santo Domingo, with its own walled *arrabal*, had been established close by San Martín, while the Franciscans had settled on steep, vacant, extramural land just below the *arrabal* and church of San Andrés, on the site where the church of San Francisco el Grande stands today.

Christian Spain had entered a new phase; although diverse forms of violence and suffering would continue to be staples of medieval life, much of the peninsula benefited from the calm at the end of the period of warring *taifas*. There would be plenty of Christian infighting too, regional power struggles, provincialism, family disputes: bastards, usurpers and the scorned. There was, however, a larger cross-peninsular project for the first time since the Romans and at the centre, after more than 300 years on a critical religious fault line, stood Madrid.

Its denomination had taken a circuitous route through the previous centuries, and explorations of the origin of the name can disappear down linguistic rabbit holes debating the transition from possible Roman-Visigoth to Arabic to early medieval Latinate verbal forms.[21] Whether real or fictitious, the Latin or proto-romance 'Matrice' was a possible starter, transmuted into the Arabic 'Mayrit'; other forms used included 'Magrit', 'Magerit' or 'Majerit'. In the absence of any standardised system of spelling, the nomenclature was a free-for-all: the old Castilian 'Matrit' still exists today in the demonym 'matritense', albeit seldom used given the contemporary predominance of 'madrileño'. Over the centuries, writing either by ear or by imagination, the forms flowered: 'Magderit', 'Mageriti', 'Matricen', 'Maydrith', 'Maydrid', 'Maiedrid', 'Mayadrid', 'Maiedrit', 'Maierit', 'Maiarid' and 'Mayadrit' turn up in medieval documentation, all travelling the path towards the final, simpler, version. Also discarded along the way, some perhaps only ever used once by anonymous scribes, are 'Majoridum', 'Majoritum', 'Mageritum', 'Magerid', 'Mageridum', 'Magritum', 'Matritum', 'Madritum', 'Mageriacum', 'Maieritum', 'Maioritum', 'Maidrit' and 'Madrit'.

To the late twelfth century, around 1194, we owe the first recorded use of 'Madrid'; meanwhile, 'Madrit' had first appeared in 1176. For the next 300 years 'Madrid' and 'Madrit' are used interchangeably until linguistic reform and evolution in the late fifteenth century saw the former take precedence. A town council document from 1477 is the last known official use of Madrit.[22] That antique form will disappear at a critical moment, with the united crowns of Castile and Aragon about to fall upon an altogether unimaginable empire.

Work and prayer

Madrid's patron saint, San Isidro, occupies both secular and holy worlds: a rural labourer, a humble figure with dirt on his hands and sweat on his brow, and an incorruptible, miraculous saint pressed into the service of a newly thriving town. Born roughly coincident with the Mozarabic *arrabal* of San Andrés around 1082 – it assists the power of his iconography to have been born coincident with the defeat of Muslim governance in Mayrit – Isidro de Merlo y Quintana was destined to join no less a figure than the miraculously rediscovered Virgin of Almudena as one of the revered symbols of Madrid. Although not canonised until the early seventeenth century, he was venerated from as early as 1212 when his body – uncorrupted after forty years in the grave – was disinterred and King Alfonso VIII recognised in this apparently healthy corpse the mysterious shepherd who had guided his troops through the narrow byways of Despeñaperros to famous victory at Las Navas de Tolosa.

Isidro was by trade a well digger, or more specifically a *zahorí* – from the Arabic *zahurí*, a geomancer, one who reveals the hidden: in this case, divining underground water sources, an important task in the expanding agricultural lands around Madrid after the pacification of the region at the end of the eleventh century. He began his working life just as the twelfth century swung into view; not being a soldier, when the Almoravid forces laid siege to Madrid in 1109, Isidro moved north to the town of Torrelaguna – nowadays

73

one of the great historic sites of the province of Madrid, it would also be the birthplace of the third Inquisitor General, Cardinal Cisneros – and there he met and married María Toribia who was to become, in time, Santa María de la Cabeza, another singular and beloved figure in the history and folklore of Madrid. Back in Madrid, in 1119 Isidro was in the service of the noble Vargas family, amply rewarded with land following their military and financial assistance in the taking of the town.

The patron saint of farmers since his beatification, work and prayer were twin staples of Isidro's life. He became so assiduous in prayer that his fellow workers complained he was never at the plough when needed. His employer decided to spy on Isidro to see if this laziness were real, or simply a matter of jealous co-workers. He indeed found Isidro away from his tasks, kneeling in prayer in the distance; in his absence the ploughs were being guided by two angels, winging their splendid way along behind the oxen. Isidro was immediately rewarded with what amounted to a promotion with the Vargas family.

Early in their life together, Isidro and María had a son, Illán. Of this young boy nothing is known until he suddenly appears, in the seventeenth century, in hagiographic accounts of his parents' lives. One day while Isidro was labouring in the fields – accompanied by angels or not is unclear – at home young Illán fell from his mother's arms and into a deep well. A mishap, a momentary distraction, a trial by an inscrutable God: the stage was set for one of Isidro's most famous miracles. Rushing home, he and his wife proceeded to pray fervently by the lip of the well, whereupon the water level rose and the baby was carried to the surface unharmed. It is said that in thanks María and Isidro swore themselves to a life of sexual abstinence. No reason is offered as to why this was an appropriate response; it has all the hallmarks of the moral purpose entrusted to the tale by its contemporary authors.

The remarkable works continued: saving his donkey, tied up outside the church in which he was praying, from wolf attack; fresh water springing from the ground at his command; multiplying bread and other foods to satisfy the hungry. Although they were almost contemporaries, his love of animals pre-dated Saint Francis, but given the centuries that passed until his life was written, medieval and early modern authors may have drawn on the same symbolic resources as Saint Francis's examples of kindness. Carrying a heavy sack of grain to be milled one morning, Isidro crossed a snow-covered field – the bright, crisp, dry cold of winter in Castile – and was moved by the sight of the birds around him pecking fruitlessly at the barren ground. He shared his bag of grain with them and then proceeded, without most of the grain, to the mill, only to find upon arrival that the sack had been replenished and was now full to bursting. Isidro was not alone in his contact with the otherworldly: María was reported to dream every night of the Virgin Mary, who spread her immaculate cloak across the waters of the Jarama.[1]

These tales have only the loosest connection to the reality of this twelfth-century farm labourer and his wife, but that is beside the point: they form part of a cultural and religious bedrock that for many over the centuries, and many still, has shaped belief and conditioned meaning. Madrid is inseparable from San Isidro and Santa María de la Cabeza, and vice versa. The meadows that took Isidro's name on the far bank of the Manzanares, where he laboured for Iván de Vargas, are synonymous with some of the brightest works of Goya; the festivals that mark his patronage of the city – the annual Feria de San Isidro – is a high point in the Madrid calendar. As a patron saint, Isidro is busy around Spain and the broader Hispanic world; in this sense, he is one of Madrid's most famous exports.

As with the life of Jesus, the miracles of the saints are ex post facto, collected and written by future generations. The more astounding the miracles, the more valuable the corpse of the saint becomes, the source of countless potential reliquaries. In Spain, not a few bodies of the holy have suffered terrifying fates after death; one thinks of Saint John of the Cross, dismembered here, dismembered there, various parts of his body spirited away, including while in Madrid in 1593 en route from Úbeda, where he had died, to Segovia, where he had expressed a wish to be buried. Centuries earlier, San Isidro faced a similar fate. He died at the age of 90 – an extraordinary longevity for the era – and was buried without a coffin, his body wrapped in a simple winding sheet. Over the following years floods played havoc with the burial ground of the church of San Andrés and yet, in 1212, when Alfonso VIII asked to see the remains of the holy labourer, he and all those with him were astonished by the perfect condition of the uncanny shepherd. He rests now, elaborately coffined, in the Collegiate Church of San Isidro el Real in central Madrid – a historic but rather ugly seventeenth-century temple in chunky grey granite – alongside María, who died just three years after him.

Isidro has not always been left in peace. As a holy figure, his corpse was in demand – faith, magic, healing – and over the years extravagant attempts were made to claim a piece of him, including by one of Isabel the Catholic's ladies-in-waiting who, while kissing the feet of the corpse, bit off the big toe of his right foot. To legend we owe the story that the queen, oblivious to what had happened, had set out for Toledo; following her, the lady-in-waiting. When the entourage reached the Manzanares, all crossed the river without difficulty except the horses of the lady-in-waiting which shied and refused to enter the water. Embarrassed and ashamed, the young woman broke down and confessed her unusual theft. The queen ordered her to go back and restore the toe. It was not affixed to the foot of the saint but placed in a receptacle that hung around the mummified neck for years until it finally, and mysteriously, disappeared.

The body was subject to an intense traffic over the years which we cannot recount in full, such were the comings and goings. The uncorrupted San Isidro was brought to the bedside of Carlos III in the eighteenth century – not a few of Spain's rulers had the habit of communing with the dead to cure in times of illness. One hundred years earlier, at the close of that strange seventeenth century of great brilliance and great darkness, one of San Isidro's desiccated fingers was placed under the pillow of Carlos II, the most unfortunate of the Habsburg rulers, likewise to assist in healing; other accounts suggest he always kept one of San Isidro's teeth under his pillow as an amulet. María also suffered the dispersal of her body after death, her head or skull being most prized as it was said to bring petitioners rain in times of drought. Her skull, too, was brought to Carlos III on his deathbed in 1788; he was reported to have kissed it with tenderness and devotion.

In 1622, just a year after the death of Felipe III, Isidro was canonised in the recently completed Plaza Mayor; colloquially, Isidro had been venerated as a saint from the early thirteenth century. It was a red-letter day for the Catholic Church, with the more recent figures of Teresa of Ávila, Ignatius of Loyola and Francis Xavier all canonised at the ceremony, together with the miraculous and proletarian Isidro de Merlo y Quintana.

Key nomenclature had by now fallen into place: the name of Madrid itself, along with Santa María de la Almudena, San Isidro and Santa María de la Cabeza. The path that winds out of mythology and towards modernity was fixed.

One of the oldest and finest examples of church architecture in Madrid, combining elements of Romanesque and Mudéjar, is found in the southern district of Carabanchel. Built over the vestiges of a Roman villa and possible traces of a Visigoth temple, the beautiful thirteenth-century hermitage of Santa María la Antigua is, according to legend, the church where San Isidro used the power of prayer to save his donkey from the ravenous wolf. San Isidro had died in 1172, so these dates don't add up; in defence of the legend, he may have attended an earlier iteration of the temple.

Like many a construction of the era, its strength is in its simple straight lines of brick and stone. Time has made a claim: a leaning side wall gives the church, from certain angles, a rickety feel. Today, it sits shyly in its perfunctory and secular surrounds; one of the architectural jewels of the city is shouldered aside by power lines, threatened by graffiti, lost at the end of a meandering road that comes to the cemetery of the Martyr Saint Sebastian after passing through one of those cityscapes so common to the working-class areas of southern Europe: open ground, high-rise apartments, the drifting unemployed, weeds and stunted trees, cars in various states of repair, dirt tracks, a sense of improvisation and abandon. Knots of teenagers conspire together, lovers sprawl on the grass of a nearby park, dogs are asleep under an intense sun: the world might be wholly at peace. Sited not far from important Roman remains and on ground occupied, recent archaeology has found, since the native Carpetanos, the later world has imposed itself on Santa María la Antigua: the municipal cemetery on one side, and the echo of the notorious Carabanchel prison, since demolished, on the other. The hermitage, declared a national monument, has never seemed more fragile or abandoned.

The emergence of Castile

The eleventh to thirteenth centuries were a time of political predominance for the medieval kingdom of Leon and, subsequently, the crown of Castile, both central to the re-emergence of Christianity on the peninsula. Madrid lay geographically at the heart of Castile, and nearby towns such as Toledo and Alcalá de Henares, both dating back to before the time of Christ, must have looked askance as the fledgling town, with its cramped streets and defensive cliffs, began to take on greater political and commercial importance in the context of a prosperous medieval Castile. Perhaps Alcalá de Henares was never in the running to be a capital, but Toledo may have laid a solid claim, to say nothing of geographically less central but historically significant towns such as Seville or Valladolid. Some have argued that were it not for Felipe II's decision in the mid-sixteenth century, Madrid would have remained a second-order Castilian town, of lesser importance than Toledo, Salamanca or Valladolid. Madrid, however, has always insisted on its independence despite the medieval influence, and even animosity, exercised by Segovia to the north, and the powerful Archbishopric of Toledo to the south.[1]

During the thirteenth century Madrid entered into serious dispute with Segovia over the rich pastoral lands, streams and forests that lay between the two towns. Segovia had sent settlers into the lovely region at the southern base of the Guadarrama to make use of the otherwise unexploited territories where a number of *sexmos* were under its control. Segovia was a region with a long pastoral tradition, and had a great capacity for the resettlement of population – numbers were streaming south with the retreat of Islam – while Madrid was, given its historic limits, an urban and agricultural region, without any oversupply of population.[2] Royal concessions from the crown of Castile, however, soon allowed Madrid extensive use of the *transierra*, in recognition of the role Madrid troops had played under King Fernando III 'the Saintly' in the defeat and return to Christian hands of Seville in 1248.[3] A generation later, in 1275, and in the face of continuing dispute and even armed conflict, King Alfonso X 'the Wise' took the lands under the direct control of the crown, giving rise to the 'royal' designation of El Real de Manzanares.[4] The dispute, however, was intractable; another decade on, in 1284, Sancho IV, the second king after Alfonso VI to carry the sobriquet of 'the Brave', found in favour of Madrid, much to the anger of Segovia. It was not until 1383 that King Juan I, who took a great interest in the development of the town, and who spent long periods in Madrid as its climate helped his tuberculosis, gave the lands by royal decree to the emerging, powerful Mendoza family, along with dominion over the feudal estates of Buitrago and Hita. El Real de Manzanares – perfect for timber, crops, fishing, sheep and cattle – was something of a jewel in the regional crown of Madrid.[5] The Mendoza family, having distinguished themselves in the service of the king throughout the fourteenth century, did not squander their good fortune, and over succeeding generations went on to play key roles in characteristic early modern fashion: in the church, the military, in government, as landowners and as patrons of the arts. An hour north of Madrid, nestling under the fantastical granite outcrops of La Pedriza, the castle of Manzanares el Real was from 1475 their family seat. It is by some distance the best preserved and architecturally most remarkable castle in Madrid, and one of the finest in Spain.

Lacking a fixed capital, the crown of Castile, which by 1400 occupied the entire peninsula with the exceptions of Portugal, Navarre,

Aragon and the diminishing Nazari emirate of Granada, hosted an itinerant court. In this way the crown kept contact with and control over its vast territories, as well as an eye on the landholding feudal families and associated nobility, influential around Madrid in the fourteenth and fifteenth centuries and particularly necessary for financing royal wars. In 1309, under the reign of Fernando IV 'the Summoned', Castile held court for the first time in Madrid. Given its geographic centrality, it was natural that over the following reign of Alfonso XI 'the Avenger' (1311–1350) the court would be held more regularly in such a convenient location.

Hosting the courts was of great importance at a time when Castile was a major player in Europe: the merino wool trade was booming partly due to England and France being ensnared in the Hundred Years' War,[6] and Spain had been opened to fresh currents of thinking and design via the intense international traffic along the pilgrimage route to Santiago de Compostela. Alfonso XI, having come of age as a 14-year-old in 1325 and assumed the throne held in regency by his grandmother, María de Molina, made Madrid one of his preferred homes.[7] Madrid has always boasted an invigorating climate, and its *alcázar* was as fine a fortification as any for the protection of the royal family. The *alcázar* would stand for 900 years; only fire, and perhaps decrepitude, brought it down as late as the eighteenth century.

The courts were hosted again in 1329; the arrival of its extensive retinue meant an increase in business for local trades, but there was a downside: not only was Madrid overcrowded, but the mass influx of strangers into the town – no matter how important they might have been – meant increasing the chance of spreading disease in an often insalubrious environment. Many residents resented being shoved aside; the lack of space became acute, and prices increased when the royal travelling show was in town. Madrid, like other medieval towns, was a tumbling conglomerate of residents, domestic animals, livestock, human waste, trade residues, building materials, mud and dust, straw, insects, feathers, animal excrement and, as a general background to the human comedy, the noise of taverns, commerce, markets, beggars, carriages, horses, players and musicians.

The dual nature of being host to the courts of Castile – economic benefit and urban congestion – would continue for centuries, perhaps even more acutely when, in the sixteenth century, Madrid scrambled to match its urban and residential infrastructure to the requirement of becoming the capital not just of Spain, but of a global empire.

By the fourteenth century further features of the Madrid we recognise today had fallen into place: the *arrabales* of San Ginés and Santa Cruz had sprung up along the roads that led, respectively, to Alcalá and Atocha. Adjacent to the Puerta de Guadalajara was the medieval marketplace, the Plaza del Arrabal; by the early seventeenth century it would become the most famous plaza of them all: the Plaza Mayor. In 1339 the original *fuero* of 1202 was overhauled, becoming a *fuero real* or Royal Code, applying not just to Madrid but all the lands under its control. In 1346 twelve governing councillors were appointed by royal decree, an early version of what would become the modern *Ayuntamiento*, or City Hall.[8] Meanwhile, a rich agricultural life helped sustain the growing population; sources from 1379 tell of extensive vineyards and grain crops, along with plums, pomegranates, cherries, figs, nuts, apples, melons, almonds and olives; lettuce, cauliflower, beans, carrots, cucumbers and turnips, all grown either within the walled town or in the dependent countryside that surrounded Madrid. The still thick forests serviced a timber industry, and all the artisanal crafts typical to a medieval economy were actively engaged, the most important of which were regulated, both in terms of scope and pricing, by the medieval town council.[9]

The horizon, however, was not cloudless. During the fourteenth century the darkest of enemies stalked the continent; in 1350 the Black Death claimed, among its countless victims, King Alfonso XI while assisting at the siege of Gibraltar. To this convulsion were added the ongoing threats of flood, drought and crop failure, along with a dynastic war of succession between Pedro I 'the Cruel' and his rival half-brother, Enrique II 'the Fratricide' of the Trastámara family, a war that set back the peaceful development of the economy of Castile.[10] Royal turf wars meant whole swathes of the Madrid region were exchanged between nobility as rewards for loyalty; the entire province, as we now know it, was a chequerboard of wandering alliances and treasons, and suffered a temporary decline in population as a result.

The dispute was settled in 1369 when Pedro I, after a decade and a half on the throne, was taken prisoner and assassinated by Enrique II, who thus earned his fratricidal sobriquet. Enrique assumed the throne as the first of the Trastámara dynasty; the family line would reach its zenith 100 years later with Isabel and Ferdinand and the union of the crowns of Castile and Aragon. Meanwhile, Enrique's wife, Juana Manuel de Villena, would be remembered for her attempt to remove the right arm from the mummified body of San Isidro – by now dead for 200 years – in order to have it as a reliquary. She may have heard of the blind man, 100 years earlier, who had wiped his eyes with a section of Isidro's winding sheet and had his sight restored. Juana Manuel could not get away with the arm, prevented from stealing it by civil officers, offended clergy, her own conscience or even supernatural forces, we do not know. The arm could only be reattached, poorly, with a makeshift ribbon.

In 1369, at the time of the ascension of the Trastámara family, the region around Madrid was under the jurisdiction of four entities: Madrid and its governing council; Toledo; Segovia; and the Order of Santiago.[11] Events continued to tilt in favour of Madrid as a centralised hub of political power; the Trastámara family made the *alcázar* one of their principal homes, carrying out reforms on the building – it took on the shape of a medieval Christian castle, with circular towers, rather than a square-jawed Islamic fortress – and frequently hosting the courts of Castile. Royal favour meant a recovery of population after the plague and ravages of the mid-fourteenth century; the *arrabales* grew steadily, in places merging to create a new extramural suburban Madrid, to the extent that the residents of San Martín and of San Ginés argued over rights to the use of the stream of Arenal. This reality, long submerged, can easily be imagined on the present-day Calle Arenal, in the heart of Madrid: on the left, the old church of San Ginés, with its documentary traces of poet Francisco de Quevedo (baptised, 1582) and playwright

Félix Lope de Vega (married, 1588) among other distinguished names from history; on the right, the Plaza de San Martín, now home to the sixteenth-century monastery of Las Descalzas Reales, housing one of the most outstanding collections of religious art in Madrid. Hospitals and convents were built to serve the needs of a growing population; the provision of basic food supplies and materials was guaranteed by municipal services dedicated to the purpose.[12] To the north of the province, in 1383 the Mendoza family found favour and lands, while in 1390 Enrique II ordered the construction of one of the great monuments of the province, the Carthusian monastery of El Paular in the beautiful Lozoya Valley. Madrid was settling in, and its boundaries were setting hard. South of the Guadarrama was its territory.

Jewish communities had remained small but strong throughout Spain, having lived alongside Muslims and Christians in Al-Andalus and participated in the steady growth of post-Islamic towns in Castile. During the fourteenth century the implicit compact of tolerance reached breaking point: social tensions, aggravated by plague deaths and common disorders in various parts of the peninsula, led to blame-shifting, paranoia, catastrophism and, ultimately, a series of pogroms in 1391. Jews were deemed responsible for food shortages and considered suspicious for their relative affluence and key role in finance; to no avail had they served as intermediaries between Muslims and Christians in matters of culture and commerce.[13] In communities across southern Spain, and in Toledo and Barcelona, Jews were killed or fled in significant numbers; albeit they only represented 5 per cent of the population, it was for the most part a highly skilled 5 per cent. In Madrid their synagogue complex, or *aljama*, was looted and trashed and, while the killings were not on the scale of other parts of the peninsula, Madrid was not innocent of bloodshed. While subsequent Castilian kings sought protection from discrimination for the Jewish community, it was only a reprieve, and the events of the late fourteenth century were to prove a precursor to the expulsion of the Jews 100 years later. There are two broad ways of understanding the lamentable cultural loss this represented for the country. The bleak view suggests Spain is a country notorious for shooting itself in the foot, periodically exiling its best, brightest and most productive; a more forgiving tone, while not excusing this historic violence, might point out that Spain, in the context of medieval Europe, had accommodated Jewish communities much longer than most other countries, where anti-Semitism had taken root earlier and lodged itself deeper. Little consolation, however: a late fifteenth-century turn toward stricter religious conformity would end the long Sephardic traditions on the peninsula.

The late fourteenth century had a further surprise in store for the people of Madrid, with an episode that began as far away as Egypt. Taken captive in battle in his own country by a force of Mamluks, the Christian king of Armenia, Leon V, was taken to Cairo in 1382 and held prisoner there by the Sultan, where he languished, his case foreshadowing the capture and imprisonment in Algiers of Cervantes 200 years later, until news of his fate reached his fellow Christian ruler, Juan I of Castile. Negotiating with merchant intermediaries, Juan I paid a ransom to secure the release of Leon, who was brought to Spain via Venice, taking up temporary residence in the market town of Medina del Campo. In 1383 or 1384 King Juan, for reasons never clarified and despite his reputation as a strong supporter of Madrid, granted title, or lordship, over Madrid to Leon in perpetuity. What the Armenian king had done to deserve this is a mystery. It was a tremendous insult to the citizens of Madrid; her native sons and daughters were not impressed by this Armenian interloper suddenly becoming their lord and master. He was granted a substantial annual pension of 150,000 *maravedis*,[14] some of which he spent on a reform of the towers of the *alcázar*. Yet this capricious experiment was doomed. By 1392 Leon was in England with Richard II, attempting unsuccessfully to negotiate a truce in the Hundred Years' War; by the following year, the often sickly but visionary Enrique III 'the Suffering' had succeeded Juan I on the throne of Castile, and Leon of Armenia was in France, granted castles and titles – the royal families looked after their own, when not stabbing each other in the back – and where, after a failed attempt to organise a crusade to retake his lands, he died in late 1393. Enrique III promptly restored Madrid's municipal rights and status, and the town could forget the whole unfortunate interlude.

Nor was this the last extravagant episode of this period. As the new king of Castile, Enrique III was known for his poor health, his efforts to halt any further violence against the Jewish communities of Spain and for his unusually broad vision of politics. He began to consider ways of connecting to the wider world beyond Europe, gathering information with all the curiosity of an anthropologist, and fell upon the idea of reaching out to the distant lands of the Timurids in Central Asia to forge an alliance, a type of pincer movement, against the threat of the Ottoman empire. An ambassador must be sent to negotiate. The very notion was daring; the journey itself almost inconceivable for the time – from Spain to the far eastern end of the Mediterranean, from Constantinople across the Black Sea via Trebizond to Armenia, Iran and Uzbekistan. For the nobleman of Madrid entrusted with this ambassadorial task, Ruy González de Clavijo, these were as remote as moonscapes; Samarkand, when he reached it in 1404, a place of untold luxury, of painted elephants and jewels and gorgeous silks.

Not to be outdone during his months-long stay at Timur's lavish court, Ruy González began to make a series of extravagant claims on behalf of Madrid and Spain. He did this carefully, for it was rumoured that the wily Timur was in possession of a magical ring whose bright stone would dim if any lie were uttered in the emperor's presence. Translating Ruy González's account for the Hakluyt Society of London in 1849, Clements Markham tells us of his strategy to avoid the sentient gemstone: 'He related many things concerning the grandeur of Spain, which, though not strictly true, were so in a metaphorical sense . . .'[15] As it happened, the stone in Timur's ring was not up to the nuances of metaphor. Clavijo claimed that his king 'had three vassals who brought six thousand knights into the field, with golden spurs' – alluding here to the three knightly Orders of Santiago, Alcántara and Calatrava. Further, 'he said that there was a bridge in Spain, forty miles broad, on which a thousand head of sheep found pasture', referring to the belief at the time that the Guadiana River, in southern Spain, flowed underground for part of its journey, only to appear again.[16] Clavijo used some simplistic wordplay to tell of 'a lion and a bull in Spain, which were maintained every day by the milk of many cows', in reference to the towns of Leon and Toro. Casting a constant eye on his informant gemstone, Timur was astonished to find it did not fade, staying bright throughout this catalogue of boasts. Lastly, and famously, Clavijo claimed there was 'a town surrounded by fire, and built upon water'. Here the reference is to Madrid, already known for its subterranean water channels and streams; the fire referred to the flinty silex stone with which the outer wall of Madrid had been built in Islamic times; it was said the metal arrowheads of besieging forces, when striking the walls, caused a spark of fire, especially spectacular at night.

The expression *Fui sobre agua edificada, mis muros de fuego son* – I was built on water, my walls are of fire – became part of the legend of Madrid, and featured on one of the city's most famous murals in the Plaza de Puerta Cerrada. For his part, Clavijo returned to Spain in 1406, the year his patron Enrique III died. He lived until 1412 and was buried in the church of San Francisco; he is also remembered by a small commemorative plaque in the Plaza de la Paja, where he had his home.

It was not until 1582, under the reign of Habsburg king Felipe II, that Clavijo's account of his journeys was first published. History reserves its ironies: while Clavijo admired the trappings of that distant, opulent empire, with its cruel and impossibly majestic leader, its lurid animals and fantastical customs, another fate awaited Spain. Barely three generations after Clavijo's journey, it was to open up an empire of its own: vaster, wilder, stranger, at times bloodier, and that was to have an impact on the future world far beyond anything in the Mongol emperor's dreams, or beyond the ken of his brooding gemstone.

The great turn

Among the patchwork of kingdoms on the peninsula – Castile, Aragon, Granada, Navarre and Portugal – Castile had assumed a clearly dominant role: larger, wealthier and, to the extent this has ever been possible, internally more cohesive. It was a centralising power that created new efficiencies and, in so doing, began one of the monstrous burdens of the Spanish state: its bureaucracy.[1] This apparatus was both cumbersome and ubiquitous, reaching into almost every aspect of life. In Madrid, laws were passed authorising a full census of residents and their properties in 1453 with the twin purpose of tracking unpaid taxes and reducing disputes over ownership; the introduction of detailed written municipal records helped to smooth out disagreements while adding an onerous red tape to civic life. From 1464 all changes of property ownership were to be reflected in the *Libros de acuerdos*,[2] an invaluable social record preserved and now digitised. As for paperwork, many would argue that in the past 600 years little has changed: Madrid sits at the very centre of an unwieldy state apparatus which seems to have no beginning and no end, but simply to exist, somehow eternal, immutable and infringing.

There was a lot to manage, even before the vast territories around the Atlantic and Pacific oceans came into view. The nobility of Castile, as factionalised among themselves as any set of Muslim *taifas*, were constantly jostling for control of land and towns; they had to be convinced, cajoled, their allegiance bought or traded where necessary. A complex system of taxes – from which the nobility was largely exempt – had to be administered. Periods of drought, hunger and crop failures continued; on top of this were the last, ragged disputes with the Muslims of Granada. In 1426 the uncorrupted corpse of San Isidro had been wheeled out again at a time of despairing drought; passing the body through the streets of Madrid, the rains began. At times, they were unwanted: in late 1434 and early 1435 three months of torrential downpours ruined crops, destroyed houses and bridges. These disasters were followed by further outbreaks of the plague, lasting for three years until 1438.[3]

By the time Enrique IV 'the Impotent' ascended the throne in 1454, a newly extended circuit of walls was in place; Madrid was in an unstoppable phase of expansion, plagues notwithstanding. The new *cerca* – a type of wall less substantial than a fortification – began at the Puerta Cerrada and now took in the Puerta de Toledo and the Puerta de Atocha (both much closer to the city centre than their present-day namesakes), then looped around to meet the Puerta del Sol, which makes its debut as part of the urban landscape of Madrid, at the very eastern edge of the town by the start of the road to Alcalá; finally, the wall enclosed the *arrabales* of San Ginés and San Martín for the first time, leaving only the Convent of Santo Domingo still outside its protective embrace. Urban development inside the walls became tighter and denser, and with this new configuration the Plaza del Arrabal, previously just outside the wall, became the most centrally located and important town square. Remodelled as the Plaza Mayor, it would remain the most important meeting point in Madrid until the nineteenth century, when eclipsed by the Puerta del Sol.

The walls erected in the expanding Madrid were not primarily defensive. Those days were long ago; the walls now operated for the better control of goods and people into and out of the city. There was also an element of public policing at a time when laws of good social behaviour might easily be flouted, but punishments were harsh. Madrid was a commercial hub, and the walls and gates were a systematic means of raising revenue and protecting local trades. Once again, location played a role: it was impossible for Madrid not to be at the centre of the manufacturing and trade networks of Castile.[4] Madrid may have been far from the sea, and thus isolated from the great medieval trade networks that benefited Barcelona and Aragon, but this was irrelevant, for Madrid was developing a different economy. It was not and never would be a Mediterranean power, nor an Atlantic one; for the moment it was busy absorbing the landless peasantry of Castile into its crowded streets and was, year by year, reign by reign, establishing itself as a diverse and dynamic centre of trade. Its time of dominance had not yet come: it was neither the most important market nor yet the biggest player in the economy of Castile, but it was at the centre of exchange, hosting merchants from all the major towns who found Madrid the perfect location for buying and selling raw materials and manufactured goods.[5] This inevitably drove population growth, reflected in the quickly expanding *arrabales* and the ever-increasing importance of the plazas within the town dedicated to different markets and fairs.

Increasingly home to the royals and nobility with all their retinue, Madrid was surrounded by a Castile that was vastly unequal in the distribution of its wealth, a rural society subject always to the vagaries of drought, disease and crippling taxes. For many in rural Castile, the only remedy to this utterly unpromising backdrop was to gravitate, despite all the risks, towards the major towns with their promise of work and food albeit, social hierarchies being as rigid as they were, the possibility of ascension was next to nil. But at least one might not starve, and carve out something, some wretched trade from some bleak corner, which might be passed on to one's children who hopefully would, successively, improve prospects. The packed urban environment of Madrid – the town now had a population of around 10,000 – not only increased the risk of illness and disease, the dangers of violence or prostitution, but also offered hope just as – all other comparisons aside – the city continues to do today. An additional drawcard from the middle of the sixteenth century was that Madrid became, and remains now, the most important place to enter the vast networks of government employment, one means of climbing the often treacherous ropes out of poverty and anonymity.

Prior to ascending the throne, Enrique IV had lived through a fruitless thirteen-year marriage to Blanca II of Navarre or, perhaps, she had lived through it with him. The marriage was annulled on the basis of Enrique's impotence, reportedly attributed to a curse, the exact nature or origin of which was never clear. The impotence was selective, as these things sometimes are: when local prostitutes in Segovia were questioned as to the king's virility, they confirmed he was indeed 'a reliable performer'. Enrique claimed the curse affected him only with Blanca, though this can have had nothing to do with her being his cousin for, having separated from her, he promptly married another cousin, Juana of Portugal, in an attempt to consolidate family connections to the Portuguese throne. Blanca, meanwhile, was submitted to the humiliating test of her virginity – it was confirmed – and then sent back to Navarre to be shut away under the custody of her sister. She remained childless for the rest of her life though, as it transpired, this was not long; she died soon after, in 'suspicious circumstances', quite possibly murdered by her sister or father. Blanca's fate has much in common with other tragic figures soon to come up over the horizon of Castilian history, such as Juana of Castile – sobriquet 'the Mad', a term now falling out of use as it reflects an age-old prejudice rather than a historical reality – and Prince Carlos, son of Felipe II. Castle walls, dungeons, weighty locks and implacable household members: these were not good years to be on the wrong side of a serious family dispute.

Enrique and his new wife, meanwhile, welcomed a daughter into the world in 1462, named Juana like her mother. This baby daughter, who would spend much of her childhood in the *alcázar*, was the origin of a long conflict that would degenerate into the War of Castilian Succession, waged between 1475 and 1479 and in which Madrid was directly implicated. After Enrique's death the right of his daughter Juana to the throne was disputed by his half-sister, Isabel. Juana, it was claimed, was illegitimate, the fruit of an affair between her mother and Beltrán de la Cueva, one of the favourites at court. This gave rise, in that Spanish love of nicknames, to her being called 'la Beltraneja', a belittling term by which the teenage Juana, her legitimacy and her right to the throne were dismissed. Rumours abounded: Enrique had confessed on his deathbed that Juana was not his daughter; alternatively, he had sworn that she was; or again, that he had obliged Beltrán de la Cueva to sleep with his wife to ensure her pregnancy when the question of his impotency, at least with his cousin-wives, became too obvious to avoid.

The nobility divided into two camps; this was, in the context of the time, a huge power play for one of the finest thrones in Europe. At stake was the crown of Castile, which effectively now had two queens: Juana, who allied herself in the most effective way with King Alfonso V of Portugal by marrying him in short order – she was 13, he was 43 – and Isabel who, back in 1469, had made a decision that was to have enormous long-term impact: she had married Ferdinand of Aragon. Should they win the war of succession, the crowns of Castile and Aragon would be united for the first time.

Not everyone had agreed with this union, and the marriage of Ferdinand and Isabel was conducted in secret. Ferdinand travelled overland to Valladolid 'in disguise and with only a tiny escort'.[6] Anything could have happened to thwart this journey – illness, banditry, accident – but such anonymous and seemingly minor events sometimes carry the weight of history. Thus Ferdinand, wrapped in simple clothes, keeping his head down as his minimal entourage passed through empty valleys and towns of towering stone, by blessed sanctuaries, through flocks of sheep, grain fields, rain storms, past the wine-laden inns to be made famous a century later by Cervantes. By night on ill-kept roads, under the weird black arms of pines, past the thick silence of oaks, hugging anonymity as best they could, they arrived at last in late autumn in Valladolid. The secretive couple wed; two teenagers brought together by powerful manipulators to serve agendas, there was no room for such quaint notions as love. And yet, inauspicious as it was, this marriage was one of the seeds from which modern Spain was to grow, and is still considered perhaps its finest royal coupling. Isabel and

Ferdinand were modest rulers, cautious yet committed to the growth of the kingdoms. The world can turn when least expected, and the passage of the years held in store for them two monumental events: the conquest of Granada and the voyages of Columbus.

In 1477 Isabel and Ferdinand entered Madrid. At last, the *alcázar* had been taken. The town had an ambivalent relationship with the Trastámara dynasty, since backing – wrongly, as it turned out – Pedro I over the Trastámara usurper Enrique II back in the 1360s. Yet all errors may be forgiven if the circumstances allow. The young monarchs aspired to much, but can have had no inkling of how their figures would flower over the coming centuries, taking on the symbolic weight of a nation and a church, a world view, a historic mission.

Castile emerged more powerful than Aragon after the union of the crowns. In his study of early modern Spain, Henry Kamen casts aside any idea that Madrid suffered for its lack of Mediterranean access: it benefited from the high volume of Castilian trade north to England, the Netherlands and France, thus rejecting 'the old image of a backward, non-capitalist and war-oriented Castile contrasted with a commercially progressive Aragon'.[7] Castile, at this point, was more dynamic and more unified politically: 'one Cortes, one tax structure, one language, one coinage, one administration, and no internal customs barriers.'[8] This substantial new crown was something of a forerunner to the European Union.

Authority, believed Isabel and Ferdinand, came from two sources: God and the people. They put themselves through a gruelling travel routine, attending wherever possible to the constant demands from nobility, landholders, clergy or simply the 'common people' across the various parts of their domains, preferring to dispense justice and wisdom in a direct and personal way. 'That was a golden time and a time of justice,' wrote native Madrid chronicler Gonzalo Fernández de Oviedo; every Friday the queen 'held public audiences in the *alcázar*, giving free and summary judgement; the humble poor were weighed along with the gentry, and received justice'.[9] Oviedo was clearly biased – he had been educated at the court of Isabel and Ferdinand – but the image holds true from other sources.[10]

While the court of Castile and Aragon remained itinerant, and preferred Valladolid when not on the road, the new monarchs did not ignore Madrid. Indeed, there was much work to do, not least as the Isabelline faction had caused enormous damage to the town and its buildings during the war of succession. Arson and looting had been rife, and much of the population had fled to the relative safety of the surrounding countryside.[11] With the courts being celebrated in Madrid in 1482 and 1499, the dregs of civil war had to be tidied up; the whole town had to be dragged from its medieval chaos into a more Renaissance sense of order. An extensive programme of rebuilding was undertaken, with an emphasis on churches, monasteries, convents and hospitals; available land on the outskirts of Madrid was increasingly occupied. A process that had begun in 1085 continued as it always has: Madrid for centuries has progressively engulfed the land around it, from the remaining fertile, watered woodlands to the north, to the parched and crumbling plains to the south.

Isabel was a highly educated woman who encouraged learning, especially among other women. She wished to run a disinfectant broom through late fifteenth-century Madrid; many of the filthy medieval customs were eliminated as a new order, led by principles of hygiene and decorum, imposed itself. From the 1490s the first roads were paved with cobblestones, and the first set of urban regulations written and enacted, dealing with matters such as the width of streets, night lighting or the circulation of carriages.[12] Madrid lived with an entire regime of smells, as various industries drenched the town with their striking odours. To this was added the animal life – pigs were banned from their muddy rootling – the foul bodies, the weird perfumes used like modern deodorants to guard against the stench; the dead, the diseased, the unwashed bodies, the mouths of rotting teeth, the wounds and sores, or the festering of poorly set limbs. The medieval street was brimming with waste, albeit in its apparent disorder it followed a particular set of rules with its own vernacular cosmography. Public orders were issued to prohibit the throwing of urine into the street, or any other human discharges such as blood and excrement, phlegm, hair or old teeth. Rubbish was to be placed in designated *muladares*.[13] These prohibitions cleaned up the town and provided a new source of revenue for the administrative coffers. For those who fell ill from any of the multiple risk factors of a late fifteenth-century cheek-by-jowl town, there awaited the crude medicines dispensed with the best will, but perhaps the worst results: mercury bichloride, once known as *suleman*, was a common crystalline treatment for syphilis, as likely to kill by mercury poisoning or internal corrosion as cure the pox; or the highly toxic *realgar*, ruby of arsenic, which, despite being a rat poison of the time, was among a contemporary medic's stock-in-trade. A modern science of health would only arrive in the eighteenth century under the Bourbon dynasty, a science that, for all its flaws and lacunae, we might nevertheless recognise today.

It is easy to walk around old Madrid unaware of the secrets of its medieval topography. Elements still break through, shyly, while others are hiding in plain sight in the curvature, gradient or naming of certain streets. As Segura tells us, the conferring of the status of capital on Madrid, for all it boosted the national and international prestige of the town and later city, was a disaster for the architectural heritage of medieval Madrid.[14] We know that much of the Islamic wall was repurposed for myriad other constructions. In medieval times, there was no modern sense of 'heritage', or of the need to preserve what had been of the enemy; the more complete the disappearance, the better. A capital demands new buildings, greater space, and lives with the ongoing urgency for change; Madrid has always loved to knock down and rebuild. The medieval footprint is there in the street layout and a few extant buildings, but has become faint with the centuries, either destroyed altogether – Madrid has additionally dealt with a series of wars on its streets – or built over in permanent palimpsest. Much, buried beneath the streets, will never be recovered. It is also true that Madrid was slow to value its heritage; in the process of rebuilding, old artefacts, walls or floors were often ignored for the sake of convenience, and priceless history lost. Until well into the twentieth century, sections of the expanded Christian walls were still destroyed, or built over, upon being found.

Who wanted a medieval artefact to ruin their plans for modern living? It has taken a long time for these attitudes, and municipal regulations, to change in order to better protect the vestiges of the ancient town.

Sometimes, one is caught between being thankful for small mercies, or aggrieved at the dimension of the historical insult. Outside the School of Architecture at Madrid's Polytechnic University there stands a Renaissance doorway, incongruously encased in brick: the beauty of the fifteenth-century stone design highlighted by the ugliness of its casement setting. The doorway could so easily have been lost forever, but in 1904, when the medieval hospital to which it belonged was being destroyed to widen the Calle Toledo, forward thinking managed to save this glorious element of Madrid's heritage. It sat in storage for years, until finally emerging again, inappropriately placed and largely ignored, but at least saved.

The hospital had been the work of the remarkable Beatriz Galindo (1465–1534), along with her husband Francisco Ramírez de Madrid (1445–1501), sobriquet 'the Artilleryman' and military adviser to the Catholic monarchs. Beatriz was from the university town of Salamanca, where from an early age she showed an extraordinary talent for grammar, Greek and Latin, so much so that she earned the sobriquet 'La Latina'. One of a significant group of talented humanist women in late medieval Spain,[15] her gifts were such that she soon found a place at court in Madrid, educating children and acting as advisor to Isabel herself. After Ramírez was killed in battle in 1501 in southern Spain during a flare-up of Moorish resistance to the new Catholic order, Beatriz dedicated herself to charitable works. Her husband had been very wealthy, and posthumously financed Beatriz's projects; to both her and her husband were attributed the since vanished Hospital of the Conception (1499) and its twin institution, the Hieronymite Convent of the Conception (1509). The always busy Calle de Concepción Jerónima was named after the convent – demolished in 1890 – while the Teatro La Latina, one of Madrid's most famous entertainment institutions, marks the site where the hospital stood until 1904. It was popularly known as the Hospital of La Latina, giving rise to the name by which this area of Madrid is still known today.[16]

Send not to ask for whom the bell tolls: the celebration of the courts in 1482 included a call for a census of Madrid's Jewish population. Despite the relatively pro-Jewish attitudes of the two kings who ruled Castile after the 1391 pogroms, Enrique III and Juan II, there was now a different atmosphere in the air. Already in 1481, the town council of Madrid had ordered the separation of Jews and Moors from Christians, claiming 'the mixing causes great damage and inconvenience to us',[17] and adult Jews were required to wear an identifying sign on their clothing. Such a separation was an own goal for Madrid given the role of Jews in business, finance and specialist trades such as tailoring. Soon a similar edict was passed for the Moors, again a self-damaging law given the prominent role of Moors as expert architects and builders. Intolerance had its dogmatic justification, but it made no sense for the commercial prosperity of the town. By 1492 both groups would be expelled in the triumphant wake of the fall of Granada; in the case of Madrid, this meant the Moors from their *morería* in the vicinity of La Latina, and the Jews – a numerically smaller group – from their *judería* believed to have been located in nearby Lavapiés.

Spain had been more tolerant than France or England, busy expelling their Jewish populations since the twelfth century. The Edict of Granada of 1492, by which the Jews were expelled from Castile and Aragon, was a turning point in Spanish social history, part of a broader attempt to standardise and unify peoples and beliefs across the peninsula. Spain's enemies used the expulsion as propaganda while turning a blind eye to abuses in their own states; once the wider maritime empire was set in motion, also was the black legend – the infamous *leyenda negra* – that was given free rein among the Dutch, French and English. A fear of Spain, born of envy, greed and bigotry, blossomed as soon as Spain had spread the sails of her ships across the waters, and sent soldiers into Flanders' fields and Aztec jungles. From the middle of the sixteenth century it was the greatest Spanish ruler, Felipe II, who was to bear the brunt of an undisguised prejudice.

In fact, initially Jews were welcome to stay, and thus preserve their property, as long as they converted to Christianity – and many did. These were the *conversos*, of which there were thousands across Spain; for those who were not particularly invested in their religion, or for whom the goods of this world were more important than those of the next, conversion was a relatively easy option. Others, for whom the world was but a transitory phase, clung to ancient scripture and teaching. Sephardic Jews, like any group of people, were not monolithic in their opinions or the application of their beliefs.

Those who refused to convert were also in their thousands, and with their families began to fill the old highways leading from Madrid – they would have departed through the Puerta de Atocha, or the Puerta de Toledo – down to the coastal ports of Valencia or, if they headed west, to Lisbon. Perhaps they filed out through the valleys of Jarama and Tajuña, up the dry and flaking hills, through pine forests, past little *posadas* and *ventas*, up onto the higher *meseta* of eastern La Mancha. As they crossed those plains and approached the escarpments that led down to the Mediterranean, they carried with them their sacred texts, their skilled hands and minds, their melancholy, the anxiety of homelessness, of stateless-ness. The unknown opened out ahead as they walked away from comfort or stability, and looked only to the immediate question of survival, beyond the exigencies of war, the ambitions of rulers, the dumb turns of fortune. The Jews, as the Moors would do a century later when they faced definitive expulsion, reached the port of Valencia, thence across the waters with their Barbary ships to Algeria and Egypt, Morocco and Tunisia. Under stars their scientists had tracked and tabulated, making calculations of curve and zenith, they moved to the soft roll of the craft, the dimensions of whose dips and rides were found among the glitter and heft of Arab mathe-matics. They all sailed away from home, watching the shapes of hills recede into darkest green, then vanished black; they travelled across the dark blue night, beginning a new search, that restless human endeavour of seeking always somewhere to be safe, to flourish, to trade, to build and to be loved.

The decision was not universally approved; even at the highest levels of government, some felt the expulsion of the Jews was a mistake.[18] Reportedly, the Edict of Granada, once drafted by Inquisitor General Torquemada, sat on the monarchs' table for days and days before they decided to act.[19] It was as if an unstoppable action were under way, one that made sense in the religious context of the time and yet was equally obviously a tactical blunder, and there was no one brave enough, or perhaps foolish enough, to try to halt proceedings. One contemporary witness, an Italian diplomat, observed that 'no one could witness the sufferings of the Jews without being moved'.[20] Some, faced with the cold reality of exile, converted in extremis on the docks, turned and headed home under a new religion. Many, finding life in exile simply too difficult to bear, converted abroad and, as was stipulated in the edict, took up the offer to return to their homes. Spain has always been a magnet, but it has also been a centrifuge: it draws cultures and peoples, both regionally and internationally, into its dynamic centre, into the hectic streets of Madrid; likewise, throughout the early modern era it spun them out, flung them away into the heavy tradition of exile.

Madrid welcomed the sixteenth century as a relatively prosperous town of some 12,000, undergoing serious urban and social reform, and a marked diversification in its professions.[21] While textiles, leatherwork, metalwork and construction continued to predominate, the fact that the town now hosted confectioners, apothecaries and watchmakers speaks to a level of sophistication Madrid had not known a century earlier. Fish, meat and game markets had become permanently established around the Plaza del Arrabal; commercial activity was intense. Madrid enjoyed a wonderful climate, a blue sky and, for all the medieval mayhem of its streets, clean air. Its nearby hunting grounds were a constant lure for royalty. It took itself more seriously as an urban environment: the stinking trades such as tanning and butchery were moved outside the city walls, distant from the homes of an ever-increasing body of nobility. Churches were many; hospitals were built; prostitution was regulated, at least to the extent it was confined to a specific site – the

Puerta del Sol. The town of Madrid had every reason to be optimistic about the new century, as did the united crowns of Castile and Aragon.

A new version of Spain was taking root at home while, at the same time, it had set out across the oceans of the world.

II

EMPIRE
1516–1759

Gold trimmed with lead

It could all have gone wrong for Madrid, and very nearly did. The first major internal conflict of the sixteenth century was another dispute over succession to the throne, and in the revolt of the Comuneros – a force of Castilian nobility, merchants and landowners opposed to a foreign head of state in Madrid – the town again backed the wrong horse.

Most rulers would surely have given up on Madrid at this point. The town had bet on Pedro I and lost in the 1360s when the Trastámara dynasty took power; backed Juana 'la Beltraneja' and lost again when Isabel and Ferdinand took control of Spain; and now, in 1520 and 1521, supported the Comuneros and lost. If the itinerant court was ever going to settle in one place, it was unlikely to be Madrid. And yet in 1528 King Carlos I 'the Caesar' fixed the town as the residence for his son and heir, Felipe II 'the Prudent', tipping the balance again in Madrid's favour. A generation later, in 1561, when Felipe sent letters to his advisers telling them to prepare the court for a permanent seat, he chose Madrid.

His decision was made in the face of his father's advice. 'If you wish to maintain the empire, make Toledo your capital,' Carlos had told his son, before going on: 'If you wish to expand it, choose Lisbon; but if it does not bother you to lose the empire, choose Madrid.' And this is exactly what young Felipe did.

A smooth succession from one monarch to another was never guaranteed in Spanish history; given medieval and early modern families were so entangled with half-siblings and bastard offspring among the affairs, illicit and open, of royalty, it is no surprise there were always a few contenders on hand to claim a throne. Ferdinand and Isabel's daughter Juana assumed the throne in 1504 along with her Belgian husband Felipe I 'the Handsome', who was king of Castile jure uxoris – by the right of his wife. Yet tragedy was in store: the handsome Felipe died in 1506 and Juana – here we peer, to the best of our ability, through centuries of myth-making – was so grief-stricken she never recovered her capacity to govern. In 1509, conveniently deemed 'mad' by both her father and son, she was locked away in a palace in the Castilian town of Tordesillas, with only her daughter for company. Juana dressed in strict black and lived isolated for the next 46 years until her death in 1555.

The succeeding monarch, Carlos, despite being the son of Juana and Felipe, was essentially an outsider, a foreign interloper who had spent most of his youth in northern Europe, for his paternal grandparents were the Habsburg Maximilian and Maria of Burgundy. The majority of Castilian towns, including Madrid, wanted nothing to do with this northerner who surrounded himself with Flemish advisers, and preferred Juana restored to the throne. Here is a persistent theme: the preference for autochthonous leadership in Madrid against outside interference. In this instance, the Flemish influence on Carlos I; the preference will appear again in the rejection of the Neapolitan advisers to King Carlos III in the late eighteenth century, of Napoleon in the early nineteenth, and in the deep suspicion, not to say hatred, of the Soviet advisers who came to work with the Republican government during the civil war and, equally and oppositely, of the Italian and German support for the Nationalist forces under Franco. Interestingly, this rejection of foreign ideas and their influence on politics did not extend to the arts, where for centuries the cross-border inspiration was intense and constant between Spanish, Flemish, Italian and French painters, designers and architects.

The Comuneros of Castile wanted nothing to do with the new king. The 1520 uprising was also a matter of finances: Carlos had sought support from the courts of Castile and Aragon to underwrite his imperial affairs throughout Italy, Germany and the Netherlands. The Castilians had no reason or desire to finance Carlos's assumption of the Holy Roman Empire[1] with all its costs, and its requirement that he spend large amounts of time outside the peninsula; memories would still have been fresh of the intimate relationship between royals and subjects during the reign of Isabel. When Carlos departed for Germany, appointing as his representative the Dutch bishop Adrian of Utrecht, a figure utterly at sea when it came to dealing with Spanish affairs, rioting broke out. The uprising was led by Toledo; in Madrid the *alcázar* was stormed – *madrileños* here anticipating Parisians by nearly 300 years – and weapons distributed. The fortress that had stood impregnable for 500 years had now been taken twice in a lifetime.

The Comuneros, however, had miscalculated. Perhaps weary, or simply wary, Juana did not back their revolt despite pressure to do so. Loyalties were split down the middle, with strong support for Carlos from the south. In 1521 outside Villalar, between Toro and Valladolid – the very heart of Old Castile – the Comuneros were defeated, and their leaders executed the following day. All lost their heads, a public act of revenge graphically rendered in 1860 by Antonio Gisbert in a work that hangs in the Spanish Congress: in a typical Castilian setting, stone church and greyish sky looming behind, one of the plotters, Bravo, has already lost his head, now held up by the executioner to a probably baying crowd; the head is a scruffy object, hair tufting atop and at the chin; blood has streamed from the neck. The other conspirators – Padilla and Maldonado – await their headless fate with impeccable calm and, it must be acknowledged, rather snappily dressed.

After the death of the leaders, resistance continued for some time in Toledo at the urging of Padilla's widow, María Pacheco – yet another of the remarkable women of early modern Castile – but this too faltered, and Pacheco went into exile in Portugal, never returning to her beloved home. There were attempts to frame the political disorder as the work of the devil shrewdly manipulating *conversos*, those new Christians who had come over, principally from Judaism, in the last few decades and whose lack of spiritual pedigree meant they could not be altogether trusted and were thus convenient scapegoats.[2] Needless to say, the evidence for diabolical intervention was nil. The Comuneros have been portrayed more recently as provincial hicks fighting against a sophisticated European model of society embodied by the emperor Carlos. This is a wilful misreading of both parties. It can be argued that, given the defeat of the Comuneros, the political evolution of Spain, and the role of Madrid taking shape within that entity, was determined towards royal power and away from parliamentary representation.[3] Within a few years of the defeat, the popular representation that was inherent to many medieval Castilian institutions was lost to the absolutism of the king. The historian Alfredo Alvar Ezquerra has made a similar point: the kingdom – plural – lost out to the king – singular.[4]

Over the years the legend of the Comuneros and their apparent anti-absolutism has occasionally been adopted by republicans and communists. This conveniently ignores the monarchic ambition of those wretched agitators. There is no surety that, even had Juana emerged from her Miss Havisham-like seclusion to lead the revolt, and supposing her faction had been victorious, she would have governed from Madrid in the open and amiable way of her mother Isabel who, for all her reputed common touch, was an authoritarian as her era demanded. History offers no such guarantees.

The Renaissance years were fast receding and early modernity loomed over the horizon. In Madrid, the transition from the medieval government of the Catholic monarchs to the bureaucratic – and absolutist – state of the Habsburgs would bring with it a wholesale conceptual shift in the role of the state.[5]

The Golden Age was approaching. The story of Spain from the early sixteenth to the late seventeenth century represents some of the most astonishing history of any nation on earth. These were splendid years, years of artistic genius and political triumph, of empire and war, of mystic, comic and profoundly moving literary creation; they were years of entropy and dynastic change, of untimely deaths, of decline and fall, of stasis and rot. They were golden years trimmed with lead: a haughty and brilliant universe dulled by lassitude, weakened by the soft underbelly of an indulged nobility and the ferocity of an increasing number of enemies. The early sixteenth to the late seventeenth century was a period both astounding and hellish: world horizons, enormous wealth, grandiose schemes, cultural brilliance, local misery and financial ruin. The triumph of forces loyal to Carlos meant Castile, often to its detriment, would be one of the principal sources for financing central and northern European wars.[6] The globe took on new dimensions; Madrid was suddenly catapulted to the status of imperial capital, amid the changing geopolitics of northern Europe and the Mediterranean, with shifting alliances from Cádiz to Istanbul, and from Madrid to the Pacific and the Americas, as Spain found itself the first properly global power.

Any one of a constellation of towns, given the right investment or the simple turn of chance, might have become the imperial capital: Valladolid, Medina del Campo, Seville, Toledo, Segovia, Burgos, Madrigal, Zaragoza. All were part of the historically expansive kingdoms of Castile and Aragon; all would lose out to Madrid. Towns such as Valencia or Barcelona were unlikely contenders for the capital, despite their medieval importance: geographically marginal and, at least in comparison to the towns of Castile, historically more independent.

Thus, with a minimum of fanfare and, to the chagrin of future historians, without documented justification, Felipe II chose Madrid to be his capital. This put an end to an anomaly: in the first half of the sixteenth century, Spain had an empire but no capital city. Carlos, never a great lover of Madrid, had moved between the Manchegan Toledo and the Castilian Valladolid, but his son opted for the town where he had lived and been confirmed as Prince of Asturias, heir to the throne. The itinerant court coming to rest at last in the centre of the nation marked the culmination of a project that for more than a thousand years had engaged, consciously or not, the myriad rulers of the territories that were becoming known collectively as Spain, from Visigoth kings to Muslim emirs and caliphs, from the counts of Barcelona, kings of Aragon and Navarre, the counts and kings of Castile, and kings of Asturias and Leon. All were finally being concentrated in one point, and under one leader.

This process was not without resistance, then and now. Felipe had made a mistake, historian John Elliott suggested, 'in assuming that residence in the mathematical centre of the peninsula would foster the impression of absolute impartiality in the treatment of his subjects'.[7] There is no evidence, however, that Felipe made such an assumption. Nevertheless, over the intervening centuries nothing has changed in this perception of centric bias, much to the bemusement of Madrid and its *madrileños*. Nor is there any evidence that can conclusively explain the specific reason or reasons why Felipe chose Madrid as his capital, giving rise to centuries of speculation. Popular theories include: Madrid's central geographic location; the limited capacity of Toledo for expansion, along with its leading role in the revolt of the Comuneros; the suspicion that fell on Valladolid after an outbreak of Protestantism; the capacity to treat Madrid as a tabula rasa; the lack of an established and meddling church authority; the compliance of local nobility; the suitability of its climate; the abundance of its hunting grounds; the abundance of water and forests; Felipe's fond memories of his earlier days; and finally, the 'Goldilocks principle': Madrid was neither too big nor too small, neither too grand nor too base. Whether any of these, or a combination of some, or even all, were factors that tilted Felipe's hand, we cannot know.

Geographic centrality has proved the most popular of these theories, but not everybody agrees. Why, asks Segura, would Felipe have bothered that the town was geographically central when he conceived of his kingdom not as Spain but as a global empire, whose centre was nowhere (unless perhaps El Escorial)? What was Castile in a Habsburg world that stretched from the Americas to Italy? And if centrality was the point, why not the ancient seat of Toledo?[8]

'The principles of mathematical harmony that obtained in the architecture of the Escorial were also applied to the selection of a capital,' speculated Elliott,[9] reminding us that, at the same time as Madrid was chosen as the capital, designers were sitting down to draft the outlines of Felipe's extraordinary palace. In 1619 chronicler Luis Cabrera de Córdoba, assuming the metaphor of the human body, wrote that 'it was right that so great a Monarchy should have a city which could function as its heart – a vital centre in the midst of the body, which ministered equally to every State in time of peace and war.'[10] Julián Marías saw a parallel between the physical reality of the peninsula, the diverse forms of its landscape and the centrality of its capital, as if Madrid were both a summation of geographic irregularity and a type of manifest destiny. Kamen was adamant that the opposite was true: 'His choice of Madrid was in no way influenced by its central location in the peninsula.'[11]

Regardless of these debates, Madrid was undeniably blessed with 'its healthy natural environment, its cheerful skies, magnificent buildings, gardens and orchards'.[12] Madrid had not simply appeared from nowhere. It had been developing, finding favour and receiving privileges from one Christian monarch after another for close to 500 years prior to 1561. It was not, despite Cabrera's seventeenth-century claims, decked with architectural or artistic glory – for the moment; it was a cramped place, and chaotic, but it was vibrant and expanding, attracting internal migrants from all over Spain. Its population was about to explode.

Another advantage of Madrid was that Felipe would be mostly free of clerical attempts to control his policymaking. It was one thing to be devout, as Felipe decidedly was; another to hand the wheel of state to clerics and bishops. Toledo, as the Archbishopric and long-term seat of divine power in the peninsula, presented too many complications. Toledo may have been the preference of his father Carlos, but the new model of the state was too complex a matter for the church. The vast array of competencies, geographic and conceptual, along with the development of new techniques of administration and the rapid increase in the number of servants of every kind that attended the royal court; in short, the arrival of the modern state meant it could not be beholden to the church, vital though that institution was. In addition, the state was, as it remains to this day, its own self-reproducing monster, multiplying its needs and its servants, its bureaucrats and planners, its codifiers of protocol and etiquette. As an expanding machine and complex organic body, the state required a stable home. It was prohibitively expensive, and increasingly inefficient, to cart the whole circus around the nation.

The idea of Madrid as tabula rasa is appealing, if somewhat in contradiction to the evidence. Felipe was attracted, some suggest,[13] by Madrid's humble, or rather undeveloped, status as a town, somewhere the new king could create a city in his own image. This seems unlikely for two reasons: despite his 42 years in power, Felipe left behind very few buildings or significant urban reforms in Madrid; and secondly, he dedicated the vast proportion of his energies to his monastery complex at nearby El Escorial. For others, Madrid was a fundamentally new city, if not ex novo; a creation built for the purposes of empire; an attempted utopia that fell back to earth amid the mess of human reality, of ambition and greed and waste, but that was nevertheless conceived as a central point from which to build and administer a new politics of absolutist glory, free from the limitations other older, more deeply institutionalised towns might impose upon the sovereign.[14]

In the nineteenth century, chronicler Mesonero Romanos had been adamant: 'One tires of hearing', he wrote, 'that Madrid was a mean village, an inappropriate choice for capital, with no political importance and without *history*; situated in the deep interior, far from the coasts, on poor and naked land, lacking a decent river and any other conditions that might suggest prosperity; equally, lacking the great artistic monuments that elevate a city, and impart to it the seal of majesty and power.'[15] Madrid's centrality was an assisting factor rather than determinant, as much symbolic as geographic. This, argued Mesonero, was a time of renewal for Spain and, within that spirit of renovation, it was logical to desire a new capital, one that would not inherit the prejudices, quarrels, rivalries and antipathies of the past. He talked up the idea of Madrid as the head of a 'one nation' conception of Spain, overriding the ambitions or anachronistic dreams of other regions. This made absolute sense within the context of mid-sixteenth-century geopolitics, a common *patria* beyond regionalism, a unity that was essential to handle the task of governing what was suddenly half the known world. A city and court were needed where the citizens of the peninsula could identify themselves not according to their regional preferences, but as *Spaniards*: a new political entity, governed by the new monarch of a new dynasty, in a new imperial capital.

Madrid, however, was not altogether ready for such a status. For all its advantages, it remained a medium-sized medieval town that had neither the infrastructure nor the necessary legal frameworks in place. There were overlaps between the laws applying to the town, and to the royal court that took up permanent residence. Madrid experienced a population explosion: from roughly 25,000 souls just after the appointment as capital, numbers more than doubled to some 65,000 by the time of Felipe's death in 1598.[16] A permanent royal court operated as a magnet for the nobility, an extensive cast of hangers-on, thousands of servants and a whole new class of professional bureaucrats; it was the necessary home for statesmen and ambassadors, and the chosen home for fortune seekers: 'If you've got your wits about you in the city it's like having a licence to print money,' says one of the down-at-heel characters in Quevedo's novel *Historia de la vida del buscón Don Pablos (The Swindler)*.[17] Many indeed had their wits about them, for they had no other means by which to survive: writer Federico Carlos Sainz de Robles, in a rather florid and arcane account, listed the new arrivals in Madrid as including 'vagabonds, troublemakers, shysters, sophists, schemers, fabulists, illusionists, conjurors, smugglers, pimps, whores and madams'[18] – a whole theatre of the picaresque, to which could be added pretenders of every class, beggars, thieves, swords for hire, card sharps and a broad range of ratbags. A large, floating population of servants and lackeys could be found congregating in the Plaza de Herradores, from where they might be selected for service by members of the upper classes; such scenes can still be found in parts of Madrid, at specific roundabouts, where drifting immigrant workers wait on their chance to be picked up by foremen and driven to a day's cash-in-hand labouring. The smaller rural towns began to empty into Madrid, supplying tailors, scribes, priests, apothecaries, cooks, ostlers, midwives, rag-and-bone men and craftspeople of every possible variety, working in the crafts that continued, along with agriculture, to buoy the economy: leather, ivory, glass, precious jewels, wood, stone, iron and steel, gold and silver and tin. The new capital attracted anyone with anything to plead; perhaps an old sea dog who had survived the Pacific and wanted to return to treasures infinite, looking to finance an overseas expedition; or monks, begging favours for a humble monastery extension. Madrid became a centre for manoeuvrings, betrayals, executions, power shifts, plots and poisonings. The conspiracies and skulduggery that had been part of the backdrop to the town as an occasional host to the courts of Castile took on greater resonance: as a national capital and imperial city following a programme of political, military and cultural expansion, the stakes were now much higher.

It is easy to get lost amid the colour; Madrid supplies it constantly. Yet not everything was confusion and trickery; serious work was being done by serious minds. The state produced expert administrators, the military highly skilled leaders, and the religious orders some of the finest intellects of the era. In nearby Alcalá de Henares the university produced or hosted a roll call of impressive early modern humanists, grammarians and theologians, to the extent it began to rival Salamanca for prominence in Spanish letters. Things built in a heady rush: in the seventeenth century, perhaps only England could rival Spain for its literary brilliance, while during the sixteenth and seventeenth centuries, its only rival in the arts were the combined republics and duchies of Italy, many of them under Spanish Habsburg control.

The advent of Madrid as capital could not but have an impact, then and subsequently, on the question of Spanish nationalism. In the early seventeenth century Juan de Mariana, a Jesuit historian and theologian educated in Alcalá de Henares, lauded 'the nation' as a Castilian entity, and Spaniards as an ancient and noble people from fertile and abundant lands, people with a combative past and deep religious faith, evidenced by their devotion to Christianity and their love of the miracle-working reliquary.[19] In *Mater Dolorosa*, Álvarez Junco has examined the conceptual shift of 'Spanish' from a dynastic-monarchic identity marker to an ethnic one. It is difficult, he argues, to pinpoint exactly the role of the throne, with its seat in Madrid, in the creation of a national identity, or how the monarchy came increasingly to identify itself as 'Spanish' – as opposed to Castilian and/or Aragonese – and how the people ruled by that monarchy came to know themselves as 'Spaniards'.[20] Not all those fighting for 'Spain' in the endless wars of the seventeenth century were doing so from patriotic duty. In another indication of the cosmopolitan reach of the Habsburg monarchy, there were countless foreign mercenaries, such as Italians or Swiss, in the armies of the Spanish generals, mercenaries who could at any time have changed allegiance, as warriors often did during the centuries when Christianity and Islam struggled for control of the peninsula.

However it was constituted or conceptualised, the Spanish monarchy was never still, and rarely at peace. From the time of Carlos I to the Napoleonic invasion, the monarchy was at least partly involved in every war on European soil, creating an almost continuous succession of 300 years of fighting.[21] Sometimes the results were triumphant, at other times not; sometimes Spain was on the defensive, at others on the attack; sometimes in coalition, other times fighting alone. This left an exhausting toll on the coffers of Castile which, for all it might have hosted the capital of a world empire, staggered under the weight. Taking on the additional task of promoting and defending the Catholic faith as part of its imperial project, Madrid, Castile and Spain all found the wealth from foreign enterprises quickly absorbed by northern wars, or by interventions in the Turkic east.

Aspiring to lead the world was an extravagant, brilliant and ruinous ambition. From twin bases – the *alcázar* of Madrid and, when it was built, the nearby monastery of San Lorenzo de El Escorial – Felipe II, a shy and cultivated man, obsessed with detail, dogmatic, stern and relentlessly at work or prayer, would take charge of this grand scheme for nearly half a century.

Strange universe

Between them they constitute just 184 years in the long history of the Iberian Peninsula, but the five Habsburg kings – erratic, brilliant, lazy, confounding – have influenced that history out of all proportion to their longevity. They were fortunate to be accompanied by the painters who rendered them – in particular Titian and Velázquez – and the writers and playwrights that blossomed in their time. After Carlos I, all the Habsburgs made Madrid their home, and in their wake followed almost all the artists of the day. The city became the site of a previously unimagined cultural richness; a golden thread winds its way through the sixteenth and seventeenth centuries. Conventional history tells us this period of splendour was followed by a long imperial decline and a lessening influence over world affairs as modernity and the Enlightenment unfurled throughout the late seventeenth and eighteenth centuries. This perspective contains elements of truth, while also reflecting an unsympathetic historiography that has systematically sought to undermine Spanish achievement.

Madrid's history as a capital city begins with Felipe II. The second Habsburg is a towering figure in Spanish and European history despite being regularly defamed, not only in his lifetime, but also for centuries since. Felipe brought the church, the judiciary, the councils of state, the parliament and the military orders under his purview; the centralisation of power was part of an efficient ordering of what had become a vast global holding.[1] His was the management of the instruments of state, while in turn those diverse instruments and their capillaries carried out the nuanced operations of power: the moral, political and economic control of the body and the soul, the life and death of the subjects of the realm.

To approach Felipe II – the original Man in Black – it is necessary to cut through the dense brambles of myth and slander put about by his arch-enemies – political and religious, domestic and international – and that have since spread, weed-like, in the untended garden that is prejudice. It is all there: the supposed gloom, the horror, the murder and incest, the fanaticism, the strangely contradictory accusations of excessive piety and excessive lust for worldly power. The empire Felipe oversaw emerged from a pre-Enlightenment world and did not carry, as baggage, many of the assumptions of cultural supremacy that came with Enlightenment thinking; it was not stained with the racist theology and crippling structural biases that came with later European empires. This has not prevented it, in contemporary times, being lumped together with the British or French empires in a revisionary understanding of the colonial past; Felipe, along with early conquistadors such as Hernán Cortés, often carry the weight of criticism, considered typical of the ills consequent upon a Spanish presence in the wider world.

Negative opinions of Felipe, his government and his empire were routine. Early in his reign he faced a serious problem with the son he had with his first wife, María Manuela, Princess of Portugal.[2] Carlos of Austria was a fragile, ill and stammering young man whose precarious physical and mental condition was worsened by a severe head injury following a fall at the age of 17. His death at 23 followed what appears to have been a harrowing life in Madrid, both for him and for those who crossed his path. A tragic figure who suffered from the era's inability to deal with mental disorders with anything other than abrupt and radical cures,[3] Carlos, whose problems may have emerged in part from ancestral endogamy, suffered miserably while reportedly making life equally miserable for those around him. Locked away by his father in a tower of the *alcázar* where he died in solitary confinement, starved and delirious, we need not concern ourselves with all the lurid details of his supposed cruelties and perversions, other than to point to the way even the most absurd accusation or rumour was jumped upon by the enemies of Spain. All was ammunition and propaganda for the likes of William of Orange, a principal enemy of Felipe, or Antonio Pérez, a traitor who fled the court in Madrid – and prison – for England, where he lived off the malicious tales Spain's enemies so enjoyed. Young Carlos's legend was distorted immediately, starting with an entry in the 1570 edition of Foxe's *Book of Martyrs* so patently fanciful as to be insulting: Carlos is presented as an amiable and learned prince who sought to blow the whistle on the gross iniquities of popery and the Inquisition. Tales were further spun by Schiller and Verdi among others, all drawing on rumour in a narrative chain in which each successive link was more and more eccentric while being ever further removed from the source; all serving to portray Felipe as a cruel and sadistic father, a fanatic and superstitious bigot.

The black legend – that historical process whereby Spain's enemies built up a case for the prosecution based on any myth, rumour, gossip or exaggeration, painting Spaniards and their representatives as intolerant and fanatical beasts, to delegitimise Spanish power and authority – had some part to play, inevitably, in the historic neglect to which Madrid has been subject. And Felipe was where the legend began. He was, for many, the source of all that was bad about Spain. In the histories written and legends invented by northern Europeans, Felipe would never be forgiven his stern opposition to Protestantism.[4] French Enlightenment writers such as Montesquieu and Voltaire, pushing the barrows of their own national propaganda, assured audiences that the eighteenth-century political decline of Spain was proof, if ever it were needed, of the detrimental impact of despotism and intolerance. An Anglo-Dutch propaganda machine turned Felipe into a monster; he was the incarnation of the 'immorality' that was inherent to Spaniards; it ran in their blood.[5] It is difficult to accept, given contemporary perspectives on the malicious construction of racial prejudice, that anyone could have taken this nonsense seriously, but take it seriously they did. Some still do.

The nineteenth century, that era of the 'discovery' of Spain, saw an abundance of travellers' accounts distorting the realities of the country to suit the prejudices and fantasies of the observer. Stendhal, in *The Charterhouse of Parma*, puts the boot in on the very opening page: the people in the realms under Habsburg rule 'had been plunged in darkest night by the jealous despotism of Carlos V and Felipe II'; once these despots' statues were overturned the world was 'flooded with light'. While monks preached obscurantism and life-denying renunciation of the world, and a slavish devotion to one's parish priest, elsewhere the French were freed by the boundless generosity of the *Encyclopédie* and Voltaire.[6]

More recently, for twentieth-century writer Carlos Fuentes, Felipe II was 'the necrophiliac monarch secluded at El Escorial'.[7] Even Jules Stewart, in his laudable history of Madrid, renders Felipe as 'ascetic, severe, bigoted, unattractive, fanatical, cruel', claiming this opinion is shared by 'most historians' who would agree those stern adjectives describe both his character and appearance.[8] Felipe as a progenitor of darkness: an embodiment of gloom, death, superstition, coldness and fear. It would not be until the latter half of the twentieth century that dressing all in black became, for a period of time, the essence of cool: in Felipe's case, so the judgement of history went, it reflected morbidity, joylessness and bigotry. And given the way his grandmother Juana had been incarcerated, and the fate of his son Carlos, why not throw in, for good measure, a suggestion of underlying madness?

Thus, his crowning achievement: the royal monastery of San Lorenzo de El Escorial, without doubt the greatest historical monument in the province of Madrid, not only for its architectural magnificence, but also for its priceless art collection and library of rare maps and manuscripts, a collection brought together under Felipe's specific guidance. Despite its splendour, the complex has not enjoyed a friendly critical reception over the years, becoming something of a punching bag; a stony dogma and symbol of all that was reactionary in Spanish history. In the 1840s Théophile Gautier found it a gloomy site characterised by 'an indefinable odour, icy and sickly, of holy water and sepulchral vaults'.[9] Others slammed it for being morbid and fanatical; an unaffordable extravaganza; hostile, dry and devoid of poetry. With their eye both romanticising and prejudiced turned on a quietly exhausted Spain, the French were implacable in their myth-making: Chateaubriand observed the palace as spider-filled and mouldy, 'built on rocky grounds among gloomy barrens'. All the stops are pulled out: 'Among these funereal buildings, one saw the shade of a man in black pass, that of Philip II, their creator.'[10] English traveller Richard Ford was of like mind: 'Cold as the grey eye and granite heart of its founder, [a] monument of fear and superstition.'[11] For journalist and mathematician Felipe Picatoste, the monastery was 'a madness and an insult to the poverty of the people'.[12] In contemporary times Jules Stewart, again: the monastery casts a 'grim shadow' across the plains; 'a pall'; it is 'as sinister as it is grandiose'.[13] An article in Spanish daily El País in 1986 opined 'its architecture reveals sexual repressions', that a crucified Christ in the monastery is 'identical to Felipe himself' and that the entire monastery is 'a condemnation of traditional magic, religious and sexual forces'.[14] Felipe's sexual repression might stem, we read – without any evidence provided – from some trauma arising from the death of his uncle Juan who died while making love to Margarita of Austria.[15] How Margarita took this singular event is not recorded.

The monastery complex has served as a blank slate on which travellers can inscribe whatever fantasy or prejudice they desire. It is revealing to observe this relentlessly negative portrayal of one of early modern Europe's most significant leaders. There are exceptions, and they have increased over the years as the remarkable achievements of Felipe II are better appreciated the closer and more fine-grained becomes the analysis.[16] He was flawed, in many ways, albeit some of those are excusable within the context of a sixteenth-century moral and mental universe. If for no other reason than the time he spent collecting art and precious manuscripts, it is clear Felipe was no narrow-minded fanatic but a patron of the arts, a highly cultured man of the Renaissance who examined for himself the relationship between faith and reason. At El Escorial the royal library, with its richly painted ceilings that celebrate the liberal arts, was situated opposite the basilica: philosophy and theology reached out to each other; learning spoke to belief; science spoke to faith; bibles spoke to astrolabes. Further, Felipe's library was the first in the world to display books with the spine outwards, in shelves along the wall, anticipating the future design of libraries everywhere. It was also the first library in Europe to be so richly decorated; as a place of learning and wonder, it also had to be aesthetically beautiful and artistically ravishing. And as so often happens in the history of Madrid, the scope of what has been lost over the years to fire, theft, ransackery and negligence is overwhelming: astonishing as the library is, we see only a portion, a shadow of its former glory.

Fresh from having overseen works on a sumptuous royal palace south of Madrid at Aranjuez, architect Juan de Herrera – a name that should be as well-known internationally as the painters and writers of his time – turned his full attention to El Escorial, eventually leaving what has often been referred to as the 'eighth wonder of the world'. It was very much Felipe's loving project, an imperial gesture that would 'integrate his political supremacy with his responsibility as a defender of the Catholic faith'.[17] Along with its unique library, its unparalleled collection of reliquaries, and the monastery itself, El Escorial also became the resting place for Spanish royals of the Habsburg and subsequent Bourbon dynasties. Visiting its mausoleum is an unsettlingly strange experience; one wanders down into a lavish crypt to find the kings and queens stacked in rows of four under a hushed umber light befitting of memorial and grandeur. The sepulchres in which the bodies are kept are rich black marble, each with its gold nameplate and ornate gold trim; in deep baroque solemnity, the royal dead are accompanied by angels and the crucified Christ.

In the haunting short story 'Joanna' by Madrid author Marcos Giralt Torrente, a young orphan lives with his austere grandmother in the town of El Escorial, 'behind which rose ominously the monastery, a fearful shadow'.[18] Here the boy endures a dismal upbringing; to seek solace, he likes to retreat with a book to a small oak wood, where Felipe had centuries earlier ordered a seat carved into the rock, a vantage point from which the king, escaping from the hectic politics of Madrid, could watch the construction of the monastery of San Lorenzo. At the seat the young boy meets Joanna, a moody and ill-fated teenager, who some years later writes to him from Tangier, asking plaintively, 'Have you gone back to read in the seat of the sad king?'[19]

A shadow and a sadness: one fearful, the other deep enough to permeate the centuries. In *Letters from Spain*, written in the early twentieth century, Czech writer Karel Čapek referred with equanimity to El Escorial as 'a miraculous sight'; a place of 'monumental solitude'; a 'castle of sorrow and pride above the parched countryside'.[20] In the late sixteenth century, barely a decade after it was completed, El Escorial was described by the English traveller John Eliot as 'the most magnificent palace of all Europe ... a hundred times more magnificent than any in Italy'. One can only wonder what Felipe, ever stern in his faith, would have thought to hear the appreciative Mr Eliot swooning that El Escorial was 'surely a terrestrial paradise, such as promiseth Mahomet in his Alcoran'.[21]

There is a seriousness and melancholy about the figure of Felipe. In the many superb portraits of the king – Sofonisba Anguissola, Titian, Alonso Sánchez Coello, later Rubens – he is never smiling, nor was this the role of monarchs. Joy and laughter in classical painting were the reserve of clowns and buffoons, drunks, musicians and angels; for Felipe, an intense and profound loneliness, for by 1584 his last and most beloved wife, Ana, had been dead for four years; his first son Carlos, for sixteen years.

Felipe's reign coincided with the height of the Spanish empire – the first on which the sun never set, for all the British later adopted this phrase – and the beginning of what we know as modern globalisation. He was the first monarch who properly understood the world-changing implications of the Americas; indeed, Felipe's motto, borrowed from Juvenal, says it all: *Non sufficit orbis* ('The world is not enough'). Limited though they were by today's standards, here were the first networks of pan-global trade, people and ideas, with all the opportunity and threats such systems suppose. For the first time, wars were fought and people conquered on the other side of the vast oceans of the planet.

Felipe was born in Valladolid in 1527, into a world strongly influenced on the one hand by the intellectual and artistic currents flowing from northern Europe as it divided, from the early sixteenth century, into Catholic and Protestant camps, and on the other from the long Catholic and humanist traditions of his homeland. Felipe was thus invested with discipline, calm and orthodoxy, edged around by elements of the fanaticism we associate with that convulsive time. For the demonic was never too far away: although Felipe was to die on the verge of the seventeenth century, with its burgeoning enlightenment, he had been born into a world still wary of the flickering temptations of the underworld. His career straddled that shift from superstition and myth to early modern science, from a world governed by absolute conceptions of heaven and hell, to one that began to be rendered – in terms defined by those doing the rendering – as rational. The European world view, allowing for nuances in different parts of the continent, had begun its inexorable move from verticality to that horizontal mode more favoured in the radical democratisation of thought and opinion. By the time of Felipe's death in 1598, God – unthinkable but true – had begun to shift and crack, albeit ever so slightly, while the people were equally on a path towards the secular; the religious wars of the seventeenth century precipitated the final loosening of the hold religion had on many societies about to radically modernise.

Felipe ruled his empire 'through the written word, with an increasingly specialized and sophisticated bureaucracy'.[22] The tasks that would confront him in government were overwhelming; a small, neat man given to reflection (and great stubbornness), he set out to govern the first global empire armed with a network of beliefs some of which, despite his humanist learning, were inherited from a medieval world thick with demons and strange punishments. Nor was Felipe alone in this: as Kamen has pointed out, the adherence of sixteenth-century Spaniards to Catholicism has been exaggerated.

Alongside conventional religiosity ran other more practical beliefs, rooted in folk traditions and remedies, 'exotic knowledge' and, where necessary, witchcraft.[23] To make matters even more complicated, Felipe's desire for control meant he attempted nothing less than to govern the world, and all the administrative complexity that would require, largely by himself. For all he was a highly sophisticated patron of the arts, this did not prevent his human flaws. Let down by himself and more often by others, Felipe was in one respect ahead of his time: he faced all the plagues of modern politics and corporate life. Plotting and scheming – to which he was not averse – jealousy and factionalism; obsessive micromanagers – none more so than himself – sycophants, ladder-climbing careerists and incompetent time-servers; international spy wars, with secrets always uncovered or betrayed; financial malfeasance; simple bungling, government agencies going into bureaucratic meltdown, and justice as slow as treacle; Felipe and much of his court would have felt at home in the modern world.

Given the recent circumnavigation of the globe, the opportunity arose to enlarge the reach of the Universal Church. Much of the expansion of the Spanish empire occurred under Felipe's rule, but it would be a mistake to consider him a colonialist driven by the sort of greed that characterised later European expansionist ventures. Felipe was not so much interested in acquisition of goods, as conversion of souls. The business of business was for others. Devoted to his father, firm in the belief that he had been endowed with a specific and sacred task, Felipe's understanding of empire was to defend and, where possible, expand the influence of the Catholic Church. The great battles of his life were primarily religious, and only took on their geopolitical dimensions by implication. His obvious rivals were two (though as he well knew, devils were everywhere): the Ottoman empire and the Protestant Reformation. Both were heresies on the edges of his European holdings. The Americas and the Pacific looked after themselves, the former in particular flooding the state coffers with wealth; it was in his own backyard that Felipe struggled to defend the faith. That his world of strictures and etiquette would unravel in the decades after his death was, from the vantage point of the middle of the sixteenth century, almost impossible to imagine.

Felipe was better suited to contemplation than extending his grasp, managerial and proselytising, around the globe. In the early 1560s, a few short years after assuming power and choosing Madrid as the fixed seat of the monarchy, he ordered a vast complex constructed to the north-west of the new imperial capital, at the base of the Guadarrama mountain range. Designed, built and decorated over two decades by the finest Spanish and Italian artists, San Lorenzo de El Escorial – monastery, palace, library, art collection, seat of learning and prayer – became the humming seat of both political and spiritual power. Never fond of the *alcázar* in Madrid – despite its constant remodelling, the ninth-century Moorish palace had never been a hospitable place – Felipe settled in to El Escorial for the last fifteen years of his life. Of necessity, he continued to travel around the peninsula attending to affairs of state; nevertheless, San Lorenzo became, in the strictest sense of the term, his spiritual home.

From the monastery he administered the empire as the bewildering complexity of globalisation began to take shape, along with the vast organisational apparatus on which it depends. Here was a splendid and obsessive monarch, dapper in black, acting as a hinge on which half the world turned. From here, on the outskirts of Madrid, emanated the orders that were nothing less than instructions to rule the world, albeit that world was more teeming than the monarch might ever imagine. From that rocky seat of power, Felipe quilled directives dealing with military movements, religious ceremony, court etiquette, marriage proposals, executions or royal pardons; building supplies, international treaties and declarations of war. He spun threads from the centre of his all-purpose granite maze that led out to the hot jungles of Peru, the swamps of Mexico, the dank trenches of Flanders, the sunlit islands of the eponymous Philippines and the fields and courts of Portugal, to say nothing of the local cat's cradle of ambitions pursued by Catalans to the north and rebellious Moriscos to the south. In his desire to be across all briefs, Felipe worked himself into the ground attempting to assimilate hundreds of parchments and their contents – complex, bloody, duplicitous, greedy, compassionate – every day. Infamously, one of the tens of thousands of documents he signed was the rejection of an application by an ex-soldier of the realm, Miguel de Cervantes, for a position as a government official in the Americas. Faced with that rejection, the now disabled former soldier was obliged to take up a role as an ambulant tax collector, wandering the plains and hills of central and southern Spain, meditating on fortune and conjuring fictions along the way.

As befitted a sophisticated Renaissance ruler, parallel to his daily tasks of government Felipe carried on a programme of cultural acquisition, including priceless collections of art, tapestries and manuscripts. Overlooking this quest to bring the world under the influence of bureaucratic order and simple piety was a series of artworks that spoke of the fundamental eccentricity of the universe – terrestrial, purgatorial, hellish and heavenly. One result of the political influence of Spain in the Low Countries in the sixteenth century was the large-scale adoption of Flemish art by the royal court. Both Felipe and his father were great collectors and patrons, as Isabel of Castile had been before them, and they accumulated work after work of Flemish art containing all the weird cosmography and loopy demons that characterise the period. While El Escorial has been conventionally labelled the geometric manifestation of Felipe's square-jawed and rigid Catholicism – the building itself laid out in the shape of a martyr's grid – such a view fails to account for the power of the art that filled the new complex. Rogier van der Weyden, Hans Memling or Joachim Patinir did not find their way by accident to Felipe's chambers. Art and prayer, albeit the two might diverge radically in content, were part of his organisational apparatus.

On his travels through the Spanish Low Countries Felipe had encountered the work of painter Jeroen van Aken of Hertogenbosch, known to us as Hieronymus Bosch. Bosch had been no struggling artisan; he had married into a wealthy family and enjoyed the privilege of belonging to an elite religious company, the Brotherhood of Our Lady. Luminaries such as Rudolph II of Prague, the Duke of Alba – Spain's chief enforcer in the Netherlands – and Cardinal Grimaldi collected his work from the late fifteenth and early sixteenth centuries, but it was above all Felipe who coveted the lurid instructional paintings that overflowed with all the curved and swerving demons of the northern imagination, bursting with hallucinatory pre-Reformation visions, shimmering colours of faith doing battle with brown devils squatting in growl and grimace and leathery intent, furious to hang, spear or bludgeon, to devour any sign of faith or modesty, to smother any light, to suck goodness up and spit it out as sin, spit out its marrow into the harrowed world. Via the Duke of Alba – this time by confiscation rather than amiable acquisition – these unearthly parables found their way to the collections of El Escorial, where they would hang for over 300 years until they were moved to the Prado Museum in Madrid. The task of ordering the world under the Universal Church meant that a will to administrative conformity and religious orthodoxy met with the profusion of difference; the straight lines of a spiritual path bordered the flux and multiplicity of the unlimited imagination. Both were deeply human.

Bosch was one of the pioneers, along with Patinir, of landscape painting. The 'garden of the world' was more than just a backdrop; it was a detailed place, gifted with shape and meaning. By the time of Felipe's reign, the garden of the world was no longer Eden, that Christian version of the ancient Persian paradise where the human soul bathed in the goodness of the natural world. Nor even a corrupted version of it: the garden was something much larger, more thrilling – when not menacing – and populated with improbable people, plants, beasts and mineral treasures. Along with his swelling collection of instruments, maps, manuscripts, codices, crucifixes and reliquaries, Felipe was surrounded by these daring visions of Bosch; they represented ideas that accompanied him as he set about administering the new Spanish globe. Bosch's circular or triptych parables were pedagogical; sober warnings against gluttony, vanity and pride, stacked with superstitions and arcane beliefs. The moral instruction called on figures from medieval folklore – still so important the length and breadth of the peninsula – and on the exaggerated beasts and fierce punishments of worlds beyond. As the empire stretched out across the last oceans of the globe, Felipe's artworks spoke of good and evil, and the possible end of the world amid a storming of crickets and amphibians of dark intent, grabbing, pulling and sucking on flesh. As he signed and signed his endless paperwork, the prudent king contemplated scenes of the black vomit, ferocious and hooded salamanders, gargoyles both sacred and profane; exotic flowers, dismembered bodies, smoky hell-fires, and sinners hung from gibbets or boiling in oil as punishment for their avarice and freewheeling sexuality.

This all sits oddly with the elegant and carefully dressed Felipe we know principally through the portraits commissioned from his favourite artist, Titian. Nor did Titian's work, despite often dealing with the agonies and ecstasies of biblical legend, flirt with the dungeons of the underworld. Yet the strangeness of the artwork with which Felipe surrounded himself was of a piece with the strangeness of the new world that his empire was unfolding, with greater or lesser levels of violence, fascination, mission and greed. These vaulting renditions of heaven and hell mirrored the terrestrial reality of the first global superpower: a brilliant ultramarine world of gold and distant clouds, of Pacific mornings, mountain silver and tropic dreams. Sailors were busy charting the world, taking one measurement after another: at sea, off brutal coasts, in bright blue waters, at the icy bottom of the world, calculating the prospect of impossible riches while monks and bishops worked on the universal acceptance of the Catholic Church under Spain. Empire was the orb that sat in the hand of God.

Paradoxically, at home Felipe had followed the example of his father in the rejection of 'corrupted' bloodlines in order to create his new bureaucracy. His European domains were extensive, taking in Portuguese, Dutch, Belgian, German, Swiss and Italian territories, yet this did not mean the bureaucracy and court administration were cosmopolitan in any modern sense. The insistence on *limpieza de sangre* – the purity or 'cleanliness' of blood – applied most specifically to the descendants of Jews, and less directly, for the time being, to Moors: dubious ancestry was believed to be intimately linked to religious heresy. Likewise, Lutherans and Illuminists, with their inclination to strip away religious ceremony in preference for internalised forms of worship, were eliminated. Perhaps those paintings, with their pedagogy of terror and wonder, had frightened Felipe, along with the very real oddities that began to return from across the seas. It was a time of astonishment and confusion: as the Spanish crown tightened its religious and administrative vision, things never before seen or imagined were now at hand: a profusion of precious metals dug from the belly of the earth; new worlds of birds and fruits and spices; animals as unfeasible as the rhinoceros; sophisticated peoples with sophisticated art and culture who nevertheless had developed for millennia ignorant of the Word of God. Felipe had reached out to embrace the world, and found it could be infinitely good; likewise, it could be deeply strange, when not surly.

The Reformation was another spectre that haunted his days. Felipe ramped up his political and religious opposition; the attempt to bring England back to the Catholic faith was a critical factor in the failed Armada of 1588. Politically, the Reformation was characterised by its direct challenge to the authority of Rome; culturally, one of its side effects was to perform a kind of demonicide: it killed off the wildly imagined bestiaries that lurked in the marginalia of monastic texts, in books of hours, or through the paintings of Bosch and his contemporaries. It was the death knell for the whiskered fish and beaky salamanders, for all the weird cats and unicorns; it was the end of griffins and monsters of the deep. Gone were the multiple grim messengers of Hades the terrified imagination had suggested might exist in lands beyond the known horizons. In separating faith from cognition, the practical burghers of northern Protestantism were part of a broader intellectual movement that did away with exuberance: God's strange creatures would henceforth be ousted by new, rational systems of science and belief. Complexity would now belong to the measurable and natural world rather than the thronging zoo-pit of devils who had entertained and threatened the pre-modern mind.

Thus, as the seventeenth century swung into view, the world was flattened out. European systems of bureaucracy, so avidly pursued by Felipe in the quietude of his mountain monastery, not only aspired to measure and manage the new globe, making it an object of European administration and control; ultimately, they were also to banish the whirly creatures of the pre-modern imagination. 'For Aristotle,' wrote philosopher José Ortega y Gasset, 'the centaur is a possibility; not so for us, as biology will not allow it.'[24]

The new secularism began a centuries-long process of increasing conformity; the world was now known and observable from west to east and back again, and the prescriptions of a new rationalism would be applied to it. The task had begun of making the world, in all its wild complexity, *manageable*. This paradox lies at the heart, and remains a key project, of globalisation today: flattening out and normalising – fashion, thought, politics – at the same time as celebrating difference. Stability is often the handmaiden of domination.

In the end, the most powerful person in the world was swamped by sadness, and the sheer impossibility of the task he had set himself. Running the world militarily, politically and commercially, while attending to its strict adherence to Spanish Catholicism, was too much. Felipe reached old age alone and died badly. His death was prolonged, one of acute pain and degradation, suffering what was likely a form of stomach and bowel cancer. As if those terrible images from Bosch were taking on a life of their own, the ruler of the world, the monarch who sent his will across the universe, put up with untreated sores and uncontrollable diarrhoea, often lying in his own faeces. For Felipe, all such suffering would lessen the price to be paid beyond this temporary life. One September morning in 1598, in the hours just before dawn, the king was dead, along with all his spidery directives and hectic administration. The age of European imperialism, however, was by now well established and very much alive; globalisation was under way and would never yet be brought back within state borders, within salty docks or granite walls, within the monastery, into its cramped rooms thick with Flemish demons and holy relics.

It is no coincidence that Felipe's death came as Cervantes and Shakespeare were at their creative height: both drew deeply on the folk wisdom of the vanishing world, and anticipated the glory and the mental despair that would accompany the newly expanded universe as people began to break free of medieval chains of dogma and astrology. Two legendary old fools, Don Quixote and King Lear, represent this fulcrum on which the world was turning towards a reality full of pluralities and contradictions, empty of old certainties. Felipe's death marked the end of the pre-modern world, with much of its remnant folklore and garish paganisms: the long transition had begun from concern for the spiritual condition of the soul to concern for the political condition of the body. The sacred, as Fuentes has written, was removed from the base of language;[25] a disjuncture arose between word and thing; a new reality intruded, secular and enlightened, to banish all the fantastic beasts and folk cures, spells and demons. The 'natural world' with its intimate connection to the rituals of the seasons and the obscure knowledge of healers, with its arcane magic and chivalries, was increasingly divorced from the new dimensions of what it meant to be human.

The birth of the seventeenth century saw a very different world come up over the horizon, a century soon overcome with war and conquest, plague, pestilence and hunger. It would also announce generations of brilliant writers, painters and poets, under skies that no longer told the fate of men and women but simply looked down, indifferent, upon their disputes and collective murders and which, along with their collective genius, now reached across the universe. Much of what Felipe had worked all his life to achieve would quickly disappear: English pirates, Dutch merchants and French nobility, none of whom could agree on, or bother with, the destiny of the human soul, took control of Felipe's globe. His old world, so overflowing with piety and devils, was gone.

As the fantastic terrors of the pre-modern imagination began to recede, also came an end to the burning of witches and heretics, an activity that, despite centuries of legend, was more vigorously and popularly carried out in northern Europe than in Inquisition Spain. The process of globalisation begun with Felipe's empire, although developing iniquities of capital, systems of expropriation and murder, and corrupted labour conditions has the virtue of embedding cultures within each other, blending them sometimes by force, sometimes by curiosity and desire. There is, eventually, no original or pure thing – such dreams belong only to unscrupulous nationalists. Whose culture belongs to whom? Those Flemish visions that accompanied the birth of globalisation were not in any way Spanish, and yet they have been assumed into its national iconography: the strange dreams and nightmares of one's neighbour, eventually adopted as one's own.

As it flooded in, the world was too vast for Felipe. Rather than drown in its multiplicity, he died in a narrow bed, with just a crucifix for company. Such objects he held to be true. Over succeeding centuries, the variety of the circumnavigated world has been made accessible; its wild oddness standardised. The bewildering world made safe, when not banal; the global is made local, and the underworld no longer exists. The melancholy that filled the hearts of Joanna and her teenage friend, reading on Felipe's ancient rocky seat outside Madrid, always remains, but we no longer need fear the leathery arm, the sulphurous tongue or the spears of hell.

We might imagine a night in 1595: the consecration of the royal Basilica of San Lorenzo, the last part of the monastery complex to be completed. Outside, a crowd of locals, among them members of the generation that built the monastery, gaze at the vast granite cage of a building, its windows lit up for the occasion with oil lamps in their thousands, throwing flickering images back onto the people there to celebrate and wonder, mixing reverence and piety with wine and cheer. Among the crowd, some of the artists who had worked, and would continue to work, at filling its galleries, such as Luis de Carvajal; two other painters central to El Escorial, Alonso Sánchez Coello and the Genoese Luca Cambiaso, had by then passed away. The main building must have worn a gaudy air that night, and the low hum of monkish song; inside, the artworks commissioned, and those already part of the royal collection, along with tapestries, ornately coloured manuscripts, astrolabes and other devices to track celestial bodies, all enriched this particular universe. By then Felipe was nearly 70, a frail man whose body was beginning to fold and collapse, coming to the end of his extraordinary earthly days.

For El Escorial, there followed years of abandon: the monastery was all the more melancholic for being so huge. It could not slink away quietly and disappear under moss, shrubbery or accumulated earth. It remained a haggard marker in grey, a sombre appointment for romantic travellers in the nineteenth century, especially decrepit after the confiscation of religious properties by the state in 1837. Later, in the first half of the twentieth century, the monastery served as a historical model for those falangists who dreamed of the construction of a new Madrid after the civil war. Juan de Herrera became, 300 years after his death and surely much to his surprise, a source of inspiration for those who found, in his exemplary works of architecture, in his unwavering line of stone, a summary of all that might be replicated in the post-war capital: order, harmony, faith, discipline. These are not inherently negative elements but depend, rather, on the uses to which they are put. In the exhausted and exhausting days after the end of the civil war, San Lorenzo de El Escorial not only harked back to a glorious past: it was itself the glorious national past, embodied.

Still one of the most remarkable amid the crowded field of Spanish historical monuments, in our secular times El Escorial is a popular day trip from Madrid. Some detour up to the panoramic views enjoyed from the stone seat where Felipe sat four and a half centuries ago, on and off for twenty years, watching the monastery transform from architectural drawing to granite reality. Its stern walls and spires look now on gentler scenes, forming a backdrop to children playing football, students filing by on school excursions, or clutches of tourists approaching Felipe's brilliant complex through sunlight, or mist, or occasional snow.

Carnival and Lent

Late sixteenth-century Madrid was teeming with life; every day its markets, squares, streets and churches witnessed the battle between the festive and the sober, between the looseness of Carnival and the rigour of Lent. Unlike the controlled architectural rectitude of the monastery at El Escorial, the capital was spreading out in all directions. A new *cerca* traced its way from San Andrés to the fountain on Calle Toledo, across to the steep street of the tanneries – the Rastro de las Tenerías, later Ribera de Curtidores, home of the famous Rastro flea market – around to Antón Martín and San Jerónimo, where the Convent of Espíritu Santo – lost to fire in 1823 – stood on the site now occupied by the Congress of Deputies; past Cedaceros to the Red de San Luis and from there, via San Martín and Santo Domingo in a line roughly pursuant to the modern Gran Vía back to the *alcázar*, passing the site where very soon the royal monastery of la Encarnación would be built, another institution remarkable for its art collection, and for its longevity, for it still stands today adjacent to the Senate. Felipe could not impose on his chosen capital the symmetry of line he had achieved for his mountain retreat; Madrid was a nest of human desire and ambition, with its own hard and sharp character established over hundreds of years before the arrival of the royal court. If El Escorial was theory, Madrid was practice; if El Escorial was prayer and wisdom, Madrid, despite its quickly growing number of religious institutions, was the tavern, the market, the theatre and the brothel. The city enters the visual record with the *View of Madrid from the west, opposite the Puerta de la Vega* drawn in 1562 by Flemish artist Anton van den Wyngaerde.[1] Madrid is a stern fortress, rising like a crown from the hills on which it is perched, surrounded by fertile plains whose various streams run down to the Manzanares. There is a significant bridge in the foreground, the forerunner to Juan de Herrera's Puente de Segovia, built two decades later between 1582 and 1584.

In 1570 Felipe's fourth wife Ana of Austria arrived in Madrid. To celebrate, a series of new fountains had been built, town chronicler López de Hoyos tells us, and Madrid was the scene for spectacle after spectacle of dancing, music, drama and military drills, even the staged storming of a 'Moorish castle' that had been placed in the middle of an artificial lake. It was a day of trumpets and drums, crimson velvet, tasselled gold and luxurious dress. The mayor kissed the queen's hand, welcoming her to her new home of Madrid, assuring her the town was entirely at her service and all its citizens her faithful vassals. Then began a royal procession, stacked with wealth and nobility, winding its way to Neptune and Sol, to San Salvador and on through a new gate built to purpose at the end of Calle Mayor. By the time she entered the *alcázar*, Ana had crossed Madrid from east to west, her route hung with rich brocades; each staging post extravagantly decorated – sculptures, arches, jewels, paintings, arms – with monuments to the epic phases of the House of Austria and of the Spanish nation, from the Visigoths to the new worlds of the Americas via, naturally, the figure of Felipe himself. One day was not enough: amid more dancing, fireworks, music and military drills, the festivities went on for a second day and night. This had been, López de Hoyos assures us, the greatest celebration Madrid had ever witnessed. The city clearly knew how to throw a party.

Ana was Felipe's niece and twenty years his junior; even Pope Pius V had reservations about approving the union. Their marriage, however, was said to be a happy one between compatible partners, and Felipe to be genuinely in love with, and faithful to, his wife.

According to the dynastic priorities of the time, Ana's most important function was to deliver a male heir; she soon bore him three sons, all of whom died in childhood. Only her weakest and youngest son Felipe would survive to assume the throne; a daughter, María, was only eight months old when Ana died of influenza and quite probably exhaustion; the infant María herself died at the age of three. Felipe was thus the only one of five children to survive. As Felipe III 'the Pious', he was to be the laziest of the Habsburgs, an unremarkable and largely forgettable sovereign who under the influence of his *valido* – a powerful royal favourite, Francisco de Sandoval, the Duke of Lerma – made the catastrophic decision in 1601 to move the royal court from Madrid to the northern town of Valladolid. This would not be his only miscalculation: he helped cripple the nation's productive workforce and economy by enforcing the expulsion of all remaining Moors from Spain between 1609 and 1614.

In the meantime, Madrid was bursting with new arrivals: the courtly, the religious, the hardworking and the unscrupulous. The supply of housing was insufficient, and what was available was mostly not up to the high standard court bureaucrats expected. The town council responded to this influx of officials and their families by imposing the *regalía de aposento*, a housing law that allowed the crown to use – essentially to requisition – half of any dwelling in order to accommodate its multiplying staff. This law had existed since medieval times and was employed in different towns around Castile to meet the demands of the travelling court; the demand in Madrid would be permanent. Royal decrees were passed in 1565 and again in 1584 that sought to guarantee housing and improve the standard of dwellings.[2] Local residents immediately sought ways either to exact maximum profit from the situation or to avoid the imposition altogether. The wealthiest families simply bought their way out of any obligation to share their homes by doing favours or making donations to the royal family. Elsewhere, the so-called *casas a la malicia* sprang up, a species of 'trick' house which appeared, from the street, to have only one storey, and thus remain exempt from the charge, while hiding a larger and more complex internal

structure. Given the compensation was poor for this rooming concession, locals who could not buy their way out of the requirement
reverted where possible to concealing their spare rooms – with
bricks, plaster, curtains, whatever was to hand – ahead of inspection
by officials, rather than having to accommodate lodgers. One or
two examples of these 'trick' houses, much changed with time, can
still be seen in the old quarter of the *morería*, in the ancient *arrabal*
of San Andrés. The best known, on the corner of Mancebos and
Redondilla in the heart of Habsburg Madrid, is one of the few
remaining civilian houses of the sixteenth century.

In 1586 Saint John of the Cross, an incessant traveller, set out from
Córdoba for Madrid. Among his many projects, he was assisting
Ana de Jesús compile and edit the works of Teresa of Ávila who
had died just a few years before. One of Teresa's desires had been
to establish a religious house in Madrid, but this had not been
possible in her lifetime; Saint John of the Cross was now in the
capital to welcome a group of nuns from different parts of Spain
whose mission was to found the Carmelite monastery of Santa Ana.
The monastery complex with its orchard and gardens stood on the
site where the Plaza de Santa Ana now stands until, like so much
else, it was torn down in the early nineteenth century during the
five years of Napoleonic ascendancy. In retrospect, at least this
vandalism gave rise to one of Madrid's most famous and frequented
plazas, with its now long tradition of bars, restaurants, music and
theatre.

The nuns, including Ana de Jesús, converged on Madrid from
different religious institutions in the Manchegan towns of Ocaña,
Toledo and Malagón. As they approached the town, just 'a quarter
of a league from the court' they witnessed a great light in the sky.
'What is that?', Ana asked the muleteer. 'They must be the lamps
of the King,' came the reply, but no: the lights were 'not of this
earth, but of heaven, and foretold in light-filled splendour the great
sanctity of the new convent the nuns had come to found'.[3]
Madrid has never been a town of dreaming spires. Religious
activity, if measured by the foundation of churches, convents and

monasteries, was intense in the second half of the sixteenth century and during the seventeenth as part of the natural expansion of the city, and as befitted the age. No fewer than seventeen new religious institutions were founded in the city under Felipe II, few of which survive, such as the royal monasteries of Las Descalzas Reales and Santa Isabel.[4] As it grew, Madrid remained a seat of secular power, of earthly administration and human desire; there is no record of a mystical tradition or community, typically associated in the sixteenth century with smaller towns such as Ávila or Úbeda. The reality of the court meant most energies were spent currying favour with the imperial family and their offshoots rather than in communion with monks, nuns and assorted priests. In the late sixteenth century, Madrid may have been the capital of both Spain and a global empire, but it still lacked two of the institutions that characterised any prominent city of the time: a bishopric and a university. Early modern Madrid hosted, as the province and the contemporary city still contain, extraordinary convents and monasteries with their glittering religious treasures, but God was never quite as present as in certain other parts of Spain, or the empire, despite the city's veneration of San Isidro.

Mysticism, in any case, had to be handled carefully. There was potential danger in an individual's ecstatic experience of union with God, in that the instructional role of the church and its intermediary priests were bypassed. Mysticism flourished among sixteenth-century Spanish visionaries, but it was private and freewheeling; it was beyond the control of authority. By definition anti-intellectual and deeply internal, the mystic experience was separate from the practical realities of regular society. Whole realms of human experience might slip away beyond the control of the church; a state of rapture allowed people 'by the grace of God' to 'function outside their natural state of being', their yearning hearts and souls answerable only to God and not any earthly institution.[5] For this reason mystics, to the extent they came back down to earth to lead active lives engaged in constructive programmes of charity and education, in the manner of Teresa of Ávila or Saint John of the Cross, were domesticated by the Catholic Church and before long the extravagant vocabulary of the mystic tradition was integrated into the orthodoxies of the church.[6] Most importantly, the poetic glow touched readers and listeners all the more deeply for being versed in the vernacular rather than obscure church Latin. Two generations before a unique combination of writers would change Spanish literature forever, the mystics helped lay the groundwork for the great blossoming of the Golden Age. It has also been suggested the influence of the Spanish mystic poets reached across the continent and found fertile territory in one of the finest English poets of the age, John Donne. This is likely: Donne was born into a Catholic family and was, among many other things, an adventurer, sailing in 1596 with the English fleet under Walter Raleigh, fighting the Spanish in Cádiz, and later studying the Spanish language. His poetry is shot through with the ecstatic, both sexual and metaphysical.

As a stepping stone to wealth and power, Madrid has never been a city in which to cleanse the sins of the mind or flesh. In his novel *Riña de gatos: Madrid, 1936* – about a bumbling Englishman abroad, a lost Velázquez, a femme fatale and the rumblings of civil war – Eduardo Mendoza makes the point that Madrid's relatively recent foundation meant it was at one remove from deeper religious traditions to be found in towns that had been saturated with the church for centuries, and that religion was kept to some extent distant from the hard politics of state and the grind of empire.[7] It imbued the daily life of the city less than in older, more pious towns; in the early months of the twentieth-century civil war the *godlessness* of Madrid was one of the qualities most held against it by the Nationalist Catholic forces who, from their older, more conservative and more deeply religious bases in towns such as Burgos, Valladolid or Salamanca, waited for Madrid to fall.

Although the proliferation of religious institutions did not convert the people of Madrid into a deeply pious collective, it nevertheless led to a flowering of religious artwork, decorative and didactic. After the magnificence of Titian, patronised by Felipe II since his earlier travels through the European Habsburg domains, came others of outstanding quality, finding employment not only in commissions for the nobility and the religious houses in Madrid, but also in the ongoing commissions for the vast spaces of the chapels, walls and galleries at El Escorial. In this environment, with a permanent seat of royal power, a settled and 'official' religious doctrine (despite occasional heresies) and, notwithstanding the drain on its resources of near constant war, there flowered in Madrid and Spain, between roughly 1550 and 1700, one of the richest and most intense periods in the history of western art.

Alonso Sánchez Coello was followed by his disciple Juan Pantoja de la Cruz; their masterpieces contribute to the unrivalled collection of the Prado Museum, along with Francisco Ribalta, Vicente Carducho, Eugenio Cajés, Juan Bautista Maíno and the master of the still life, Juan Sánchez Cotán. Even those painters who stayed mostly within regional centres, such as Luis de Morales, Juan de Juanes or the brilliant but largely forgotten Pedro de Orrente, were influenced by the developing dimensions of the royal collection in Madrid with its Flemish and Italian masterpieces. All of these names, talented as they were, would be relegated by history to remain in the shadow of the following generation, for in the first half of the seventeenth century there arrived Francisco de Zurbarán, Diego Velázquez, José de Ribera, Alonso Cano and Bartolomé Esteban Murillo.

As so often happens, there was an exception shimmering on the edge of convention. El Greco, an odd Cretan mystic who had found his way by the mid-1570s to Toledo, did not work in Madrid or draw his inspiration from the artworks collected in the royal galleries. In his travels from Greece he had admired and learned from Titian in Venice, and drew from the deep Roman well of Raphael and Michelangelo, but he never found favour at the court in Madrid. It was not for lack of trying; in a serious error of judgement, Felipe II dismissed the possibility of hiring El Greco as a court painter, reportedly not finding his outlandish forms and the striking chroma of his palette to his sober liking, a decision all the stranger when we consider the attraction Felipe felt for Hieronymus Bosch.

From his studio in Toledo, however, El Greco was loved and supported; local commissions flowed in. In consequence, while for the art lover the Prado Museum remains the undisputed temple for both Velázquez and Goya – as would be expected, given the close relationship of both painters to the royal court – the collection of El Greco, while necessarily superb, needs to be complemented with explorations to the surrounding towns of El Escorial, Illescas and, of course, Toledo.[8] El Greco had been no secret to the Spanish painters of the eighteenth century, but later in the nineteenth, when Spain was 'discovered' by Europeans and Americans, their painters were mesmerised by his unfamiliar work. Developed beyond the parameters of fashion, correction or approval, it was unlike anything they had seen, and to find El Greco in his full array it was necessary to track down his masterpieces that were scattered about, a series of moody jewels tucked away in the darkened corners of provincial churches. To come across them for the first time must have been startling, as they were found to be serving, as they had done for centuries, as a living part of the faith and daily practice of their community. This is the case with various works by El Greco in the church of Our Lady of Charity in Illescas, just beyond the provincial border of Madrid. The church, founded by the indomitable Cardinal Cisneros, allows us the rare opportunity to view El Greco's art interwoven with the community for which it was created; it functions here outside art history, art theory or the politics of museum management. His paintings in Illescas are humble and quotidian sacred objects, and precisely therein lies their power.

The influence of El Greco on painters of the late nineteenth and early twentieth century was profound: Manet, Cézanne, Zuloaga and Picasso, to name just some; the French were particularly enamoured. As established notions of space, figure and surface were broken up, this forgotten visionary surged back from his sidelined position to take a place as one of the four revered revolutionaries of Spanish art, along with Velázquez, Goya and Picasso.

By the green skirts of the Guadarrama range, in the heart of the Lozoya Valley, amid a beautiful landscape of forests, lakes, stone walls, rich meadows and fast-flowing mountain streams, is the fourteenth-century Carthusian monastery of El Paular. Its cloisters contain one of those art treasures that against all odds was saved from the vicissitudes of the centuries, and which cannot but offer a melancholy suggestion of everything that, as a counterpoint, has been lost. Indeed, given the fragility of documents and canvases, the easy lure of jewels and gold, the centuries of fires, rains, rodents and pillaging armies, to say nothing of hostile administrations, theft of church property and a rolling series of civil wars, it is miraculous that any of these materials have survived until our times.

The Italian-born Vicente Carducho arrived in Spain as a young man in 1585, accompanying his older brother, one of the many Italian artists commissioned by Felipe to decorate El Escorial. Carducho had an outstanding career in Spain as a painter, teacher and theorist, albeit as an artist he was eclipsed later in life by the upstart talent of Diego Velázquez. The last great commission of his career was a series of fifty-six large-scale canvases for the monastery at El Paular, narrating the life of Saint Bruno, founder of the Carthusian Order, as well as the subsequent history of the Carthusians. Today, one walks clockwise around the cloisters of El Paular admiring the ambition and scope of this storyboard. Brilliant though the artworks are, they do not tell a uniformly happy story; canvas after canvas displays either a miracle of the faith, an ecstatic vision or a brutal murder; there are deaths by bludgeoning – mostly at the hands of infidel Turks or the heretical English – and a morbid series of torture chambers where monks meet awful ends, only to be winged up into heaven by cherubim and angels. The virulently anti-Catholic English do not come out of Carducho's series well, portrayed as a cruel, fanatical people in thrall to religious fervour and intolerance. The inescapable irony: this was precisely the denunciation directed at the Spanish by their historic enemies.

After suffering from centuries of damp and deterioration, and their confiscation and redistribution following the closure of the monastery in 1835 and the state seizure of church assets in 1836, the Carducho series languished. Two canvases stored in the municipal museum of Tortosa, in eastern Spain, were suspected of being burnt by Republican forces during the civil war. Finally in 2011, after years of painstaking restoration work, fifty-two of the original scries were once again hung in the cloisters of El Paular, where they constitute one of the lesser-known but more spectacular cultural treasures of Madrid.

Madrid had begun the sixteenth century as an expanding Castilian town under the Trastámara dynasty; now it entered the seventeenth century as the Habsburg capital of Spain and its global empire. The skeleton around which the modern city wraps its body was firmly in place; major religious institutions and hospitals aligned with major roads. One of the most important of its time was the Hospital of the Annunciation, founded in 1596 in the neighbourhood of Atocha, where the walls of Madrid gave access via the Puerta de Vallecas. This would later become the General Hospital of Madrid and, after various lives and reconstructions, the Museo Nacional Centro de Arte Reina Sofía. Throughout the town, streets still followed the path of old streams and former city walls, while an increasing traffic in goods and people filled the roads that led north to Segovia, south to Toledo or Vallecas, east to Alcalá de Henares or Valencia, and west to Extremadura.

Not all was smooth in the process of embedding the faith during such turbulent times, with wars and heresies abounding; across Europe, the battle for the modern human soul was in full swing. The antagonists for Spain were still Protestants and Muslims, the latter of more concern now in Turkey than in Spain itself. Some pockets of resistance remained: in 1567 a delegation of Moors entered Madrid from the Alpujarras in the far south of Spain to plead for the suspension of a directive that outlawed Moorish dress and the use of the Arabic language. Their presence would have been a reminder of *Madrid árabe*, those days now not only lost, but increasingly denied altogether by the flattering pens at the Habsburg court; Moorish Spain was part of a quickly vanishing past. The delegation was rejected and soon returned from whence they had come; as they crossed the plains on their journey south, they might have seen two indistinct, dusty figures in the distance, quick scrawls or pen marks against the horizon.

Sic transit gloria mundi

aving conferred capital status on Madrid and built an artistic and religious complex without parallel on its outskirts, Felipe II was a figure both impregnable and on borrowed time. Politically at his apogee, throughout the late 1570s and 1580s his control over events began to loosen at the same time as he began to diminish physically. In 1578 a major political murder took place in Madrid that would implicate and unsettle Felipe. The capital has a long relationship with different forms of disorder: military coups, social upheaval, anarchism, civil war and terrorism, domestic and international, have all stained the city with blood.

The incident might have been simply another act of skulduggery shadowed by malice, jealousy and ambition, were it not for the profile of the actors involved. The victim was Juan de Escobedo, a powerful secretary to Don Juan of Austria, half-brother to Felipe II. His appointment had come on the recommendation of another powerful secretary of state, Antonio Pérez, and was made with the idea that Escobedo would keep tabs on Don Juan whose success leading Spain and its allies to victory over the Turkish fleet at the Battle of Lepanto[1] had given rise to excessive vanity and scheming that troubled Felipe. Don Juan was widely admired as one of the finest military leaders in Europe, and in 1576 was named governor of Flanders at a time when Spain's northern dominions were facing a revolt led by William the Silent, Prince of Orange. Escobedo travelled regularly between Spain and Flanders, where Don Juan had begun to formulate an elaborate plan to cross the Channel, invade England, release Mary Stuart from prison, marry her, throw Elizabeth I off the throne and declare England a Catholic nation, creating a Catholic league of England and Flanders over which he, naturally, would rule as monarch. Felipe could not tolerate this combination of ambition and insubordination. Far from carrying out his principal task which was to cool Don Juan's fervour, Escobedo fell under his spell. Pérez, meanwhile, had reportedly been negotiating with the rebels of Flanders against his king and employer; no treachery could be discounted. Uncovering the plot, Escobedo threatened to expose Pérez before the king; Pérez, who controlled all communication with the king, quickly turned the tables, convinced Felipe that it was in fact Escobedo who was plotting treason and royal overthrow, and between the two of them, history tells us, they ordered the murder of Escobedo. Felipe could not be associated with anything so sordid; Pérez was tasked with the deed.

He first attempted to poison Escobedo who, Rasputin-like, refused to die. Pérez was either using the wrong kind of poison or mistaking the fatal dosage. In his account of these events, Gregorio Marañón – scientist, medic, essayist, historian and one of the most brilliant minds of twentieth-century Madrid – tells of various attempts to bring Escobedo down until, exasperated by his resistance, Pérez decided to hire a gang of cut-throats, one of whom was a master swordsman.[2]

On Easter Monday 1578 Escobedo made an evening visit to the one-eyed Princess of Éboli, another of the exotic characters who peopled late sixteenth-century Madrid: born Ana de Mendoza, she was by all accounts an extraordinarily attractive and energetic young woman, married at the age of 13 to the Prince of Éboli, had ten children in quick succession, was rumoured to have been Felipe's lover, spent three years in a convent and then rejoined civilian life, only to become involved in the court intrigues of Pérez; she spent the last decade of her life in prison, and died at 52. It is possible that Escobedo had been with the Princess of Éboli to reveal he knew of her liaison with Pérez and of his treasonous intrigues with Flemish rebels. One imagines Escobedo casting an eye up to the heavens as he left the house of the squinty princess, perhaps sensing rain. He spent a short time at the nearby house of his mistress Brianda de Guzmán then, on his way home at last, the assassins fell upon him.

Representations of the murder emphasise the menace and shadow of narrow alleys near the church of Santa María. Even the most important of statesmen can be killed in an instant; behind the church, the shadows closed around Escobedo. His murder antici-pated one of the most famous murders in literature, when hired assassins fell on Macbeth's old friend Banquo: the theatricality, the immanent thrill, the foul night sinister, a sense of the tragic bordering on comic; the plotters in wait; the forbidding Insausti, the master swordsman, driving his blade straight through, the outer walls of Santa María spattered with blood, Escobedo unseamed and bleeding out by the flicker of torches, prayers diminishing to uselessness.

Don Juan also died in 1578, in the Netherlands. His string of military conquests was almost as long as the list of his illicit affairs with women of the noble houses of the day. For reasons never clear, his body was cut into three sections – or four, depending on the version – and taken back to Spain where it was sewn together again for his burial. He was just 33, and is the only technically illegitimate Habsburg buried in El Escorial. Under suspicion of involvement in the scandal, the Princess of Éboli was imprisoned in the tower in the town of Pinto, south of Madrid. The magnificent tower, some-what reformed, still stands today.

Such events unsteadied Felipe, at the apex of his reign. The slow decline of his physical strength soon began, as he retreated in the following decade to a life more governed by prayer. A waning man, he developed a late interest in the gardens of the royal monastery. The Armada in 1588 was his final epic; that it ended in failure takes nothing from his greatness. In his last decade there was one skirmish after another, but it was by now all sound and fury. 'My son,' he is reported to have whispered on his deathbed to Felipe III, 'see here now, the fate in store for all the kingdoms of the world.'[3]

It is to take nothing away from the magnificent, historic city of Valladolid to admit there were no good reasons to move the capital there from Madrid in 1601. Felipe III, just two years on the throne, had in his indolence delegated much of his authority to Sandoval, the Duke of Lerma. The next Felipe was interested above all in hunting and, like most *madrileños* of his time, the theatre. These pastimes, along with the pious foundation of another scattering of monasteries and charitable houses, at least meant the new monarch was not pursuing war; during his largely peaceful reign, the Spanish empire reached its greatest extension, thus making even stranger his agreeing to move the capital a few hours north to the flatlands of Castile, as if while expanding the empire he were simultaneously downsizing its most important city.

Valladolid was smaller, drier in summer, mistier, damper and colder in winter: other than an illustrious past as host to assorted monarchs, it had little to offer. The transferral of the court was to last only five years, much to the relief of the people of Madrid and, it was said, to the relief of Felipe III, who found himself bored to tears by provincial life, far removed from the variety and spectacle of Madrid. The excuse that Valladolid was a necessary escape from the vices of the capital was only ever that – an excuse, the cover for an elaborate real-estate *pelotazo*.[4] Madrid was indeed full of vice: precisely for that reason, the indolent king wanted to get back as soon as he could. In Valladolid, much closer to the town of Lerma where the duke had his base, Felipe could be kept in tighter check.

The five-year episode allowed Sandoval to carry out a series of property speculations that made him enormously rich. With advance notice of the transferral – a textbook case of insider trading – he made a fortune first buying up cheap homes and buildings in Valladolid ahead of the royal move and then, five years later, performed the same operation, purchasing choice sites in Madrid that had been massively devalued when the court decamped. He additionally received substantial bribes from prominent Madrid businesses and the town council to engineer the return. A more perfect, and more corrupt, business operation is hard to imagine.

All those who made the move, under one obligation or another, had no choice: not just the court apparatus, but also all the useful and parasitic who fed from its needs and desires. The tradespeople and bureaucrats trudged off, along with the crooks and charlatans that existed in the long shadow of the court, the matchmakers and delivery boys, the entire servant class, and the criminal and indolent attracted to the flame. The streets and people of Madrid were bereft: 'deprived of the court, the town has suffered the greatest calamity that any locality has ever experienced, because everyone of every category found some way of making a living.'[5] Even allowing for the hyperbole, the effect was pernicious for Madrid. The largely forgotten seventeenth-century Madrid playwright, Agustín de Rojas Villandrando, reflected on 'the enormous solitude that overtook Madrid, where one saw scarcely a soul in the streets, and all was sadness and melancholy . . .'[6]

Not only the artisans and servants moved to Valladolid; many of the cultural class also made the visits necessary to keep up flattery and patronage: writers Góngora, Quevedo and Cervantes all spent time in the northern town, as did the young Flemish painter Peter Paul Rubens. To Rubens's stay in Valladolid we owe a stunning equestrian portrait of the Duke of Lerma, the royal favourite in immaculate armour atop a creamy, muscular, bright-eyed horse against a backdrop of blue so strangely electric, Rubens might have been rifling through El Greco's paintbox, a portrait that breaks the mould of so many tedious portraits of dignitaries atop their chargers.[7] Despite his youth, Rubens was a diplomat who knew the royal courts of Europe; he was reportedly nonplussed by the power the duke exerted over the king. Sandoval was the de facto ruler of Spain for the first two decades of the seventeenth century, and Felipe III was far from the last of Spanish rulers – absolutist or democratic – to employ the figure of the *valido*. Such figures, now masquerading as political 'gurus', have always stalked the halls of power.

In 1605 a delegation of some 600 persons visited Valladolid from England as part of ongoing peace negotiations. This visit has given rise to speculation that William Shakespeare was among the retinue of the famous, worthy and noble, and that he might have met Miguel de Cervantes, in Valladolid with his family at the time, and who had just published *Don Quixote* that same year. Much effort has been put into trying to trace evidence of such a contact, without

success. What is more certain, however, is that the English delegation, upon returning, carried in their baggage the very first copy of
Don Quixote to reach British shores.

After a couple of seasons, the royals were bored in Valladolid.
They filled the empty hours with frivolous entertainments, wasting
'both energy and money'.[8] Memorably, their son Felipe IV 'the
Planet King' was born there in 1605, but by then the town council
of Madrid was urging Felipe to amend the error of the dislocation,
the absence of the royal court having devastated the city and the
economy of its surrounding towns.[9] A substantial bribe was offered
to bring the court back; the Duke of Lerma could not resist another
lucrative real-estate deal and it was duly agreed that in early 1606
Madrid would once more become the seat of royalty and by default
the national capital. The royal party packed up and returned to
Madrid; their northern adventure ultimately pointless. For months,
lines of carriages threaded the roads southwards, through Tordesillas
and Medina del Campo, Olmedo, Arévalo and Segovia, over the
mountain passes and down to El Escorial, arriving eventually into
a mostly abandoned Madrid. Carriage by carriage, mule by mule,
all the human paraphernalia wound its way back: the chancers and
poets, administrators and thieves; the courtesans and prostitutes,
the tradesmen and jesters. The city did not take long to recover its
festive spirit: the royal return was soon celebrated with theatre,
street dancing, bullfights and general partying.

Once back in Madrid Felipe was to pronounce, famously, that
sólo Madrid es corte: only Madrid is the court. And in Madrid the
court was to stay, albeit at certain historic moments there have been
brief governmental sojourns in Cádiz (1810–13) and Republican
Valencia (November 1936–October 1937), both a side effect of war.
In *Los años de Madridgrado*, his study of the emotional battle for
Madrid during the civil war, Fernando Castillo discusses how
Francoist leaders considered changing the capital of Spain from
Madrid – a city that, in giving itself over to Republicans and Soviet
military advisers had in their eyes proved undeserving of the role
– in favour of Seville.[10] The temporary capitals of the armed rebel-
lion, Salamanca and Burgos, were both saturated with symbols of

nationalist sentiment, yet were too small and ultimately too provincial, as Valladolid had been 300 years before. In the 1930s these debates did not affect the court as the royal family were no longer in Spain, but they demonstrate how periodically, whether under a monarchic or republican system, there are always forces in Spain wanting to defenestrate Madrid as the national capital.

In these years Madrid made a quantum departure from what had always been its bigger, smarter and more beautiful neighbour, Toledo. The two towns were on opposite trajectories. In the first three decades of the seventeenth century, as the reign of Felipe III gave way to that of Felipe IV, the population of Madrid increased from 65,000 to 175,000, while that of Toledo plummeted from 80,000 to around 25,000.[11] It would be safe to assume the vast majority of those who left Toledo went to Madrid. While Madrid had been an ugly duckling, Toledo had drawn people to her; now the flow was opposite, from the Tagus north to the Manzanares. An increasing number of privileges was granted to Madrid and the town began its transformation into a city, withdrawing from the long shadow of Toledo and towards its own light and high blue sky. For a thousand years the Visigoth 'Matrice', the Islamic Mayrit and the medieval Madrid had been inferior. Toledo, the ancient seat of learning and ecclesiastical power, was airy and opulent, altogether richer and more sophisticated; when Madrid had been a grubby village with pigs rootling around the streets, Toledo had been a town of translators and synagogues, of high medieval scholarship. But history had other plans: wrapped around by the noble Tagus, Toledo was preserved, a lovely monument in stone and steel, in carved wood and jewellery, in sacred and scientific texts, a town of narrow streets where Hebrew and Arabic still resonated. Madrid, thick-skinned and warty by comparison, rose to the status of capital, cloaked in all the vestments of power. The rulers of the church stayed in Toledo; the rulers of the nation, in Madrid. For the royal family, for every ambitious schemer and statesman who flocked in the wings, and for all the brilliant poets, artists and dramatists who were beginning to populate the Spanish stage, home was Madrid.

Perhaps symbolically, given the eclipse of Toledo, the first of the great sixteenth-century artists to die was El Greco, in 1614. His collected portraits of saints, along with Velázquez's portraits of buffoons at court, are without peer in western art. The views he painted of his adopted home have been always admired, often imitated, but never equalled. Toledo may have been destined to recede into the role of historic artefact, splendid in its Roman, Visigoth, Hebraic, Muslim and Christian heritage, while the main show moved on to Madrid, but one thing could never be taken away: the town would always have El Greco.

In the repeating cycle of the years, economic crises were never far away: failed harvests, treasure galleons lost to pirates or sunk at sea, inadequate tax collection, or the cost of ongoing conflict across Europe to which the Habsburg regime was inevitably committed financially and with the supply of troops. Wealth from the new world was not used efficiently; rather than being dedicated to 'nation-building' projects, much of the gold and silver from America 'was hoarded in the form of jewellery, household furnishings and liturgical objects; great amounts of silver were stored in Spanish monasteries, convents, palaces and churches'.[12] This basic mismanagement of resources left an unequalled heritage of religious art and architecture, but little capital available for the broader project of national development.

If Felipe II had fudged his way along with a largely overspent credit, deepening the Spanish debt, and Felipe III had mostly ignored matters of international consequence by living between peace treaties, the theatre and the hunting lodge, under Felipe IV the state budgets were strained beyond bearing. The glittering stars of seventeenth-century Madrid lit up a night sky of war, of international conflict and regional revolt, of plague, pandemic and falling birth rates, of inflation and bankruptcy and the self-inflicted wound that was the expulsion of the Moors. Removing such large numbers of the productive class left whole regions much the poorer. Facing hunger, rural Castilians abandoned the countryside to congregate in Madrid, for centuries a magnet for internal migration, or left by the boatload to the Americas. Nor was it only the landless; the traditional towns of Castile suffered a decline as noble families left behind their provincial estates and windswept rural castles to move to the capital.[13] So acute had this problem become that by 1619 the Council of Castile had to order numerous nobles back to their home towns, along with an oversupply of ecclesiastics who had come to Madrid attracted by the new religious houses.[14] The nation simply did not have the resources, or did not allocate them efficiently enough, to maintain the strength of nation and empire. Only along the fertile northern coasts were there positive demographics in this period;[15] in Madrid, after the sharp rise in the first decades of the century, the population fell from the 1630s due to plague, emigration and the recruitment of males into the armies of the Imperial Alliance fighting the hugely destructive Thirty Years' War.

Only Madrid was the court, but by no means was Madrid *only* the court. Not everyone lived amid brightly coloured tapestries and perfumed silk, warmed by massy fireplaces, their ancestors looking down from oil and canvas upon the subsequent generations. Madrid was experiencing a new, refined and baroque glimpse of capital life – tree-lined avenues, splendid horse-drawn carriages, public fountains, palaces and a selection of beautiful new homes and stately buildings – yet for many life remained basic, cramped and poor. The new magnificence, moreover, came funded by increased taxes on basic goods such as meat, water and wine. Upward mobility from the lower rungs of society was next to impossible; injustice was common, not least as an illiterate underclass lacked the resources by which to challenge unfair treatment. This is not to say life was uniquely miserable: life has always been celebrated to the full in Madrid, and there has never been a direct relationship between prosperity and enjoyment, as many royal lives will testify. The nobility lived safer lives, to the extent they were less exposed to everyday violence, disease or privation, but those who could not afford such luxuries did not live any less intensely. Madrid embodied a highly ceremonial and hierarchised society: those lower down the ranks were often treated poorly, but there was absolute co-dependence. One could not live without the other, and the presence of the well-to-do afforded an array of strategies for survival for those needing to live off their wits. It was not only the upper classes who observed the etiquette of hierarchy: as Galdós would show in his late nineteenth-century novel *Misericordia*, wherever half a dozen persons come together for any purpose, there will always be one who will attempt to impose their will on the others.[16] Among beggars there existed strictly applied rankings as much as among the flatterers at court.

Thousands of peasants, artisans and their families continued to flow into Madrid, not least as town after Castilian town was devastated by the bubonic plague that raced through Spain – leaping from body to body, from skin to skin, a time of blood and rats and fleas. The peasantry continued to bear an inordinate burden of taxation; they were the bottom and most essential rung in a feudal structure that generated, but did not redistribute, significant amounts of wealth. In 1593 the courts had highlighted the excessive contribution of 'the people who sustain this kingdom'.[17] The great mass of anonymous Castilian peasants and labourers 'supported Spanish government and society, financed the armies and fleets, and subsidized the allies' along with a network of aristocratic layabouts, the church and clergy, bankers and assorted moneylenders.[18] Madrid society obeyed the pyramidal structure so typical of early modern societies: the baseload of work was carried out by the most poorly paid, including the harvesting of crops, the construction of buildings and ships, the skinning and butchering of meat, the cooking of food, the paving of streets, the weaving and cutting of cloth, the chopping of firewood, the turning of pottery, the making of shoes, the collection of taxes and the burying of bodies. This imbalance was accentuated in a Madrid society dominated by, and in service to, the court and its crowded schools of attendant officials and, during the reigns of Felipe III and Felipe IV, the array of often extravagant entertainments that kept an idle nobility amused. In 1616 Madrid magistrate Mateo López Bravo argued the debilitating effects for the nation of the concentration of riches in few hands: 'The maldistribution of wealth is very harmful: it creates power, arrogance and idleness among those who have it and misery, humiliation and despair among those who do not.'[19]

Madrid was bursting against its walls, crowding its streets and markets and charitable houses, its bars and brothels and theatre corrals. Felipe II had realised that 'liveability' was one of the major challenges facing his new capital; legal and technical systems were put in place in an attempt to regulate the profusion of the town. Building programmes to house the swelling population were mostly a matter of private initiative and necessity acting as the mother of invention; to his credit, however, Felipe III also understood the centrality of water to Madrid, and that a clean water supply and hygiene were essential to underwrite successful growth. The old Islamic water channels needed to be expanded as the tenth-century system, brilliant as it was, could not adequately supply the much larger seventeenth-century capital. Three major works were undertaken around 1617 to bring an improved supply of fresh water to the centre: the channels of the Castellana, the Buen Retiro and the Abroñigal.[20] Professions associated with water became more closely regulated and supervised: well diggers, plumbers, pipe layers and water carriers were all vital to conducting the efficient flow of water through the city, with its streams, underground channels, wells, waterwheels, drains and pipes and still, not altogether yet controlled, the effluent produced every day by more than 150,000 people milling around the administrative centre of the largest empire in the world.

Hygiene was not just a matter of the body, but of the physical appearance of the city. Madrid aspired to be clean as well as beautiful, majestic, splendid. Two decades after the decision to settle the capital in Madrid, an urban works committee was established under the watchful eye of Juan de Herrera. There was a need to spruce up the streets and buildings. A new set of urban laws came into force placing restrictions around common and private space and with it, as ever, new layers of administrative complexity.[21] Infrastructure projects were unfurled and the image of the town polished, though it was never possible, however much the old regime tried, to banish the unsightly poor to the margins. Madrid's homeless, uprooted, vagabond and picaresque were a permanent feature and have taken an equally permanent place in the literature of the period. The early modern vagabond – the *pícaro* – spawned a literary genre for which Spain became famous even if, as is likely the case, their literary fame was out of proportion to their actual numbers.[22]

Antonio Mancelli's 1623 bird's-eye map shows Madrid as a compact organism, cramped within its restrictive walls yet surrounded by orderly gardens, parks and orchards.[23] The fundamental morphology of the centre was settling deeper; it is clearly recognisable as the Madrid of today, with the tight clustering of buildings and its maze of crooked streets; a town both compact and haphazard, a small and already infinitely complex object on the central *meseta*. Work was carried out on facades and balconies; a clampdown followed on illegal dwellings or unpaid urban taxes. As part of the facial scrub and general body work, a document of 1661 lays out the ideal profile of a master builder: 'Required to know how to read and write, to draw, to know Geometry, Perspective and Arithmetic; to have read History, to have listened to Philosophy, understand Music and something of Medicine; to have an understanding of Law, with a knowledge of Astrology and matters of Heaven.'[24] A master builder in seventeenth-century Madrid, then, must be ready to create works of beauty, harmony and of the highest principles. Obviously not all buildings in the capital benefited from the input of a culturally sophisticated master builder, but baroque Madrid flowered with superb churches and convents, palaces and offices of state. Some splendid examples remain but many did not survive the vicissitudes of the nineteenth century.

The project of beautification was one thing; another was daily hygiene. Along with human waste, which was not only effluent but also the bloody aftermath of childbirth, primitive medical procedures and arcane dentistry, the city produced great volumes of construction debris – Madrid was, is and seemingly forever will be under construction – food scraps, market refuse and all the detritus left behind by crowds and street vendors. Building rubble was particularly awkward for pedestrians and horse-drawn vehicles.[25] Some necessary trades were noisy – blacksmiths and associated crafts – while others, such as bakeries or ceramic kilns, ran the continual risk of fire. Others, such as tanneries, stank to high heaven and left organic waste behind, to say nothing of the accumulated excrement of horses, cattle, dogs, pigs, cats and rats and, inevitably, the carcasses of dead animals, not all of which were immediately retrieved from the public thoroughfare.[26] Many of the worst trades had been moved outside the city walls, but their polluted overflows still ran into the Manzanares or one of the other smaller streams. Adding to what seems an enormous and fetid chaos was the constant dust or mud from streets, many not yet paved or cobbled. A vague idea of this disorder – without the overpowering stench or animal waste – can be gleaned by hanging around after the close of the Rastro, Madrid's Sunday flea market: in the Plaza de Cascorro, down Ribera de Curtidores, in the Plaza del General Vara del Rey, all the way down to the cluttered stalls by Ronda de Toledo, the long tradition of street cleaning begins, with brooms and high-powered water hoses amid piles of trash, lost garments, unidentified shreds, dirty plastics, stolen goods, loose items bouncing around, papers, food scraps, the odd shoe, abandoned phones or emptied wallets, hair ties, bottles, alcohol and urine. Madrid has always been a city where people live intensely; consequently, it often has the appearance of being intensely *lived in*.

Along this often murky corridor of the seventeenth century, dim and earthy, running through palaces and slums, ripe with all the smells of splendour and decay, ripe with fruitful abundance and shrunken with ailment and disease, went the human body. In the town of Corpa, half an hour east of Madrid, healing waters high in sodium, potassium and magnesium cured the constipation of various Habsburg rulers.[27] At the La Margarita spa in nearby Loeches, the corruption of the body eased by the waters is an inventory of early modern illness: cataracts and scrofulous ulcers, tumours, eczema, impetigo, scabies, psoriasis and other itchy sores, necrosis of the spleen and liver, haemorrhoids, gout, constipation and venereal diseases. All afflicted early modern residents of Madrid; only the select few, however, had access to the 'quickening of the digestive system' provided by the springs of Loeches, a magical water that emerged from underground to carry away those inescapable conditions to which flesh is prone. In showers or baths, taken with a dash of sugar or mallow flower to hide the sulphurous flavour, or even gargled, the waters were renowned for flushing away every debilitating condition, active or passive, apparent on the skin or creeping its silent way through the internal organs, softly rotting the body. Thus passes the glory of the world.

For years historians have debated the extent to which the seventeenth-century downturn in the Spanish economy was due to a systemic indolence among the nobility, the alleged disdain of the Castilian ruling class for commerce and manual labour. There is some truth here, though the debate itself gives rise to stereotypes, rehashed in the argument that the 'laziness' and 'inefficiency' of Spaniards contributed to the country's financial crisis in the early twenty-first century. A country, the cliché runs, where the spark of innovation was dampened by a regressive and inquisitorial clergy determined, along with a domineering military, to keep Spaniards fearful, obedient and illiterate. In hindsight, Spain's major error was the very uneven distribution of the riches of empire, but such concentrations of wealth were consonant with the times.

An empire of world significance, for all it might subsequently have been lost, and a culture of enduring world importance, cannot be raised by layabouts and shirkers. Despite all the problems it faced, the magnificence of early modern Spain did not come about by accident, but through ingenuity, sacrifice and labour. Elliott floats the idea that Spain was poor precisely because it was wealthy: riches made it indolent.[28] This is not necessarily a Spanish trait, or flaw: that people tend to work less the wealthier they are is mostly true for any culture. There is no doubt that many of the nobility were inefficient estate managers; it is also true the nobility was indulged, especially when it came to exemption from taxes and immunity from the conventional legal processes that applied to farmers, merchants and peasants, but this was only a small percentage of the populace and cannot in itself be an explanation, for it neglects the fact most people were hard-working and by necessity innovative. Survival in the pre-modern era required effort, adaptability and patience.

The economy of Madrid was intimately connected to that of Castile, and by extension to the vicissitudes of climate, plague and the volume of imperial trade. Madrid also generated its own local economy, trades and activities related to the court, its provisioning and maintenance, and its extensive hinterland of domestic servants. By the late sixteenth century a raft of administrative and clerical trades flourished and there developed, underwriting the banking, finance and administration of church and empire, the infamous and endless bureaucracy of Madrid, a multiplying of parchments, of wax and ink and ribbons, scribes and lawyers, accountants, agents and secretaries. Like interleaving flowers and curling vines that embellish medieval manuscripts, a woven garland of paperwork threaded its way through the town, papers of denial, stipulation and concession, papers that settled disputes, demanded compliance, granted titles, ordered executions; papers that directed the home, the street, the world, the soul. As the site to which all manner of legal complaints might be directed, the court attracted litigants from within Madrid and its surrounds; the wheels of state moved slowly, and in 1603 one parish priest read the funeral sermon for a petitioner who had waited in vain for eleven years for the resolution of his case.[29]

Serving the aristocracy was a cast of thousands, for the court also demanded doctors and apothecaries, barbers, tailors, chaplains, chefs, cooks and sommeliers, along with wardrobe assistants, clockmakers, architects, builders, painters, engineers, carpenters, foresters, game-keepers, dog handlers and ostlers, and all the employees who worked beneath these key posts. The staff at Madrid's court numbered around 1,500, an endlessly humming nest of intrigue. Meanwhile, an array of practical professions had long since established themselves in specific areas of the capital, now remembered by street names that marked the locus of those *gremios*, or guilds. The most famous in the old city include Bordadores (embroiderers) and Hileras (spin-ners), kept busy with cottons, wool, silk, pearls and gold braid, preparing the sumptuous garments of the court; Tintoreros (dyers), Cuchilleros (cutlers), Yeseros (plasterers), Botoneras (button makers and sellers), Latoneros (tinsmiths or coppersmiths), Herradores (farriers), Esparteros (weavers) and, with a nod to the new admin-istrative roles demanded by the court, Relatores (clerks and secretaries).

By the middle of the seventeenth century, Madrid had assumed economic leadership of Castile, surpassing many of the formerly thriving towns such as the market centre of Medina del Campo. In an atmosphere of general Castilian decline, and despite the drop in population due to plague and war, the economy of Madrid expanded, drawing in the resources of surrounding towns. Hungry nobles continued to leave their poor estates to search for favour and employment at the heart of the government machine. The collapse of trade and agriculture in the north of Castile saw merchants and bankers move their business to Madrid.[30] The expanding church presence in the capital was another factor; as one of three common occupations for the sons of the upper classes, along with the army and civil administration, the church played its part in the drain from the countryside, providing a means by which, in an increasingly uncertain world, the sons – and occasionally daughters – of the rural nobility might find the tasks to fill their days, the food and shelter to survive, and the prayer with which to maintain the good reputation of a family name. The idea was thus cemented in the seventeenth century that Madrid was fundamentally vampiric; British historian John Lynch described Madrid as an essentially parasitic community, a focus of consumption rather than production.[31] This jealousy of Madrid would continue through the centuries and until the present day; the often rehearsed argument that the capital hoovers up resources from the towns and regions surrounding it ignores Madrid's enormous capacity, as a capital city, to generate opportunity, wealth and employment.

By the seventeenth century it had become necessary to furnish the capital of empire with a splendid origin story that matched the glory of a global power, a classical past that befitted the royal family. Eager chroniclers cast their minds back towards a mythical figure known as Ocno Bianor, whose lineage was traced to Homeric times and the Battle of Troy. When Trojan leader Bianor the First was killed by Greek warrior Agamemnon, his son fled to Albania, founding a new family and dynasty.[32] Subsequently, one of his sons had an affair with the seer and magician Manto, daughter of Greek prophet Tiresias. Later – some suggest around 789 BCE – Manto's son Ocno founded two cities in honour of his mother: Mantua, in modern Italy, and Mantua Carpetanorum, or modern-day Madrid. This legend of the Carpetanian Mantua thus dates the city at the centre of the Iberian Peninsula as older than Rome, founded in 753 BCE. No evidence of any sort has backed the mythical Carpetanian Mantua; it remains a fanciful amusement.

Flattery has no truck with facts. One of the earliest chroniclers, Juan López de Hoyos – otherwise famous for counting the young Miguel de Cervantes among his pupils – also asserted Greek origins for Madrid, claiming in 1572 that the discovery of an image of a dragon among the granite waste of a demolition site was proof positive, as the Theban general Epaminondas had flown such an image on his battle standards in the fourth century BCE, and had been in the habit of immortalising the dragon in stone on any construction he oversaw.[33] Nineteenth-century chronicler Ramón de Mesonero Romanos condemned such efforts to falsify the past. 'Adulation and panegyric' had been pressed into service of the Spanish capital, he claimed, to enhance its reputation, linking the origins of Madrid to 'mythological and fabulous heroes' via 'hyperbolic and gratuitous conjecture'.[34] Writing from a time of more sober rationalism, Mesonero indulged, but equally scorned, those pen-pushers who, at the height of the Spanish empire, 'with more enthusiasm than good judgement' and inventing 'a thousand confusing traditions' had sought to provide the city with suitably epic origins. How apposite was his warning against those who, perhaps even in good faith, build chauvinistic dreams from 'the delirium of fable and false chronicle' and 'the disfigurement of otherwise respectable accounts'.[35]

Regardless of the way its origins were constructed, Madrid was now a significant force. It was a world view, an established order, a dynasty, a structure of state power, an administration and an aesthetic and cultural project. It was surrounded by beautiful parks and palaces, from Aranjuez to El Pardo to Valsaín, and in El Escorial provided a home for both God and human wisdom.[36] The urban now dominated the topographic: the city was no longer a product of the cliffs, gullies and streams that had shaped its development for the past seven centuries, but was increasingly determined by specific planning and ideology.[37] The Habsburgs varied in their capacity or desire to enhance the city, but what never changed was Madrid as a concentration of power. There was no *trompe l'oeil*, no obfuscation: power was squat and absolute, embedded in hierarchies and architecture. As the early modern world advanced towards the project of the Enlightenment, the urban was where human behaviour could be more tightly controlled through frameworks of law and order, and its energies harnessed; the human subject set on the path to its modern consecration as political being.

The prestige of the city emanated not only from its baroque splendour and its implacable royal power, but increasingly from its celebrated artists and writers. Sixteenth-century Castile had seen a concentration of extraordinary literary talent – the first such in modern Spanish history – with Teresa of Ávila (b. Ávila, 1515), Fray Luis de León (b. Cuenca, 1527), Alonso de Ercilla (b. Madrid, 1533), Saint John of the Cross (b. Ávila, 1542) and Mateo Alemán (b. Seville, 1547). The late sixteenth and first half of the seventeenth century would see Madrid as the permanent or temporary home to another two generations of genius: Miguel de Cervantes (b. Alcalá de Henares, 1547), Luis de Góngora (b. Córdoba, 1561), Lope de Vega (b. Madrid, 1562), Tirso de Molina (b. Madrid, 1579), Francisco de Quevedo (b. Madrid, 1580) and Calderón de la Barca (b. Madrid, 1600) represent an embarrassment of literary riches. To political and economic power was now added an undeniable cultural dominance; through the authority and magnetism of the court, Madrid drew unparalleled talent to its streets and salons. Among these brilliant artists there were friendships and also jealousies and rivalries aplenty, even an occasional simmering hatred. Some of the famous writers, painters and playwrights of this Golden Age were schemers and climbers at court, dependent on the crumbs of patronage; they praised, flattered and begged when necessary. An artist was a labourer, and had to eat and feed a family. What they shared, beyond their talent, was the need or desire to be in Madrid. The galaxy of painters, some of whom spent their entire careers in Madrid, others significant parts of it, include Alonso Sánchez Coello, Juan van der Hamen, Juan Pantoja de la Cruz, Bartolomé and Vicente Carducho, Eugenio Cajés, Francisco Rizi, Juan Bautista Maíno, Juan Carreño de Miranda, Diego Velázquez, Francisco de Zurbarán, Alonso Cano and Claudio Coello; Rubens travelled multiple times to Madrid as both painter and ambassador.

All these writers and painters, through their own lives and the lives of those they documented, serve as a priceless window onto their time. Quite apart from their formal and technical brilliance, in the novels of Cervantes, the works of Quevedo and Lope de Vega, the paintings of Velázquez or the dramas of Calderón, to name just some, we glimpse the customs of the day, and the citizens whose labour held aloft the entire structure of the court, the church and its authority.

Despite the historic association of his name with the region of La Mancha, Madrid would be a major part of Cervantes's life, dramatic as it was with its episodes of warfare, injury, imprisonment, frustration, jealousy and disillusion. For the major part of his life, the *Quixote* was absent, for it only came into being in the final decade, by which time Cervantes was exhausted and poor. He had run dozens of plays across the Madrid stage without any recognition; even his application to work in the Americas was a failure. When he came to publish *Don Quixote* in Madrid in 1605 – printed in a workshop on Calle Atocha – he was somewhere between an unknown and a has-been.[38] Cervantes lacked access to the charmed inner circles of the court and its influence; even after publishing a work immortalised by the years, he found it difficult to find patronage. It came at last in 1610, when he was 63 years of age and near the end of his life. In 1616 he was buried in Franciscan robes in the Convent of the Barefoot Trinitarians of San Ildefonso in what is now the literary quarter of Madrid; his wife Catalina Salazar was buried alongside him a decade later. In death, Cervantes's treatment, or at least that of his remains, matched the humiliations of his life: his bones were lost for some 350 years until finally uncovered in a crypt in 2015.

The man, with all his flaws, ambitions and disappointments, is difficult to separate from either the myth or the overpowering presence of his own creations; his work along those ragged country roads, in flea-bitten inns, or by the attenuated light of a prison candle, represented a shift in the intellectual conception of the universe, translated into and at the same time overcoming the limiting framework of the medieval chivalric romance, infusing it with modern doubt and ancient satire. In this fresh ontology, understanding was distinct from believing;[39] men and women were released from the sway of Gods and cast onto the stony ground of Reason. Reason itself would claim three victims: the firmly held Christian beliefs of the early modern world; the pagan rituals that had existed prior to and, to some extent, survived alongside the teachings and rituals of the church; and Reason itself. In an eternal play of mirrors Reason, that doubted all truths, had necessarily to doubt its own claims to wisdom. After Erasmus, Reason was suspicious of appearances, including its own reflection: truth was dual, appearance illusory; there were no longer solid underpinnings to a world that was ambiguous and mercurial. Everything was possible; freed from the limits of faith, the new parameters of the universe were simultaneously beautiful and absolutely terrifying, comic and despairing. Suddenly Felipe II's old motto of *Non sufficit orbis* ('The world is not enough') takes on a new meaning in a new age, radically reinvented by Cervantes.

Beyond such abstractions, the human was still all too human. Among his torrential output of comedic plays, novels, novellas and poems, Lope de Vega's *Sacred Rhymes*[40] includes the heartbreaking lament of a father for his dead son, *A la muerte de Carlos Félix*; like many poets of the age, his work dealt with the precariousness of life, the pervasive presence of grief and death, the intensity and paradoxes of love. 'To faint, to dare, to rage / rough, gentle, outgoing, shy / lively, deadly, dead, alive / loyal, traitorous, cowardly and brave', he opens one of his poems on the definition of love – the urgent, percussive hammering of his language calling to mind his English contemporary, John Donne – before concluding 'to believe that Heaven fits in Hell / offers life and the soul to a deception / this is love, and who has tried it, knows it'. This last line, where experience is offered as the guarantee of knowledge, echoes the conclusion to Shakespeare's famous Sonnet 116: 'If this be error, and upon me proved / I never writ, nor no man ever loved.'

Love was not only an abstract, but a sparring partner in the daily round: Lope de Vega had a seemingly unending appetite for affairs, licit and illicit, matched only by his overflowing literary output. He married twice, had dozens of partners and fifteen children. The streets and houses, the inns and alcoves of Madrid were his playground; he also possessed a fine three-storey house in the city centre that remains today a museum featuring the author's library, study and his patio garden, a point of peaceful reflection in the midst of the billow and swirl that was his life, that was his native city. Lope de Vega is, like Cervantes, a figure impossible to compass: his masterful poetry, his transformation of the dramatic form that underpinned much of the theatre of the Spanish Golden Age, his complex relationships with impresarios and actors, the various personal tragedies that befell him later in life. His passage from prodigious youth – Cervantes referred to him as a freak of nature – to care-worn old man can be traced through various portraits, from the upright and fresh-faced gentleman of the late sixteenth century, to the sterner and successful man drawn by Francisco Pacheco, to the works of Eugenio Cajés and Juan van der Hamen, who painted him with a heavier frame, wearied, serious, aware of his particular deepening twilight.

Francisco de Quevedo was an altogether different character, comic and bitingly satirical, short-sighted and club-footed, a stumbling bundle of intellectual nerves. Another prodigious mind, talented in various languages from the age of five, at home across all literary genres of the day, he nearly entered the priesthood – a common calling for any literate person of the time. He was too enamoured, however, by the wild profusion of life in Madrid, with its shocking contrasts of lovely silks and bloody rags, of the smooth and scented skin of noble women and prostitutes, of the scabbed and wretched flesh of delisted soldiers; the perfumed décolletage, the rotting gums and missing teeth; the polished uniforms of court lackeys. He rose high, fell from grace, made enemies, spent time in prison, wrote endlessly, prayed to God, knelt before his patrons; he was both aggressive and servile, constantly observing the lay of the land, working the contours of the street and court, rendering human desire and stupidity in all its forms.

The squalid side of Madrid, its illusions, its obsession with status, honour and surface appearances, and its inventory of petty criminals is brilliantly told through his accessible novella *The Swindler*.[41] 'I told myself I was going to Madrid where nobody knew me ... and I would get on through my own merits,' the young boy recalls as he leaves behind one of his adventures in Alcalá de Henares.[42] 'In Madrid you can find all types, half-wits and sharp minds, the very rich and the very poor. The city hides criminals and a good man's qualities are not appreciated ... Some of us are gentlemen without funds, others empty-bellied, half-baked, scabby, skinny and wolfish. We live by our wits.'[43] Again and again, the emphasis is on those who survive by getting by on their own shrewdness, turning to their advantage whatever the unpredictable street throws up before them. Nowhere is the disjuncture between appearance and reality better illustrated than in the episode where a friend resorts to an old trick of scattering bread crumbs over his chin and clothing for no other reason than that others would assume, on seeing him, that he had just eaten, and would have no inkling of the wretched and starving beggar he really was.

Quevedo was a rowdy figure, known for settling disputes with his sword. On Easter Thursday of 1611, seeing a man strike a woman in the church of San Ginés, and that no one stood to defend her, Quevedo intervened and challenged the offender to 'take things outside'. They did; tempers and abuse flared as they moved across Arenal and up into the vicinity of the Plaza de San Martín where Quevedo drew a *florete* (a light sword) and killed the other man.

There was, in Quevedo, a blend of the prickly genius, the jealous bastard and the obsequious lackey. When necessary, he could be the servile scribe, flattering members of the court – in particular Felipe IV's royal favourite, the Count-Duke of Olivares, for whom he became a significant propagandist. His medium was verbal genius; the art of survival offers us works of lucid cleverness and beauty. In daily relationships, there was another side to Quevedo, on display in his rivalry with poet Luis de Góngora, who lived in the heart of the literary quarter, then a hive of taverns, brothels, cheap inns, courtyard theatres and gambling dens, along with its resident religious houses, and where any Golden Age poet would have felt at home. Quevedo could not stab Góngora like a common thug, but he did something perhaps even worse: on hearing that he was experiencing financial difficulties and could not keep up the payments on his rent, Quevedo purchased the house where Góngora lived and then proceeded to throw his rival poet out into the street.

We are fortunate to know Quevedo through the wonderful portrait by Juan van der Hamen, a copy of a lost original by Velázquez. The writer, wearing the insignia of the Order of Santiago to which Velázquez would later aspire, looks out through his characteristic pince-nez, his hair receding, a look of infinite patience on his face, as if daring the viewer to make any comment to which he could immediately reply with caustic tongue or sharpened sword.[44]

The stern and somewhat gnarled poet Luis de Góngora had carved out a splendid career in his native Córdoba until in 1617, in his mid-fifties, he moved to Madrid in the expectation of being granted a royal chaplaincy. Rather than confirming his person and status at court, this was the start of a rolling wave of disappointments. Góngora divided opinion: his often extravagantly baroque work, pushing the boundaries of the language and its uses was, in the words of his Andalusian compatriot Federico García Lorca, 'either treated with disdain or defended with a burning passion';[45] Lorca was one of his ardent twentieth-century defenders. Góngora had a weakness for cards; indeed, when we consider his brilliant writing, his gloomy portrait, his addiction to gambling and his being permanently in debt, Góngora presents as a kind of proto-Dostoyevsky. Another error, though he could not know it at the time, was to make the wrong alliances; some of those closest to him did not fare well when the regime, and with it the person of the royal favourite, changed from Felipe III to Felipe IV in 1621. In 1625, defeated by the disappointments of life, he suffered a stroke and with it a partial loss of memory. His edges were blunted; one can only imagine what thoughts or visions, what bitter regrets, passed through that brilliant but now slightly impaired mind, as he turned for Córdoba and home. Arguably the most innovative poet in the Spanish language[46] must have looked from the coach at the scruffy villages of La Mancha as they passed, at the Cervantine characters, the swarthy muleteers and prisoners trudging their way to the galleys, the bumbling clerics and modest ladies, and he would surely have turned a verse or two in his mind, before they were lost forever.

Madrid was alive with conversation. Then and now, the city is dedicated to endless conversation. Today's wall-to-wall radio, television and social media *tertulias* are a modern and more formalised form of gossip, replacing the café *tertulia* – the tradition of long, often themed conversations among selected and invited friends – and earlier still, the *mentidero*. Neither a soapbox nor a speaker's corner, the *mentidero* was a place where people came together to join in conversation and debate – artistic, literary, political or perhaps nothing substantial at all – contrasting views, sparring verbally, laughing together. Everything from birth to death, from the midwife to the priest to the gravedigger, every jealousy and sexual escapade, every theatrical gesture or knife thrust, every glimpse or wink or gasp, all the reek and squalor of Madrid: in the seventeenth century, the *mentidero* was the place to gather, to spread rumour, scandal and prattle, to hear the latest news of the court or updates on Spain's military adventures.[47] It was where wits and tongues became sharp as razors, giving practice to poets and pithy wordsmiths. One of the most frequented was by the *alcázar*, another by the vanished church of Royal San Felipe, where Esparteros now meets the Puerta del Sol; a third, in the Calle del León in the heart of the literary quarter, where actors came to exchange gossip in the fervent atmosphere of theatrical Madrid. And with this abundance of street life came the taverns, bars, bodegas, dens, dives and all the associated business for which Madrid was, and remains, rightly famous.[48] It is one of the hallmarks of life in Madrid that people gather at the end of the day to discuss events, to argue ideas and politics, to gossip and flirt, to preen and display, to vent, to give solace and advice, to share anxieties and pain; to celebrate, as they always have, the simple joy of being alive.

The court of the Planet King

In 1634 the courtier Juan Mateos authored an obscure treatise on the art of hunting,[1] a favourite pastime for many a monarch in the rich forests surrounding Madrid. As master of the hunt, one of Mateos's principal tasks was to ensure Felipe IV had ample prey; a series of long snares or floating fences was set up that impeded the escape of boars or stags, driven into the *tela real*, the 'royal canvas'. The king might then, from a sheltered space, hunt down these animals at his leisure while members of the court looked on in admiration. How easy it was, taking pot shots at frightened and bewildered prey, trapped inside these false surrounds. One of Velázquez's works,[2] commissioned to decorate the Torre de la Parada, a royal hunting lodge in El Pardo, shows this sport, and the hundreds of high-society spectators who milled around, engaged in their own busy social activities of conversation, plotting and seduction.

Prepping the hunt has a long history; reality staged to placate and flatter, to boost the ego of kings and dictators. Royalty enjoyed their own reality and a distinct relationship to the world, separated as if by a force field of reputation from the more prosaic existence of others. Countless servants were tasked with the protocols that ensured this separation stayed in place. The seventeenth century was an age of peak artifice, illusion and tricks of the light; an age of theatrical effects, mirrors, gilded speech, flattering tongues and shameless verse. Mendoza refers to Velázquez as a man 'who spent his life caught up in the labyrinth of ceremony, false appearances and concealments that characterised the Spanish court'.[3] Image and reality battled together in baroque Madrid, a constant interplay of truth and falsehood: the world as theatre, in which nothing was quite as it seems, and theatre as a representation of the world. Power gave special access to leisure and entertainment, a delightful way of passing through a world that was all too often brutal and unsophisticated. In Madrid, theatre was also a leveller, available not only to the royal court but also, through the *corrales de comedia*, or domestic corrals, to everyone.

Two courts were effectively in operation: at the *alcázar* and, from the mid-1630s, at the newly built Palace of the Buen Retiro. One was for the business of government, the other for the business of pleasure, drama and spectacle. During the central years of the seventeenth century, with Madrid at its baroque height, the court was both the centre of operations for the politics of the day – and these were complicated by international war with the Dutch and the French, and by the regional revolts in Catalonia and Portugal – at the same time as it doubled as a stage full of illusion, farce, fantasy, sleight-of-hand and trickery. Felipe IV was both real – he was the most powerful being in the nation, with the right to assign life or death to his subjects, one of the foremost sovereigns of his time – and unreal, in that he was mostly invisible, elusive, unreachable for all but the most select officials. He appeared in public only in relation to religious matters, such as a celebratory mass or an auto-da-fé or he might, as in the case of the rigged hunt, appear briefly before selected nobility and upper-class ladies to show off his riding and shooting skills.

Madrid was the heart of this fabricated enchantment, the stage on which the tricks were performed. Vast crews were required to plan, design, build and operate the ongoing performance. The city, or that part of it where the court and the nobility were entertained, was a city of magic that served to divert attention away from the economic decline of the period and, in the second half of the century, the faltering nature of the Habsburg dynasty.

Yet not everything was artifice. There remained the cold hand of absolutist power: the reign of Felipe IV had begun in 1621 with a bloody execution. Two years earlier, Rodrigo Calderón – First Count of Oliva, Marquis of Siete Iglesias – had been one of the most powerful men in the Spain of Felipe III. Possessed of enormous riches, titles and collections of art and fine furniture, he was also widely disliked for his insolence and corruption. Overnight he was imprisoned, his goods embargoed, and in a matter of hours he fell from the heights to the bottom of the deepest pit.[4] Two and a half years later, possibly still unable to process the turn of events, he was led to the scaffold in the recently inaugurated, splendid surrounds of the Plaza Mayor.

His letters appealing for clemency had found no sympathetic ear with the 16-year-old king; given the politicking and labyrinthine ambitions of the time it is quite possible the letters never reached the king at all. Without his former protector and close collaborator, the now-fallen Duke of Lerma, Calderón found himself alone in a Madrid where the regime had changed. Others had scores to settle. He was arrested and tortured, first in Valladolid and then in Madrid, accused of murder, poisoning, conspiracy and witchcraft. One of the 244 charges against him went back to the death during child-birth eight years earlier of Felipe III's wife, Margarita of Austria,[5] a death now attributed to the influence of Calderón's sorcery.

His death, like most that took place over the years in the Plaza Mayor, was a spectacle of revenge.[6] Unshaven and dressed in a black-hooded robe, he was mounted on a mule and led from the place of his arrest to the Plaza Mayor accompanied by seventy town sheriffs and twenty monks, all the while devotedly kissing a crucifix in his hand. A crier went before the procession, announcing both the crime and the impending manner of execution. Seeing his calm, piety and dignity, the crowd turned their hatred of this once arro-gant man into pity and admiration. Having arrived at the plaza and mounted the scaffold, he spent some three-quarters of an hour in Latin prayer, after which the executioner asked for his forgiveness. It was granted warmly and, blindfolded with a handkerchief, Calderón's throat was cut. He was heard to pronounce the name of Jesus twice, the second time mid-execution, drawing an affecting response from the crowd. Many of those in attendance, having come to enjoy the spectacle of seeing Calderón put to death, found themselves weeping and wondering whether the crimes of the man or the hatred of his enemies had played the greater part in his downfall. The manner of his death was the forging of his legend; nevertheless, such a singular act expressed the incontestable will of the king over his subjects, even those – perhaps especially those – who had risen to great heights in their service to the crown. When that crown changed from one head to another, one's service, no matter how loyal, might count for nothing.

In 1619 Madrid had inaugurated a dazzling new heart, the Plaza Mayor. For hundreds of years a market place, first outside and then since the fifteenth century within the city walls, the reform of the Plaza del Arrabal was a project conceived and begun by Felipe II. Put on hold while the court wandered off aimlessly to Valladolid for five years, the project was revived once Felipe III had settled back in Madrid, charging his chief architect Juan Gómez de Mora[7] with its completion. It is something of a historical injustice that the equestrian statue that takes centre place in the modern square is of the unimpressive Felipe III rather than his father.

The plaza is admired for its imposing presence, its monumentality, its arcades, its beautiful symmetry, its granite and earthy tones that complement the brilliant blue of the skies above Madrid; it is spectacular in aerial photographs, a mathematical perfection providing a locus of order within a jumble of orange, rust-red roofs and twisting streets. It never ceases to be a joy to enter the Plaza Mayor, along crowded and narrow entranceways that open up suddenly to square and sky; from within a series of tight restrictions, there is a flowering of space and light. The creation of the plaza had angered many residents of Madrid at the time, as houses had to be demolished to allow the expansion and straightening of the square. Appointed *alarifes* – from the Arabic *al' arif*, expert or master builder – prepared a report for the mayor which provides an insight into the social environment of the plaza in 1617, with houses described, their occupants named and their professions listed. For most, the dwelling and the business were one and the same: confectioners, jewellers, pastry cooks, butchers, fruiterers, herbalists. 'The house of Antonio Rodríguez is in danger of collapse, and must be knocked down'; 'the house of Juan de Oviedo is in poor condition and about to collapse'; 'the house of María de Bolivar on the corner of the alleyway of the taverns is on the point of collapse'; 'the house of Melchor Ruiz is new and in good order'. Some of the houses were reported as having collapsed roofs, sinking walls, no windows or proper flooring.[8] Given the plan was for a major new showpiece for Madrid, any such defects needed to be eliminated. It would not be the last time those with an interest in developing real estate in Madrid declared an occupancy invalid, dangerous or in need of removal. The *pelotazo* has always been alive and well; the urban history of Madrid is filled with places 'needing to be pulled down' and countless irreparable mistakes have been made. At the same time, it is not hard to imagine the crumbling adobe structures around the Plaza del Arrabal, many very old and built to house merchants, labourers and ordinary citizens, being a rickety and weather-beaten mess.

The Plaza Mayor, in its elegant stone eminence, is one of the great public squares of Europe. In use for 400 years, its buildings have served as a market, a stables, an arts academy, a history academy, royal apartments, municipal library and archive. It remains one of the city's finest constructions and, along with the fountain of the goddess Cibeles and the Puerta de Alcalá, has come to symbolise Madrid. An intense human traffic reflects its role as one of the major tourist drawcards of the city; visitors and locals stroll among portrait artists, costumed entertainers, vendors peddling bullfight and flamenco paraphernalia, buskers, overpriced cafés and restaurants. In the seventeenth century, a Christmas market was celebrated in the nearby Plaza de Santa Cruz; since the nineteenth century, the market has been held in the Plaza Mayor, one of Madrid's most beautiful traditions. At such a time, seduced by the seasonal sense of well-being and comforted by the smell of roasting chestnuts, it is difficult to imagine the uses to which the Plaza Mayor has been put, the displays of life and death. The square served as a gateway to both Heaven and Hell: a year after the execution of Calderón came the canonisation of San Isidro; whether popular drama, bull-fight, canonisation, parade or public execution, the Plaza Mayor tended, until our more secular times, to be the stage both for enter-tainment and the brutal spectacle of power.

Like a glutton letting out the notches on their belt, Madrid required yet another encircling wall, for a certain disorder was spreading out beyond the strictly controlled etiquette of the royal court. The 1625 *cerca* of Felipe IV enclosed a significantly larger area than the previous version built to accommodate urban expansion in the time of his grandfather. Thirteen kilometres in length, this new wall embraced a tripling in Madrid's population and revealed a new emphasis on parks, gardens and splendid buildings. Like Felipe II's wall, its gates operated as control points for goods and tariffs, a checkpoint against potential criminality, and as a last line of defence against external diseases. This wall was to last until 1868, and bare remnants still stand in the Ronda de Segovia, near the Puerta de Toledo, one of the key entry and exit points from the seventeenth-century town. The *cerca* took in all of what is now central Madrid; its path can still be clearly traced, from the Royal Palace down to the Puerta de Toledo, via Embajadores to Atocha, up the World Heritage avenues past the Botanic Gardens, the Prado, Neptune and Cibeles, the Buen Retiro complex as it was built, the original Puerta de Alcalá, then north along Serrano as far as the former Portillo de Recoletos – now Colón; via Génova through the former Puerta de Santa Bárbara – Alonso Martínez – and the former Puerta de los Pozos de Nieve – Glorieta de Bilbao – through San Bernardo, then by Conde Duque to Princesa and the Plaza de España.

The vast majority of what tourist guides recommend as Madrid is to be found within this encircling belt, for here are the oldest quarters, the narrowest streets, the beautiful baroque architecture, the world-renowned art galleries and museums, the famous hotels and cafés, the legendary Plaza Mayor and Puerta de Sol, the Congress of Deputies, the Royal Palace, the Almudena Cathedral, the oldest churches, the Retiro Park, the major commercial streets and thoroughfares, the theatres and cinemas, the bars of the old

literary quarter, and the traditional nightlife districts of Chueca and
Malasaña. It is also an area in which it has become prohibitively
expensive to live. Like many cities in Europe, the old centre is
increasingly dedicated to tourism – with thousands of apartments
reconverted – commerce, politics, gastronomy and the big business
of culture. That is, it continues to follow Felipe IV's example, and
remains dedicated to power and spectacle.

Two years into his reign, in 1623, Felipe was witness to a bizarre
event known to us as 'the Spanish Match'. It is hard to disagree
with Laura Cumming who calls it, in her wonderful book on
Velázquez, 'one of the high farces of European history'.[9] In the way
of European royals, with their intermingling of bloodlines, for some
years negotiations had been carried on between London and Madrid
regarding a marriage between the young Prince Charles and María
Anna, Felipe's younger sister. There was mention of peace, of union,
of mutual interests, but the talks dragged on for years. Finally fed
up with waiting, Charles allowed himself to be talked into the
harebrained scheme, probably the idea of his close friend the Duke
of Buckingham, of travelling to Madrid in disguise to woo the
infanta in person. Somewhere the notion had been floated that
Prince Charles would convert to Catholicism and that English
Catholics would thereafter enjoy better treatment. What could
possibly go wrong? As it turned out, everything.

Assuming the names of 'Mr John Smith' and 'Mr Thomas Smith'
the two set out from England, for all the world a pair of village
idiots. Cumming provides an incomparable summary: the prince
and the duke adopted wigs and false beards; on the crossing to
France they were both violently sick; on the outskirts of Paris they
were identified by German tourists (one wonders, how?) and forced
to change their English wigs for voluminous French periwigs; they
brawled with locals along the route, at one point had to steal goats
in order to eat and finally arrived 'at the most rigid court in Europe
without invitation or warning'.[10] Felipe and his court were embarrassed by the appalling lack of protocol, and attempted to hide these
importunate visitors until they could be formally received, an
arrangement requiring strict planning and etiquette.

Letters in English archives show how things went from bad to worse: the Duke of Buckingham was essentially a hooligan. Cumming relates how he committed one faux pas after another, his behaviour helping to undermine any possibility of a union, albeit both parties continued to negotiate. Beyond the hope for improved conditions of trade, one party saw as their endgame an English conversion to Catholicism, the other a possible union of Spain to the ranks of Protestantism. Neither was ever going to happen; apart from anything else, María Anna sternly refused to marry a non-Catholic. In a moment largely lost to history, Prince Charles, haughty but polite – as was the surrounding court – sat for a portrait by Velázquez who had been brought to Madrid by young King Felipe's new royal favourite, the Count-Duke of Olivares, like Velázquez a native of Seville.[11] Buckingham, meanwhile, was reported to sit when he should have been standing, to be loud when he should have been quiet, to slouch around putting his feet up on royal chairs, to abuse Prince Charles, to bring prostitutes into the *alcázar*, to walk around half-naked, to intimidate the local priests and to whinge constantly about the formalities of the Spanish court.[12] The Spanish, ever polite as per rigid etiquette, and displaying the legendary hospitality of Madrid, continued to entertain their guests with banquets, theatre and tourneys, but their patience began to wear thin. The Count-Duke of Olivares faced the tricky diplomatic task of getting rid of these visitors, particularly the uncouth Buckingham, without offending the English monarchy. In October of 1623, seven months after they had set out as John and Thomas Smith, Prince Charles and the Duke of Buckingham returned to England. Nothing had been achieved; there was no improvement in relations between the two countries. Charles, however, took with him a lesson in decorum; the tightly prescribed manners of Habsburg Madrid for some decades provided a model for the court at London.[13]

Neither of the Smiths ended well: the Duke of Buckingham was assassinated in 1628; King Charles lost his head in 1649.

Spain and its capital city had changed radically in the previous hundred years, symbolised in royal portraits by the transition from the so-called major Habsburgs to the so-called minors: from Titian's armoured, steed-bound monarchs to Velázquez's relaxed royals in hunting gear,[14] not as upright or rigid as their forebears, in soft leather rather than steel, accompanied by one of Velázquez's inimitable dogs. Baroque Madrid was not only rigid in etiquette but also wilder in its entertainments and extravagance. Statesmen and diplomats rubbed shoulders with entertainers in this blend of enlightenment and chaos, of the religious and the carnivalesque; it was an age of belles-lettres, court dwarves and busy taxonomers.

Felipe IV was not an idle ruler. Inheriting one of the most powerful institutions in the world as a teenager, he relied heavily on Gaspar de Guzmán, Count-Duke of Olivares, the older man who had guided his childhood. Ambitious, vain, greedy and divisive, Olivares was also a shrewd and hard-working politician who held sway in Madrid for twenty years, advising Felipe even as the young king grew into the role and became wiser in the ways of the court, domestic and international politics.

It was Olivares's suggestion that one of Felipe's priorities should be to centralise and homogenise the state along the lines of his French counterpart and contemporary, Cardinal Richelieu.[15] Madrid, in this vision, would be as powerful as Paris. Yet, just as Madrid and Paris are two very different cities, Spain and France are two very distinct political entities. Olivares faced enormous resistance in his battle against regional privileges. Centralisation proceeded much more effectively in France; from Madrid, Olivares was up against a raft of deeply embedded regional traditions, power bases and languages. If he could domesticate these disparate elements and tighten them under the corsetry of the Habsburg monarchy, Olivares flattered to deceive, Felipe might become 'the most powerful prince on earth'.

Yet his mind was on other matters. On the eastern edge of Madrid, Felipe decreed the construction of a series of stately pleasure gardens, fountains, hermitages and a palace complex, the Palace of the Buen Retiro. While Felipe II had ordered an ascetic temple dedicated to God and learning, his grandson ordered a lavish amusement park. Although mostly destroyed over the years, what remains of this complex is, along with the artwork of Velázquez and the literature of the Golden Age, the most enduring legacy of Felipe IV's reign in Madrid. The private and exclusive wealth of one century may become the common wealth of another, and so the Retiro Park, created as part of a royal pleasure complex in the 1630s and 1640s, was opened to the public by Carlos III in the late eighteenth century, and by the nineteenth was in municipal hands, despite the best efforts of the French to destroy it during the War of Independence.[16] This lung and green jewel in the heart of Madrid survived the years of ruin.

The Retiro is a magical place at any time, but perhaps Sundays and late afternoons are its most popular, among the rays of the westering sun, among the crowds, thronging or lazily stretched out upon stone benches. The great public gardens of Europe are extraordinary feats of the imagination, gifts passed down from history that have ended up as acts of generosity – unintentionally, yet gifts nonetheless – from autocrats and absolutists from whom history and time have wrested their private domains and made them available for all. They are also monuments to years of dedicated, anonymous work. The Retiro is symmetry and mathematics; statuary and the beauty of channelled light; the harmonies of landscape tamed carefully to provide a backdrop to leisure and delight. The garden as an area for shared relaxation, contemplation and pleasure is an inheritance from Persians, Babylonians and Umayyads, filtered through the Christian Renaissance and the practical wisdom of the secular: here are paths and chambers of greenery, flowered tunnels and boughs, the curve of classical flesh or the sterner bronze of the historic figure; here are grottos, a crystal palace, lakes, fountains and wrought iron. The city park or garden may be regimented and abide by rules, but that is part of its charm. It is nature as a gentle human invention: the garden as paradise and repose, a stage for love and laughter and tenderness. Everyone is welcome; in the Retiro, even Satan himself stares down from a plinth.

The escarpments on the western edge of Madrid, vital to its defence in earlier times, were now an impediment to growth. Only to the east of the city could Felipe and his planners lay out the rolling acres of a pleasure palace with its sundry buildings, gardens, lakes and parks, sufficient to match the splendour of the Planet King. All the tropes of the Renaissance garden were deployed, along with palaces and hermitages of the baroque. A place of statuary and fountains, walls of art and tapestries, of lovely paths and terraces, grand balconies and entrances; a place of stagecraft and effect.

The opportunity to oversee the works provided Olivares with one of the greatest challenges of his career. Done well, enormous credit would accrue to him, entrenching his position as the most powerful figure in Madrid after the king and one of the leading statesmen of Europe. His idea was not just to build the complex, but to deliver it to the king 'dressed and furnished'.[17] Overseeing the physical construction would not be enough; Olivares needed to source an extraordinary quantity of paintings and furnishings to fill the echoing spaces.

Contemporary commentators tell us the grand palace complex was disappointingly plain on the outside. This was in part due to the construction being a rushed job, and to the cultural preference sometimes applying in Spanish architecture for internal over external decoration. This element of modesty can often be observed: plain appearances hide glorious inner patios; humble village churches burst with priceless carvings, sculptures and artworks. Faceless mortar often hides dense flowerage, an abundance of gold and silver filigree. The new complex had a seeming infinity of interior walls, galleries, corridors, salons, reception and dining rooms; the blank space could be measured by the square acre. Felipe was not one for a series of discreet decorations; the mode of the day was for walls to be filled to the ceiling with artwork, whether paintings or tapestries, the latter often serving as insulation in the winter months. Salons might feature intricately patterned tilework up to a metre and a half; from there to the ceiling was space to be filled. A century later, this dizzying method of arranging art was to cost the royal collection in Madrid, and the Spanish nation, hundreds of masterpieces, lost forever.

Like his grandfather, Felipe was a great patron of the arts. No ignorant autocrat, he had, it has been agreed by experts down the years, a remarkably good eye, and loved music and painting almost as much as he loved women. It helped that his government had agents all through the Netherlands and Italy – including, at one point, Velázquez himself – buying up the very best artwork from Flanders, Rome or Naples to accompany the works supplied by commissioned local painters such as Carducho, Cajés, Maíno, Zurbarán, Orrente and Cano. These roving agents, cheque books in hand, were progressively helping to create one of the finest art collections in the world. The superb offerings they sent back, including Claude, Poussin, Rubens, Guido Reni, Ribera, Giovanni Lanfranco and Artemisia Gentileschi, would fill the royal collection and, in time, grace the walls of the Prado Museum. Along with those existing works already collected by Isabel of Castile and Felipe II, the intense commissioning of the seventeenth century helped lay the foundation for one of the undisputed cultural triumphs of the Spanish nation and of the western world.

Olivares had been told he could not take artwork from other royal palaces in order to decorate the Buen Retiro. He tried at one stage to loot the collection at El Escorial, but the friars sent him packing.[18] The Buen Retiro complex contained half a dozen hermitages; these too had to be filled. Whole themed series of paintings were ordered; apart from those works that glorified the Habsburg family, landscapes were popular, as were still lifes, floral arrangements, battle scenes – military victories, naturally – biblical scenes and didactic moments from classical history. Allegories of virtue, faith and justice abounded. Another series, commissioned specifically for the queen's apartments, was Velázquez's set of court buffoons, painted with a psychological insight, tenderness and compassion towards the disabled unheard of in that age, and rarely equalled since. Royal portraits were added: brilliant but often gloomy or, in the case of the royal equestrian portraits, simply dull. The bloody heroics of mythology or Christian martyrdom were there, and tales of Roman splendour and decay. Paintings mass-produced in Rubens's workshop in Flanders arrived and, in the Landscape Gallery, the natural world was idealised as a lovely thing, a site for penance and withdrawal from the world. Poussin and Claude were among those whose works promoted the notion of a splendid arcadia.

To acquire further paintings, there was the trusted technique of bribery and extortion, at times indistinguishable from theft. Felipe's agents made sure to scour the collections of the nobility, both living and recently deceased, in search of quick gains, twisting arms to pick up spectacular artworks for a song. There was no reason, they argued, why a duke or marquis would not want to donate from his own collection to enhance the glory of the king's new palace. Sometimes, extortion was a little gentler; a treasure might be gleaned from a private collection with a promise of future and ongoing patronage, or a royal expropriation carried out under the guise of a gift to the king. Olivares, says Elliott, 'dragooned his unfortunate relatives, along with the entire Spanish establishment, into providing furniture, tapestries and paintings'; around 800 artworks were acquired for the palace alone, helping fill the blank acreage.[19] Olivares was highly effective as a hunter-gatherer of classical art for it was not only a service to the king, but a passion of his own. Inspired by his example, and the growth of the collection at the Buen Retiro, art collecting became fashionable in Madrid,[20] giving rise to a series of superb collections that drew on the finest works from local painters and those from Naples, Rome and Venice, Antwerp and Amsterdam.

The Buen Retiro was thus the centrepiece of a broader cultural renovation, by which the royalty, the nobility and the church entered on a period of active baroque acquisition. Seventeenth-century Madrid was unquestionably the artistic capital of the nation, and the demand for artwork was acute; the spaces to be decorated were multiplying with new buildings, monasteries and private palaces, and the advent of an economically powerful upper middle class. Art became not just a matter of decoration, and in some cases veneration; collection became a matter of display and prestige. All followed the lead of Felipe and the royal court, and as the local community was not sufficient to meet demand, artists arrived from other countries, principally Italy, just as they had during the years of the construction of El Escorial. Madrid was 'an environment receptive to innovation'[21] and the artwork of the period reflects not just the royal fervour, but the broader political reality of the Spanish empire, European and intercontinental, where Spain's role and status were constantly changing.

After three hectic years of building works, the Palace of the Buen Retiro was ready in December 1633. If anyone believed in omens, they might have looked to the sky: the day prior to the inauguration the heavens opened, creating a quagmire in the main plaza where entertainments such as jousting and bullfighting were planned. Nothing, however, would halt the displays: Felipe was installed in a special balcony fitted with glass panels hung rich with red and gold trimmings. 'To one observer,' write Brown and Elliott, 'the seated king looked like a holy relic in a reliquary.'[22] There he sits, the most powerful monarch in the world, glassed in as a museum exhibit in the fairground of his own magnificence, trapped behind rain-lashed glass, frosted, distanced from the spectacle, fringed with gaudy bunting. Simultaneously both thrilled and bored: thrilled by spectacle, by theatre and by global power, with servile legions at bended knee; bored by the simple fact of being human, and subject to humours, aches and unfulfilled longings. Felipe, however, was more than just the frontispiece of a court-as-spectacle: a skilled horseman, he later joined the jousting himself. The king inevitably won a number of prizes; one assumes concessions were made by his opponents to avoid an accidental regicide. The court later adjourned to a different part of the palace complex to enjoy a fight to the death between a bull and a lion; amid a tearing and a goring, from the violence of beast on beast, the lion emerged victorious.

Prior to the inauguration of the Buen Retiro, the sixteenth-century palace at Aranjuez had been a favoured venue for theatrical performances, with an island in the middle of the Tagus often serving as a stage. The Buen Retiro was now more convenient; entertainments included intricately planned mock naval battles enacted on the artificial lake. Just as Felipe II had brought the finest Italian painters to decorate El Escorial, so his grandson with his sidekick Olivares now brought the finest designers to Madrid, including the Florentine engineer and scenographer Cosimo Lotti, to ensure the brilliance of the stage sets. Rivers, gardens, forests, palaces, storms, descending gods and crashing sea waves:[23] these were new techniques that astonished audiences as one replaced the other in the blink of an eye; behind the scenes and below the boards, improbable machines managed one optical illusion after another; a combination of controlled magic and disorder. In these days before the birth of modern science, storms and lightning retained the primordial power of divine anger; special effects to create tempests for the theatre must have been among the first artificial amplifications of sound. Where would people have heard ear-splitting noise other than from natural and usually terrifying sources: from the sky, in the roll and dark grey break of thunder, upon the battlefield, on deck the splintered, smashed and burning ship, amid the fiery riot, or during acts of surgery and childbirth, unaided by any calming anaesthetic?

Consonant with its artistic pre-eminence, Madrid was home for the high point of early modern Spanish drama. The seventeenth-century stage was glorious and prolific. Along with the unstoppable Lope de Vega and the redoubtable Francisco de Quevedo, two further giants of the Spanish stage were native *madrileños*: Tirso de Molina and Pedro Calderón de la Barca. These were the famous names; around the entertainment industry milled an enormous cast of lesser playwrights, poets, actors, designers, engineers, painters, carpenters, dressmakers, wig makers and costumers. The theatre provided an extra source of income for highly skilled artists, such as the *madrileño* Francisco Rizi; there were always decorations needed and extravagant sets to be completed if art commissions with churches or the nobility tailed off.

The theatre, however, was not only for the elites. The works of the great playwrights of the Golden Age were performed for local audiences, as the theatre became a popular addiction in baroque Madrid. The *corrales de comedia* – there were up to six of these open-air theatres in Madrid at the height of their popularity – were set up in tight urban settings, a kind of improvised stage surrounded on three sides by the balconies of the *corral*, or inner patio, of a block of houses; or a stage might be set up in a vacant space between houses. These structures evolved in sophistication over the years, some eventually becoming standardised, conventional theatres. In some cases, where one side of the *corral* was the wall of a house, the owners quickly realised how they might create viewing platforms – and thus revenue – by putting in new windows and constructing balconies. Democratic though the popular theatre might be, there were still hierarchies and separations: the *celosías* were private viewing areas where the guests could see but not be seen; the *cazuela* stands reserved exclusively for women; the *aposentos* the equivalent of a private box for the wealthy; the *gradas* for merchants and artisans; the *bancos* for literary critics; the *desvanes* for clerical workers and students; and finally, a general standing area was for the 'popular classes', those who did not merit any of the above categories.[24] One's station in life thus determined one's place in the theatre, but the event itself, both before and after, allowed for a wholesale mixing of social classes, an opportunity to talk and drink, enjoying wine, sweets, chestnuts and pine nuts.[25] The theatre was necessarily a highly social occasion.

The *corrales* were clustered around the literary quarter where writers, poets and satirists gravitated; the news and gossip of their hectic world was exchanged at the *mentidero* in Calle del León, abuzz with scandal and lies, where deals were brokered, verbal contracts negotiated, hearts broken, swords sharpened. The plays themselves, abounding in acute wordplay and poetic skill, explored popular themes: the newly opening field of human psychology, the infinite ways of triumph and tragedy, the mazy trails of love and the endless comedies of manners; injustice, violence, heresy, courage, seduction, reputation, honour, liberty and betrayal. A generational body of work that brought together tremendous energy and a worldly sadness; that debated, in the words of Francisco Umbral,[26] between eloquence and bitterness, from the classical world to the fruits of a contemporary transoceanic empire.

The famous playwrights were rightly celebrated, but in their battle for patronage they were characters in their own drama. To be favoured by one of the influential elites was to ensure one's name and reputation – and for a time, one's income – though such patronage could not ensure one's immortality. Quevedo and Lope de Vega were notorious court hustlers, the quality of whose work has saved them from anonymity; others, such as Antonio Hurtado de Mendoza or the tragic figure of the Count of Villamediana, are today mostly forgotten. The quest for glory worked both ways:

members of the nobility also fought over access to the cleverest and most honeyed tongues to sing their praises.[27]

This was a brilliant and opulent time in Madrid: animated and elegant, its haughty style would be eclipsed only by the incoming neighbour, Louis XIV. For a time, nothing was as spectacular as the court of the Planet King: 'a magnificent theatre in which the principal actor was permanently on stage'.[28] At times of celebration – and these were frequent – parties might last for days on end, a rolling banquet of comedies, masques, bullfights and re-enactments from history. Long gone was the sober and obsessive administration of Felipe's grandfather, managing the world from the sculpted gardens of El Escorial.

Historically, detractors have sought to belittle Madrid by arguing that, without the royal court, the city lacked sufficient charms or historic claims to eminence, that the court was the only reason for its existence – as if this were not reason enough. The nation and the empire needed to be administered from *somewhere*; in any case, Madrid fast outgrew the court. The notion that Madrid 'had come into existence to meet the needs of the royal household and of a privileged court elite'[29] is misleading: it ignores the long history of Madrid as a strategic defensive town in the Islamic and immediately post-Islamic era, as a medieval centre of Castilian commerce and as the site for regular visits of the royal court since the early four-teenth century. Naturally, the fixing of the court boosted Madrid and was an integral part of its identity, but it was not the singular reason for the city, which had developed both in parallel and beyond the royal presence.

There were multiple Madrids. Below the glitter and charm, below the baroque gold and polished marble were the thousands of *madrileños* who fed the hungry machine of spectacle; a vast supporting cast and crew to manage the daily performances of etiquette, extravagance and display. The court was said exaggeratedly to contain all of humanity; by the definitions of the day, its cross-section tended to either extreme, from the quasi-divine king, the royal family, a clustering of wealthy nobles, key statemen, priests, confessors, the literati and artists in favour at the time, to the other extreme where, like any centre of power, it drew in chancers, shysters, quacks, vain fools, flatterers and idiots. Some fitted both categories: equally flatterer and statesman – Olivares was the classic example – or vain fool and *literato*. The court employed a cast of minor bureaucrats, musicians, medics and surgeons, along with all the florid entertainers, the dwarves and simpletons and jokers, there to assert the paradoxically provisional nature of surety. In short, the privileged, the beautiful and the damned.

Because the Planet King shines so bright, a star whose gravity dragged in all those who sought to represent the world and gain favour from it – being also those in a position to leave written and visual record of the time – history has eclipsed the crowded others. It was still nearly two centuries before anyone would 'write the city' in our modern sense; we are still a century and a half before the social consciousness of Goya. The inner life of the seamstress, kitchen hand, brick layer or page is still inaccessible, though here and there the anonymous peer through: we catch glimpses in Velázquez's revellers or spinners, among the filthy street life of Quevedo's *Swindler*, or Murillo's somewhat sweetened child beggars. A very wealthy upper class made their presence clear in fine buildings and patronage of the arts; a conventional middle class did not yet exist. Representations of Madrid under Felipe IV gave us royalty, nobility, military and the priesthood, and then poverty, the picaresque, the outlawed, the illusory. The latter are all forerunners to Pío Baroja's early twentieth-century wretched of the earth living among the grime of Madrid's southern outskirts.

Thousands lived beyond the reach of the administration; the cracks to fall through were wide and many. However, the popular notion of Madrid as an unproductive, parasitic city is belied by an examination of the professions of property owners in 1650. This clearly excluded a large percentage of the population, but is nevertheless instructive. Only around 1 per cent of this population was engaged in primary production, as would be expected of an urban capital, while around 17 per cent were engaged in artisanal work and construction; 8 per cent were merchants, vendors or involved with other types of commercial activity, 15 per cent were servants, including to the royal household, 18 per cent bureaucrats, 13 per cent belonged to the nobility and the remaining 27 per cent fell under a diverse category that included 'widows, foreigners, artists, priests, health workers and the military'.[30] Among property owners, the class that had grown most rapidly since 1620 was the nobility, while other sectors were mostly stable, with the exception of primary production, which declined. These are all consistent with a capital dedicated to the administration of a country and an empire.

Of the professions exercised by all those who were not registered as property owners, including those dedicated to labouring, entertainments, theatre and prostitution, we have no reliable record. Of the plasterer, working the endless walls of the Buen Retiro; of the tailor and the dressmaker, confecting the garments of the impossibly rich; of the cleric charged with the care of one of the hermitages in the Buen Retiro, such as San Juan or San Blas, polishing statuary and chalices, musing on biblical passages, sacred hymns or the political squabbles of the day, or dreaming of erotics in the dusty sacristy. These people carried out the quiet ceremonies of daily life, turned the wheels of empire, oiled the machinery, rowed the empire ships from below deck, fired the muskets and arquebuses, repaired the equipment of the battlefield, dressed and buried the bodies; cooked the rations on the march, tended to shattered bones or heard the lightly voiced confessions of the dying; nursed the mothers in childbirth; held close the coughing children; slept with the smell of the unwashed, the abattoir, the tannery. They did not sit to have their portraits painted. For these citizens life was difficult and materially poor, but they retained traditions of festivity, song and celebration; they met and wed and baptised their children, drank and laughed amid the work. Even in the poorest circumstances, humour was present as an essential tool for a life which was never dull and rarely still.

Any governing elite is removed from the daily cares of its citizens. It is easy to suppose that Felipe's court and those gathered around it were divorced from reality, and that given the passion for spectacle and representation, they lacked a grasp on the social order of the day. The Spanish court of the high baroque created its own reality, as much a part of seventeenth-century Madrid as the lives of the anonymous. For the court, like the street, contained all the pride and folly of human relationships. Among those who lived and worked under the broad royal umbrella, including the buffoons – to a degree exempt from the strict etiquette and protocols – there were fierce jealousies and rivalries, plotting and alliances, love affairs, betrayal and despair. As a focus of aspiration and, on many occasions, a graveyard of hope, the court was all too real.

Velázquez and Teixeira

One day in late 1628, two men travelled in a carriage from the *alcázar* in Madrid along the forested road to El Escorial. We might imagine the day as autumnal, the sky bright: ahead loomed the Guadarrama mountains, always splendid in their bulky threat. One gentleman was older, more robust and experienced; the other was smaller, shyer, yet no less calculating or observant than his companion. Notwithstanding the lack of any facial resemblance, they might have been father and son. The conversation was lively, dealing with the gossip of the court, the latest international intrigues and alliances of war-torn Europe; an appraisal of fashionable women; and questions of painterly technique: how to render the divinity of a king, or best portray a psychological state through the expressions of a face, the posture of a body, the distribution of light across a canvas? Was royalty indeed divine, or simply flesh and blood, prone to disease and angst like other mortals? What other subjects, from the carnal to the divine, were permissible? Was their profession a noble calling, or simply another manual trade dedicated to the greater glory of the powerful?

Along the king's road they rolled, through Las Rozas and Torrelodones before stopping at a tavern for refreshment. Over lunch and a glass of wine, it was clear to bystanders in the roadside tavern that one of these men was experienced, gregarious, accustomed to moving among exalted circles; the other was a timid yet graceful partner, ambitious and eager to learn. The older man was Peter Paul Rubens, diplomat, spy, courtier and painter; the quiet companion a man whose person, if not his works, has been largely lost: Diego Velázquez.

Having acquitted themselves at luncheon the two men, unknown to those around them though commanding the respect due to higher rank, stepped back into their carriage, the older man standing aside to allow his young charge to enter first. Settled, Rubens and Velázquez rolled on towards the great monastery, bearing down upon the subject of their visit: the royal art collection.

Rubens had first visited Spain in 1603, bringing a crateload of paintings from Italy to Felipe III and the Duke of Lerma, then at Valladolid. His second visit was longer, a stay of nine months between 1628 and 1629, during which time he established a studio in the *alcázar* at Madrid and had extensive contact with his patron, Felipe IV, and Velázquez. There is no doubt Rubens was an inspiration and a huge influence on the younger painter, both for his worldly ways, fine-tuned in the courts of Europe, and for his knowledge of art history and the Italian masters that Velázquez knew only tangentially. At the conclusion of Rubens's longer sojourn in Madrid, Velázquez left for Italy, already a great painter in his own right but wise enough to appreciate all he could still learn at the feet of the Italian collections. Following Rubens's example, it was now the young court painter from Madrid who wished to be at the forefront of current representational practice, and to bring back from Italy the finest artworks he could lay hands on, along with a refined technical skill to enhance his own work and, by extension, the decorative glory of Felipe's court. In time, the pupil overtook the master: for all Rubens's talent and influence, it is Velázquez's outrageous skill that now overshadows the famous veteran. Three works he produced as a man in his early twenties, well before he met Rubens – *The Waterseller of Seville*, *Old Woman Frying Eggs* and *Christ in the House of Martha and Mary* – stand in the highest ranks of European art; all three, through the vagaries of history, were lost to Spain and are held in collections in the UK.[1] After his visit to Italy, Velázquez produced over subsequent decades a relatively small but astonishingly innovative and complex body of work that has no seventeenth-century equal.

Despite his attachment to the court, much of his career spent inside a golden cage,[2] Velázquez was essential to bringing alive the otherwise anonymous people of his age. The Renaissance brought a different and multidimensional energy to European art, breaking away from the two-dimensional surface of medieval painting towards a socially more diverse range of subjects, with previously ignored or unsuspected persons beginning to enter the frame. A new joy in the triumph of the human lay beyond the erstwhile overriding theme of Jesus' crucifixion and the associated agony, with its sallow and morose attendants. Such pessimism was not surprising at a time when the world was stalked by war, plague, exhaustion, hunger, fear and death; in medieval paintings, almost no one laughs or smiles. The default is a kind of humourless rictus. A rich and compassionate post-Renaissance humanism bursts through the works of Velázquez. The enquiring minds of his age were deepening their examination of the human condition, and he renders this candidly: nothing human is alien to the painter. The faces of his subjects are fully realised, full of doubt, enquiry, wonder, arrogance, lust, joy, boredom, laughter and astonishment. These are not the two-dimensional grimaces of the medieval, nor even the ecstatic, transfixed bodies and faces of El Greco's swooning subjects – his models reportedly taken from an insane asylum – but were rounded human beings in all their shape and complexity. Their faces are pocked and scarred, their hair messy, their teeth uneven, their clothes old rags, yet they beam out towards the modern viewer with urgency: see, they seem to say, this was us, and we drew every ounce of pleasure we could from a life that was often painful and bewildering.

This humanity is apparent in the faces of the men who gather around Bacchus in *The Triumph of Bacchus* or the astonished metalworkers who have looked up to witness the sudden arrival of Apollo in *Vulcan's Forge*.[3] This capacity is most evident in his portraits of the court entertainers – actors, buffoons and dwarves. Not only did Velázquez see those who were considered inappropriate subjects for art; he saw how they embodied the same depths of humanity of any pope, nobleman or royal family member. In *Pablo de Valladolid* we find not only the genius of technique – Manet famously called this the most astonishing picture ever painted – but also a miracle of sympathy.[4] The body of the actor floats in space, unmoored from the conventions of perspective, held only by the smudge of his own shadow. There are none of the usual contextualising devices, such as the icy peaks of the Guadarrama or the fiery denouement of Lepanto. Pablo stands alone; other than his collar, he is dressed from head to foot in black. The simplicity of the work combines with a melancholy gentleness, a humanity expressed most softly here by both actor and artist. For these persons, wit and wile were vital to maintaining a place within the hallowed surrounds of the court; they had to work to keep their status. Nothing was given out of commiseration, for all 'defects' were the work of God and thus part of the natural order of the world. Velázquez sees beyond this convenient fiction: his portraits of court jesters and dwarves are ahead of their time not by years but by centuries.

Painters of genius fall in and out of favour, their works lost amid the spare wreckage of attics and the deepening grime of years; intellectual and cultural fashions dictate the level of grace afforded any artist. 'Some people', wrote Laura Cumming, 'knew Velázquez chiefly as a painter of dogs.'[5] This remark is not as dismissive as it might seem, for the dogs who appear in the corners of multiple Velázquez portraits are some of the most beautifully rendered in art history. Nevertheless, the artist fell from notice after his death and the eclipse of the Habsburg dynasty. Like El Greco, Velázquez has come to his singular status at the heights of the European classical tradition after being forgotten, unknown and unobserved, and thus not valued, assessed or appreciated. For some two centuries, until well after the age of Napoleon and the birth of the modern museum, Velázquez was scarcely known outside Spain other than, perhaps, at the court of Naples. The death of his patron and friend Felipe IV in 1665, just five years after Velázquez's own death in 1660, was followed by a period of political uncertainty and dynastic change; amid these troubled times, the artist was ignored. Velázquez's style did not match that of the incoming Bourbon regime at the start of the eighteenth century, and thus historical circumstances served, for some time, to bury him.

Madrid had initially drawn in the young Velázquez only to send him away. The capital would do this to artist after artist, seeking their fortune amid the dense human traffic of the city. Madrid was no place for the faint-hearted provincial: life on its streets and in its corridors of power was fast and brutal. Powerful friends were necessary; the city operated through connections and influences. The setback was only temporary: the year after leaving Madrid Velázquez was back, at the right hand of the omnipresent Olivares, and this time he came blazing into the companionship of Felipe, otherwise so inaccessible behind successive doors, controls, galleries, corridors, guards and officers. He upset the apple cart, usurping the established court painter Vicente Carducho and the highly regarded Eugenio Cajés. To rub salt into the wound, Velázquez triumphed over both older artists in a 1627 painting competition whose theme of 'The Expulsion of the Moors' was a celebratory glance back at the Habsburg role in defending the purity of faith in Spain.[6]

It is possibly best to approach Velázquez sideways: not as the illustrious court painter and royal administrator, but as a man engaged in everyday acts, troubled by pride, envious of others, aspiring to social position. He may not, like countless artists over the years, have been a very likeable person: capable of being a servile humbug – who was not before the Planet King? – and status-conscious to the extreme. Some of this would have stemmed from his hectic workload serving the king, finding little time to paint. One cannot imagine he would have had the time or inclination to suffer fools.

Early twentieth-century novelist Vicente Blasco Ibáñez suggested Velázquez's was, in some senses, a wasted life, accursed by the age in which the artist was compelled to live. 'Unhappy Diego!', he cries out to him, one Spanish artist ruefully looking back across the centuries to another. 'He had been born into the great melancholy period of our history.' Velázquez was a painter given an almost divine gift for rendering the human form, yet fate landed him in a period in which 'the women looked like tortoises', their heads and arms barely escaping from the hard shells of their corsetry, while the men had 'a priestly rigidity, holding their dirty heads erect above dismal garments'. What Velázquez might have done with the human form, had he lived in a less tetric age, is suggested by the lovely eroticism of his rendering of Venus before the mirror, a gorgeous work that war and history would place in English hands. Blasco does not hold back his pessimism – somewhat typical of the time – towards the Spanish seventeenth century and the decline of the Habsburgs: 'a moribund nation, finding entertainment in the monstrous and ridiculous, revelling in buffoons, idiots and disabled clowns . . . the hypochondriac humour of a monarchy sick in body and soul, terrified of Hell . . .'[7]

This damning portrait of the dying Habsburgs is only one, very narrow window onto seventeenth-century Spain, written by a twentieth-century novelist who had his own axes to grind. According to Blasco, the entire Spanish seventeenth century would have been forgotten had it not been for Velázquez, a claim as absurd as it is hypothetical. His suggestion that Velázquez might have been a greater painter had he lived in a less repressive and more sensual age is a pointless speculation; and given the works by Velázquez lost over the years, we have only an incomplete view of his genius. We have *Las Meninas*, thrumming as the radiant core from which the entire collection of the Prado extends; the enigmatic family of Felipe IV has taken on the mantle of being the ground zero from which Spanish art emerges and is measured; we have the dark pulse of the venerable Mother Jerónima de la Fuente, before whose terrifying gaze it would be impossible to contemplate a heretical thought; or Don Diego del Corral, before whose profound integrity it would be impossible to contemplate any infraction of the law;[8] we have the miracles of human expressiveness drawn from his palette of warm browns and reds, hard blacks and softest pinks; we have the glint of emotion he lured from the surface of the canvas; we have the shimmering skies above Madrid and the Guadarrama range; the royal children, beggars, saints and philosophers; the classical world of gods and wine, the profane world alongside the Christian and orthodox; we have the echoing and gloomy interiors of the *alcázar*, we have the vanishing of backgrounds and contexts that simultaneously bring forth the psychological and the markedly physical: the runnels on a forehead, the slightly bruised skin, all the imperfections that life and worry and misfortune and excess might bring to a face, full of pride, exaltation, fear, joy, arrogance or humility. We have the quiet contemplation of the world, the subject alone amid the frame.

The painter was buried, in 1660, in the church of San Juan Bautista, which once stood close by the *alcázar*. He lay in peace until, like so much else in Madrid, he was disturbed by the ongoing effects of the Napoleonic invasion in the early nineteenth century. French king José Bonaparte, determined to 'clean up' Madrid by running a formal French eye over the rowdy Spanish capital, ordered a series of demolitions around the Royal Palace with the intention of opening up the cramped landscape of the city. The twelfth-century church was razed, and the remains of Velázquez and his wife Juana Pacheco, who died just a week after her husband and was buried beside him, were lost. No one, at the time, bothered to mark or preserve their graves; until quite recently, Spain was dismissive of its dead and Madrid careless with its heritage. A small monument marking the site where the church of San Juan Bautista once stood declares that 'his glory was not buried with him', a noble sentiment but only partly true, for like any artist, Velázquez has had to suffer the whims of taste. While the search for his body carries on inter-mittently, it is quite likely his bones were milled about with earth and rubble, and have contributed to the landfill foundations of a nineteenth-century redevelopment. As a fate, it is absolutely in keeping with the history of Madrid; indeed, the very same awaited another master painter more than 100 years later, when the remains of the Venetian Giovanni Battista Tiepolo, responsible for a superb body of work at the eighteenth-century court of Carlos III, were lost amid the dust and debris of yet another demolished church.

Felipe IV's long reign bequeathed another of the most important artefacts in the history of the city. The first surviving image of Madrid is a simple engraving by the Flemish painter Jan Cornelisz Vermeyen in 1536, but by the early seventeenth century, in the interests of politics and empire, there was a need to inscribe Madrid as monumental. In the 1620s two histories of the city had appeared, the works of Gil González Davila and Jerónimo de la Quintana, the latter narrating an especially epic past in the mists of Greek mythology that thereby avoided any mention of Islam in the long ancestry of Madrid. In 1656 the Portuguese cartographer Pedro Teixeira turned in the opposite direction and, eschewing all myth and fantasy, applied the forensic eye of the cartographer-scientist to Madrid.

In a period overflowing with beautiful art, objects and furnishings, Teixeira's twenty-panel map of Madrid is outstanding for its technical bravura and originality. Amid a city famous for simulacra, here was a rigorous presentation of the facts. Teixeira engraves Madrid in great detail: every house, street, square, palace, church, convent, hermitage, hospital and fountain, along with the city walls and gates, gardens, orchards, small lakes and streams. The city is tightly built, full of crooked medieval streets and early modern churches; indeed, Madrid is packed with religious buildings, reflecting the wealth that had been poured into their foundation and development over the previous century. No fewer than thirty-one male and twenty-six female convents are shown, quite apart from the parish churches. Civil buildings are detailed, including the two prisons and an abattoir, a customs house and grain exchange. The structure of the houses and their courtyards allows us to see how easily the *corrales* were adapted for local theatre; a mock galleon sails on the waters of the lake of the Buen Retiro. The broad avenues that run from the heart of the city out to Atocha and the Retiro are now a permanent and defining feature of the capital, as are the roads leading to Toledo to the south, to Hortaleza and Fuencarral to the north and the Puente de Segovia crossing the Manzanares on the western edge of the city. The Buen Retiro complex enfolds the city to the east; to the west and north-west a series of fields and orchards border the river towards the rising hills of Moncloa, where the map ends in a nondescript fade to rural Castile. Teixeira's map inspires a sense of longing: the whole is unmistakably Madrid, while being at the same time an altogether vanished city.

Along with tapestries that told appropriate historical narratives, such maps were increasingly part of the royal furnishings; they were a validation of the Planet King and a confirmation of the grandeur of the city, no matter how much this grandeur might have been at odds with prevailing economic conditions and the social reality for many of its residents.[9] This transcription of the built world of Madrid reflected 'the practice of cosmography as both a humanistic and scientific pursuit'.[10] In the spirit of the age, art and science came together to render homage to Habsburg greatness. Equally, Teixeira's bird's-eye view of the city suggested a sense of control, a methodical taxonomising of the built environment.

What the splendid map – it is, first and foremost, an object of great beauty – could not detail was the level of poverty on the streets. In the latter half of the seventeenth century Madrid still attracted the destitute as much as the upwardly mobile. Begging became institutionalised, a guaranteed form of income.[11] There was a common belief that God spoke through the poor, the blind and the lame, and these had to be provided with protection. Inevitably, in a city and country renowned for the picaresque, there were all manner of con jobs and deceptions; one of the tasks facing authorities was to sort the genuinely needy from hustlers and scammers who knew a gullible charity when they saw it. The tricks of appearance and shape-shifting were not only a matter of baroque art or dramaturgy, but were on display in the filthiest tavern.

Equally invisible to Teixeira's cartographic eye were the networks of passageways beneath Madrid. These had served different purposes over the centuries, most particularly for the distribution of water and the discreet movement of royals from one part of the city to another, such as from the Royal Palace to a church or convent. In 1611 Margarita of Austria had ordered one such passageway built, unusually above ground, allowing her to move in complete privacy to and from the monastery of la Encarnación, her personal project. Not content with being simply a passageway, its walls were hung with sumptuous art: yet another site that demanded new paintings. Indeed, royal patronage would assure the monastery a stunning art collection over the years; unfortunately for Margarita, she only saw the beginning of the works, for later in 1611 she died in childbirth, not before having arranged a series of wealthy donations to the incipient institution. Another tale tells how, a generation later, Felipe IV used the channels that snaked beneath the city, large enough to serve as candle-lit canals, to move discreetly from one amorous assignation to another in a purpose-built gondola. One of the women he pursued became so tired of his molesting that, in the manner of Juliet, she staged her own death. Felipe, we are told, came across this macabre, subterranean, candle-flickering tableau and was so terrified he fled, never to return.

During the combined reigns of Felipe II, Felipe III and Felipe IV, from the mid-sixteenth to the late seventeenth century, the artistic and cultural gravity of Madrid was the equal of any city in Europe, or indeed the world. It passed its zenith and began to trail off in the 1670s; the Golden Age grew overcast as its galaxy grew old. The seventeenth-century losses were irreplaceable: aside from El Greco, Cervantes had been the first major artist to die, in 1616; then followed Góngora and Lope de Vega and before long Quevedo, Tirso de Molina and the political master, the Count-Duke of Olivares. Young Prince Baltasar Carlos, the brilliant and promised heir, had died suddenly; Felipe's pan-European wives Isabel of France and Mariana of Austria passed into history, the latter not before overseeing the regency of Carlos II; Felipe himself died mid-century, as did Ribera, Velázquez, Zurbarán and Alonso Cano. A generation of painters without peer was gone. By the late 1670s only Francisco Rizi, Juan Carreño de Miranda and Claudio Coello were still working in Madrid. Of the writers only Calderón de la Barca remained, and he was on his last legs. By the end of the century they would all be dead, and the Spanish arm of the Habsburg dynasty that had settled in Madrid nearly 200 years earlier fell silent.

Regime change

As ever, things might have turned out differently: of Felipe IV's seventeen legitimate children by two wives, Prince Baltasar Carlos was the sixth born, in 1629 – the first male, and the first to survive beyond infancy. He is the subject of one of Velázquez's finest portraits; at the age of seven, he stands under an oak tree at El Pardo, hunting rifle in hand, a collared dog asleep at his feet, the unmistakable Guadarrama behind him.[1] There is a gentleness and beauty to his face unusual for the Habsburg line which tended to stern ugliness; it is easy to see why such dynastic hopes were placed in this golden child. While tender-faced, he appears confident of the world, sharp of mind, discerning and with a clear physical capacity for outdoor pursuits; he proved himself a skilled rider and hunter before the age of ten. The entire Spanish empire was to be his inheritance, and there is every chance he would have ruled into the eighteenth century, providing the Habsburg dynasty a strong line of succession, had the young prince not died of smallpox at the age of 16. The throne passed on, after the death of Felipe in 1665, to his half-brother Carlos.

Felipe might otherwise have entered middle age content with preparing his magnificent son to rule, learning statecraft and diplomacy, the rigours of court, the endless pleasures of absolutist power. The death of his son came just two years after the death of his first wife; the world was no longer at his beck and call. Any of the playwrights of the day, or any of the fools and buffoons, could have told the Planet King what darkness lay in store beyond the frivolity of the Buen Retiro. Finding himself suddenly without a male heir, he remarried at the age of 44, his new wife his 14-year-old niece, Mariana of Austria. Only two of their children survived infancy, and only one was male. The next occupant of the *alcázar* in Madrid would be historically one of the most maltreated of rulers, subject to mockery, calumny and rumours of witchcraft. Every possible cliché about the decadence of Spain was served.

Open season was declared on Carlos II: no adjective too extreme, no description too outlandish. He was variously described as 'weak and incapable', 'degenerate and pathetic', 'disabled and abnormal', 'mad and sterile', 'a pale and sickly relic', 'wretched', 'mean and paltry, the height of Spanish misfortune', 'descended from the deranged Juana la Loca', 'psychologically disturbed', 'a rachitic and feeble-minded weakling', 'the last stunted sprig of a degenerate line', 'retarded by rickets and mentally subnormal', 'a freak', 'a shadow king', 'unhappy and neurotic' and 'an invalid' who lived his life 'under the shadow of death'; 'his days were few and evil'.[2] The miracle of Velázquez, argued Trapiello, allows us to forgive all the other sins of Felipe IV, including the worst, which was his failure to disinherit his son.[3] 'Never were a people so overrun with fools in all states as they are,' wrote Samuel Pepys.[4] If sobriquets are our guide, Spain was in a parlous state, moving in the space of a generation from the 'Planet King' to 'the Bewitched'.

By definition, such bigotry and simplification leave out the close detail. Were it not for the smallpox that carried off Baltasar Carlos, the universally mocked Carlos would never have ruled; indeed, he may never have been born. Carlos was without doubt unfortunate in many ways, but he was by no means incompetent, and recent historiography has been more generous to him. Like his Habsburg predecessors, he sat for an outstanding painter. Where Felipe II had Titian, Antonio Moro, Sofonisba Anguissola, Alonso Sánchez Coello and even, as one-offs, El Greco, Rubens and Juan Pantoja de la Cruz; where Felipe III had Velázquez and Pantoja de la Cruz; and where Felipe IV had Velázquez – the Planet King allegedly would allow no other painter to do his portrait – Carlos stood for a number of the most haunting portraits of any Habsburg, at the hands of Juan Carreño de Miranda and Luca Giordano.[5]

The machinery of foreign propaganda that painted Spain as an obscure hotbed of superstitious and retrograde necromancers went into overdrive. Like many a topic in Spanish history, the lurid and the exaggerated went hand in hand, and when he came of age and assumed the throne in 1675, Carlos began a reign that was nothing like the catastrophe such descriptors might anticipate. He may have been unwell for much of his life, but Carlos was not stupid. The last two or three decades of the century were positive for Spain, led by growth in peripheral cities such as Barcelona; after the radical centralisation attempted by Olivares a generation before, regions such as Catalonia and Valencia appreciated the greater freedom they had to trade and manage their own affairs with less direction from Madrid. Economic reforms were enacted in an attempt to reduce both inflation and the tax burden on citizens and agricultural outputs such as wheat and wool showed clear increases.[6] Spain was not, despite opinion to the contrary, closed to the burgeoning ideas of the Enlightenment in either science or philosophy.

Popular accounts said otherwise. As English, French, Italian and German courtiers and nobles went about the continent in the seventeenth century, they produced a voluminous travel literature, and Spain was often in their cross-hairs; their counterpart Spanish travellers, however, did not produce a corresponding literature reflecting the society of those they encountered.[7] The Grand Tour as a social phenomenon of the upper classes was just beginning – it is worth noting that Spaniards had been sending their finest to learn from Italian arts and manners for centuries before the Grand Tour became a staple for the wealthy northerner – and with it a new genre of travel writing emerged as the literate statesman, businessman or member of the idle gentry began to report on their journeys.

Madrid entered travellers' journals described mostly as a primitive place: rude, harsh and for the most part uncivilised, located in a central Spanish landscape that was itself a wasteland of privation, a semi-barbarous space where Europe had expired, exhausted by the heat and touched by the long and dusty arm of Africa. It was all wretched villages – 'the villages and houses exceed in dirt and nastiness anything I had conceived,' wrote one English diplomat[8] – and rough, indigestible food. In short, the approach to Madrid was a bad recreation of the toughest pages of *Don Quixote*, a place of no beauty or comfort: miserable, desolate and melancholy. A strange transposition of responsibility took place among many foreign observers, whereby so-called defects of landscape or comfort were indicative of defects of national character. When convenient, and drawing on prejudice rather than evidence, this was put down to one of a series of usual suspects: laziness, ignorance, authoritarianism or religious extremism. 'The very name of a Spaniard is reckoned to be frightful and terrible to all people of humanity, or of Christian compassion,' wrote the otherwise laudable Daniel Defoe in *Robinson Crusoe*.[9] A nation and a dynasty that were not only political enemies, but were also by nature flawed and bordering on evil.

In France, meanwhile, the young King Louis XIV had an eye on the Spanish throne; in 1660 he had married his first cousin María Teresa, daughter of Felipe IV, at an elaborate ceremony on the Bidasoa River that marks the border between the two countries. The ceremony, held mid-stream on the Isle of Pheasants, was designed and organised by Velázquez, a task so all-consuming and strenuous it is thought to have contributed to his death a few months later. Louis XIV thus laid the groundwork through marriage for one of his children or grandchildren to accede in time to the Spanish throne. The path was not smooth – it would take a decade-long war to settle the succession – but this is indeed what eventually happened.

The English had been worried for some time by events in Madrid. As early as the 1670s ambassador William Godolphin – who converted to Catholicism and refused to return to England when recalled, preferring to live out his life in Spain – had written, 'By all the notices I have of the present temper of this people I am persuaded, if it should happen that the young king dye as things now stand, they would tamely goe into the obedience of France.'[10]

The 1690s was a critical decade, a time of continued economic and demographic recovery after the wars, plagues and famines of the seventeenth century, while equally a decade of frantic spycraft and diplomatic jockeying as it became clear Carlos II would die without an heir. After ten years of marriage with his first wife, Marie-Louise d'Orléans, the couple had been unable to produce a child when Marie-Louise, aged 26, died suddenly in the *alcázar*, most likely of an acute appendicitis. A hastily arranged second marriage to Mariana of Neuburg again failed to produce an heir, despite Mariana claiming to be pregnant on eleven occasions. Control of the great Spanish empire was up for grabs, and the succession became a matter of the utmost international seriousness; foreign diplomats descended on Madrid, and where there are diplomats, there are spies. Madrid in the 1690s was a veritable nest.

The court and city were full of intrigues, Madrid alive with secret commissioners working on behalf of European nobility, all jostling for the spoils of the Habsburg throne, all negotiating – mostly in vain – and preparing deals, scenarios, agreements, many of which changed regularly as the diplomatic environment shifted one way, then another. The future of Madrid was now debated backwards and forwards in London, Paris, Vienna and The Hague, the other great centres of European political power of the age. England and the Netherlands wished at all costs to avoid a union between Spain and France, or between Spain and Austria, for either scenario would significantly weaken their own positions.[11] Nor were the Spaniards keen on union with France, according to the English ambassador in Madrid, Alexander Stanhope, who wrote in 1698 to his son: 'What I can discover of these people's inclination is for a French Prince, provided they can be assured the same shall never be King of France . . . they would rather have the devil than see France and Spain united.'[12] Carlos, meanwhile, was growing weaker, and government was in the hands of the Count of Oropesa who, lost amid a web of political intrigues at court, had ignored the basic needs of the people of Madrid. Major bread riots would soon see him removed from his position.

Much of the ridicule and condescension heaped on Carlos stems from the infamous attempt in 1699 to exorcise him. Suffering from ill health and convulsive fits, and with the successional horse trading in full swing, the *alcázar* 'pullulated with confessors and exorcists and visionary nuns employing every artifice known to the Church to free him from the devil'.[13] There were two principal curses to be addressed: impotence and social unrest. Various persons, including the king's confessor, Froilán Díaz, attended to the enfeebled king. In the course of their questioning of the demons inside Carlos's twitching body, it was revealed that the king was indeed the victim of malevolent forces, one of whom was his Austrian wife, Mariana. The queen did not take this well and had the exorcist dismissed.

On the streets of Madrid other matters were more pressing than the haggling and skulduggery among the elite families of Europe. Wasteful expenditure by the crown – the queen's party were guilty of pillaging both royal and public revenues – along with a series of failed crops and a mismanaged distribution of essential foodstuffs led to increasing hunger and despair. Stanhope reported in 1694: 'This country is in a most miserable condition; no head to govern, and every man in office does what he pleases, without fear of being called to account.'[14] Fed up with the shortages they had to endure while greed and wastage were evident among the aristocracy, in April 1699 – end of the reign, end of the dynasty, end of the century – rioting broke out in the streets and crowds stormed the *alcázar* in the so-called *motín de los gatos*, the uprising taking its name from the popular usage, dating as far back as the eleventh century, of *gatos* (cats) to refer to the people of Madrid. Stanhope reported that the mayor of Madrid had rudely dismissed a woman who had approached him in the marketplace, pleading hunger and complaining of the husband and six children she had to feed; the mayor retorted she ought to be thankful bread was not even more expensive, cynically adding that she might consider castrating her husband to prevent him giving her any more children.[15] She responded by calling him a thief and a cuckold, and throwing a pair of pigeons in his face; the crowd – Stanhope says 'the rabble' – pursued the mayor, pelting him with stones and came close to killing him.[16] Matters escalated; 5,000 – 10,000 in French ambassador Henri Harcourt's account – rampaged through Madrid shouting for bread, denouncing bad government and yelling 'Death to the dog who has brought this ruin upon us!'. Siege was laid to the Count of Oropesa's home; shots were fired from within, killing various members of the enraged crowd. Religious orders rushed to the site with images of the crucified Christ in the hope these might calm the anger; they had no effect. The crowd was pacified only by the eventual appearance outside the *alcázar* of the king in person, who pardoned them, asked them to pardon him in turn, and promised to attend to their needs. The Count of Oropesa, on whom bad government could be blamed, was dismissed.

By late May, hunger was driving more and more desperate people into Madrid: some 20,000 'flocked from the country round, to share in that little there here is, who were starving at home, and look like ghosts'.[17] Stanhope describes sending his servants two leagues to Vallecas for bread, carrying 'long guns to secure it when they have it, otherwise it would be taken from them, for several people are killed every day in the streets in scuffles for bread', later reporting that his secretary Don Francisco had seen five women 'stifled to death' by people crowding around a bakery.[18]

Nothing was going to save Carlos, albeit there was a resort to oldest of miracles – the uncorrupted bodies of the dead. Carlos's mother Mariana had died in 1696. A week after her death, Stanhope writes of the 'great noise of a miracle': an old lame nun had taken a piece of the waistcoat the queen mother had been wearing when she died and, putting it 'in great faith' to her lips, 'she was perfectly well, and immediately threw away her crutches'.[19] In late 1699, it was rumoured at the court that a temporary reprieve in Carlos's wasting illness was thanks to a visit to the royal pantheon at El Escorial, where all the coffins were opened; the queen mother, barely three years in the grave, was said to have been found in perfect condition, while the body of Felipe III, Carlos's grandfather, fell to pieces when it was moved. Stanhope, to his credit, dismisses as a 'romantic story' the rumour that Carlos, upon viewing the body of his first wife, Marie-Louise d'Orléans, and finding it in perfect condition – she had been dead for ten years – rushed out of the vault exclaiming, 'I shall soon be with her in Heaven!'[20] In the nineteenth century, English historian Thomas Macaulay had possibly been reading Edgar Allan Poe before sitting down to pen this gothic account: 'Into these dark vaults the unhappy monarch descended by torchlight, and penetrated to that superb and gloomy chamber where, round the great black crucifix, were ranged the coffins of the kings and queens of Spain. There he commanded his attendants to open the massy chests of bronze in which the relics of his predecessors decayed.' Macaulay gives full credence to the legend of Carlos's extravagant reaction: 'The awful sight completed the ruin of his body and mind.'[21] This type of nonsense would be nothing more than a humorous aside, a forgotten slander, had it not been presented to generations as serious history, adding yet another layer to the construction of Habsburg Spain as both wretched and apocalyptic, a crumbling and exhausted state overrun by bed-hopping ministers and Jesuits, and ruled by fanatics. Here in Macaulay, prejudices were presented as conventional wisdoms that, for all their obvious hyperbole, were to become fossilised as articles of truth.

Carlos's painful life came to an end a year later, in November 1700. The warp of genes was done, and no longer laid crooked waste to his exhausted frame. He died in the *alcázar* and was buried, as per custom, along with his forebears in El Escorial. Just four weeks earlier, under great pressure from the powerful Archbishop of Toledo, Cardinal Portocarrero, he had signed a will passing his throne to Philippe d'Anjou, grandson of Louis XIV; after years of jostling, there had finally been a factional victory. This gave preference to the French line of the family over the previously dominant Austrian. Two centuries of Habsburg rule from Madrid would give way to the Bourbons, though not without a fight.

Absolutism would remain the order of the day, but the early modern world with its emphasis on faith and miracle, with its abundance of the lurid and sinister, was quickly fading. The deep curve of the oral tradition had long begun to give way before the flat surface of the written word. Prayers and potions would start to give ground before the microscope and the sextant; dead bodies would cease to offer miracles and cures. War, hunger and pestilence were far from done – war would occupy the government of Madrid for the first decade of the eighteenth century – but a new era was breaking in Europe that would eventually bring alternative forms of government and radically different conceptions of the human, further centred as a social and political being.

And Madrid, under French rulers with visions of Versailles and a half-Italian ruler with visions of Naples, would undergo a century of facelift.

New absolutisms

In April 1701 the people of Madrid were out on the streets to observe the arrival of their 17-year-old king, fresh from the ambience of Versailles. Felipe V – yet another Felipe – had arrived in February, but went straight to the Buen Retiro for a period of adjustment before making his grand entrance into Madrid in April. There was a party atmosphere, of course, as the entourage moved through the rain from the Buen Retiro across the city, via the Puerta del Sol, to the *alcázar*; ink drawings of the time show the gaudy procession, all rearing horses and plumes. A triumphal arch was erected to mark the occasion, the work of the baroque painter and architect Teodoro de Ardemans, who would go on to have a distinguished career under Felipe's royal patronage. The following day the king crossed the city again in the opposite direction, passing through the Plaza Mayor on his way to a celebratory mass at Our Lady of Atocha.[1] Once the flags and bunting were put away, and the revellers returned to work, the mood remained positive but with notes of caution. While parts of Spain had made an economic recovery towards the end of the previous century, in Madrid there was still an atmosphere of exhaustion and distemper following the riot-filled last days of the Habsburgs. Felipe V 'the Lively' was on probation: the citizens of Madrid welcomed the idea of modernised governance, at the same time as they disapproved of the king's French retinue who spoke no Spanish and clearly looked down on the city and court in which they found themselves.

The arrogance of the French towards the Spanish at court – those outside of it did not exist – was part of a longer tradition often complemented by a cultural and intellectual deference of Spaniards to their northern neighbours. For some, the French assumption of the Spanish throne split the country down the middle, not so much politically as culturally, opening up a division between two elites: the progressive and outward-looking, pro-French camp – the so-called *afrancesados*, whose role in Spanish history will continue to be debated even until our times – and a conservative, nationalist, pro-Castilian camp.[2] The two were not entirely exclusive, and the pro-Castilian temper, suspicious of outside interference and so often denounced as provincial, will have its counterpart in the development of Basque and Catalan nationalism. Yet these two ways of seeing laid down a fault line that reflected a deeply complex relationship between Spain and France, one expressed too often from the Spanish side as inferiority, an assumption that would colour intellectuals and their work until well into the late twentieth century.[3]

Thus, Mesonero Romanos's imagined account of the arrival of Felipe V in Madrid: 'raised amid the splendour of Versailles, he must have longed for its magnificence as he crossed the dead-looking fields, miserable villages and appalling roads, only to arrive in the ancient and collapsing Alcázar; or as he passed along the wasteland of its tortured and gloomy streets, its wretched housing, its unsophisticated avenues, its frail walls and gates, its lack of fountains and public monuments, its lack of ornamentation or public comfort . . .'[4] The young French royal, in summary, must have wondered what he had let himself in for.

This anguished self-criticism is not uncommon in Spanish letters, and Mesonero makes his sympathies clear: the supposedly perverse darkness of Carlos II had given way to the flooding light of Versailles, albeit it remained unclear how far the benefits of absolutism, for all it clothed itself in Enlightenment thinking, could extend: the oxymoron of the so-called 'enlightened despot'. The new dynasty was the driving force behind a wholesale architectural and institutional renovation of Madrid that would take place over the coming century, reaching its zenith during the reign of Carlos III (1759–88).

Such renovation cannot take away from the extraordinary cultural achievement that had already taken place in Madrid over the previous centuries. It is one thing to knock down the old, another to disown it altogether. Regardless of all the French and Italianate layerings the Bourbons brought to Madrid, the city would always rest on Muslim, medieval Christian and Habsburg foundations.

The city continued to grow, not so much by stretching out its arms and legs as going upwards. One-storey dwellings began to be replaced with taller structures, and remaining vacant lots or former vegetable gardens were progressively used up for residential purposes. The modern city was on its way; the bones of Madrid hardened into shape and its culture seeped into every pore and fissure, its identity moulded in the salons and palaces, in the convents and marketplaces, the taverns and courtyard theatres. The Golden Age might have been over, along with the roller-coaster ride of the Habsburgs, but it all lived on as part of the bedrock and undeniable heritage of Madrid.

Again, Macaulay could not miss a chance to reflect poorly on the Spanish, more so if it allowed him to be equally dismissive of the French: when young Felipe – 'a lounging, moping boy' whose 'mind was naturally feeble' – arrived in Madrid, he writes, 'the disorders of the capital were increased by the arrival of French adventurers, the refuse of Parisian brothels and gaming-houses. These wretches considered Spaniards as a subjugated race whom the countrymen of the new sovereign might cheat and insult with impunity.'[5]

If *madrileños* did not take to the hundreds of French officials who came with the young king, the antagonism was mutual: the officials did not take to the city or its royal court. They found Madrid unfamiliar and antiquated: everything from clothing to etiquette to the palace decorations seemed 'relics of a past age'. Felipe, most shockingly, 'refused to accept food cooked in the Castilian way'.[6] The ruling class of Castile wanted no part of French style in manners and dress, rejecting them 'as contemptuously as they had those of the Dutch in an earlier period'.[7] Here writ large was the pride and independence of Castile, its satisfaction with the values of its own culture and tradition; a pride that, over the coming centuries, would at certain times and in certain hands morph into an exclusionary nationalism.

Young Felipe was homesick. Surrounded by luxury and comfort, he was nevertheless a stranger in a strange land. The French courtiers would not adapt to the Castilian ways they thought so beneath them, so they set about imposing Paris and Versailles on Madrid. The project of reform, however, could not be fully embraced until Felipe was properly settled on the throne, and he had to face a contender, Archduke Carlos of Austria, who also laid claim to the Spanish title on the basis of being the closest available Habsburg. A vast empire of land, sea and resources was at stake; European powers could see themselves partaking in a colonial carve-up of the Spanish Americas. There was the very real prospect of French dominion over the continent: Europe, neither for the first nor last time, divided into warring camps, with an alliance of the pro-Bourbon Spanish and the French entering battle against the pro-Habsburg Spanish, the Austrians under the banner of the Holy Roman Empire, the British and Spain's old foe, the Dutch. Between 1701 and 1715 the conflict dragged on, resulting in close to a million entirely unnecessary deaths. The war has its echoes in contemporary divisions: the fact that Castile and Madrid backed the Bourbon claimant, while Catalonia backed the Habsburg pretender, still resonates in Spanish domestic politics 300 years later.

At the height of the war, Madrid changed hands various times as troops loyal to Felipe or to the Archduke Carlos variously held the upper hand. In 1706 and 1710 Madrid was occupied by Carlos's forces, each time only briefly, as the *madrileños* did all they could to sabotage the Austrian presence. As either Felipe or Carlos entered or retreated from Madrid, the people came out onto the street, jeering or cheering as the Great Powers' display of ping-pong became an almost annual event, comic were it not so serious.[8] With Felipe absent during much of the early stages of the war, his teenage wife María Luisa of Savoy acted as regent, winning the affection of the *madrileños*, regularly appearing on the balcony of the *alcázar* to read dispatches from her husband, earning the nickname of 'La Saboyana' and being seen by the locals not so much as a queen as a conventional and loyal wife whose husband was abroad, soldiering in the interests of Spain.[9]

In 1710 Madrid witnessed a replay of the events of 1601, as the court and some 30,000 officials and citizens decamped to Valladolid ahead of the imminent fall of the city. Austrian and British troops arrived to find a hostile population; citizens refused to acknowledge or cooperate with the new military authorities. Before too long, food supplies were running low, and the *madrileños* grew even more adamant in their opposition after episodes of looting and vandalism, drunkenness, debauchery, destruction of sacred images and sacramental objects.[10] As the supply situation became acute, the occupying forces withdrew from Madrid and Toledo, a ragged, exhausted and starving army. Some ten days after the unsuccessful hooligans had left, and in the company of Louis Joseph, Duke of Vendôme, Felipe V arrived back in Madrid, pausing at the little chapel that marked the entrance to the city at Atocha. He was met with universal joy; his coach was thronged with a cheering crowd, blessing and acclaiming the king; a long night of fireworks and partying began.[11]

In the merry-go-round of history, the roles would be reversed 100 years later, when Madrid would rise up against the occupying French under Napoleon.

Diplomatic settlement was reached in 1715 through the treaties of Utrecht, Spain giving up much of its territory in the Netherlands and Italy but keeping its American domains intact. With Felipe agreeing that the crowns of Spain and France would not ever be united – a direct threat to British aspirations to hegemony – the continent, minor skirmishes aside, settled into a peace that had proved evasive during the previous century. For his part, Felipe continued his project of reforming Madrid and creating a Spanish court along the administrative and aesthetic lines of Versailles. An important step, according to nineteenth-century French historian Arthur de Boislisle, was 'to make the peoples of this monarchy cast off their black clothing in order to adopt our fashions and dress in the French way'.[12] Or in the words of French ambassador Saint-Simon, to be rid of 'this great nunnish paraphernalia'.[13] Indeed, some felt that Madrid was 'entirely governed by directions from Versailles' and that the French-speaking Felipe was not so much king of Spain, as the figurehead, or ambassador, of French sovereignty.[14] It was notable how much of Madrid's administration was run by the French courtiers who had come to Spain with the young king. The Habsburg royals, for all that they belonged to an Austrian house with roots that traced back to eleventh-century Switzerland, had become deeply Spanish over time, in language and modes; the first Bourbons were part of a new era in which Spain was imbued, at least at the upper levels of its society, by French customs and, most particularly during the reign of Carlos III, the finest Italian style.

Changes were both minor and major: there were simple acts of beautification, such as new fountains in the Puerta del Sol, or entertainment, such as the construction of the Teatro de los Caños del Peral, over which the Royal Theatre would later be built. There were superb private palaces, including that of the Marqués de Villafranca, in use today as the Royal Academy of Engineering. Above all, the reign of Felipe V was an era of institutional central-isation, for in the absolutist century knowledge was intimately connected to scientific and economic control. The National Library of Spain (1711) and the Royal Academy of Spain (1713) were both founded before the end of the war; the Royal Academy of History followed in 1738. With peace in view, and a new dynasty, there was a nation to be catalogued and taxonomised, a language to be reined in and ordered, and an erstwhile chaotic history upon which a sense of meaning needed to be placed.

There were also regional wings to be clipped. Part of the consol-idation of Bourbon power in Madrid meant the ending of what, for Felipe and his government, had been seditious tendencies in Catalonia. The *Nueva Planta* decrees ended the regional autonomy and location-specific laws of Valencia, Aragon, Majorca and Catalonia, drawing them all under the umbrella of the absolutist monarchy. By the end of his long double reign in 1746, Felipe and his ministers had succeeded in reinforcing Madrid as the focal point of a centralising state to a much greater degree than his Habsburg

1 & 2. Commissioned by Felipe IV in 1656, Portuguese cartographer Pedro Teixeira produced the first, and still perhaps the most beautiful, map of Madrid. While the majority of the buildings of the mid-seventeenth century have been lost, the view is unmistakeably Madrid, with the city flanked by the Buen Retiro to the east, the Manzanares River and the Casa de Campo to the west, and the hills of Moncloa to the north-west.

3. A section of the original Umayyad walls are preserved in the Parque del Emir Mohamed I (who ruled 852–86) in central Madrid. Rising above is the Cathedral of La Almudena, built on the site where an image of the Virgin is said to have miraculously appeared when Christian troops captured the town in 1083.

4. Built between 1563 and 1584 in the mountains north-west of Madrid, the royal monastery of San Lorenzo de El Escorial is the crowning monument of the reign of Felipe II. The site contains a monastery, a royal mausoleum, a dazzling art collection, an archive and a library, and is often termed the 'eighth wonder of the world'.

5. By the middle of the eighteenth century Madrid was undergoing significant urban and architectural change courtesy of its new Bourbon rulers with visions of Versailles. Antonio Joli here depicts the Calle de Alcalá, with the soon-to-be-remodelled Plaza de Cibeles in the foreground and the church of San José (1745) visible on the right.

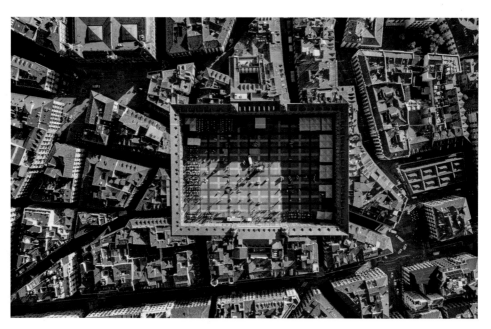

6. Madrid's Plaza Mayor (1621) is the most famous in Spain and served as the model for dozens of plazas in Central and South America. Witness over the centuries to religious ceremonies, executions, bullfights, riots and the always busy commerce of the capital, it is now one of the top tourist attractions of Madrid.

7. Goya's late eighteenth-century paintings of social customs and leisure pastimes in and around Madrid remain one of the best sources for a glimpse into the world of *majos* and *majas*. These elaborately costumed working-class characters would become central to the development of Madrid folklore and identity.

8. Madrid painter Aureliano de Beruete produced a series of views of the city, including this light-filled masterpiece from 1904 of the *View of Madrid from the Meadow of San Isidro*. The painter has overlooked the slum underworld by the Manzanares River so vividly portrayed at this time by writer Pío Baroja.

9. The Royal Palace of Madrid was built between 1735 and 1764, replacing the original Moorish *alcázar*. It was first occupied by the Bourbon reformer and 'enlightened despot', Carlos III. The western face looks down on the Campo del Moro gardens from where, in 1109, Almoravid general Ali ibn Yusuf laid siege to the town.

10. The fountain of Greek goddess Cibeles is one of the best-known sites in Madrid. It is surrounded on four sides by the Bank of Spain, the Palace of Communications, the Palace of Linares and the Buenavista Palace. The fountain is also famous as a centre for the celebrations of football club Real Madrid.

11. Jubilant scenes in the Puerta del Sol on 14 April 1931, as crowds thronged central Madrid to celebrate the declaration of the Second Republic. Despite its political errors and violence, the Republic represented a turning point in Spanish history, and in Madrid coincided with the final years of a 'Silver Age' of culture and science.

12. During the Spanish Civil War, Republican-controlled Madrid resisted the siege of Nationalist forces for close to three years. The first six months were the most violent: in the second half of 1936 the city was marred by street fighting, daily assassinations, aerial bombardment and regular artillery attacks from the nearby Casa de Campo.

13. The Noviciado Metro station on Calle de San Bernardo in 1955. Madrid had come through the civil war and its difficult aftermath, including the damaging effects of Franco's ill-conceived attempt at autarky. Alongside terrible poverty and deprivation, a middle class was re-emerging whose children would lead opposition to the regime.

14. In the late 1970s and early 1980s the post-dictatorship cultural explosion across Spain was best and most famously represented by the *movida madrileña*, a generally leaderless movement based in central Madrid that blended rich Spanish cultural expression with heavy stylistic doses of punk and new wave.

15. Madrid has always been famous for its relentless enjoyment of conversation. The Plaza de Santa Ana, created in the early nineteenth century by occupying king José Bonaparte, is home to bars, terrace cafes, theatres and clubs that are typical of Madrid's love of socialising, entertainment and nightlife.

16. In twenty-first-century Madrid, the economic boom of finance and digital high-tech has brought a new skyline to the city. Here, the Four Towers business district seen against the backdrop, so beloved by Velázquez, of the Sierra de Guadarrama. In the middle distance, the high-density apartment living that is so characteristic of the city.

predecessors who had ruled over a land that was still an assemblage of disparate regions. The centralisation of Spanish institutions, with direct effects on industry, trade, culture and politics – a centralisation for which Madrid is so often reviled from the periphery – stemmed from this French passion for concentration of power. The language of Castile, *castellano*, became the language of the state, the church and the law; the first step to streamlining the bulky awkwardness of a national bureaucracy was to homogenise the language of transmission. It is no coincidence that the *kilómetro cero*, the central point in the Puerta del Sol from which the six major radial highways in Spain are measured – the commemorative plaque is a whimsical tourist attraction – was established in 1720. This network fans out across the whole nation, reaching each extremity. Numbered clockwise, it ignores other, more naturally occurring phenomena such as the Mediterranean corridor from Catalonia down the length of eastern Spain and thence to the southern exit ports to Africa, or the east–west flow of major rivers: the Tagus, the Ebro and the Guadalquivir; even the old Roman roads that led north from Cádiz and Seville to the mines of Galicia, a major thoroughfare that had no contact with the centre of the peninsula; or the many winding paths of the transhumant sheep migrations, routes that in some instances are pre-Christian. The *kilómetro cero* was a symbol that the long process of measuring, cataloguing and classifying the material realities of Spain and its empire had begun. This was a project in which science would play a major part, and would reach its eighteenth-century climax in the five-year Malaspina expedition (1789–94), a maritime journey of exploration around the entire Spanish globe. Under the patronage of Felipe's son, Carlos III, this huge undertaking sought to mirror the classificatory efforts of linguists, geographers, surveyors, administrators and historians, bringing order to the world and documenting the wild natural and human diversity of the empire, even as that empire was under threat from political developments that would reach their fruition in the near future.

Peace brought the opportunity to expand the economy; as part of the effort to improve commercial productivity, Felipe established a series of royal manufacturing sites, the *manufacturas reales*, including the Royal Tapestry Factory, one of the most important extant institutions of Bourbon Madrid. Other factories were later established in Madrid and distributed around the peninsula, producing textiles, porcelain, weapons, tobacco, glassware, paper, machinery and silverware, all goods that were central to life in the eighteenth century.

This strong will to centralisation along the French model established by Richelieu and Louis XIV, and resuscitating the old dreams of Olivares, led to new questions, always relevant in Madrid, as to the nature of the Spanish nation. Depending on one's geographic position on the peninsula, or one's ideological position on a broad spectrum, this was either the consolidation of a historic mission begun under Ferdinand and Isabel, and thence the Habsburgs, or was the birth of a modern system of repression directed against cultural, political and linguistic diversity. Under the first Bourbon rulers there was a tendency 'to present power in terms of lineage or collective culture, which furthered the development of the ethnic patriotism initiated under the Habsburgs'.[15] In the artworks that adorned the buildings of the regime and the books that filled its libraries, there was a clear preference for a pedagogical narrative that reinforced the idea of the Spanish nation.[16] The new academic institutions in Madrid were part of the development of a national culture closely identified with the monarchy. Whether this was a good thing or not is the subject of ongoing debate: was a stronger and more centralised Spanish state part of the celebration of a nation, or was it to the greater glory of the absolutist monarchy?[17] Perhaps this is not so important: the great academic institutions headquartered in Madrid are no longer associated with the royal family, nor is their contemporary purpose, it goes without saying, to glorify the monarchy.

The establishment of *castellano* as the national language with its codifying body in Madrid, much as it has been scorned over the years as an absolutist outrage that sidelined other languages such as Catalan, Galego and Basque – a discrimination, say its critics, perpetrated by the Bourbons and pursued centuries later by General

Franco – ignores the benefits that have accrued to Spanish as a global language of literature and communication. Another of the languages sidelined in these reforms was Latin, a move that brought a range of cultural and spiritual resources away from an educated elite and closer to the broad mass of people.

The impact of the reforms introduced fitfully across the eighteenth century would resonate long into the nineteenth. The territory of reform was slippery, and when based on imported models – in this case French – provided ammunition for an opposition wanting to frame any proposal to modernise or reform as antipatriotic, heretical, atheistic or immoral.[18] This happened again in the early nineteenth century, when those Spanish liberals who wished to maintain a programme of reform found themselves denounced as an elite, out of touch with those who fought so courageously in Madrid and elsewhere against Napoleon's troops. Again, the inversion from one century to the next: the French state and its rulers, with whom Spain continued an anxious relationship often expressed as unequals, were either the designers of the future or the destroyers of the glorious national past.

Physically, Madrid began to evolve beyond the tightly packed environment of the Habsburg capital. In the early eighteenth century the long arc to the immediate south and west of the city centre, swooping anti-clockwise from Atocha to the Hermitage of San Antonio de la Florida, was improved with new bridges over the Manzanares and a series of gardens and roads that better connected the whole curve to the historic centre and out to nearby towns such as Leganés and Carabanchel.[19] This is today one of the most beautiful areas of the city, restored to parklands and walkways along the river via the extensive Madrid Río regreening project of the early twenty-first century, that wanders along a series of landmarks such as the Puente de Toledo with its statues of San Isidro and Santa María de la Cabeza, the Puente de Segovia, the Hermitage of La Virgen del Puerto (reconstructed after the civil war), the revitalised Campo del Moro with its long, graceful vista up to the western side of the Royal Palace, the reconstructed Puerta de San Vicente and the Hermitage of San Antonio de la Florida, whose beautiful frescoes by Goya are one of the lesser-known treasures of Madrid. Much of this work was begun under city mayor Francisco Antonio Salcedo, the Marquis of Vadillo, whose name is honoured by a Metro station and a roundabout at the start of the road to Carabanchel; the Marquis himself is buried at the base of the main altar of the lovely, self-contained Hermitage of La Virgen del Puerto, under a slab of dark green marble. Architectural design was either carried out, or inspired, by two important native architects of Madrid – José Benito de Churriguera and Pedro de Ribera. Churriguera, whose work is to be found across Castile, left a style that carried his own name, the Churrigueresque, being the highly ornamental, exuberant and overflowing endpoint of Spanish baroque.

The first half of the eighteenth century was a quiet time in the cultural history of Madrid; nor was it a bad thing that little seemed to have happened. The city had still not caught its breath after the painters and writers of the seventeenth century. Felipe brought few artists to the court; perhaps the best-known was the Frenchman Jean Ranc, who produced colourful but wearyingly dull rococo portraits. Ranc is not forgotten to history as he might otherwise have been, for he was destined to play a small but critical role in one of the most significant events in the history of Madrid, shortly before his death in 1735. It would not be until the second half of the century that a new generation of painters, brought to the court under royal patronage, would set Madrid alight once more with the brilliance of their work: Corrado Giaquinto, Giovanni Battista Tiepolo and Anton Raphael Mengs. The Italian cultural influence came to dominate Madrid through the powerful personality and reach of Isabel de Farnesio of Parma, second wife to Felipe following the death from tuberculosis in 1714 of María Luisa, the popular 'Saboyana'. It would not be until the end of the eighteenth century that a number of Spanish painters, the *madrileño* Luis Paret, the *valenciano* Vicente López and the *aragonés* Francisco Goya, would again place Madrid as one of the principal sites of European art.

The style of entertainment in the absolutist court changed too. The theatrical fever had died down during the decade and more of war, though it was not extinguished; Madrid has always been a city enamoured of the dramatic arts. The change of regime resulted in a sweeping clean of the jesters, fools and dwarves who had peopled the edges of the Habsburg court, free to whisper hard truths into the ears of those who laughed at them and with them. Felipe wanted no part of this tasteless Spanish buffoonery; the French love for the exotic did not embrace local eccentricities but favoured instead a servitude that included 'Negroes', Moors and South American Indians bearing brightly coloured parrots.[20] The Habsburgs, we might conclude, found both solace and a hard-edged truth in their freaks and jesters, while the Bourbons preferred the colour and excitement of dark skins from the distant corners of the globe along with, in time, the explosive thrill of Italian opera. This was a more obvious form of racialised colonialism, as befitted a new European era: the Spanish-inflected Austrians, with their roots in Flemish art and bloody crusades, their fear of God and the fires of hell, gave way to the French Bourbons, with their own desires swayed by the exotic brown skins of the tropics, the deserts or the jungle. These were two very different ways of viewing the world, playing out within the confines of the court at Madrid: both absolutist, both edged with cruelty, both using 'strange' bodies as a regime of entertainment within a broader universe of meaning.

The young, beautiful and graceful María Luisa of Savoy had been able to utterly dominate her husband Felipe, who suffered not only from the strangeness of his Madrid environment, but also from the bullying oversight of his grandfather Louis XIV. Matters were no different with Isabel de Farnesio, who found a husband suffering episodes of manic depression and outbursts of bipolar aggression. Both of Felipe's wives were reputed to have controlled him through the supply or withdrawal of sexual favours; the king was reportedly voracious but straitjacketed by piety into being faithful to his wives. In 1724 he suddenly abdicated in favour of his teenage son, Luis, and retired to the relaxing grounds of the royal palace at La Granja de San Ildefonso, just over the Guadarrama range in the province of Segovia, a site he had ordered built to purpose by his architect

Teodoro de Ardemans very much in the style, though without the degree of lavish excess, of Versailles. The palace boasts a beautiful natural setting and spectacular gardens and fountains; unfortunately for Felipe, his rest was brief, as new king Luis I 'the Beloved' died eight months after ascending the throne, the victim of smallpox at the age of only 17. Felipe resumed his role as Bourbon king at the end of 1724, and was to rule for another twenty-two years.

Isabel de Farnesio was an ambitious woman, and put up with her husband's erratic behaviour, including episodes of violent beating, in order to keep her eye on a longer game: to see her sons grow up to rule in her native Italy. Meanwhile, one of the only soothing balms for Felipe as he battled with mental illness and physical wasting was the voice of Farinelli, the legendary castrato who had made Madrid his home in 1737. Both Farinelli and his compatriot, Domenico Scarlatti, became fixtures at the court, serving the royal family in their separate ways while enjoying a close friendship. Farinelli sang nightly for the melancholy king, and would do so for twenty years, singing also for his melancholy son, Fernando. The Neapolitan Scarlatti had been employed in Lisbon as music master to the young Portuguese princess Barbara, and when she married Fernando in 1729 at the age of 18, Scarlatti accompanied her to Spain, living first in Seville and then Madrid, where he would live and compose for the rest of his life.

As the newest member of the family and partner to the heir to the throne, Barbara clashed with Farnesio, a rivalry that would continue for years. Farnesio was determined to keep the Portuguese princess away from the intimate details and power plays of the court; Barbara, for her part a highly accomplished and sophisticated young woman, was content to further her close relationship with Scarlatti, performing the sonatas composed by her friend and master, many of which were dedicated to her. Upon the death of Felipe in 1746, Barbara joined her husband Fernando VI 'the Prudent, the Just' on the throne, ushering in a reign of a decade and a half characterised as splendid precisely because absolutely nothing happened.[21] While still in the absolutist tradition, Fernando was the first bourgeois ruler, calm and contented with his lot. He did not look to

fight wars, waste huge amounts of money on unnecessary extravagances, or even exhume the bodies of the dead to cure or sanctify
the living. Perhaps the budget for entertainments had been used up
in the days of the inauguration: an elaborate series of festivities,
over the course of four days, marked the entrance of Fernando into
Madrid, a splendour confirming Madrid as one of the great cities
of pre-industrial Europe.[22] Day one was an elaborate royal procession through the city; day two featured a gigantic masked parade
sponsored by the major guilds and the town hall; day three was a
day of fireworks; and day four, a marathon double session of bullfighting in the Plaza Mayor, at which no fewer than thirty-one
bulls were killed before it became too dark, and everyone too
exhausted, to continue the spectacle.

Bourbon Madrid continued to attract internal migrants in search
of opportunity. Eighty per cent of the population were engaged in
trade and commerce, construction, domestic service, entertainment
or simply relied, as ever, on charity and wits, on theft and trickery,
to make ends meet. The modernising French and Italian turns in
administration and culture were alien and irrelevant to the labouring
or begging classes. Italian opera was hugely successful in the eighteenth century, just as Spanish drama had been in the seventeenth,
but it did not have the same popular or democratic reach. Kamen,
who suggests this embrace of opera was a symptom of the broadening cultural horizons of the ruling class, identifies at the same
time a gap opening up between a modernising elite and the traditional culture of the masses, a culture that, for all their otherworldly
distance, some of the Habsburg rulers had shared with their people.[23]

The War of Spanish Succession had left a trail of negative demographic effects; it was not until the middle of the century that the
population of Madrid was restored to its late-Habsburg levels, before
rising to around 200,000 by the end of the century. Plague loomed
again, while years of drought or locusts led to poor harvests and
famine. When the burden of agrarian work, back-breaking and
miserably paid, became unsustainable, many sought out the precarious streets of the capital. In addition, Madrid had its share of

ex-soldiers, many without employment, or wounded and disabled, reduced to begging and vagabondage. The sick too, and the mentally disturbed, might wander the streets if they had not found any charitable institution to take them in. Some, if remotely fit enough, were recruited from aimlessness and placed into the army. Early forms of policing sought to keep the streets of Madrid safe from both physical and moral danger: the *Ronda del Pecado Mortal* – 'doing the rounds' against mortal sin – was a voluntary group of black-clad men who from 1733 specifically targeted the thriving trade in prostitution, walking the streets late at night, accompanied by a mournful bell, intoning warnings in sombre verse against sin and the punishments of hell. The hope was that not only would the prostitutes leave off their trade and repair to a special safe house set up for them in the Calle Hortaleza, but that the sinning clients would also be discouraged by dark threats of damnation. Apart from sporadic victories, there was no indication the doomsayers enjoyed success. At the same time, the Brotherhood of Refuge and Piety, founded as far back as 1615, was active on the streets providing for the destitute; from the first to the third decade of the eighteenth century, as the after-effects of a fourteen-year war played out, the need for its charity increased more than tenfold.[24] Four hundred years after its founding, the Brotherhood is still active, operating out of its base in the historic church of San Antonio de los Alemanes.

There were significant improvements in the streetscape of Madrid, with updated drainage, better street lighting, increased paving and the refurbishment and beautification of houses and noble mansions. Where possible, streets were widened, as befitted the seat of a highly ceremonial court. Given the restrictions of space, it was impossible for the increasing number of noble families to build in the vicinity of the old *alcázar*; they began to look to the east of the city, around the Buen Retiro, emphasising the status of this green and pleasant zone as one of the most exclusive of Madrid, as it remains to this day. The improvements in facilities and infrastructure showed what could be attended to when a state is not at war; in 1753 the governing council of Madrid recorded a financial profit for the first time since its foundation in 1346.[25] These changes to the physical aspect of

Madrid prepared the way for the even more significant reforms that would come with Carlos III later in the century.

Along with the beautiful Church of San Marcos, one of the first creations of Madrid architect Ventura Rodríguez, the legacy of Fernando's reign includes what has become one of the finest, yet most overlooked, art museums in Spain. Tourists who come to Madrid for the world-famous galleries gravitate to one or all of the Prado, the Thyssen-Bornemisza and the Reina Sofía, often ignoring altogether a gallery with an outstanding collection of Spanish art that stands nearby, adjacent to the Puerta del Sol. The Real Academia de Bellas Artes San Fernando, founded in 1752 and located since 1773 in the Palace of Goyeneche, is one of the great legacies of Fernando's time: an art academy that attracted an extraordinary list of students and teachers and built up, over the years, a dazzling collection of painting, sculpture and drawings.[26] In keeping with the newly enlightened times, there was also the first attempt at a Botanic Gardens along the banks of the Manzanares close to El Pardo, later moved by Carlos III to central Madrid where it remains, a close partner to the Prado Museum and the Retiro.

While she held sway at court, Isabel de Farnesio had kept Fernando and Barbara at bay by installing them at the royal palace of La Granja – a type of lazy and luxurious exile – over the mountains and out of the way of any palace conspiracy. After Felipe's death, the couple reversed the roles and sent Farnesio to her own exile from court at La Granja. She was too well connected, however, not to remain active in international politics, engineering her son Carlos's rise to the kingdom of the Two Sicilies – essentially Naples and Palermo – in 1748. Her time in Madrid would come again, after the death of Fernando, when Carlos was brought, much against his will, from Naples to take up the Spanish crown.

In that same year of 1748, the Convent of the Salesas Reales was founded under Barbara's patronage. She died a decade later, in 1758; the death of his wife left Fernando prostrate with grief. Melancholy by nature, he was never to recover from the shock, and spent the last year of his life consumed by sadness. He is reported to have abandoned any self-care, wandering the gardens in his nightgown without rhyme or reason. Sainz de Robles presents a more colourful if voyeuristic picture based on correspondence of one of the royal doctors: the king became unhinged, accosted by nightmares and visions; he was constipated for thirty-six days, fasted for long periods, and hit himself repeatedly.[27] His father Felipe V had ended his life in similarly distressing physical circumstances, unwashed and full of sores, raggedy and swollen, unable to speak; now Fernando gave up all will to live and slouched to the grave in grief, his heart broken and his world closed down.

He and his queen now lie in peace, amid a certain late baroque glory, in the church of Santa Bárbara in the lovely Plaza de las Salesas; the convent that accompanied the church is now the home of the Supreme Court of Spain; indeed, the whole Salesas quarter is one of the loveliest in Madrid. This cultured and peaceful couple died not long after their great friend Scarlatti, in 1757. Magnificent sepulchres were carved for them; on his, Fernando is represented supporting the fine arts. Scarlatti's grave, meanwhile, was lost. A plaque marks his former residence behind the Gran Vía in Calle Leganitos, between a Chinese hairdresser and a hardware store.

A conflagration

By 1734 the French painter Jean Ranc was a 60-year-old man, suffering from shortness of sight. He had come to Madrid a decade earlier as part of the Bourbon cultural overhaul, leaving behind the court of Louis XV. He had not enjoyed his years in the capital, fighting with jealous rivals and never feeling at home despite being with his five children.

By the early eighteenth century the royal *alcázar* bore little resemblance to the original Islamic or later medieval Christian fortification. Over 900 years it had undergone countless rebuilds and extensions: without changing location, it had evolved from a squat and flinty Moorish keep to an elongated baroque palace with hundreds of rooms, many stacked to the rafters with precious art, furniture, tapestries, porcelain, jewellery, documents and historical archives. From the point of view of any archaeologist, historian or architect, it was a living palimpsest of Madrid past and present, a trove of clues and treasures, many of which were about to be lost forever.

We cannot know for certain how Jean Ranc passed Christmas Eve 1734. He might have been in his room, stoking the fireplace against the winter night; he might have been drying one of his French wigs, or mixing paints and chemicals, perhaps alcohol. He might have been in another part of the *alcázar* complex, with his children or in consultation, if not celebration, with court officials;

he might have been in argument with his nemesis Michel-Ange Houasse. Whether he was in his rooms or not, this seems to have been where the great fire started, and it caught with a combustible rage.

Certain events act as catalysts that lurch history forward. The catastrophic fire that broke out in the *alcázar* that evening would be another turning point in the history of Madrid. As often in moments of crisis, one error led to another, until the errors added up to a comedy, and then the comedy to a tragedy. In a single incident nine centuries of history were lost.

When the fire alarms were set off just after midnight, a great clanging of bells, there was immediate confusion: many thought it was the call to the *misa de gallo* – the Midnight Mass. Precious time was lost as the danger of what was happening was not at first perceived; it was easy enough in a palace complex of such size for an incident in one part to go unnoticed in another. The crowds outside knew the gravity of the situation straight away. Now came a second error: palace officials were cautious about allowing members of the public admittance, not because they were concerned for their safety, but because they suspected many of being potential looters. The anonymous of Madrid – the 'common people', the servants and labourers who kept the machines turning – wanted to throw themselves into the task of saving religious and cultural inheritance, which was sanctioned by God. The rigidity of hierarchy and its obsession with process and rank slowed any chance of extinguishing the fire, which grew thick on oil and timber, tables, bedsteads, a thousand embroidered chairs, frayed tapestries, the long drop of drapery and curtains. It was one thing to save artistic treasures, another to allow the crowd into the royal compound, to tramp the corridors, blaspheme the order of things. Those few who were available set to work, and more important than human chains to relay buckets of water were desperate human chains to pass out items of incalculable value.

By four in the morning, the sky now a furious smoky orange, the main chapel had gone; many of its religious treasures, perhaps being of higher priority than human life, were saved. In the Great

Salon, with its different aesthetics, and where the walls teemed with paintings from floor to ceiling, there were no ladders available. Rescuers frantically ripped the canvases from their frames and threw them out the window into a courtyard to keep them from the unstoppable greed of the flames. Only those paintings within some two metres of floor level could be saved. Among the paintings rescued in this way was Velázquez's *Las Meninas* and the superb Titian portrait of *Charles V at Mühlberg*. Up to 500 works of art were lost, some vaguely known from copies or preparatory sketches, most beyond our imagining.

Had *Las Meninas* been reduced to ash, could we even imagine those young maids, and the enigmatic painter himself, peering from around the corner of his stand, adding to the wild geometry of that canvas? The painting of *Las Meninas* is basically inconceivable; were it not to exist, such a painting could not be invented. Also up in flames went what was considered one of Velázquez's greatest works, his *Expulsion of the Moors*; other paintings, possibly less remarkable to contemporaries, may with the passage of time have become works of unquestionable genius. Inventories from the *alcázar* allow us to know that works by Ribera, Guido Reni, Artemisia Gentileschi, Veronese, Tintoretto, Raphael, Leonardo, Rubens, Titian, Sánchez Coello, Carducho, El Greco, Hans Holbein and others were among those lost. Often, these were works that had only been in existence for a generation or two; in some cases, the paint would barely have been dry. Given the restricted nature of art display, they will have been viewed by only a few individuals, then lost, never having the opportunity to add that glaze of age which alters aesthetic perceptions. They would never know the consecration of the nineteenth and twentieth centuries, the boast of the catalogue, the eye of the modern critic, the adulation of crowds. In this sense, they are among the most exclusive of artworks, with their ephemeral and barely witnessed beauty. There may have been other works as spectacular as *Las Meninas*; perhaps it owes its absolute uniqueness to an accident and a fire. Countless works were only ever seen within the close spaces of the royal court, enjoyed – or frowned upon – by the royal family, their entertainers, lovers, servants and visitors. These artworks never had a 'public' in the modern sense of the word. Visual documents that might change our understanding of European art in the sixteenth and seventeenth centuries would never reach the triumph and glare of public display, or be subjected to historical and symbolic exegesis; would never be cleaned, restored or brightened. These paintings never built up the dark patina of time.

Lost also were documents of incalculable historic value, archives of the South American empire, Indigenous artefacts, papal bulls and the entire collection of sacred music from the royal chapel. Silver chalices and crosses were melted by the blaze, falling to the charred floors with precious stones.

The fire took four days to be brought under control. When the smoke had cleared, Felipe saw the bright side of the disaster: here was an opportunity to build an entire new royal palace, less gloomy, more in the airy and sumptuous way of Versailles. An initial plan was drawn up by Italian architect Filippo Juvara who had recently remodelled sections of the palace-retreat at La Granja de San Ildefonso. Juvara proposed an edifice of absurd dimensions; the Spanish purse did not reach that level of splendour or, more to the point, could not match that level of sheer waste. Juvara died soon after in mysterious circumstances and another Italian who had been working with him at La Granja, Giovanni Battista Sachetti, was called upon to revise the plans and continue with the work. Juvara had initially thought of placing the palace in a different location, but this idea was also discarded. The new royal palace was built over two and a half decades, begun in 1736 and finally inaugurated, with Carlos III as its first resident, in 1764.

Jean Ranc had died, overwhelmed with depression, barely six months after the fire.

Such devastations of cultural heritage affect all countries; Spain and Madrid have had to endure one after another. Less than half a century after the inauguration of the new palace came the theft and pillage of Napoleon and his marauding troops; three decades later, the national confiscation of religious property under prime minister Mendizábal which, while having the noble objective of raising finance and better spreading the national wealth, had the inevitable side effect of the destruction – accidental or otherwise – of count-less artworks and objects of enormous cultural value and the sale, to boost the national coffers, of items of incalculable value that now grace foreign museums or are hidden away in private collections. In the third decade of the twentieth century came the wreck of another civil war, further years of ultimately pointless destruction of artistic heritage, sometimes carried out deliberately – especially in the case of church property – and at other times as the collateral of bombing, fire, or both, further depleting the cultural heritage of the nation.

The fire at the *alcázar* destroyed evidence of a world view. The royal collection as it then stood might only have been one cross-section of a cultural period, but such collections are windows through which broader cultural assumptions around work, hierarchy, status, wealth, gender and systems of belief can be viewed. Absences mark out the shape of what we eventually manage to know. Much of pre-Enlightenment Madrid had been consumed in the fire, count-less images and religious or decorative items turned to ash amid the stench of chemicals and the hot flow of molten lead, silver and gold. The decision to build the new palace atop the ruins of the old meant surviving materials were repurposed for foundations, and one of the richest archaeological sites in Madrid was buried under the new royal home.

As the monarchy had been transformed over the past century, so the royal family now had a new residence in accord with the times. No longer needing to adapt an ancient and patched-up conglom-eration, the Bourbons could enjoy a palace in Madrid entirely their own, and Carlos III would bring in his most distinguished architect from Naples, Francesco Sabatini, to add beautifying elements. A new time was beginning; for the moment the politics remained absolutist, but were opening up to the currents of the age that would bring social, political and intellectual changes as the old regimes staggered to their end. None of this would be easy, but much of Madrid, physically and mentally, was ready to be rebuilt. The anon-ymous would demand to be named. Over the next century and a half, the city would experience the fusion of its rich popular culture and its often volatile politics; new waves of thought meant the way a society should be organised was no longer a matter of a sovereign and their ministers, but a matter of popular will. While a new palace would be built from the ground up, others had begun to dream of doing the same with the nation, its capital city and its history.

III

CITY

1759–1975

The spring of hope

Throughout the latter half of the 1770s Francisco Goya, who had arrived in Madrid in 1775, created dozens of light-filled paintings that throw open the social world of Madrid's popular classes at leisure: drinking and dancing by the banks of the Manzanares, playing games, singing with guitar, attending markets and fairs, hunting and fishing, flying kites, washing clothes, brawling outside inns; posing, seducing and being seduced.[1] The world is full of optimistic bright reds and yellows, fresh greens, lovely blue skies. There is a sense of warmth and springtime; clouds accentuate the blue rather than threaten storms. The people of Madrid are as they always have been: confident with a touch of arrogance, committed to pleasure. The gentle tone of these works does not disguise what must have been, for some of those who appear in them, a life of poverty and privation, especially among the fighting wretches outside the highway taverns. At the same time, these paintings are anthropological documents, introducing us to some of the stock characters of Goya's time: the *majos* and *majas*, the legendary members of Madrid's popular classes and, above them in wealth and hierarchy, the French-influenced *petimetres* and *petimetras*. Many of these works were base drawings to be developed later into tapestries and focused on the pleasant side of life; Goya was many years away from his darker galleries, portraying the dispossessed, the unwanted, the persecuted, the victims of war, the inmates of the mental asylum with all its unthinkable grimness. Young and splendid, he had not yet learned the close details of atrocity.

Up at the Royal Palace, seen in the distance from the meadows of San Isidro, Carlos III is served his lunch or dinner; the hour of the day is unknown, or simply irrelevant, as absolutism ran to its own time. The pleasures of the court are rolling and infinite in this crowded and rococo setting.[2] The walls drip with mythology and gold, or swirl in a greenish-greyish cloud of opulence. Where Goya's *majos* and *majas* turn, dance and play, and even the *petimetres* have their fun, the courtiers here follow rigid ceremonial protocol. The painter of this other work is Luis Paret, a native son of Madrid, gifted from a young age at rendering the world around him, which is astonishing for its luxuries and utter misery. Paret was both brilliant and status-conscious; aspiring to this grand life, to rub shoulders with the nobility, to breathe the scent of their perfumes, Paret became a procurer for the king's younger brother, the Infante Luis; an *alcahuete*, from the medieval Arabic *al-qawwad* for messenger. Kindlier versions see in this etymology the evolution of the matchmaker; the harsher reality is Paret was a pimp, a trafficker in young women served up to the prince.

For all his reputation as an enlightened reformer, it is hard to square this extravagant, even absurd image of Carlos: what could possibly be enlightened about this lush reverence, this world of velvet, jewels and rich wall hangings, of endless servants, of whim and desire. Carlos is dining before his court, a room full of lackeys and flatterers; a room groaning with image, yet somehow weightless; a chamber loaded with meaning and intent, yet frivolous. Very little light slipped through the armoured walls of absolutism.

Luis Paret was one of the finest artists of his age. His later life being ruined by a concocted scandal, he was exiled to Puerto Rico for three years and then banned from the court for the best part of another decade. This genius did what he could, given the circumstances life threw at him; he died, back in Madrid at last, of tuberculosis at the very end of the century, and has since suffered the common fate of being largely forgotten. His painting of Carlos eating, as much as any other, points to the unsustainable absurdity of late eighteenth-century Europe: how could such a society not have some type of revolution brewing? Such stratification was not ordained by God, or even in the teachings; it was the extreme perversion of power. Over the coming century and a half, others would wrest this power from the aristocracy, at gunpoint and in violence. The butcher's block did not play the role in Madrid it played in Paris, but the transition would not be peaceful.

A conventional summary of this period might run as follows: Madrid swerved from an enlightened and rapidly modernising city in the late eighteenth century into over 100 years of stasis and decline. A long nineteenth century leads from the invasion of Napoleon in 1808, and the city's legendary resistance, to the birth of the Second Republic in 1931, where a flowering of progressive change, building on broader cultural developments across Europe and North America, was stamped out by the Francoist victory in the civil war, leading to another four decades of cultural and political inertia, including two decades of international ostracism.

Inevitably, Madrid's evolution was more complicated and nuanced than this, and indeed more optimistic. The expansion of the capital of empire from town to city coincided with an age of great tumult. From the timid enlightenment of the late eighteenth century, with its embrace of a universal science, to the ferocious and, for Madrid, character-defining defeat of Napoleon; thence from the illiberal early nineteenth century to the civil disorder and wars of the mid-nineteenth; the expropriation of monastic properties and the declining power of the church; the arrival of the modern age; a comfortable bourgeoisie, beautifully described and parodied by Spain's finest writers, gloriously painted by her artists; electricity, railways, street lighting, sanitation and a new water supply; modernism, male suffrage and anxiety for revolution; a republic, female suffrage and civil war. Not, by any means, Spain's only civil war, but by far its deadliest and most infamous, for it coincided not only with a new era of war reporting and media coverage of atrocities, but also laid out a blueprint for the ideological clash soon to engulf the entire continent. Never before had a war attracted so many celebrity visitors and denunciations; Madrid, especially, became the stage for a host of international commentators and fighters who joined the battle against fascism. The war was followed by a decade that was deadly, leaden, painful and slow; then, from the 1950s, the gradual reopening of Spain; the slow death of the regime from the 1960s; the death of the dictator in 1975. From the reign of Carlos III to the death of Franco are two centuries of enormous upheaval and conflict, of change and suffering, and of the survival and reinvention of a great city. These are remarkable years, at the end of which Madrid emerged, with a shout and a scream, and came roaring back into the world.

Following the death of his half-brother Fernando VI, Carlos was not especially keen to return to his birthplace of Madrid. His mother Isabel de Farnesio had secured the leading role of southern Italy for him, where he lived and ruled in extraordinary comfort and style. He might have been, like all royals from the time of the *antiguo regimen*, a fundamentally lethargic person – other than when it came to hunting – but he was not incompetent. Coming to Madrid from Naples in 1759, he brought with him great experience, for he had already governed in Italy for twenty-five years, and he knew – he may have been lazy, but he was not stupid – that good government requires delegating the right tasks to the right statesmen. Carlos had an entire reform programme to unfold in Madrid and Spain, and knew he could not do it all himself. He brought some excellent state servants from Naples, and to them he would add a cohort of very fine statesmen in Spain. Theirs were, in hindsight, chequered careers. These senior administrators and state planners rose and fell according to the circumstances in which they found themselves, or into which others engineered them; when their downfall came it tended to be the result of jealousy, ambition, scandal or changing fashion, rather than an inability to do their jobs to the highest level of expertise. Various names are outstanding in this history: the Counts of Aranda, Campomanes and Floridablanca, and the untitled but equally brilliant Gaspar Melchor de Jovellanos and Pablo de Olavide. All had moments of triumph and moments of distressing difficulty; all enjoyed support and garnered enemies along the way.

Madrid was already the nexus of a complex state bureaucracy, and this would now increase substantially. Over the following decades it would be politicians and statesmen taking centre stage, rather than a powerful royal favourite fending off jealous nobles and scheming his way to fortunes and disgrace. Men like the economist Campomanes, the lawyer and land reformer Jovellanos or the lawyer, politician and urban reformer Olavide were not in the mould of Lerma or Olivares, the powerful dukes of old. The new class of statesmen were of appropriate stock – society was not yet secular enough to admit those without breeding into the higher ranks – but they were also extremely competent, well read and keen to put social and administrative reforms in place. Olavide was heavily influenced by Voltaire and Rousseau, while Jovellanos drew partly on the work of Adam Smith. All were keenly aware that the nature of society and governments was changing; their role was to facilitate these changes within the context of a reactionary system without upsetting the foundations of the church or monarchy. Perhaps an impossible task, and one that would suffer setback after setback, but under Carlos III that long path was begun.

Spain's Enlightenment intellectuals may have been fewer in number and less famous than their French neighbours, and faced sterner opposition, but they had a practical strength the Frenchmen lacked.[3] As art historian Robert Hughes points out, the French Enlightenment intellectuals were mostly impractical dreamers who had no idea of the day-to-day business of government. They were utopian fantasists who 'couldn't run a provincial restaurant, let alone a country'.[4] The Spanish intellectuals, however, were both intellectuals *and* politicians; men like Campomanes or Jovellanos understood the practical nature of power and its administration, and just as importantly, 'they knew how easily the *pueblo*, the people, could turn into the *populacho*, the mob'.[5] Historical processes unfold differently in different environments and Madrid, in this respect, proceeded more cautiously towards regime change than Paris.

The reigns of Felipe V and Fernando VI had begun to modify the baroque deficiencies of the Habsburg capital, but much remained to be done; Madrid needed major infrastructural reform. Carlos III, who earned the sobriquet of 'Madrid's greatest ever mayor' – a popular but disputed title – undertook wholesale changes to the physical appearance of the capital. Other tasks pending were an overhaul of government finances, desperately needed agriculture and land reform across the country, reform of law, industry, international trade and relations, and of the overwhelming influence of the church. In summary, the path chosen was paradoxical: a modernisation both cautious and profound. Additionally, with the spectre of broad-ranging social discontent on the horizon, further measures were required to marshal and manage the still considerable numbers of poor and destitute. This was both a moral and a political obligation: despite the popular cliché of the Inquisition preventing all modern-ising knowledge from passing over the high dark wall of the Pyrenees, the leading Spanish statesmen of the day knew perfectly well what was taking place elsewhere in Europe.

As political and administrative reforms took shape, Madrid became a thriving hub for lawyers and clerks, attorneys and govern-ment agents, all professions that experienced strong growth parallel to an expanding state apparatus.[6] These were part of a professional cadre that developed beyond the old ties and obligations of noble and royal patronage. Although these professions were in their bourgeois infancy – social ascent still commonly revolved around family and connections, and noble titles could be purchased at the right price – the estates of the *antiguo regimen* were beginning to be left behind. Madrid became further entrenched as the capital from which the nation was administered, petitioned, judged, ruled and legislated. It was the home of the State Treasury and the majority of financial brokers and instruments that kept the nation financially afloat.

Since the middle of the seventeenth century, the *cinco gremios mayores* – the five major guilds of jewellers, silk merchants, haber-dashers, textile makers and pharmacists – had captured the Madrid market with absolute control of supply to the royal family and the state, cornering local production and the import trade. Given their power, they also began to operate as financiers to the state. The profile of these guilds gives an insight into the trades that held sway: there was no manufacture, no agriculture or fisheries; industrial production as it would come to be known did not yet exist, or barely; the five major guilds represented luxury items rather than essential goods, and operated with the close support of the state.[7] Just as importantly, tight control of this closed shop meant any 'suspect' or 'wandering' blood was kept out, for fear of both impurity and the spark of true competition.[8] Members of the corporation of the five major guilds wound their tentacles through the municipal government, the state administration and even the nobility. As always, business was smoothed by knowing the right person in the right place, and profitably placing a key person or family member ensured an ongoing institutional preference. Over time, the hermetic nature of the guilds was their undoing; such a closed shop could not survive a changing and expanding society. The pre-modern guild system lacked the flexibility to adapt to new ways of doing business, and eventually others simply went around them, or parallel to them, in creating new goods and artisanal services. These competing interests included the royal manufactories, with various centres of production in Madrid such as the Royal Tapestry Factory and the Royal Porcelain Factory, the latter located in the Retiro and responsible for exquisite creations, until destroyed in an act of malice by British forces in the early nineteenth century; a glassware factory in La Granja, a silverware factory and workshop. These factories produced goods for the international market as well as supplying the royal family and nobility. Elsewhere, the daily economy of Madrid carried on via family and small businesses, ambulant street vendors, markets and fairs, produce merchants and all the traditional crafts and trades.

The eastern edge of Madrid remained a place of airy green retreat from the thick atmosphere of the town; alongside Felipe IV's palace complex ran a broad avenue from Atocha to Cibeles, established as one of the vital social gathering places of the city, a place for strolling, meeting and seducing, for conversation and showing off from gleaming carriages. Now part of the *Paisaje de la Luz*, the world heritage-listed cultural landscape comprising the Paseo del Prado and its galleries, the Retiro Park and the Jerónimos quarter, it is at its most magnificent when closed off to traffic, and residents and tourists are free to wander the spectacular tree-lined avenue, as *madrileños* have done for centuries, rich now with some of most concentrated history of the city, stacked with palaces and galleries, monuments and fountains.

The Paseo del Prado was the first tree-lined boulevard in a major European city – a surprise for those who have painted Madrid as a dusty or concrete-ridden wasteland. The role of the Paseo del Prado as an emblematic component of Madrid's social and cultural landscape was central to the urban refurbishment of the city under Carlos. His legacy is a scattered galaxy of sites across central Madrid: from the fountains of Cibeles and Neptune to the accompanying Botanic Gardens, moved from the vicinity of El Pardo to its current and permanent site in 1781. Close by the Retiro Park was the Palace of Villahermosa (now the National Thyssen-Bornemisza Museum), the General Hospital (now the Reina Sofía Art Museum), the Puerta de Alcalá, one of the most beloved symbols of Madrid, the Astronomical Observatory in the gardens of the Retiro itself, and next to Cibeles the Palace of Buenavista, a military headquarters since the nineteenth century. In the Puerta del Sol, the Casa de Correos, perhaps the most famous building in Spain (for Spaniards, if not for foreigners) given its role in annual New Year's Eve celebrations; the permanent home given to the Academia de Bella Artes de San Fernando at the top of Calle de Alcalá in the Palace of Goyeneche; the Royal Customs House, also on Calle de Alcalá and now the Ministry of Treasury; and on Calle Fuencarral, the magnificent Hospice of San Fernando, now the Madrid municipal museum. Elsewhere around the edges of Madrid were the church of San Francisco el Grande, and the Palaces of Grimaldi and Duque de Liria. This suite of new buildings and fountains added heft to Madrid, a sense of neoclassical muscle to outdo the more ephemeral follies of the baroque, forming part of a tradition of 'imperial grandeur'[9] common to much of Madrid's governmental architecture.

The great majority of these projects were driven by two outstanding architects: the Italian Francesco Sabatini and the *madrileño* Ventura Rodríguez. They – and in turn Juan de Villanueva – took up the baton and carried on the great municipal tradition of Pedro de Ribera, bringing Madrid from the baroque into the neoclassical. The Sabatini Gardens, built on the western side of the Royal Palace over a former stables complex in the 1930s, are named in honour of the Sicilian architect who had come to Madrid at the behest of Carlos. The gardens, with their mazy hedges, sandy paths and pond reflecting the palace walls, overlooked by a selection of medieval kings and queens, embody the neoclassical elegance and simplicity that Sabatini so skilfully imparted to the palace. Together with the adjacent Campo del Moro, the gardens form one of the loveliest retreats from the noise of central Madrid.

The cramped city centre, while enjoying improvements in paving, lighting, sewerage and rubbish collection, did not change its fundamental topography. Madrid was, and remains, a city whose oldest streets recall the tight curves of the Islamic and the cluster of the medieval. Much as Carlos's new buildings and decorations might nowadays be central to Madrid both physically and conceptually, this rectilinear monumentalism was then on the edges of and external to the old city; such grand perspectives might belong in Versailles, St Petersburg or Aranjuez where space imposed no limits, but they were not a natural fit with Madrid's ancient zigzag of streets, its clustering of convents, markets and dwellings, all still constrained by the *cerca* of Felipe IV, now over 100 years old. Urban design assumed three principles: the straight line, the grand perspective and uniformity,[10] thus serving dual purposes: a clear statement of and hymn to absolutist power, and an opportunity for air to flow through the newly opened spaces. Power and hygiene ran hand in hand, in theory if not always in practice.

From the exquisite work of Pedro Teixeira in 1656, the age of science had moved on, by 1761, to the first geometric map of Madrid, produced on Carlos's orders by the French cartographer Nicolas Chalmandrier, followed in subsequent years by more detailed and precisely measured maps by Antonio Espinosa in 1769 and

Tomás López in 1785. In all of these maps the constraint to growth of the old walls was evident. The mathematical exactitude on display in gardens and parks – the Retiro to the east, the palace gardens to the west – would not be applied to street layout until the nineteenth century when more spacious, grid-like suburbs such as Salamanca, Chamberí and Argüelles began to take shape.

Carlos is faulted by some contemporary historians who see his building programmes as leaving Madrid with a showy display of power but no deep structural reforms; a friendly face cast towards the people that was a smiling justification of absolutism, a cementing of ancient hierarchies.[11] And yet, historical change was on the way, regardless of Carlos's actions. It would not come as quickly as some would like; for others, naturally enough, it would come too quickly. For both reformers and traditionalists, there would be a high price to pay.

Carlos was determined to control what he considered some of the more outlandish festival pursuits in Madrid. Seeing himself as the sophisticated king of Naples and Sicily, he believed he had a duty to *civilise* the unruly populace of his home town. Like all who leave their places of birth and return years later, his judgement was clouded by his experiences in another land; for all his Italian worldliness, he was liable to miscalculation. Six years into his reign, in 1765, in an attempt to separate the sacred religious and the theatrical profane, a range of religious dramas such as the *comedia de santos* or the *auto sacramental* were banned, as was gambling (poor Góngora would have been turning in his grave). Much of the local carnivalesque was in the cross-hairs of this enlightened puritanism: other bans applied to burning effigies of Judas and to the papier-mâché giants brought out on festive occasions. The banning of untuned instruments exemplified the demand for harmony over noise, for mathematics over chaos. Also banned were dancing in churches, cemeteries or before sacred images; processional flagellants and others tied to penitential crosses – this was not the way to treat flesh, and was redolent of fanaticism, and fanatics troubled leaders; bullfighting to the death (again, the flaying of the body, whether man or beast);

swearing and abuse was banned at Christmas; representations or performances of magic: in short, any activity that spoke to older, more visceral traditions, edged with paganism or a too excessive religiosity. Thus one aspect of Carlos's particular form of 'enlightenment' was a scourging of the popular forms of liturgy, of unbridled celebration. Masks were banned, as were fireworks and the throwing of eggs. Street theatre was to be closely monitored for moral and political content; any stage, or potential site of representation, was bound with more tightly enforced and extensively applied rules.

Amid all the order was disorder; much of this social ferment was leading up to riots in Madrid in 1766. That great political actor of the mid- to late eighteenth century – known conventionally at the time as 'the mob' – was claiming a role in politics. One of Carlos's enforcers of these new codes, Leopoldo de Gregorio, a Neapolitan statesman known to us as the Marquis of Esquilache, had alienated a cross-section of the nobility and the clergy with his rejection of any traditions he felt might be in the way of his reforms. Being a foreigner is often listed as one of the main charges against him, but his origin was not so much an issue as his being a despotic busybody who sought to interfere in cherished local customs. In a move that brought to mind Peter the Great's assault on the Russian beard, Esquilache decreed that the long Spanish cape was to be cut, and the broad-brimmed hat no longer allowed to cover the face; it was believed the cape permitted the concealment of weapons, and the broad-brimmed hat allowed criminals to disguise or hide their faces. In both Russian and Spanish instances, autocratic rulers were pursuing the beloved European project of standardisation, moving away from autochthonous modes to the modernising centre ground. Esquilache's decree was not well met in the capital, and combined with broader social discontent over rising bread prices, the fuse was lit. Nor did it help that municipal officers were out on the street fining those infringing the new dress codes, even removing their broad hats and cutting their capes to length in situ. Beyond these humiliating impositions was a more important question: it was all very well to be reforming people's daily practices, but what about the cost of bread?

On 23 March a crowd stormed towards the Royal Palace, not to overthrow the king – the riots were not anti-monarchical – but to petition for the deposition of the extravagant and arrogant Esquilache. Not placated, a crowd of hungry workers from various trades thronged to the home of Esquilache, the sixteenth-century mansion known as the *casa de las siete chimineas* – the House of Seven Chimneys – which still stands in the historic Plaza del Rey, just behind the Gran Vía. The house was ransacked and a servant killed; the riots continued for another two or three days before their principal demand, that Esquilache be dismissed, was granted. Not merely forced from his role, Esquilache fled Spain altogether, bemoaning the ungrateful citizens of Madrid: 'I cleaned up the city and paved its streets, I created boulevards and promoted public works. They ought to erect a statue in my honour rather than treat me in this undignified fashion,' he wrote just prior to boarding a ship for the return voyage to Naples. He embodied the vision of the enlightened despot: governing for the people, but without the people. His erstwhile patron was no different: Carlos is reported to have complained paternalistically of his subjects behaving like spoilt children.

Following the days of sound and fury, some forty deaths among soldiers and rioters, and vague promises from the king, the crowds settled back to their routines. The hunt for those responsible for the riots began with a commission of investigation headed by Campomanes. The uprising had been 'popular' to the extent it had drawn thousands onto the streets, but in the background there was a web of possible puppet masters among disgruntled nobility and clergy. Suspicion fell – once it had fallen, there was no turning back – on the Jesuits, in part due to their control of significant grain fields that supplied the city and surrounds with wheat, in part also as a result of the jealousy felt by the Enlightenment reformers towards the religious order that had such close control over the education – humanistic and religious – of large sectors of the nobility and their children.[12] The order had many enemies, and despite no evidence ever having been found to suggest the Jesuits were behind the riots, they were a convenient scapegoat for ministers such as Aranda and Campomanes who opposed them and resented their influence at the highest levels of power. Having previously been expelled from Portugal and France, the Society of Jesus was expelled from Spain in 1767; following a series of lightning raids on their institutions they were placed on ships at different ports around the country and sent into exile. Two generations later, after the collapse of Napoleon's regime, they would be back.

There remained, as always, the poor and the dead; both presented problems of different orders of magnitude. The riots against Esquilache had flared up in a context of enormous privation and hunger following years of drought and bad harvests, coupled with the decision to remove controls on the price of grain. Dating back to the Habsburg years, charitable associations had provided a form of social safety net as best they could. The charitable institutions served a double purpose: they provided sustenance and shelter to the poor, or the temporarily unemployed labourer or domestic servant and, just as importantly, they provided a platform for the wealthy to display their charity, which was intimately linked to piety. The poor served, then, in the remission of others' sins.[13] Their policing was necessary as both political and moral obligation: a wide array of hospitals, hospices, boarding houses, orphanages and asylums sought to cater to the multitudes of needy. One institution in the 1740s reported a death rate as high as 80 per cent of all those admitted to it, and these institutions were often desperately short of funds themselves.[14] The church and the state debated their respective responsibilities, and their regimes of punishment or reform, caught between the need for order and the moral requirement to provide charity and shelter. Any plan to clean beggars and the homeless from the streets usually proposed one of three destinations for them: the hospital, the asylum or the army. The impoverished, however, will remain a feature of Madrid's streets: in the late nineteenth century, a beggars' collective is superbly drawn in Galdós's *Misericordia*; in the twentieth century, the years during and beyond the civil war were marked by a high degree of destitution as the city, broken to pieces, then swamped with internal migrants, struggled to house, feed and find employment for its population.

Meanwhile, the dead were everywhere. In a city still medieval in much of its urban design, and with a high mortality rate, burials were a constant problem. With the first extramural cemetery of San Isidro not established until 1811, Madrid was running out of space to house its dead. A royal decree of 1787 demanded bodies be buried outside the city walls, given both a lack of space and an increasing awareness of hygiene and public health. It took another generation before the dead were finally placed outside the city, as there was some resistance to the idea of no longer burying bodies inside the church: customs relating to funerary practices do not lend themselves to easy amendment.

Given the long-established connection between the general cemetery – an anonymous dumping ground – and the poor of society, which member of the nobility or the wealthy classes would consent to such a common resting place? As hierarchies existed both in heaven and on earth, so they ordered life and death. Where one was buried was critical: the more hallowed the ground, the better the chances of a smooth passage to heaven, or at least a shorter stay in purgatory. Churches understood they could increase their funding by using the prospect of purgatory as a type of spiritual tax that needed paying prior to entry into heaven; a tax paid in cash and worldly goods in return for guarantees of a swifter passage to eternal bliss.

The corpses of those designated as deserving were buried inside churches, the closer to the main altar the better, a privilege largely reserved for the noble classes, the priesthood, the wealthy and the highly devout; a common labourer such as San Isidro was the exception that confirmed the rule for those of his class. Adjacent to the main altar was said to be where saints ushering folk to heaven had better access to cadavers, a curious belief that established a limitation on the physical reach of supernatural beings. The highway to heaven was facilitated by the intercession of prayers, a type of 'solidarity between the living and the dead'.[15] There was also – it might seem obvious – a relation between the speed of the passage to heaven and the size of a monetary donation to the church.[16] Space under church floors was limited; two centuries of devout Habsburgs had given Madrid plenty of churches, but they were mostly small, and in a crowded city, even allowing that burial under consecrated flooring was reserved, demand outgrew supply. One workaround for this problem was that bodies would be left a specific time (enough, perhaps, for the tax to be acknowledged and passage to heaven assured) and then the flagstones were lifted up, graves emptied out and reused. Burial spaces were in a constant process of recycling.

The capacity for shortcuts and picaresque malpractice is obvious. To hasten the decomposition of the bodies, quicklime was used as a dissolvent. To save time or money, not enough quicklime might be used, or the grave not dug deeply enough, or the sepulchral stone not be properly sealed over the remains of the dead. Or simply, bodies were disinterred before time, as if the newly dead were impatient, clamouring to make the passage through the dark chamber of burial and into the pearly light of paradise. Thus arose an extraordinary problem of public health in the city: the 'cadaverous stench' of half-decomposed bodies filling churches with the reek of hell. As graves were opened up to exhume bodies, as if forcing a guest to vacate a hotel room in order to accommodate the next client, the air became rank with poisonous vapours; churches became unusable for a period of time, and the narrow streets around them equally uninhabitable.[17] Churches were generally not well ventilated, and the smell of rotting cadavers mixing with burning candle wax and the humidity of damp stone created an environment perfect for the transmission of any disease, or propagation of any plague. Fainting in church was common, and if a priest might look around and wonder where his flock had disappeared to, the explanation was usually in the toxic air of the church itself.[18] What is unclear is how the priests managed to work under such pestilential conditions.

For some churches in the heart of Madrid, such as the historic and beautiful San Ginés, overcrowding was a constant problem: the interior of the church had only 110 allocated spaces for burials. This led to an occasional wholesale 'clearing out' of the graves, regardless of how long they had been occupied. Inevitably, the fully desiccated emerged along with the half-decomposed; all were piled together 'large and small, red bloods and blue bloods' in a 'repugnant mixture' and taken to common ground below the Puerta de Toledo.[19] Logically, it was in this direction, south across the river, that the cemetery of San Isidro was planned and opened in 1811. Meanwhile, no opportunity for profit-taking might be wasted: accounts from the 1770s and 1780s reveal how, during the emptying of graves, coffins were often found to be in good condition; less scrupulous gravediggers saw the chance to profit from their resale. A black market in used coffins grew up, strongly opposed by the carpenters' guild, for whom the recycling of wooden coffins was a threat to the strength and security of their business.[20]

Not all bodies were buried inside churches; this was simply a preference for those who could afford such a luxury. Yet even outside the small, consecrated churchyards might at times overflow. The cemetery of San Martín was the resting place for a high number of the poor, and in the nearby Buena Dicha cemetery – Our Lady of Good Fortune – 'the neighbours complained of the excessively turned earth, and the high number of cadavers there, being more than could reasonably fit, being then an extra trench opened up and the bodies covered with only the thinnest layer of earth, such that a repugnant smell, a fetid air emanated from the earth, causing health problems for those who lived in the vicinity.'[21]

Madrid's two great cemeteries – San Isidro and La Almudena – are now an intimate part of the city's cultural heritage. Other sites of singular importance include the cemetery of La Florida where those executed by lamplight on the morning of 3 May 1808, commemorated in Goya's famous painting, are laid to rest. Elsewhere, Madrid's cemeteries are a roll call of the famous and infamous who have lived and died in the city over the past 200 years. Aside from the dictators buried at different locations around Madrid – Ante Pavelić, Fulgencio Batista, Rafael Trujillo and, of course, Francisco Franco – the cemeteries, highly recommended in tour guides, are a cornucopia of film stars, artists, entertainers, scientists, poets, novelists, playwrights and bullfighters. No fewer than 5 million people lie, or have lain, under the earth in Our Lady of Almudena, Europe's largest cemetery.

Carlos died in 1788, on the cusp of the French Revolution, leaving behind a much-enhanced Madrid, for the city was embracing a confidence and awareness of itself as a European capital with one eye on an incipient modernity, part of a larger network of cities looking to the future by grasping, knowing and administering the natural world.

We find this enquiring mind in the breathtaking still lifes – *bodegones* – of painter Luis Meléndez. While Carlos's court had been dominated by the great Italian masters, Tiepolo and Giaquinto, and the Bohemian Mengs, some of the finest works of the period came from the brush of Meléndez. Born in Naples of Spanish parents, he was brought back to Spain when only one year old and grew up in Madrid, training under the French master Louis-Michel van Loo, painter at the court of Felipe V. When his father, also a painter, had a falling out with the director of the recently established Academy of Fine Arts, both father and son were expelled from the school. Meléndez went back to Italy for five years, among other clients producing work for the king of Naples, Carlos, who a decade later would become king of Spain.

Settled back in Madrid, many of the still lifes for which he is famous were painted on the order of the Prince of Asturias, the future Carlos IV 'the Hunter', to grace the royal natural history collection, established in 1771. The collection was more a cabinet of curiosities than a museum, though in time it would contribute to the collections of many nineteenth-century institutions, including the Naval Museum, the Prado Museum and the National Archaeological Museum. The Spanish Enlightenment was at its height, and Meléndez approached his commission to paint forty-four still lifes with the exacting eye of a botanist, and the hand of a Zurbarán or a Sánchez Cotán. His works show both austerity and abundant beauty; there is a will to scientific reproduction beside an abandonment to colour. The fruits of the earth and the world – a watermelon, a cut of salmon, a jug of drinking chocolate, a lemon, a brass dish, a silver fork, a gnarly lump of bread, a glass, a floral cup, a wooden table – are rendered with a pure architectural and compositional force: that combination of exactitude and love that characterised the finest nature artists of the time.[22] Luis Meléndez died, ignored and in absolute poverty, in 1780.

One of the last acts of Carlos's life was to commission a scientific journey around the entire Spanish empire, taking account of its vast complexity and variety, measuring the winds and tides and river mouths, classifying all the coloured birds and insects from the Philippines to Mexico to Tierra del Fuego; collecting flowers and seeds, recording the depths of ocean straits; recording fauna, trees and mineral wealth. Led by navigator Alessandro Malaspina, the highly successful five-year voyage would have a tragic postscript when the expedition returned to Madrid in 1794. Malaspina fell victim to a series of court intrigues; he was accused of plotting the overthrow of Carlos IV's new favourite, Manuel Godoy. He was jailed, then exiled; the extraordinary scientific record of the expedition was spitefully locked away for decades. What behaviour will not be swayed by vanity? Malaspina had allowed the sweet perfume of conspiracy to persuade his thinking, and got it into his head that he might oust Godoy from both his prominent positions – as secretary of state and prime minister, and as the queen's lover. He was enormously naive, for Malaspina was at home behind the capstan, charting stars and foreign coasts. Having dominated the lonely oceans of the planet, he was suckered into thinking he could navigate the clotted schemes of the royal court. Amid whispers, knives and webs of treachery, his sea legs were found wanting; he tottered and was caught out by the all-seeing, all-knowing Godoy.

Over the years, countless sailors had made their way back to Spain, travelling from Cádiz or Seville up to Madrid to seek the favours of the king, for they knew there were treasures in the antipodes: half-blinded with the light of the Pacific, half-mad with unimaginable distances working a curse on their leathery souls, they had mostly been unsuccessful in their search for funding. They begged, they wrote pleading letters, they muttered of strange new lands, but to no avail. Malaspina returned triumphant and completely compos mentis, yet nothing he had experienced on the vast oceans of the world prevented him from being dragged under by the machinations of the court at Madrid.

Carlos's death allowed the ascension to the throne of his somewhat hapless son, Carlos IV, whose reign began overshadowed by the spectre of the French Revolution. Madrid continued with a programme of urban reforms, but the confidence of Carlos III's reign was shaken by a nervous sovereign; the city limped, rather than strode, into the nineteenth century. For such a quintessentially Spanish city, the eighteenth century had seen Madrid assume a significant French and Italian cultural bedrock. In the first decades of the nineteenth, the French influence – or interference – would be even more direct, in the figure of Napoleon. His attempt to take Madrid and seize the Spanish throne would prove a short-term disaster for the people of Madrid and their cultural heritage, yet a disaster from which they would in the longer term emerge triumphant, and with a series of mythologies that continue today to define Madrid as a city of a defiantly independent character.

The winter of despair

Francisco Goya's portrait of statesman Gaspar Melchor de Jovellanos is one of the finest representations of dignity in resignation and exhaustion committed to canvas.[1] This saddened Enlightenment figure, wearied by work and lost opportunity, scorned finally by the conservative elite of his own society, allegorises the wasted life of a wasted man. Everything, he seems to be sighing, has been for nothing. It is one of the most fully dimensioned of Goya's portraits; Jovellanos emerges from deep within the canvas, wearing a shimmering lilac coat and black velvet breeches, head propped on his hand. One of the clearest thinkers of the Spanish Enlightenment, a champion against vested and reactionary interests in trade and the economy, a brilliant and versatile writer, Godoy would soon have him arrested and imprisoned. Painted in Aranjuez amid the conflict over his too radical plans for agrarian reform, Jovellanos assumes a pose of beautiful melancholy; at the age of 54, many of the final years of his life would be spent in prison, with a brief flickering of the light before dying of pneumonia. Albeit he was able to survive in more comfort than the average prisoner, his health would never recover from the years in confinement.

Jovellanos was only one of the reformers from the reign of Carlos III who were lost to the country as darker clouds gathered north of the Pyrenees. The counts of Floridablanca and, eventually, Aranda, were also cast aside as the brash new royal favourite, Manuel

Godoy, made his way into the royal chambers. There had barely been time for some reforms to be put into place – taxes and bread prices – before the European sky grew sombre for members of the *antiguo regimen*. Everything that had seemed solid, or at least hopeful – institutional reform, international trade, the continuing programme of public works – was under threat from twin dangers. In the first instance, the ideas of the Enlightenment and the French Revolution, which promoted only 'insolence in deeds, words and writings against legitimate powers'[2] and which, putting deeds into practice, meant Carlos IV observed from afar the beheading of his cousin Louis XVI in the French capital. In the second instance – if the first did not make Carlos skittish enough – his unspectacular reign would be overrun by an expansionist French army, a treacherous son, a conniving royal favourite and the humiliating concession of his rights to the throne to Joseph, the brother of Napoleon.

For the citizens of Madrid, the new era had begun with a terrible fire that raced through the western side of the Plaza Mayor in 1790. Starting among the bolts of a fabric retailer, the fire took off through the wooden beams of the plaza, jumping from house to house, from retailer to retailer, burning for nine days before being finally extinguished. So fierce was the blaze it burnt through to houses on the Cava de San Miguel and the nearby church of San Miguel de los Octoes. Dating from the early thirteenth century, the church could not withstand the damage and was knocked down in the following years, opening up space for the Plaza de San Miguel and eventually a market of the same name, converted in the twenty-first century into one of Madrid's most popular gourmet destinations. Neoclassical architect Juan de Villanueva, after Ventura Rodríguez and Francesco Sabatini Madrid's next great urban designer, took charge of the rebuild of the Plaza Mayor; it is to his vision that we owe the current plaza, with its uniform three-storey height and closed corners, its mathematical charm. This redesign created two of the most famous entrances to the plaza: the Portal de Cofreros, which opens on to Calle Toledo, and the Arco de Cuchilleros, famous for its hefty postcard beauty and for its intimate connection with the heroine of Galdós's classic *Fortunata y Jacinta*.

Madrid entered the nineteenth century with close to 200,000 residents, the beginnings of a proper sewerage system, a growing suite of national scientific and cultural institutions, and a strongly developing sense of itself not merely as a court, but as a home. Always a town of immigrants, there was nevertheless a distinct culture and folklore of Madrid that had been building through the seventeenth and eighteenth centuries. The city was not only a destination but a point of origin, of cultural rootedness. The opening decades of the nineteenth century would see the development of a specifically Madrid identity that was distinct, while still enveloped within a broader Spanish identity.

The French occupation of Madrid in 1808 played a foundational role in this new sense of self. The raffish young secretary of state Godoy, who had enjoyed an astonishing ascension at the court and into queen María Luisa's bedchamber, had set his mind on a Spanish takeover of Portugal, reviving memories of Felipe II some 200 years earlier. The apparent excuse for such a move was Portugal's refusal to stop trading with the British, who had recently inflicted a serious defeat on the French and Spanish fleets off the Cape of Trafalgar. This was not to be just any takeover: in Godoy's feverish and arrogant plans, Portugal was to be divided into three, with one part Spanish, one part French and a third part for the exclusive reign of Godoy, who imagined himself a flamboyant King of the Algarve. From such fantasies are born the worst of historical errors, and Godoy fatally underestimated Napoleon. Having signed into being this fantastical notion of a tripartite Portugal via the secret Treaty of Fontainebleau in 1807, Napoleonic troops proceeded to enter Spain, supposedly en route to Portugal. They did go on to take Lisbon but, with a wobbly king on the throne, Napoleon could see the whole prize of Spain before him; there was no reason why he should not topple the Bourbon regime and include Spain as part of his broader conquests. Having fled to France, Carlos abdicated in favour of his son Ferdinand, an arch-enemy of Godoy who was alleged – with some justice – to have sold out Spain to the French. At Napoleon's insistence, Carlos retracted his abdication and instead passed the throne to Napoleon, who promptly placed it in the hands of his eldest brother, Joseph. In hindsight, none of the actors involved in this ridiculous drama were remotely suited to running a country.

The reputation and behaviour of occupying armies is rarely good. As new columns of French troops descended on Madrid from the north, they were attacked and harassed again and again: the impending war would introduce the word and concept of the *guerrilla* into the English language. Marshal Joachim Murat arrived in Madrid in late March, with the rumour that Napoleon was soon to arrive. As the days passed, he failed to materialise, and it was obvious the *madrileños* wanted no part of the underhanded machinations that had led to this occupation. The French troops, initially met with bemusement, soon faced open hostility. Apart from anything else, they represented a pressure on food supplies for the capital, and these were not times of abundance. Affrays and scuffles were commonplace, and increasingly led to deaths in knife fights, gun fights, ambushes and tavern brawls. It was to no avail that in early April the municipal government of Madrid called for peace between the parties, claiming the French troops would soon be gone.[3] Rumours spread of a major uprising planned for the Thursday before Easter; in the event, like Napoleon himself, it did not materialise, but matters were moving in only one direction. Napoleon was implacable, believing fear was the only means by which to earn the love of the mob and thence the nation;[4] one of his aides-de-camp, general Auguste-Julien Bigarré, had threatened that should the people not submit, he would 'set fire to all four corners of [Madrid] and put to the sword everybody found within it'.[5] If Godoy had underestimated Napoleon in his feverish plan to subdivide Portugal, Napoleon likewise underestimated the people of Spain. And he seriously underestimated the people of Madrid.

The uprising eventually took place on 2 May, triggered by the fear the last member of the royal family, the 14-year-old Francisco de Paula, was being removed from Madrid and that the city would be left in the hands of Murat and his troops; this was the last straw for an angry populace. Crowds streaming to the Royal Palace were fired upon by French artillery. While the Spanish army had orders to remain neutral, the people of Madrid were not so sanguine, or cowardly. The revolt that followed, the bloody street fighting, the repression and subsequent executions are all the more deeply etched into the legend of Madrid for having been graphically captured by Goya. Around many of the classic sites of the old city centre – the Royal Palace, the Plaza Mayor, the Puerta del Sol, the Puerta de Toledo and the Monteleón artillery depot, later redesigned as the Plaza del Dos de Mayo – the people of Madrid launched themselves upon the French with anything to hand. Men and women fought together, furious and insulted by the affrontery of the enemy; there were acts of extraordinary bravery and extraordinary brutality; this was hand-to-hand combat in tight, closed street environments, exacerbated by the use of guns and cannons. There was terrible carnage at a time of primitive medical aid; the wounded were bandaged with strips of old sheets or clothing, or went untended. Between 400–500 citizens died on that day and subsequently, as all those who had been caught carrying arms were sentenced to death by firing squad. Many injured in the fighting refused to seek treatment for fear of exposing themselves as participants, thus risking a death sentence.[6]

The most famous victim of the violence on 2 May was the young seamstress Manuela Malasaña, a 17-year-old working-class woman from Maravillas – since renamed Malasaña, one of Madrid's most famous inner-city districts – who has come to symbolise the local resistance to the French troops. Here was an entirely new and secular heroine in the national pantheon: young, female and working-class, Manuela Malasaña did not carry the imprimatur of royalty, such as Isabel the Catholic or Catherine of Aragon, nor the weight of tragedy so favoured by the Romantics in their obsession with 'mad' Juana of Castile, nor even the mysticism and piety of Ana de Jesús or Teresa of Ávila. While the exact manner of her death is in dispute – one popular account has her being executed on the spot having been found carrying her work scissors, which were treated as a concealed weapon – she certainly fell in active confrontation with the enemy. The site of Malasaña's original home, just off the Plaza del Dos de Mayo in Calle de San Andrés, carries the typical golden memorial plaque used by the town council of Madrid to celebrate singular sites, but the building itself is — like so many others — marred at street level by meaningless graffiti tags and cheap advertising stickers. It is perfectly possible to walk past such a historic site without even noticing.

In the Plaza del Dos de Mayo stands a monument to Luis Daoiz and Pedro Velarde, the two artillerymen who led the fighting. Daoiz was bayonetted to death, Velarde shot; one of Joaquín Sorolla's historical paintings depicts the scene as Velarde died, amid the heat, confusion, gun smoke, dead bodies, broken equipment and exhaustion of the day.[7] An altogether different image, one of the most famous photographs representing the new liberty Madrid enjoyed after the end of the Franco regime, was taken during the local *barrio* festivities of 1976, when two young anarchists climbed stark naked and stood, with everything hanging free, one on top of Daoiz, the other on top of Velarde, as a crowd cheered them on.[8] One suspects the artillerymen would not have minded at all. The jubilant anarchist performance was typical of the defiance and celebration of the time, in one of Madrid's most intense areas of nightlife. It remains one of those images that is immediately recognisable as part of the city's history, and while it quickly dated, it nevertheless recalls with precision a celebratory moment in the capital, the stirrings of what soon become the legendary – and like all legends, somewhat over-hyped – *movida madrileña* of the late 1970s and early 1980s.

Meanwhile, back in May 1808, those rebels executed by lamplight at Príncipe Pío were immortalised by Goya in their terrified final moments.[9] Even greater numbers were put in front of firing squads around the Prado and Retiro districts and other sites scattered throughout the capital. It was an eerie look forward to another time of 'organised' street executions that would arrive in 1936.

On 3 May Madrid was a city in silence, its streets empty and shops closed, cadavers being cleared away. It must have stunk of gunpowder, burnt buildings, dead animals, blood. On the following days, to simulate some kind of normality, Murat demanded the theatres be opened; they were, but no public came.[10] The people of Madrid had been momentarily paralysed, but when they recovered their senses, it was not in submission, but in order to resist with even greater determination. The national capital was the centre of a broader revolt that spread quickly, starting in the nearby town of Mostoles and thence out to all corners of Spain. The insurrection of Madrid had been brutally put down, but the Spanish War of Independence, which would last until 1814, was just getting under way.

Those in Madrid who favoured abandoning Habsburg and Bourbon absolutism in favour of the ideas of the French Enlightenment faced a serious quandary. After all, just how modern and liberal was an occupying army? The city of Madrid knew from first-hand experience what others felt in their bones: the Enlightenment was fine in theory, but left a lot to be desired in practice. Again, the eternally vexed question of Spain's relationship to France, and of the country's political and cultural elite with their northern neighbour. For the *afrancesados* – a term used disparagingly of those who looked admiringly to French cultural ideas and political thinking – Napoleon was the worst that could happen. The ideals they wished to promote were being betrayed by the very source of those ideals; how might they champion a society and culture that produced such monsters?

The broad outline of the debate was simple: the *afrancesados* could claim they were in favour of liberty and progress, and of bringing an end to the dark absolutism of church and monarchy, while the traditionalists could claim they stood in patriotic duty by their national leaders against a foreign invader who had burnt towns, killed innocent civilians and was seeking nothing less than to overthrow the entire system of government. For traditionalists, Bourbon absolutism imposed through royal birthright was preferable to Napoleonic absolutism imposed at the end of a gun; if Spain was to change, it would do so in its own way, and without instruction or obligation from the French. Here are the seeds of the twentieth-century charge levelled against Spain of being somehow outside the mainstream of liberal progress in Europe during the nineteenth century; further, for some observers, this chaotic period of history contributed to the creation of a hardy stereotype: 'Spaniards as excessive in their passions and lacking in the sort of rational control required of civilized nations, opening the door, from the 1820s, to Orientalist constructions of Spain.'[11] Thus, the Napoleonic invasion was disastrous for Spain and Madrid in multiple ways: it led to completely unwarranted death and destruction in human lives, property and priceless cultural heritage; it fortified the most reactionary forces within society, as the French excesses gave their opponents' illiberalism an added veneer of legitimacy; and it allowed the British and French to deal with Spain contemptuously, as they had not been able to do in previous centuries. Pale echoes of this winter of despair can still be heard in the subterranean chambers of the nation.

Joseph Bonaparte ruled as King José I from 1808 to 1813. Like Carlos III fifty years earlier, he had been serving as king of Naples and only came reluctantly to Madrid. As an imposed French king who represented the forces that had invaded the country, he was barely welcomed, as per the traditional ceremonies by which the people of Madrid greeted the entrance into the city of their new monarchs. When he arrived in July of 1808, there were fireworks, orchestras and bullfights as protocol, but many of the local nobles and grandees absented themselves from the receptions and welcoming committees.[12] He had barely sat on the throne before he was forced to leave Madrid again due to the exigencies of war and the trouncing of the French at the Battle of Bailén in Andalusia; while he was gone, the people of Madrid rebuilt the barricades. After a further six months of war, during which Napoleon himself finally reached Madrid, spending two weeks camped on the outskirts of the city at Chamartín de la Rosa, from where he directed an artillery bombardment of the capital, José Bonaparte was finally able to secure a certain resigned submission and promise of loyalty from the people of Madrid after resistance in the Retiro and at key gates to the city such as Alcalá, Atocha, Recoletos, Fuencarral or Conde Duque had been crushed.[13] He entered the city with greater fanfare in January 1809, and this time the streets were decked with lights and colours, purpose-built arches, music and dancing. Much of Madrid was in ruins – the palace of the Buen Retiro that had so delighted Felipe IV 200 years earlier was largely destroyed and all the trees of the royal park had been cut down for firewood – yet somehow Madrid put on its finest, and got ready for the party.

José I had an enormous impact on the shape and feel of Madrid in just five years. His model was Paris – that persistent obsession of enlightened Madrid. He earned the epithet of 'king of the plazas' for his determination to open up the cramped spaces within the city walls, creating more and larger public squares. Writing in 1868, liberal politician and journalist Ángel Fernández de los Ríos claimed that José Bonaparte had made the first serious attempt to 'dignify' the Spanish capital. Never mind the insult this supposes to Carlos III and his brilliant neoclassical Spanish and Italian architects; like many progressive Spaniards of the nineteenth century, Fernández de los Ríos was a committed Francophile; he wrote of Bonaparte's move from 'the splendid court of Paris to the misery of Madrid'.[14] Apart from the obvious bias of the comment, he has elided all mention of the fact that Madrid's ruinous state was a result of French military invasion.

José and his planners went at Madrid, widening streets, planting trees and knocking down many old churches, sometimes for reasons of public safety, other times to open up plazas, and other times no doubt out of simple bloody-mindedness: if a religious building stood in the way of some grander Parisian vision, it had to go. In some instances, whole blocks of houses were cleared. It is true the 'king of the plazas' created a number of Madrid's favourites, such as the Plaza de Santa Ana or San Miguel, and he laid the plans, without staying long enough to see the execution, of the splendid Plaza de Oriente, opening up the eastern face of the Royal Palace, providing it with the grand approach it enjoys today and lining the plaza with statues of Spanish royals. It is equally true his desire to 'open up' the city meant Madrid's medieval and baroque religious architecture suffered heavily, and often unnecessarily; a long list of churches were destroyed in the years between 1809 and 1814, including the razing of the twelfth-century church of San Juan Bautista by which the bodies of Velázquez and his wife Juana Pacheco were lost. Elsewhere, cemeteries were moved outside the city walls, reforms were put in place for the tax system, and feudal and provincial customs – especially those beloved around the periphery of the nation – were eliminated in favour of a strongly centralised state along Napoleonic lines. As always, progressive French governance ran parallel to some interest groups in Spain and Madrid, and perpendicular to others.

Bonaparte's entire rule was provisional: constantly subject to satirical abuse through popular verse and song, he never won over the people, nor did he ever fully control the country. The war dragged on, and after the British under Wellington had been victorious at the Battle of Vitoria in northern Spain in 1813, he abdicated from a throne he had never wanted in the first place. Spain had been something of a nightmare, albeit he had made progress in Madrid, notably with the abolition of the Inquisition. This might sound an epochal achievement, but it was no more than easy pickings: the Inquisition had for many years been barely relevant.

The French withdrawal in defeat after Vitoria saw a desperate scrambling of troops northwards, taking with them whatever they could carry: cart after cart of looted goods. Mules were loaded down with priceless art, tapestries, icons, gold and silverware, ceramics and jewellery. In the roiling aftermath of war, wrote Laura Cumming, 'works by Velázquez turned up on battlefields or in soldiers' baggage, like a hoard of bright treasures suddenly emerging out of ploughed soil'.[15] Spain was pillaged disgracefully. European nations – some more than others – had developed an expertise in the art of global plunder, and they showed no compunction in practising that sordid theft upon each other's art collections, state and private, sacred and profane.

As a final indignity, Napoleon ordered a selection of the finest works of Spanish art shipped to Paris to be displayed as a symbol of the friendship between the two nations. Some friendship; this was a not-so-carefully disguised looting of art heritage. The British blew up the Royal Porcelain Factory in the Retiro, a spiteful act of industrial sabotage, yet were otherwise slightly less avaricious than the French, perhaps because Catholic art did not have the same appeal to them. Wellington, some years later, offered to return a number of the Spanish masterpieces that had come into his hands. The new king Fernando VII, in all his vanity, arrogance and ignorance, showed no interest in recovering the items.

Even the deepest winter has its moments of brightness; not all is dark skies and shivering limbs. Carlos IV had made one good decision, influenced or not by those around him: the appointment of Francisco Goya as painter to the court. He would undoubtedly have triumphed elsewhere in any capacity, but in the late eighteenth century royal patronage was still vital. It provided career stability for Goya, and saved Carlos and his family from disappearing from history altogether.

Madrid between 1775 and 1825 remains so alive for us today partly thanks to the voluminous and extraordinary work of Goya as witness. He was the last great painter before the invention of photography changed the representation of the world forever. Indeed, if we admit the first photograph as dated to 1826 or 1827 and place this beside the death of Goya in 1828, it is appropriate perhaps that the great documenter of life, of beauty and savagery, of manners, of vanity and cruelty, of hope, joy and deepest sadness, overlapped the birth of modern imagery, as if passing on a baton to the new alchemy that was to burst upon the world. Modern imagery begins not with photography, influential as it has been in changing entirely the perspective of the world, but with Francisco Goya. Of all the superb nineteenth-century painters across the globe, none had his range or urgent sense of witness.

Goya is a fulcrum around which western art turns; and despite his Aragonese origins, he is a thoroughly Madrid painter. His cartoons for the Royal Tapestry Factory that document social customs in and around the capital are saturated with the city's clear, beautiful light, and with the optimism of the time: wonderfully elegant people pose wonderfully. His work on war, murder, possession, madness, banditry and the breakdown of reason depicts the hellish conditions into which the city and its residents could also be plunged. His is a body of work that tracks the consequences and direct human impact of decisions made in the capital, or of the murderous attempts made on Madrid by a foreign invader. Despite living through a period of political turbulence, Goya worked constantly, as he was compelled to do: he painted, drew, etched, engraved. His colossal body of work continually branched into new fields. By the time he was preparing his *Disasters of War*, coinciding with the French invasion, it was half a lifetime since he had received guidance from two very different but equally exceptional painters at the Madrid court: Giovanni Battista Tiepolo and Anton Raphael Mengs.

Goya had left the exuberance of the rococo Tiepolo and the grammatical accuracy of the neoclassical Mengs behind; he absorbed their knowledge and moved beyond both. His emotional range was unlike that of any other artist: the lovely scenes for the royal tapestries gave way to the commissioned portraits of Carlos IV and the royal family; high-ranking persons such as Godoy, Jovellanos or Floridablanca, the Duke and Duchess of Alba; the naked *maja*; then on to the satire of the *Caprichos*, a vast range of works dealing with every possible aspect of Spanish life, from the most profane to the sacred; and on to the *Disasters of War* and the late black paintings from the Quinta del Sordo, the property across the river from central Madrid where Goya lived briefly towards the end of his life before going into exile. In his war etchings and across the surface of his darker works, Goya announced the coming century and held the horrors it would contain up to close inspection. Emerging from absolutism, the newly modern citizen would walk straight into alternative forms of tyranny, while practising the arts of cruelty upon enemies and the innocent alike. The first war reporter, Goya's work described and denounced the extent of destruction without purpose, of killing without reason. There was only so much the mortal frame could bear.

In the twentieth century, Goya was adopted as the war artist *por excelencia*: the precursor to Picasso's *Guernica* or any of the famous photojournalists who captured the explicit horror of a century of warfare across the globe. Goya had seen it, and rendered it, first. Indeed, given the brutally visceral nature of nineteenth-century war, with its shattered limbs and garrotted necks, its disembowelled soldiers and civilians hanging from trees, its lack of basic medicine or any anaesthetic, its filth, its stench, its harrowing unravelling of the body, Goya was a messenger of the most direct and startling kind, speaking to the modern world where medicine and rituals protect us from the dead, while at the same time killing becomes more efficient than ever.

Goya outshone his contemporaries, some of whom were outstanding artists, such as the two Valencians, Vicente López – author of the finest portrait of the artist[16] – and Mariano Salvador Maella, who painted at the court with Goya. Was it merely his range and originality that allowed him to stand out from his contemporaries? Art historian and critic Francisco Calvo Serraller suggested there was more to it, that the significance of Goya within the context of nineteenth-century European thought and taste was linked to a romanticised view of Spanish eccentricity. There was nothing specifically 'exotic' about a contemporary such as Vicente López. He was a brilliant painter, but in that respect like many others; his content did not bear the untamed strangeness with which many of Goya's canvases overflowed, and which so appealed to the Romantics in their 'discovery' of Spain. Goya was valued not so much for his astonishing pictorial skill, nor because he embodied certain notions of 'Spanish painting', but because his work seemed to express a kind of unsophisticated rawness that fitted with Romantic notions of Spain as a throwback, a rarity, a nation that was not yet ready for the dawning of the modern era that was fully upon Europe by the middle of the industrial – and industrious – nineteenth century.[17] All those images of war, bloodshed, witchcraft, dismemberment, madness: there was something atavistic there, a deep ancestral aggression. One went to Goya as if to view a new species at the zoo; in short, there was a hint of condescension, not so much towards Goya as towards the Spanish nation and its people, in the way the deaf and grumpy Aragonese was adopted by modernism and its aesthetic and intellectual interests.

This fascinating proposition can be observed elsewhere. Hughes's study of Goya, with its superb and nuanced appreciation of Goya's art and its context, nevertheless veers at times into a sneering condescension towards Madrid, as if Goya existed despite rather than because of the city in which he worked. Yet geniuses do not spring up separate from their native soils, and Goya was very much the product of late eighteenth- and early nineteenth-century Madrid, with all its flaws and triumphs, oddities and injustices. Hughes's unwritten notion is that Goya was too good for the Madrid that helped create him. While it is true Goya transcends the city where he worked, as he would have any other, it was precisely the social and political context of the city, first with the balmy pleasures of Carlos III's reign and the lazy family of Carlos IV, the characters at court, the reformers and inquisitors, the saints and beauties and madams and crones and executioners, the brigands and brawlers and picnickers, all followed by the tragedies of war and occupation, that provided the source material for his colossal body of work. For a prickly critic like Hughes, Madrid lacked the benchmarks of modernity to be found in London, Paris, New York or – the subject of another of Hughes's books – Barcelona. This is a recurring theme of the last 200 years, an attitude common among foreign writers on Madrid but equally often expressed by local writers and thinkers. In the case of Goya, it is true that for the general international public the darker and stranger works hold the greatest appeal. This is partly a reflection of contemporary tastes that preference the radical and destructive: Goya as witness to domestic pleasures is a less attractive proposition. It is foolish, however, to believe the late black works hold some essential truth about Spain that is more profound than the truth contained in his light and airy scenes of semi-rural domesticity. It is the latter images, less well-known, less reproduced and less popular, that provide a more faithful representation of the nation and its people – optimistic, celebratory, sharing company – than the dark outliers of his work.

In May 1808 the 'common people' of Madrid, rather than the political class, nobility or royalty, had risen up and led the country by example.[18] Yet coming out of the invasion would not be easy. Years of war meant fields went untended and food supplies, often consumed by invading forces, dwindled to nothing. In the last months of 1811 and the first half of 1812, Madrid was devastated by famine. People from all social classes were reduced to begging; bodies lay in the streets, the exhausted unable to move. It is estimated some 20,000 people died of hunger and associated infectious diseases. Any animal – cats, rats, dogs or donkeys – were food, as were roots, flowers, vegetable scraps or anything people thought might alleviate their maddening hunger. Mesonero recounts the day his father, taking note of families in crisis to organise some charitable assistance, no matter how paltry, observed a family of eight in dire need. Returning the next day to offer help, he found only one of the eight still alive. The parishes sent out carts twice daily to collect the dead from the streets; sometimes, only a faint groan offered any indication a bunch of rags was a living person. Like so much else that happened in the city, Goya was witness to this side effect of war: his etching *They do not arrive in time*,[19] from the *Disasters of War* series, is typical in its scenes of abject human collapse. Conditions eased only when Wellington, with assorted Spanish troops and guerrilla fighters, entered Madrid in August 1812, freeing up supply lines and enabling food once more to enter the city, increasing availability and reducing the cost of bread.

The reversion to the petty absolutism of Fernando VII 'the Felon' after 1814, and the rejection of the revolutionary constitution drafted in Cádiz in 1812,[20] suggested a backwards step for the nation. It was certainly an attempt to seek security in the known – embodied in the monarchy and, above all, the Catholic Church – in the face of the uncertainties of a modernising programme driven by liberal thinkers and secular politicians. The latter were tainted by association with models of society and governance based on France, the longed-for dream of Spanish reformers, rejected by both illiberal conservatives and the national peripheries who loathed its centralising tendencies. Fernando was notoriously opposed to constitutional change; under his rule, Spain continued to disappear from the front line of European politics it had occupied for the last 300 years. For all the restless activity within the nation and its capital, from the outside it might have seemed Spain had gone into hibernation; we recall Manuel Azaña's claim in 1920 that life and events had stalled in Madrid for some 200 years. A corollary of this disappearance from the centre of European affairs was a general ignorance of Madrid at precisely the same time as, post-Napoleon, to be a *madrileño* or *madrileña* was no longer a matter of chance – a provisional necessity forged by the need to be close to the opportunities of the court – but increasingly a matter of pride. The city and its people had survived too much not to be proud, and during the nineteenth century developed an increasing consciousness, an identity taking shape as the character of Madrid and its citizens entered popular literature, art and entertainment.

Stasis and discovery

Despite twenty or so years of Fernando VII's deeply reactionary reign, there was movement below the absolutist surface; society was changing irredeemably. This complex period saw the start of the political zigzagging and yo-yoing that would characterise the century; under pressure from military leader Rafael del Riego, Madrid experienced the first instance of the *pronunciamiento*, the means by which the military forced a change of government, later a commonplace process in Madrid in the nineteenth century. During the brief 'liberal triennial' from 1820 to 1823, Fernando signed back into law the 1812 constitution, that abhorred document of iniquitous liberties he had previously dissolved. Such lenience in an absolutist would be short-lived: three years into the period of liberal government, and with Fernando's connivance, Louis XVIII of France invaded Spain with the so-called 'hundred thousand sons of Saint Louis'. These were understood not to number 100,000, and neither to be sons of any saint; just whose sons they were was open to satirical conjecture. The liberal triennial in Spain had inspired new constitutions and political movements throughout Europe and South America: it had to be stopped. Proving writers can be as base and immoral as any politician, this French operation against social progress and liberty was directed in part by Chateaubriand, once described by Napoleon as a vile and untrustworthy person who suffered from the additional weakness of writing books. Chateaubriand later boasted of how he had achieved in six months in Spain what Napoleon was unable to achieve in seven years; it would not have occurred to him to imagine what the Spanish thought of his achievements or his bragging. As for the charismatic Riego, he was captured in Andalusia and taken to Madrid in chains, where he was sentenced to die a traitor's death: to be dragged, hanged and quartered. Only the first two were applied: he was hanged in the Plaza de la Cebada, after suffering the final humiliation of being dragged through an abusive crowd, in a basket tied to the back of a donkey, to the foot of the scaffold. The Plaza de la Cebada itself, which had assumed the role of hosting public executions after they were moved out of the Plaza Mayor had an air, wrote Galdós, of villainy, decrepitude and irregularity in all its dimensions; it was lugubrious, insalubrious and repugnant.[1]

To every absolutist his due: there were positive changes in Madrid in the years up to Fernando's death in 1833. Urban landmarks included the last constructed of the great gates into Madrid, the Puerta de Toledo, replacing an earlier and more modest gate; the Red de San Luis; the Monument to the Heroes of the Second of May along the Paseo del Prado; the Royal Conservatory of Music under the patronage of Fernando's fourth wife – and niece – María Cristina; the beginnings of the Royal Theatre, built over the old theatre of los Caños del Peral; and the Scientific, Literary and Artistic Athenaeum, for the next hundred years a key cultural institution in the city, a home for the expression and development of ideas, not the least of which was the promotion of intellectual debate as a contribution to society and politics.

The moment that redeems Fernando's legacy – to the extent that is possible – was the decision to transform Juan de Villanueva's Museum of Natural Sciences into a home for the royal art collection. The building had only recently been completed when the French occupied Madrid and trashed the museum, using it as a stables and recycling the lead in the roofing to make bullets. Encouraged now by his second wife – another niece – Isabel of Braganza, Fernando had city master architect Antonio López Aguado rebuild the whole structure, following the original plans of his former teacher Villanueva. Initially known as the Royal Museum of Painting and Sculpture, it belonged to the royal family, unsurprisingly given it housed their art collections, and was passed on as an inheritance to the nation decades later in 1868. It was not long, however, before the institution became known as the 'Prado' in honour of the *prado* – field or meadow – of San Jerónimo where it was built, and consistent with the splendid avenue of the same name. The people of Spain now possessed what twentieth-century artist Antonio Saura would describe as the most intense art collection in the world. Not the most extensive, but the most concentratedly brilliant.

The royal collections had always been private affairs for a limited public; it took until the twentieth century for a broader public appreciation of the scope and value of this legacy and its role in the fixing of national identity through pride at cultural achievement. The collection, which survived its serpentine travels during the civil war, is perhaps one of the national collections most closely identifiable with the nation that holds it and, over the 200 years since its foundation, the Prado Museum has been central not only to the identity of Madrid, but also to Spain and the stories the country tells itself and others. While that identity has been challenged from different corners of the peninsula, the museum has stood constant, for it rises above the nation, however defined or disputed, as a reference point for universal cultural achievement. The Prado is not only important for what it objectively is – magnificent enough by any measure – but for where it has come from, how it has survived and what it represents. Here gathered together is the very peak of human endeavour in this particular field: the classical art of Spain and Europe. Having survived the vagaries of history the collection is, to paraphrase Don DeLillo on the Parthenon, what we have saved from the madness. It is these things: beauty, dignity, order, proportion.[2] No one has destroyed or diminished the artefacts of western civilisation so much as western armies themselves, with their fire and looting and their illegal traffic. The collection that has come to rest in the Prado has been attacked, burnt, maltreated, partly stolen and partly destroyed many times, and what survives to us from Spanish royal collections is startling for the fact that these fragile treasures have somehow managed to pass through those centuries of countervailing pressures: war, theft, dynastic and regime change, climate shifts, rough handling, misappropriation. What we see, in all its brilliance, is perhaps only a whisper, a pale resemblance to the full extent of what has been created, then lost.

The immense value of the collection – not just intrinsically, but also as a symbol of Spain's cultural heritage – was never so clear as during its evacuation from Republican Madrid in late 1936. The operation was precarious, truckloads of hastily boxed art treasures making their way to Valencia, including a difficult crossing of the Jarama River at Arganda del Rey. Armed, smoking men sat on the back of the trucks, laden with odd shapes wrapped in cloth and paper. In these hurried and basic conditions, part of the collection of the Prado was removed from the threat of bombardment and fire. The crossing of the Jarama was slow, uncertain; there were heart-stopping moments; at any stage the entire cargo could have crashed down into the river. Some of the paintings hauled from the burning *alcázar* were outside again for the first time since that fiery December night 200 years before, *Las Meninas* among them. Trucks inched across the bridge; the armed men remained impassive, perhaps even indifferent.

In Republican Valencia, the magnificent Torres de Serranos, a section of fortified gates from the fourteenth-century wall around the town, had been roughly conditioned to receive the artworks. Over the next year and a half, the major pieces – Goya, Titian, Dürer, Mantegna and Velázquez among them – would be taken load by load to Valencia; some would then go south to Cartagena, others north to Barcelona, then via the castles of Figueras and Perelada into France and Switzerland, where they would form part of an exhibition in Geneva of over 150 paintings and tapestries. After three years of peripatetic wandering and questionable custodianship, they eventually made their way back to Madrid, via Irún and Burgos, in September 1939. There is much that is miraculous about the Prado collection, and this was perhaps its luckiest hour. Had the works still been in Switzerland when the full European war broke out, anything might have happened to them. The train carrying them home to Madrid, a four-day journey, was travelling as the opening shots of the Second World War were fired.[3]

With its focus on European art from the fifteenth to the nineteenth centuries, the collection at the Prado reflects what many consider the grandest period of Spanish history, and provides an extraordinary narrative of continental art and of Spain's central role in that history. In a nineteenth century where writers and thinkers, foreign and domestic, often bemoaned Spain's late development into the conventions of modernity, the Prado Museum was one reference point that showed Spain at the very height of European culture, and the desperate moves to save the collection from the threat of bombardment during the civil war suggest how closely the nation identified with it, and how critical this cultural survival was for the government. There had been excessive sacking and burning of churches, often with terrible loss of cultural heritage, yet when the Republican government left Madrid and retreated to Valencia, it made sure to take a selection of the treasures of the Prado Museum with it. In a country so often divided, this cultural inheritance unites like few other institutions. Debates over art, history and meaning come and go, shifting with intellectual trends that preference one form of telling over another; as every generation brings its preferences and lenses, the collection at the Prado Museum remains impervious.

Madrid and Spain might not have been on the conventional itinerary of the Grand Tour, yet they began to come into sight for the northern European traveller. Eighteenth- and nineteenth-century accounts were both damning and romantically orientalising: according to Montesquieu, 'he who sits for ten hours a day is doubly respected than he who only sits for five'.[4] Montesquieu may be using Spain here in the abstract, highlighting the dangers of a society dominated by an intolerant clergy, a lazy aristocracy and an absolutist monarchy,[5] but such prejudice is damaging regardless of nuance. For such an influential thinker to deride Spain and its people in this way helped set a precedent. The idleness of the Spaniard became dogma. Backward, forgotten and indolent: what possible interest could their capital city hold?

Following the works of Lord Byron and Washington Irving – the latter spending three years in Madrid from 1826 to 1829 and later four years from 1842 to 1846 as a minister of the US government – Mesonero warned of foreigners' easy misconceptions of Spain and Madrid. They saw, essentially, what they wanted to see: 'The French, English, Germans and other foreigners have tried to provide a *moral* description of Spain,' he wrote in 1832 in his article 'The Customs of Madrid', 'but they have either created an idealised romantic and quixotic country or, ignoring the passage of time, have written not as it is but as they suppose it might have been back in the "Felipe" years.'[6] True to this choice between romantic clichés or anachronistic descriptions of a vanished country, he lists some of the images these writers trotted out: blind singing beggars, young women knifing their lovers out of jealous fury or workers taking a break from the arduous task of doing nothing. These writers first created then reinforced a framework of stereotypes that would serve for at least another century. Rather than a generous, frank and courageous people, these foreign observers, claimed Mesonero, tended to ridicule, presenting Spaniards or *madrileños* as obstinate, mean-spirited and stupid. 'First let us advise the mere Idler and Man of Pleasure to go rather to Paris, Vienna, St. Petersburg, Florence, or Rome, than to Madrid . . . Madrid itself is but a dear, second-rate European capital,' wrote Richard Ford in the 1840s; 'the capital is without industry or resources,' he claimed, 'and poorer than many of our provincial cities.'[7] This stands in stark contrast with the observations of Scottish journalist Henry Inglis, who wrote in 1830 that he had 'purposely walked several times into the lowest quarters of the city, but I never encountered any such pictures of poverty and wretchedness as are to be found in Paris, London, Dublin, Manchester and other great towns of France and England'.[8] Inglis found Madrid bustling and alive, its streets full of elegant men and women. If the people were not as busy as in Britain, and dedicated more than a usual amount of time to enjoyment and pleasure, this was the result, he believed, of the lack of a significant manufacturing sector. For other Britons, fresh from the increasing regulation of urban life supposed by the Industrial Revolution, this love of calm idleness suggested a moral flaw, but Inglis was impressed, noting an 'air of ease and pleasure to the pursuits of the inhabitants of Madrid'.[9] Other visitors were equally enthusiastic, including Russian composer Mikhail Glinka, who in 1844 considered Madrid and Aranjuez a southern version of St Petersburg.[10]

The prevailing tendency in the first half of the nineteenth century, however, was for writers to be disappointed by Madrid. What they found most alluring about Spain was a fiction they created in their own minds: a dusky and exotic Islamic past, now crumbling and ruined, its very decrepitude its main attraction, part of the floral sensuality of southern Spain. Madrid, in contrast, lacked any beauty and was surrounded by dirty villages, dry and monotonous landscapes, and where the line between reporting and condescension was fine: 'these women, so beautiful in their rags, these men, so proud in their tatters, these children already clothed in the shreds from the paternal cloak,' wrote Alexandre Dumas in 1846, 'all indicated to us not only a different people but a different century.'[11] In short: nineteenth-century poverty tourism.

Scholars for many years interpreted Spanish history 'from a premise of backwardness'[12] and this deficit model allowed the old canard of Spain and its capital city as sidelined from the flow of modernisation. Its liberal revolution had apparently failed, its industrialisation was tardy and its empire in steep decline: these served to 'relegate Spain's presence in dominant historical narratives'.[13] Having seen its empire already come and go before the age of the Industrial Revolution rather than parallel to it, Spain differed from northern European models of colonialism, and was thus considered to be excluded from the conventional paths to modernisation followed elsewhere. Like the Ottomans and the Russians, the Spanish were 'peripheral' to Europe,[14] a people tinged with an obscure barbarism like the Muscovite or the Turk.[15] Despite having been historically central to the political and cultural development of European sensibilities, Spain was sidelined; the essence of Europe was to be found principally among the French, Germans,

Dutch, Flemish, Swedes and Italians. Indeed, in the fifteenth century Spain – or Castile, Aragon and Navarre, to be precise, albeit the entity was often referred to from outside as 'Spain' – was not considered especially 'European', being a country, in many a northern imagination, that was overrun with Moors and Jews. A strange land, below the conspicuous barrier of the Pyrenees, too tainted with 'Africa' and all the late medieval prejudice the name implied. Consistent with this thinking, Madrid was considered unfit to share the company of London or Paris, Rome or Venice.

The sources that support this view are copious; the new always casts a patronising view back on the old. The end of the Spanish empire came to be interpreted not as the inevitable decline to which all empires are destined, but as indicative of a character flaw in the Spanish people themselves. A historical process, common to all ages, was read by Spain's multiple enemies – and by the end of the nine-teenth century even by some Spaniards – in moral terms, suggesting the wastefulness and corruptibility of Catholicism, the laziness of Latinate southerners drugged by sunlight, wine and popery; their leaders a troop of inbred misfits easily lampooned, despite marriage between cousins being common across the royal houses of Europe for centuries as part of the construction of political allegiances. It was not unusual for Spain to be considered an outlier among the civilised on the basis of modes of behaviour or governance that were common elsewhere: the expulsion of the Jews and the burning of heretics are two examples where, rather than set a fierce and bigoted precedent, Spain followed the example of other European powers. Within Spain, as the nineteenth-century science of history began to formalise a version of the past, some saw this propensity of others to opine unfavourably on Spanish matters as providing a reference point for ways to improve the nation, learning from the advice and observa-tions of outsiders. It also encouraged a nationalist inversion, a kind of fierce 'doubling down' in the protection of the autochthonous.

For a people apparently in thrall to religion, Madrid has a consid-erable track record of destroying religious property. In the summer of 1834, in the early days of María Cristina's regency – the future

Isabel II was only four years old – anticlerical riots broke out in Madrid amid a widespread cholera epidemic. After thousands of deaths, a rumour got about that certain religious orders, in particular the Jesuits, had poisoned the public drinking fountains. This was false and absurd, yet nearly eighty clergy, including a dozen Jesuits, were murdered amid the reprisals that followed, and religious buildings burnt to the ground.

Only two years later, amid a financial crisis brought on by empty state coffers and the need to finance a civil war against the Carlists – those who supported the claims to the throne of Fernando VII's brother, Carlos, over the claims of Fernando's daughter, Isabel – the moderate liberal government appointed highly regarded financier Juan Álvarez Mendizábal as treasurer. In one of the most significant moves in Spanish political history, and as part of the so-called Liberal Revolution of 1835–37, Mendizábal ordered the confiscation and sale of huge numbers of religious properties, both buildings and land, including all convents with fewer than twelve members. This helped ease the finances in Madrid in the short term, but the effect in rural areas was to transfer ownership of vast tracts of land from the church to wealthy oligarchs; the humble farmer was usually left with nothing. Not even the small numbers of emerging middle-class investors were able to take advantage of this ecclesiastical fire sale. Large areas of land previously held static by the church were made fertile; however, the multiplication of olive fields and vineyards meant the clearing of older forests. Inevitably, art treasures that had belonged to the church slipped into private hands; many items were lost or destroyed, while others eventually found their way into museums. There were further confiscations of religious property in 1841 and again in the mid-1850s; governments of one stripe or another came and went, first enacting such laws, then abrogating them. The sale of religious property carried on regardless, so vast was the material at hand, until late in the nineteenth century; in total, well over 200,000 properties of every conceivable size and shape, from chalices to farmlands to paintings to entire monasteries, were sold. The crippling Spanish debt was paid down, for the time being. Little attention was paid to the numbers of religious persons, particularly older monks, who were effectively made homeless, and forced into an immiserated existence.

Parallel to the nineteenth-century construction of Spain in the popular imagination went the renewed physical construction of Madrid. The administrative capital, even of a shrinking empire – the South American colonies had almost all fought and won their independence by the end of Fernando's rule – was equally monumental and magnificent as it was a busy, crowded, dirty and mostly unhygienic place, still straining at the *cerca* with which Felipe IV had encircled the town in 1625. Through fits and starts, a limping process of trial and error and the contributions of a series of highly talented if often frustrated statesmen, the dream of a liberal and modernising society was revived after the last nervous kick from the dying animal of absolutism. The European revolutions of 1848 were just over the horizon; there would be no return to the stasis, controls and certainties of the *antiguo regimen*. There would be reversals – progress is never without interruptions – but the transformation of the city, in both physical shape and political thinking, was unstoppable, despite the lack of suffrage or, for the moment, organised political resistance to the ruling classes and their assumption of power, for whether monarchical or liberal and republican, the actors were sometimes indistinguishable. The political, philosophical, scientific and cultural modernity that was moving across Europe, bringing atheism and political disillusion in its wake, reached Madrid; world views that would mark the intellectual parameters that frame our understanding of the world for the next 200 years were set in place.

A superb linguist and inveterate traveller, the Englishman George Henry Borrow arrived in Spain in late 1835 and spent the next few years exploring the country with the apparent objective of promoting a more vernacular and accessible version of the Bible. In this, he was mostly unsuccessful, yet his remains an enormously valuable, if obviously biased, glimpse of a nation undergoing change. Despite its eccentricities, Borrow's account contains magical and priceless tales as he slums it with rural gypsies, stealing along the barren roads and across the pitch-dark nights of the nineteenth-century countryside. When he comes to Madrid, he loves the city. 'I have visited most of the principal capitals of the world,' he writes, no doubt exaggeratedly, 'but upon the whole none has so ever interested me as this city of Madrid.'[16] His first significant encounter is a failure; seeking support from prime minister Mendizábal for his mission, he is sent on his way without too much contemplation. 'Yours is not the first application I have had,' Mendizábal tells Borrow; 'ever since I have held the reins of government I have been pestered in this manner, by English calling themselves Evangelical Christians, who have of late come flocking over into Spain. Only last week a hunchbacked fellow found his way into my cabinet . . . and told me that Christ was coming.'[17] Borrow insists part of the solution to Spain's internal conflicts – the first Carlist war was in full swing – was the better distribution of the gospels. 'What strange infatuation is this,' replied Mendizábal, who had spent years in London as a businessman, including a brief spell in a debtors' prison, 'which drives you over lands and waters with Bibles in your hands.'[18] Forget the bibles was the essence of his message, and bring us guns.

In Madrid, Borrow observes the city to be diverse in its Spanish population, drawn from all over the peninsula, but with few foreigners other than 'French tailors and glove-makers'. The city is 'strictly Spanish', and he finds 'no colonies of Germans, as at Saint Petersburg; no English factories, as at Lisbon; no multitudes of insolent Yankees lounging through the streets as at the Havannah'.[19] He soon falls into the company of one Baltasar who, his mother tells Borrow, 'loves Englishmen on account of the liberality of their opinions'.[20] The two spend some time together, a pair of opposites attracting with a mutual fascination; Baltasar is short, rather overweight and with a 'yellow and sickly' face; shabby, extravagant, boastful and proud. He laments that, it being winter, he is unable to take Borrow to see a bullfighting spectacle, but all is not lost, for 'happily tomorrow there is an execution'.[21] This, it turns out, is one of those moments where the brutal past is on display: the execution is a double garrotting – two brothers had been found guilty of breaking, entering and murder – carried out amid a priestly chanting of litanies, as if those voices might carry the soul of the executed prisoners to heaven, having reconciled their sins and received spiritual absolution. Observing the powerful role in the ghastly spectacle of the priest, who seemed 'to have the power of shutting the gates of heaven or of hell', Borrow cannot help but use the occasion to have a swipe at 'the Popish system whose grand aim has ever been to keep people's minds as far as possible from God, and to centre their hopes and fears in the priesthood'.[22]

Borrow no doubt developed a connection with the people he encountered that was richer than that of many of his fellow-travellers of the era who did not have the same grasp of the language, nor had they explored the sometimes dimly lit corners of the nation and its capital into which Borrow took himself. English and French travellers came from empires reaching their apogee, and passed through a Spain not only with her empire lost, but charred and smoking from Napoleon's vain and pointless incursion, and the equally pointless Carlist wars. In addition, these writers saw Spain with eyes washed in the milky light of softer climes; their vision was accustomed to mists and gentle greys; they found Madrid left them gasping in the bare heat. All the references to Spain, or Madrid, as a furnace or a frying pan are typical of those who do not know how to navigate these temperatures. Landscape had assumed its romantic dimensions with its preference for the pretty rustic, appealing for its distance from the refinements of perfumes, silks and etiquette. The land around Madrid was repeatedly considered antagonistic to all serious human pleasures, and travellers damned the arid centre of the peninsula, lacking in glades and pretty crags, in gentle greens. It had blue, but it was of a burning kind, as were its yellows, sands and ochres. The description of Lynch is typical: 'Visitors enjoyed the social life of Madrid but not its environment. The surrounding landscape was desolate and melancholy, the outskirts were uniformly miserable.'[23] Or, elsewhere: '. . . the road to Madrid looked out at a large, barren country, devoid of anything green except occasional olives, oaks and cork trees.'[24] This was, apparently, a land in decline, a wasted and depressed nation suffering chronic misrule and injustice – and, by extension, a lack of productivity.

Amid these and similar descriptions, Spain was established as a victim of history; a species of beautiful corpse, or heroic lost cause. It remained stubbornly outside the inclusive embrace, an unimaginably strange place on the edge of Europe. Precious few, in consequence, were bothered with its capital city.

The emerging metropolis

A new air flowed into the tight spaces of Madrid; the following decades saw a liberalising period in politics along with an enthusiastic modernisation of the city's infrastructure. These reforms were driven by an opening of the political spectrum at home and abroad, by new technologies of engineering, construction and transport, and by domestic necessities: the 1834 cholera epidemic that had led to the murder of Jesuits and other clergy was a sanitary wake-up call.

The urban landscape of inner Madrid was, as always, in flux. After the widespread demolition of churches and convents in the first decades of the nineteenth century, the 1836 disentailment and confiscation of religious property freed up further tracts of land for redevelopment, precisely at a time when a strong bourgeoisie was emerging, a professional class requiring new urban and commercial developments in which to live, work and invest. By the 1860s, under the guidance of civil engineer Carlos María de Castro, plans were drawn up to substantially increase the size of the city, drawing on the Haussmann model of Parisian development to create new districts such as Chamberí, Argüelles and Salamanca, the latter named after the Marquis of Salamanca, the principal financier behind the project which eventually bankrupted him. Districts of broad and, in time, regular tree-lined avenues would occupy what had been fields and gardens, pastures with a scattering of hovels, warehouses, forges and kilns, and other elements of the still insignificant industry Madrid had gathered around it. Parallel to these changes, poverty became entrenched on the outskirts of Madrid, particularly in the districts directly south of the centre – the slopes that led from the old medieval ghettos down to the Manzanares, mostly contained within the contemporary administrative district of Arganzuela – an area which would remain associated with poverty until the second half of the twentieth century, and whose abject living conditions would be amply documented by Galdós and, after him, Pío Baroja. From the middle of the nineteenth century other districts, housing another influx of internal migrants who would start arriving on the recently inaugurated train lines into Madrid, grew up beyond the planned symmetry of the bourgeois city: districts such as Prosperidad, La Guindalera and Ventas, or the former military camp of Tetuán, were all swelling the size and population of Madrid. In the eight years between 1852 and 1860, Madrid grew in population as much as in the previous fifty years; equally, in the two decades between 1870 and 1890, the population increase equalled that of the hundred years between 1750 and 1850.[1] A city of 300,000 in the 1860s became a city of over half a million by the end of the century. For many, the modern city that was coming into being might represent the best opportunity for advancement, of whatever sort, but it contained large areas of wretchedness. 'Taken altogether, Spain was a poor nation and its capital was inhabited, above all, by poor people. There's not much more to it than that,' wrote the historian and anthropologist Julio Caro Baroja.[2] Indeed, it was a lack of finance that held back many of the urban reforms in post-Napoleonic Madrid; in the long half-century from Fernando VII to Alfonso XII (ruled 1874–85), not only did Madrid experience spectacular change and growth; also remarkable are the number of urban schemes that did not make it beyond the drawing board. Of all the Madrids – there have been dozens down the centuries – there exist also the spectral versions of the city that never took shape, and that might have had a profound effect on its morphology.

The form of provincial Madrid within the larger territory of New Castile was established by 1833, following the shape it had acquired during its medieval disputes with Segovia, Toledo and Guadalajara, gaining territory here and ceding territory there.[3] From the richly pastured, mountainous north to the long plains of the south, a broad collection of towns fell within the gravitational influence of the capital. This capacity for attraction was evident in 1836 when, after a few false starts, the government decreed the transfer of the University of Alcalá to Madrid, with the relocated institution to be known as the Universidad Central. The transition occurred faculty by faculty over a decade; Madrid now had the university it had lacked for centuries, despite Spain boasting in Salamanca, Valladolid and Alcalá some of the oldest universities in the world. Teaching and research were subject to centralisation, and the university would soon be closely linked to those staples of Madrid life that were politics, media and *tertulia* cafés.

At this time Madrid was also home to one of its most famous sons, and certainly its most famous chronicler, Ramón de Mesonero Romanos, whose work laid down frameworks for understanding the urban profile and development of Madrid for decades to come.[4] This journalist, prolific writer and enthusiastic walker dedicated much of his life to descriptions of the city and its history; more than this, he was influential in helping determine urban policy. In the mid-1830s he travelled extensively throughout Spain, France and England, taking notes on urban landscapes and planning, and found support for his ideas from one of Madrid's most reform-minded mayors, Joaquín Vizcaíno, the Marquis of Pontejos.[5] Under Pontejos's brief mayoralty, and at Mesonero's urging, a significant repaving of streets was undertaken, along with improved street lighting and sewerage services, public baths and a large-scale planting of trees, as well as taken-for-granted initiatives such as street signage and the numbering of houses.[6] Having suffered from but survived the cholera epidemic of 1834, Mesonero was an enthusiastic promoter of the relatively new science of public hygiene and its intimate link to urban planning; he campaigned for the city to improve its management of human and animal waste.[7] Among his many achievements, Mesonero helped invent modern conceptions of Madrid; his ideas 'would operate as both a future blueprint for architects and urban planners and a powerful narrative of traditional Madrilenian identity'.[8]

Mesonero was the first major exponent in Spain of the literary style known as *costumbrismo*, a form of proto-anthropology combined with the observational journalistic article, a genre that explored the customs of long-established working-class Madrid, but did so for a middle-class audience. It was, essentially, a series of field reports as entertainment: the beliefs, rituals, festivities, costumes, styles and habits of *castizo* Madrid, with its *majos* and *manolos*, its *majas* and *manolas*,[9] its dances, music and forms of speech; a panoply of working-class authenticity, later adopted as fashionable by the upper classes, that was verified by writers such as Mesonero and to a lesser extent his approximate contemporary Mariano José de Larra. These social customs were accounted for, described and codified, as if setting them in print established a form of law or right. Here was old Madrid: the nineteenth-century bourgeois audience received a history of the city and an explanation of its most famous rituals. *Costumbrismo* was a form of nostalgia for a Spain that would disappear under the incoming wave of industrialisation and urban development, as well as providing not a few of the stereotypes that foreign authors were only too ready to indulge and promote.[10] Mesonero placed into words what Goya had placed into pictures: it was both a reflection of reality and the construction of cliché. Of course the *majos* and *manolas* existed and yet, picturesque as they could be, they represented only a relatively small percentage of the population of Madrid. Beyond these considerations, the *costumbrismo* of Mesonero represented a move towards another new literary form: the study of the city as a being in and of itself. As with the natural sciences, so with this form of burgeoning social science: the urban world was an object to be observed, studied, analysed, understood, classified and, eventually, tamed. Mesonero would be followed by countless other observers of the social world of Madrid; none would be as important and prolific as Benito Pérez Galdós.

Fernando's daughter Isabel finally ascended the throne in 1843 at the age of 13, following the regencies of her mother María Cristina and of General Espartero. By the age of 16 her marriage had been arranged to the unremarkable Francisco de Asís – almost inevitably, her cousin – after a series of potential candidates was considered, then discarded for one reason or another. In a raffle of mediocre European nobles, one of the least impressive – perhaps chosen for that very reason – ended up as Isabel's partner. She was not happy with the choice, and allegedly whispered to a friend not long after their wedding night: 'What can I say about man who was wearing more lace than I?'[11] Throughout her reign, which would end amid financial scandal and revolution in 1868, Isabel was notorious for her love affairs, her husband either impotent or homosexual. Officially, they had twelve children, though the parentage is questionable, and only five lived into adulthood. Isabel is an easy figure to caricature; evidence suggests she was neither intellectually sharp nor morally firm. An absolutely *ordinary* majesty;[12] immature and unfit to lead the nation through the political complexities of the mid-nineteenth century.

To the outsider, and not a few insiders, the politics of the second half of the nineteenth century, played out upon the Madrid stage and in the reactionary Carlist wars, was a form of *trastorno*: a disorder of chaotic alignments and realignments through which the nation, in fits and starts, left absolutism behind and began to develop its own constitutional regime based on a series of freedoms and representative institutions. The path from absolutism to an imperfect form of parliamentary democracy took a number of generations, and was not without violence. Many, with good reason, have baulked before the hall of mirrors that is this period: the revolving panel of generals, politicians, chancers, royalty; the sense of a nation running a furious treadmill. It might all have been great fun – the stuff of *zarzuelas*[13] and period dramas, smouldering romance and royal sex scandals – were it not for the fact people were being killed, again and again, and always uselessly, while the economic development of the country and its capital were held back by an anachronistic elite.

Isabel at times imposed her will on political decision-making but was for the most part lost to affairs and financial corruption; she had, ultimately, little impact on the political fortunes of Spain, other than when her incompetence or lack of serious leadership made difficult matters worse. Against a background of ongoing Carlist wars and regional instability, governments in Madrid alternated between moderate and progressive liberals. Both were elite forma-tions that kept suffrage limited to property-owning males, yet they at least understood that political progress was essential for the economic progress of the nation. The moderates, more inclined to a French model of highly centralised administration, and the progressives, more inclined to the British parliamentary system and the school of Adam Smith,[14] were each backed in turn by military generals; governments swung back and forth between progress and reaction, aided and abetted by the likes of Baldomero Espartero and Juan Prim, who supported the progressive liberals, Francisco Serrano, whose loyalties wandered over the political spectrum, Ramón María Narváez of the moderates and the liberal unionist leader Leopoldo O'Donnell.[15] If nothing else, this period of musical chairs of prime ministers, politicians and generals reads like a street guide, for the political history of the nineteenth century runs through the city's nomenclature, especially in the rectilinear bourgeois districts that were growing at roughly the same time: the Canal de Isabel II; Argüelles; Fernández de los Ríos; Donoso Cortés; Alonso Martínez; Ríos Rosas; Diego de León; Salamanca; Serrano; Narváez; Martínez Campos; Prim; Cánovas del Castillo; Sagasta; O'Donnell; Emilio Castelar; Canalejas; Eduardo Dato and more. The century of coups and generals, monarchs and pretenders, reformers, anar-chists and violent dreamers – these latter without streets named in their honour – left its leading gentlemen across the landscape. And as was commonly the case, precious few women.

Despite the political confusion, the second half of the century opened new opportunities for economic development: industrial capitalism had arrived, and a quickly swelling population required a substantially new city to be built. For Mesonero, writing towards the end of his life, the two signature events of the nineteenth century in Madrid were the sound of the first train whistle blown at Atocha in 1851 and the arrival of the water supply from the Lozoya River in 1858. Both were critical to urban expansion and industry, for population growth, urban development and changing environmental conditions had left those aquifers and original streams, such as the Fuente Castellana, the Abroñigal, San Pedro, Leganitos or the Manzanares, either exhausted, contaminated or both. They were no longer fit for purpose.

Mesonero might have added, given its lasting effect on the city, the thorough redesign after 1855 of the Puerta del Sol. In a city increasingly moved by political discontent, the Puerta del Sol had become a strategic nexus. Not only was it a place of constant social gathering, of crowds, rumour mills and agitation; it also faced the Ministry of the Interior which had moved into the famous Casa de Correos in the late 1840s. The chaotic streets around Sol were cleaned up and, in some cases, realigned; the square itself was enlarged, and by the 1870s a degree of uniformity imposed on the buildings that surround it. These are now one of Madrid's most impressive architectural sights, fanning in semicircular fashion from the Calle Mayor at one end, via Arenal, Preciados, Carmen, Montera and Alcalá, to the opposite end of the semicircle at the Carrera de San Jerónimo. Visiting in 1870, the Italian writer Edmondo de Amicis left a vivid impression of Sol via an early example of modernist literary list-making, a dense scramble of details piled one on top of another in blurred imitation of the hectic life before his eyes: 'It is not a square like others,' he observes correctly; it was not then nor is it now. 'It is a mingling of salon, promenade, theatre, academy, garden, a square of arms and a market.' Giddy with the movement, the constant thronging of people from dawn until after midnight, he observes the gathering of 'merchants, the disengaged demagogues, the unemployed clerks, the aged pensioners, and the elegant young men; there they traffic, talk politics, court girls, promenade, read newspapers, hunt down their debtors, seek their friends, prepare demonstrations against the ministry, coin the false reports which circulate throughout Spain, and weave the scandalous gossip of the city.'[16] Social divisions and hierarchies were obvious, yet this did not prevent such a diverse range of citizens and visitors from coming together, shoulder to shoulder, on the very same stretch of pavement. The square is an aural experience, full of the cries, shouts and shrieks of vendors, the blast of horns, cracking of whips, clanking of sabres, strumming of guitars and the singing of the blind.[17] It is a sensory overload; he is pushed and shoved, shouldered and elbowed through this carnival of life and commerce, ambition and pleasure; a hum, a racket, a fever and a commotion.

Not everything was fun and games, nor was the atmosphere of the Puerta del Sol always one of sunny chaos. Since the 1850s it has witnessed most of the significant social and political moments in Madrid, many of them of national importance. The square has never ceased to be the most vital meeting point of old Madrid and a centre of social protest, yet it changes with remarkable regularity. It is more heavily policed and surveilled now than at any time, as it is one of the essential tourist sites of the capital, inevitably tamer than in de Amicis's time. No municipal government, it seems, can leave the square alone; it had undergone another substantial redesign even while this book was being written.

Elsewhere, during Isabel's reign, Madrid added further buildings appropriate to a modern capital: a Royal Mint, a new Royal Theatre some thirty slow years in the construction, a new home for the fifteenth-century Court of Audit, and a Congress of Deputies, built over the burnt ruins of the convent of the Holy Spirit in Carrera de San Jerónimo between 1843 and 1850. Under the progressive minister of finance, Pascual Madoz, a further-reaching expropriation of religious property and church land was passed into law; convents were demolished as much of the clerical seventeenth and eighteenth centuries disappeared. Squares that would become central to the life of Madrid appeared, such as the Glorieta de Bilbao, site of the former Puerta de los Pozos de Nieve, and the Plaza del Progreso, later renamed Tirso de Molina, forming an urban partnership with the nearby seventeenth-century Plaza de Antón Martín.

As de Amicis's description of the Puerta del Sol confirms, Madrid was a city as much dedicated to pleasure and amusement as to business and government. The emergent bourgeoisie enjoyed a series of gardens and pleasure parks developed around the zone of Alcalá, Recoletos and the Retiro; this green and elegant parkland was no longer the eastern edge of the city but had become fully integrated within it. For a decade and a half, the Campo Eliseo gardens, just to the north of the Retiro, were a brilliant playground with a gamut of entertainments: open-air theatre, dancing and fireworks, a shooting range and a roller coaster,[18] to say nothing of the age-old pursuits of gossip, display and seduction. Women were elegant and sharp, wore their finest mantillas and astonished foreign observers with their use of the fan, 'an art completely unknown in France',[19] while men dressed soberly, if often beyond their means. The nearby bullring, standing just behind the Puerta de Alcalá for nearly 150 years before its move to the district of Ventas, was equally part of the entertainment.

When engineers moved in to build the Salamanca quarter, the pleasure gardens quickly disappeared; at around the same time, the Retiro park came under the full control of the town council, another popular place for the people of Madrid to stroll and take the cool air of an evening, to flirt, relax and show off. In the centre of the city, and especially around the Puerta del Sol, café society became a new focal point – mostly male – for social gossip, political plotting, wasting time and, via the wonderful Madrid institution of the *tertulia*, intellectual and literary discussion at cafés such as the Príncipe, Fontana de Oro, Lorenzini, Suizo or the restaurant Lhardy.[20]

Parallel to the friendly pleasures of the upper classes, the machinery of the city turned: a railway line was built between Madrid and Aranjuez; the waters of the Lozoya River were channelled and brought to Madrid in a major feat of engineering; and the districts surrounding the centre filled with an underclass, the ongoing generations of the Madrid working poor and homeless swollen by the numbers of migrants from rural Spain. Once the old walls were down, there was potentially no limit to the city's growth. Technology was changing the face and conception of the city; with increasing industrialisation came a new proletariat that had swapped the plough and sickle for the regime of machinery. A different kind of daily repetition, but one that offered opportunities for social mobility and political organisation.

Vital to the movement of the new industrial class, the railways were to have a huge impact on the social reality of the country. Azorín quotes from the short-lived publication *El Siglo Pintoresco*, in 1845: 'We have seen more new business enterprises in Spain over the last month than in all the years since the end of our civil war.[21] Capitalists and foreign engineers have been visiting the capital; everywhere one sees the will of the British and the whole peninsula has been covered – on paper at least – with a complex network of railways.'[22]

Two elements were essential to a Spanish railway system: it would connect Spain to France and vice versa, and all lines would lead into, and out from, Madrid. The enthusiastic Marqués de Pontejos had tried as early as 1829 to float the idea of a railway, but progress was stalled, not only for reasons of finance; it was only a generation since Spain had been invaded by France, and for some conservative politicians the thought of opening up paths to the northern neighbour was anathema. Why should a welcome mat be laid out, given the track record of the French? One senator commented that 'it would be to our benefit to be as isolated from France as possible.' As for the Pyrenees, suggested another, 'it would be convenient if they were to be twice as high.'[23] In 1845, just a few years before he died, English railway engineer George Stephenson was in Madrid to discuss the construction of a Madrid–France line, which surveyors had recommended could be built without much difficulty. The government, however, would not commit, gave his party the run-around and, while they waited, offered them entry to the bullfights to alleviate their boredom. Stephenson refused, and soon returned to England after a fruitless mission. Nevertheless, the first stations were built: Atocha, sometimes known as the Mediodía or South station, in 1851; Príncipe Pío, also known as the North station, in 1861 and significantly enlarged in 1882; and in 1880, the Delicias station. Between and around them all grew Madrid's first major urban industrial zone.

Apart from the monumental buildings of government and finance that would come towards the end of the century, the next version of Madrid, serving as a bridge between the mid-nineteenth and twenty-first centuries, would require a series of complex networks, above ground and below, around which the city could expand. These were the veiny system of water supply, the dark and wandering network of the Metro and eventually the great commercial avenues, lit up by twentieth-century neon, along which commerce, cinema and spectacle would flourish.

The new water supply, known as the Canal de Isabel II, was a major engineering feat and an important contribution to the nineteenth-century commitment to public sanitation. The water carriers of Madrid who so amused Gautier during his stay in 1840 with their clay pitchers, wicker baskets, glasses, sugar cubes and occasional pieces of orange and lemon, shouting their wares along the streets, would soon disappear. During his period as Minister of Public Works, the moderate politician Juan Bravo Murillo ordered an engineering project that would bring plentiful water from the beautiful Lozoya River down to the capital. The Guadarrama mountains again enter the story of Madrid: having been a line of defence, a source of rich pastures and a safe haven for bandits, the range now provided Madrid with one of the finest water supplies in the world, a tradition of which the city remains proud. In 1858, following the construction of an extensive system of dams, aqueducts, pipes, pumps, controls and storage facilities, the water of the Lozoya arrived and began to flow, bursting 20 metres up into the Madrid sky from a fountain on the Calle San Bernardo. A work by Madrid painter Eugenio Lucas Velázquez shows the moment and the enthusiastic crowds, which included the queen and dignitaries, flags waving, a jet of water rising into a light blue sky outside the baroque church of Our Lady of Montserrat. While the supply would still take some years to reach most citizens, the beneficial effects were immediate: not only did Madrid have an excellent water supply that helped to mitigate common diseases, the supply also facilitated much-needed industrial development around the city.

The former was vital to the question of public health. For centuries monarchs and civilian leaders had sought to reform the often toxic streets. Hygiene was now a matter of will or decorum, as well as of science and control, linked to sewerage, street lighting, health, industry and prosperity. Social class played its part too: the air needed to be clean, the water supply pure and the streets washed to maintain the moral standards of the newly expanding proletariat, for whom uncleanliness might be part of a broader pattern of laziness, depravity, godlessness and social dissatisfaction. At least by the latter part of the century the question of the cemeteries had been resolved, with the construction of a second major *camposanto* in 1884, the Almudena, to the east of the city, home now to an extraordinary range of funerary architecture, at times as extraordinary as the biographies of its silent population.

Parallel to the passing of the nineteenth century went the decline of that most popular figure in Spanish legend, the *bandido*, a figure eventually made obsolescent by the advent of the railway, better systems of security and a professionalised police force. The last great bandit of Madrid had been Luis Candelas, though he was less a highwayman than a city thief, making daring raids on jewellery collections and wealthy retail establishments. Goya, again providing testament to the range of his subject matter, had portrayed the late eighteenth- and early nineteenth-century *bandoleros* who were an integral part of the Spanish countryside, especially prevalent after the war against Napoleon. Hundreds of armed men were left unpaid and without employment once their guerrilla tactics had helped expel the French; their skills were perfectly adapted to raiding coaches and unwary travellers. At the same time, their exploits enriched a new romantic literature; armed with horses, muskets and knives, they created their own legends on the mountain roads around Madrid. Driven by necessity, greed or a sense of injustice – sometimes the motives were mixed, and no matter how noble a bandit leader might be, the same purity of motives was not always shared by his followers who were often vagabonds and common criminals – they were both dangerous and a staple of folklore; both romanticised and feared. Gangs knew the hidden ways through sharp terrain; against the brusque and knobbly backdrop of La Pedriza they used their intimate knowledge of forest paths and stacked tors to hide after their robberies, or melted away among their supporters in villages such as

Miraflores, Guadalix, El Escorial, Torrelodones or Soto del Real.[24] Often redistributing their gains among the villagers ensured legend, popularity, a blind eye and a silent tongue.

Candelas was a native of Lavapiés, in the heart of old Madrid. His was not a childhood of penury; indeed, he was well educated for the time, literate and an enthusiastic reader. Whether he formed his notions of social justice from readings, social observation or in the company of friends is unclear; his altruism might have been merely a romantic smokescreen behind which to hide his addiction to robbery, for he had formed part of local gangs from the age of 14 or 15, much to his respectable father's chagrin. When he was just 19 his father died; Candelas tried his hand as a bookseller, but the lure and excitement of crime was too strong. It is alleged – though the dates don't quite match up – that he spent time in the El Saladero prison, a substantial building designed by Ventura Rodríguez in the Plaza de Santa Bárbara that had been used for salting pork, hence its name; it was later converted into a prison that housed many of the *bandidos* of Madrid, along with forgers and corrupt politicians. El Saladero was known as a focus of vice, filth and infection, a lock-up typical of an age only just beginning to consider concepts such as prison reform or criminal rehabilitation. Candelas used the money he extracted from his raids to fund his lifestyle, for he had always loved to dress smartly, eat well and entertain women lavishly. In a stroke of luck he inherited a fortune from his mother but this was not enough to deter him from a life of crime; on the contrary, it signalled a transformation in Candelas's life. By day, he assumed a pseudonym, setting himself up in society as one Luis Álvarez de Cobos, gaining access to the living rooms of the elite; by night, he carried on his double life of stealth and robbery. Such a life was unsustainable in the longer term; Candelas fell foul of the aristocracy by assaulting a tailor to the queen in her workshop, and holding up the carriage of the French ambassador and his wife. There was a fine line between romanticism and outrage; Candelas was widely celebrated in popular verse and song, but his fate was the scaffold at the age of 33. He begged for clemency from the regent María Cristina on the basis of his crimes having been committed without bloodshed – something on which he prided himself and rested his reputation – but his appeal was denied, and he was executed by garrotte in 1837. Candelas was, in many respects, an eighteenth-century character, a figure from the Goya handbook; everything about him was original and yet, through no fault of his own, his story contains all the elements of cliché. His passing into *costumbrismo* folklore was just that: the confirmation of a legend divorced from reality. Even as he lived through it, the age in which he could operate had vanished.

As part of nineteenth-century secularism, land in Madrid continued to be cleared of religious property. In 1869 the church of Santa María, sited at the farthest end of Calle Mayor where the original mosque was believed to have stood nearly a thousand years before, was torn down, as was the church of Santa Cruz. New plazas opened out where convents had stood: the Plaza del Dos de Mayo replaced the convent of Maravillas, and the Plaza de Santo Domingo replaced the convent of the same name. Everywhere, remaining walls and gates were removed, including the old wall around the Retiro, allowing municipal planners to lengthen and broaden streets in all directions. New suburbs sprang up, new gardens, avenues and elegant districts such as Chamberí and Argüelles. At the same time, the removal of the walls not only meant the city could grow outwards; it also meant the poorer *arrabales*, semi-rural or semi-industrial, always semi-developed, would merge with Madrid and add substantially to its size. Thus, districts which are now considered quintessentially Madrid were incorporated into the body of the city, including Tetuán, Chamartín, Hortaleza, Guindalera, Concepción, Vallecas, San Isidro and Imperial.[25] The city was now surrounded by a series of demarcated working-class districts whose social and political influence would increase significantly in the coming decades.

The mad medley of governments – a carousel of privileged actors swapping seats on the merry-go-round, yet never getting off or demanding the infernal machine come to a halt – was unsustainable. Change was coming from below; new forms of social consciousness were taking hold that could not be undone; new forms of organisation took shape, community groups stitched together. Many among the nobility and ruling classes found the entry of the proletariat into Spanish politics disturbing and abhorrent; no one, however, could have been surprised, given the inability of the liberal system to provide the country with any long-term stability.

Between 1823 and 1865, Madrid saw sixty-five heads of government – some of them repeating various times, others lasting just one day; in the period from 1868 to 1874, the so-called 'democratic sexennial', which included the short-lived First Republic, there were seventeen heads of government (seven of these were presidents); during the years of the Bourbon restoration, from 1874 to 1931, another fifty heads of government, many serving more than once on the political roundabout. The period is a bewildering one for students of history and politics – the list of national leaders every bit as challenging as the list of Visigoth kings – and was a long-suffering one for the people of Madrid, albeit the satirical press had never had it so good. Práxedes Mateo Sagasta, the first Spanish leader who lived into the twentieth century, occupied the role seven times over a thirty-year period; Antonio Cánovas del Castillo, shot dead in Mondragón in the Basque region in 1897, served six times.

The hall of mirrors had its darker side. Writing his memoirs, Galdós recalls the sergeants' revolt of 1866 against Isabel II, an uprising that led to a wave of executions. Such events were typical of the time; 'the habitual recourse to violence' as a nineteenth-century means of advancing political solutions to national problems.[26] The old Galdós recalls his younger self, recently arrived in Madrid, amid 'the thick revolutionary atmosphere of those turbulent times', witnessing a day of 'groaning victims, violent imprecations, streams of blood, voices of hatred . . . Madrid was hell', By night, 'we saw the plundering of the dead' and then later, the procession, 'tragic and sinister' of defeated military rebels, carted two by two down the Calle de Alcalá, 'to be shot against the walls of the old bull-ring'.[27] Nearly seventy rebels faced the firing squad; Isabel had wanted to see a thousand or more executed, only to be advised by the general O'Donnell that this would release a wave of blood that might rise and drown the queen herself.

Pleasures and anxieties

Until the late 1980s one might still encounter very elderly persons who had, in their distant childhoods, known the Madrid of Benito Pérez Galdós. Not as an abstraction or an imagined place recreated through literature or film, but as a tangible city environment, with all its poverty and style.

Galdós was, like Dickens in London a generation before him, a capaciously brilliant novelist with a background in journalism. Both were politically active and engaged, Galdós more directly so than Dickens. Both authors have exerted a powerful influence over the memory and conception of their respective cities, yet neither Galdosian Madrid nor Dickensian London exist now other than as reliquaries, constructions for period drama, literary tourism – the houses, the squares, the fountains – or as academic specialism. The contemporary cities are beyond anything they might have imagined. Galdós's beloved city has been overwhelmed by the vast spread of the modern metropolis with its skyline, extensive outlying suburbs and flourishing, cross-cultural blending. If the Madrid of Galdós lingered in tiny pockets until late into the twentieth century in haberdashers and confectioners, in ink-stained bureaucrats and parish priests, in a certain formality of manners, in a haughty *manola* or *chispera*, a lame beggar or a whiskered paterfamilias, then the brutally unsympathetic twenty-first century has been erasing it completely. There remains the occasional business to cast us back to that era, such as the *almacén de Pontejos* – a classic haberdashery from the early twentieth century – but Madrid today is as much its newer developments such as Sanchinarro, Montecarmelo and El Cañaveral, or a Warner Brothers theme park, as it is the Plaza de Pontejos or the Arco de Cuchilleros. This does not mean the novelist and his work are any less relevant or any less magnificent. In 2020, the anniversary of the death of Galdós was both a celebration and a closing. One hundred years encapsulates four generations; beyond this, literary genius exists only in the most diffuse way, through the work, the social commentary, the imaginary characters as they parade across an altogether vanished Madrid: the proud and stormy generals, the lazy bourgeoisie, the humiliated bureaucrats, the miserable beggars clustered in church portals and on street corners, the elegant ladies or the 'fallen women' who so fascinated and populated the nineteenth-century novel.

Politically, the Madrid of Galdós coincided with the half-century from the restoration of the monarchy – Isabel's son, Alfonso XII 'the Pacifier', ascended the throne in 1874 – to the dictatorship of Miguel Primo de Rivera, who in 1923 assumed control of Spain from Alfonso's son, Alfonso XIII 'the African', albeit the latter did not abdicate until 1931. These were fifty years of ferment; the explosion of a new world with its new technologies, art forms and demands for representation. The failed First Spanish Republic – so few would fight for it, and so many against it – was followed by the Restoration, the collapse of the remaining overseas empire after the Spanish–American war of 1898 in Cuba, and a period of national reflection, anxiety and doubt. How had the country managed to lose every last component of empire? How and why were other European nations' empires booming while Spain's had ended in defeat, ignominy and the embarrassing poverty of troops arriving home after the Cuban disaster, sick and ragged and broken? During these years Madrid played host to the corrupted system of political turns – the two main parties swapping in and out of power by mutual agreement – followed by a dictatorship. Years of torment and high pleasure, of modernist and avant-garde art and literature, of intellectual ferment, of rapid urban expansion and collective working-class organisation; of developments in literacy, medicine and science. When it arrived in 1923, the rule of Miguel Primo de Rivera was hardly the first experience of authoritarianism, given the centuries of absolutist kings, but it was Spain's first dictatorship of the modern era.

Madrid was endlessly criticised for broader national failings. If Spain was in a precarious condition after its Cuban crisis, some argued, much of the fault lay with Madrid for having been unable to provide the models of leadership and governance necessary to maintain an empire and its prosperous trade networks. Those hostile to the city argued Madrid had once again proved to be nothing but artifice, a city that knew how to be a court but not a capital, and which, without either empire or court, had no important role or meaning.[1]

These are, of course, the views of detractors. Madrid, meanwhile, was adding further defining public and private monuments to its streets: the Bank of Spain at Cibeles, the Palacio de Linares and a new home for the National Library and Archaeological Museum, both on the Paseo de Recoletos; the Palacio de Cristal in the Retiro park; the imposing Palacio de Fomento close by Atocha, the neoclassical Madrid Stock Exchange, the Palacio Cerralbo, the first phase of the Royal Basilica of Atocha and finally, over a thousand years after the virgin first appeared miraculously among the broken walls, her candles still aflame, the Cathedral of La Almudena. Some of Madrid's wonderful covered markets were built, such as La Cebada, Chamberí, Mostenses, Mercado de la Paz and, early in the twentieth century, San Miguel – all significantly reformed and modernised in subsequent years, and in some cases rebuilt entirely. The great project of the *ensanche*, the enlargement of the city with middle- and upper-class districts of uniform residential buildings and broad, regularly spaced and tree-lined streets – open to the fabled and prophylactic breezes of the nearby *sierra* – continued apace, if not always strictly to Castro's original 1857 plan. Change was constant: 'Everything nowadays is new,' wrote Galdós in 1870, reflecting vague anxieties before an entirely new world bursting in upon the certainties of the old.[2] Madrid may have been slower than others, such as Bilbao and Barcelona, to start this metamorphosis brought by new forms of capital and industrialisation to the physical geography of cities. Even if not experiencing an intense industrialisation in the form of hulking smoke stacks or dark satanic mills – Madrid had no coal mines, no steelworks – the urban growth required to house a new proletariat nevertheless pushed the city, free of her ancient walls, in all directions. The incoming version of Madrid would shake the self-satisfied slumber of her *tertulianos* in their cafés. 'Different times will surely come, other ways of being, other customs', suggested Galdós in *La de Bringas* (1884), predicting surprises and disturbances amid the 'disordered and unthinking movement of a society that has lived for years impatient for change'.[3] In fifty years, the population of Madrid passed from some 400,000 at the Restoration to 1 million during the dictatorship of Primo de Rivera. The city was waking from a period of occasional sleep into a new era of ceaseless movement; leaving behind the comfort of nineteenth-century liberalism to become a dynamic twentieth-century metropolis with all the social, cultural and political conflicts, and triumphs, such a radical change would suppose.

'Every day the growing mass of bricks covered up another thin layer of the landscape.' Galdós, here in *Fortunata y Jacinta*, sounds a note of melancholy for the loss of habitat. The construction of a church is consuming the views of Madrid the frail Maximiliano sees from Cuatro Caminos: 'At last the roof of the church swallowed everything, and all that could be seen was the clear light of the sunset, the tail of the day being dragged away by the sky.'[4] The view had been a loving one: looking west from Cuatro Caminos out onto the Castilian countryside: '. . . the stark tones of the Moncloa landscape and the admirable horizon that looks like the sea: gentle wavy lines from whose apparent unsettledness there rose like the masts of a boat towers of nearby towns.'[5] Perhaps Maxi was looking wistfully at the towers of Villaviciosa by the former Qal'at Jalifa of Islamic times, or Boadilla del Monte, or even Las Rozas, suspected by some of being the site of the lost Roman town of Miacum.

Despite its contemporary status as one of the city's finest residential districts, Chamberí had begun life as a northern fringe where the city walls gave way to the countryside. In Galdós's *Tristana*, we first meet co-protagonist Don Lope living in Chamberí, in a 'cheap, plebeian rented room, with, as noisy neighbours, a tavern, a café, a shop selling milk fresh from the goat, and a narrow inner courtyard with numbered rooms'.[6] This combination of poverty, noise and overcrowding, with its domesticated goat nodding to the rural, is not uncommon in accounts of life in Madrid beyond the mansions and living rooms of the wealthy. In the case of Chamberí, however, there is the saving grace of 'the better light, the fresher air, and the broad, smiling horizon'.[7] Not so the cramped and winding streets of old Madrid, the most common setting for Galdós, where the picturesque, the miserable and the contentedly comfortable live side by side. In *Miau*, his splendid novel denouncing bureaucratic corruption, we meet young Luisito Cadalso, a proto-flaneur on the streets of Madrid. Carrying the humiliating letters in which his unemployed grandfather begged charity of his former friends and acquaintances in government employ, the dedicated pedestrian

acquired a thorough knowledge of the city's topography, as he was up and down every quarter without ever getting lost, and although he knew the shortest route, he would often take the longest, out of habit and following his instincts as an *observer*, enjoying the shop window displays, and listening, without missing a single syllable, to the charlatans selling elixirs or con artists at their tricks. He might, perhaps, come across a monkey astride a dog, or turning the handle on a chocolate grinder . . . at other times an unhappy bear, chained and skinny, or Italians, Turks or false Moors performing any kind of trick for money. He was also entertained by funerals, troops marching to music, construction sites, tramlines, the washing of the streets, a candle-lit Viaticum; in short, all the random events that make up life in the public thoroughfare.[8]

Here was all the confused glory, the music and riches, the colour and misery and layered oppressions of the late nineteenth-century street.

Given his background in journalism and his dedication to social commentary, Galdós also confronted the disadvantage of Madrid's underclass, descending, along with two of his protagonists, into the squalor of Las Cambroneras in *Misericordia*, a novel that portrays the life of beggars in the church portals of the inner city and slums that lay below the Puerta de Toledo, the dumping ground for the poor through the lower reaches of Imperial, districts to which Pío Baroja would return a generation later. Anecdotes serve to highlight social conditions for the less fortunate: in *Misericordia*, two women are mentioned in passing as having died from eating cats. A perfectly fine dish in normal circumstances, it is pointed out, but when the cats are ridden with rabies, three days is all it takes to send a person feverish to the grave.[9] The heroine of the novel, Benina, is a household servant who secretly goes begging to support her employer fallen on hard times. When an inheritance allows her employer's family to come once again into money, Benina is ostracised by those she formerly maintained, partly because of her kindness towards a fellow beggar, a blind Moor named Almudena. One of Galdós's finest novels of sustained, compassionate observation, *Misericordia* is equally a denunciation of middle-class hypocrisy and the triumph of 'comfort' over charity. The underclass might display the virtues of Christian tolerance and kindness, but would not yet be beneficiaries of a rapidly changing Madrid.

It was even possible to overlook the slums in the broader context of Madrid's striking physical setting: an aesthetic pleasure available to anyone regardless of their station in life. At the end of *Miau*, the dejected, humiliated public administrator Ramón Villaamil experiences a sudden flaring up of the otherwise forgotten beauty of life, shortly before taking his own. He sees, pristine and splendid, the clear blue, snow-capped mountains that rear up behind Madrid. 'How beautiful is this!', he exclaims, looking out from where the long incline of San Vicente falls away to the Manzanares. 'It seems as though I were seeing everything for the first time in my life, or as if those mountains, trees and sky had only just been created' and shone with all the light of the new.[10] Below him, but not entering his view, are the packed slums and hovels that border the river.

Having climbed to the top of the hill, he enters a tavern for what has all the hallmarks of a last supper – or in this case, last breakfast. On the point of leaving this world, he is not averse to offering advice on the iniquities of Madrid to a group of young soldiers who

Villaamil at first assumes to be country bumpkins, come to the city to escape 'the dark poverty of their villages' and who might now be looking to find, in this Babel, a way to varnish themselves with respectability. 'Unhappy men! What a favour to disabuse them of their illusions!' He warns them to flee the 'deceitful abyss of Madrid, which will swallow you and make you unhappy for the rest of your lives . . . You must loathe the State, and rebel against your bosses', the wretched Villaamil advises, in an outburst of proto-anarchism.[11] The State, so dominant in Madrid, was for Villaamil a cruel and uncaring behemoth, ever ready to discard its servants when required.

Following the restoration of the Bourbon monarchy in 1874, Madrid hosted one of the least proud periods of political evolution: the system of turns that operated for nearly fifty years either side of the new century. This national political swindle provided for two pro-monarchical forces – conservatives and liberals – to exchange government in a form of carefully managed musical chairs. Excluded from power-sharing in Madrid were any remnant Carlists, republicans – their moment had been brief – and other formations making their appearance in national politics such as socialists and anarchists, the brash young children of nineteenth-century philosophy arriving to stake their claims for a role in the acquisition and distribution of power. The system of turns was rotten to the core: nepotism, fraud and incompetence were rife; elections were rigged, votes bought, ballot outcomes tightly controlled. It was a manifestation, if not also a justification and enforcement, of the idea – to prove so nefarious in the twentieth century and even into the twenty-first – that there were 'two Spains'. Not the two parties brazenly and anti-democratically taking turns at power, but simply those who held power and those who did not. The dividing line, for all it can be diffuse, and for all that people and parties might shift from one side to the other given changing circumstances, nevertheless in time became an unfordable trench. This system, led by the conservative Antonio Cánovas del Castillo and the liberal Práxedes Mateo Sagasta, may have been an improvement on the military coups that had preceded it, but it was to prove insufficient for a new urban modernity; it could not handle all the enquiry, the flux, the urge to innovate and explore, that came with a more educated and demanding citizenry. Likewise, the system did nothing for the increasingly organised working classes from the outer districts or, as in Galdós's *Misericordia*, for the residents of the slum-dark streets, the broken hovels, the dirty, overcrowded *corrales* that filled the unpaved districts, without squares, fountains, parks, street lighting or sewerage, clustered around the Manzanares, their residents prey to cholera, tuberculosis and malnutrition.

Walking the pleasant streets, extensive gardens, sculpted parks and refurbished industrial warehouses in the districts along the Manzanares River in an arc between Santa María de la Cabeza and the Puente de Segovia, it is nowadays difficult to imagine the Madrid that existed here little more than a century before. The lower reaches of what were Las Injurias, Las Peñuelas, Las Cambroneras or Gil Imón have long since been tamed, drained of damp and infection, resurfaced, rebuilt and reimagined. Artist Aureliano de Beruete painted a superb view of Madrid from the meadow of San Isidro in the first decade of the twentieth century,[12] which nevertheless begs the question: where are the slums? Beruete comes a century after Goya, looking across at Madrid from beyond the river, a busy city on a distant hill. It shines under a beautiful sky with a village-like innocence: a clustering of white buildings, a series of church towers in the near distance; the Royal Palace like a beacon; in the foreground a gentle pastoral, a clear stream, the green banks and the San Isidro meadows, all washed in sunshine. Madrid shows off its monumental architecture, including the huge military barracks on the Montaña del Príncipe Pío, now the site of a reconstructed Egyptian temple; the poverty of the city, however, is invisible to Beruete's friendly eye, albeit it must have been staring him in the face, just across the river from his tripod and easel.

In the same decade, novelist Pío Baroja descended, literally and metaphorically, into the insalubrious *barrios*, charting the struggle of young provincial Manuel Alcázar, come to Madrid in search of a living, following the footsteps of his mother who is employed as a household servant. 'They asked me if I wanted to stay there [in the rural town] or move to Madrid, and I told them I'd much prefer to move to Madrid,' he explains to her when she meets him upon his arrival at the Mediodía/Atocha station.[13] Thus begins *La busca* (*The Quest*), where Manuel finds himself among the familiar over-crowded rooms and grimy taverns, observing and learning from street-smart peers to navigate his way among alcoholic card sharps, boasters and swindlers, ruinous women and razor-tongued ladies, immersed in the rich Madrid slang with its catalogues of invective: a whole teeming lower-class life, as textured, intense and dignified as any other, yet full of despair. Just another anonymous boy from a rural backwater, another migrant to swell the hard streets of Madrid and learn its often brutal ways, Manuel Alcázar is a species of Oliver Twist without the optimistic outcomes of Dickens's orphan boy; Baroja's Madrid in *La busca* is a dark city, greasy, aggressive, fundamentally cruel and filthy, a considerably more miserable place than Dickens's London where the light of charity, despite everything, shines through. There are no such sweet trimmings to *La busca*, although the characters retain a sense of humour, an ability to laugh at the absurd circumstances of life and the equally absurd vanity of people. Baroja, wrote Michael Ugarte, was operating as a biological investigator as much as a novelist, applying the principles of science to people and their social settings to describe their realities, the better to diagnose their illnesses: 'Baroja lived in a city that had discovered sociology; it was a city that was both the site of the promotion of the new social understanding as well as a perfect atmosphere for the laboratory itself, the breeding ground of crime, poverty, disease, deviance, and pathology.'[14] Baroja's denunciation was categorical: 'Who concerns themselves with them? Nobody, absolutely nobody. I myself have walked through Injurias and Cambroneras at night, mingled with the lowlife in the taverns of Peñuelas and the bars at Cuatro Caminos ... I have seen women cramped together in the cellars of the government offices and men thrown naked into cells. I have seen ragged street urchins crawl from caves in the hills of San Blas and watched as they devoured dead cats ... nowhere have I seen anyone take a real interest in all this wretchedness and poverty.'[15] Little wonder that infant mortality was still high. 'Haven't you seen the constant procession of little white coffins?', Tristana asks her lover, before adding, bleakly and exaggeratedly. 'A child born is a child dead.'[16]

The first book in the trilogy *La lucha por la vida* – *The Struggle for Life* – *La busca* does not follow any conventional narrative arc. It begins roughly where it ends, with the exhaustion, misery and whip-smart repartee of those who inhabit the deprivation of the lower reaches of Madrid. It features the old iron aqueduct over the Calle Segovia – the current aqueduct would not be built until 1930 – where Manuel wanders to enjoy the brief pleasure of the evening sky. Yet splendid sunsets and their fiery, roiling clouds were not always enough to raise the spirits: the sky might be limpid, burning, pure, but the earth below was still subject to human miseries: the highway to Extremadura in the distance was 'a broken line with two sets of grey and filthy houses ... That severe and depressing landscape on the outskirts of Madrid, in all its cold and sullen grimness reached into Manuel's soul.'[17] Baroja does not let up: only a few moments later, Manuel is to find out one of his best friends, in an excess of envious rage, has murdered his former girlfriend and then killed himself.

After a series of misadventures, Manuel finds a temporary home with Custodio, a rag-and-bone man, along with his wife, dog, donkeys, chickens and pig. They inhabit a world of filth, leftovers and rubbish, and have settled into a small black depression near the river into which is brought and processed every discarded object, every bottle or shred of tin, every bone and shard and strip of dirty cloth, every rotten vegetable; even human waste, resold as fertiliser in the market gardens along the river bank. Here it is Baroja rather than Galdós (and without the dramatic, sentimental plot twists) who brings to mind the Dickens of *Our Mutual Friend*, with the great piles of refuse from the modern city carted to the outskirts to be transformed into a type of base gold. Around 10,000 rag-and-bone men operated in Madrid at the opening of the twentieth century, their mules constantly hauling rubbish to the periphery.[18]

At the dusk of one century and the dawning of another, Madrid was overflowing with every kind of seller, trickster and huckster: all means of making a living were valid. If the life of a working-class family was difficult, it was worse for the underclass of beggars, homeless and unemployed. There was little work in rural Spain – the adolescent migrant Manuel is typical of his time – and the loss of colonial markets had a depressing effect on trade and sectors of the economy.[19] Trying to find his way towards steady employment, in the second volume of the trilogy Manuel goes to work for the eccentric Bonifacio de Mingote, who has set up the pompously titled 'European Agency of Business and Placements', a species of talent agency – or simply rogue's den – of various facets and opportunities: available for clients of all social classes were 'medicines, meats, fruit, seafood, funeral wreaths, false teeth and women's hats'. Bonifacio's multifarious services also ran to analysis of saliva and urine; prepared course notes were offered for those studying law or medicine; loans, mortgages and other financial instruments were offered; advertisements that were 'monstrous, sensational, moving . . . all available at ridiculously low prices'.[20] Here is ingenuity gone wild, a world teeming with both abstract concepts and concrete objects, a city full of speculators and grifters, scoundrels and opportunists, along with honest others, all following that crooked path towards modernity.

Not all was bleak in the *fin de siglo* city; bourgeois Madrid had entered one of its finest periods. Graceful residential architecture blossomed across the city, as did new opportunities for the secular pursuits of consumerism and entertainment. As the bourgeoisie moved increasingly into positions of political and financial power, a business elite was overtaking the traditional aristocracy at the top of the social pecking order, sometimes by the direct method of marrying into nobility.[21] Madrid was not only a fine city for the wealthy; it was a place of leisure, to observe and be observed. For men, the cafés and the *tertulias* functioned as a key point of social connection, display and for negotiating placements for family members; for bourgeois women, more restricted by conservative social protocols, there were the pleasure gardens and tree-lined avenues, the magnificent and fashionable Paseo de la Castellana, the opera and theatre, the markets and, increasingly, shopping arcades. Parsons suggests that in the novels of Galdós, while men are often static, at their business or their *tertulias*, women are in constant movement across the city, engaged in shopping at markets and boutiques, attending Mass, visiting friends or performing acts of charity.[22] Further, there is a preference shown for the sociability of 'old' Madrid, with its tight network of streets, balconies and small squares, over the 'new' Madrid of the *ensanche* districts such as Salamanca where neighbours had greater space between themselves and there was less mixing of social classes. The old city had always been a blend of aristocracy and vagrancy settled atop the rich compost of tradition; the new city was still in the process of definition.

The chance to relax and breathe 'country air' was important for those entirely removed, on a daily basis, from nature. In *Tristana*, the eponymous heroine loves to spend her afternoons walking not in 'Madrid proper' but in the area around Cuatro Caminos: 'a walk in the country, usually with a picnic, moments of healthy relaxation'.[23] On Sundays, this area 'thronged with people' as the residents of Chamberí headed out to picnic in Tetuán, and the Calle de Ríos Rosas is described as a 'lovely, broad, straight, sunny road, which looks out over a vast expanse of countryside'.[24] Meeting her lover Horacio for evening strolls, Tristana wanders past a fairground at rest, 'plunged in lonely gloom, the massive bulk of the carousel where the wooden horses stood poised with their galloping legs outstretched as if bewitched', while to the west a typically spectacular Madrid sunset played out, 'the sky in flames'.[25]

The late nineteenth century was a time of new consumerist habits: in a change that would work its way through the city over the following hundred years, the small family businesses integral to the fabric of Madrid life – tailors, haberdashers, greengrocers, jewellers, cabinet makers, silk merchants – would begin to be overtaken by the department store and, eventually, the supermarket chain and the multinational retailer. The women and men who patronised these small businesses used them as a system of navigation for moving around the city; location in Madrid was described not by the street name or number but by reference to surrounding cafés, stores or bars. The fully glassed shop window and its display became part of the visual enticement of the street, with fashionable boutiques clustered around the Puerta del Sol and adjacent streets such as Carmen, Montera, Carretas or Hortaleza. Shopping for luxuries rather than essentials – for trinkets and furs rather than milk, meat and chickpeas – was obviously a matter of status, but equally of pleasure, and of knowing oneself as *modern* and necessarily *cosmopolitan*: what better than to be able to dress in the latest fabrics and designs from Paris?

Madrid also exerted a cultural influence on smaller, provincial capitals. In another of the great nineteenth-century Spanish novels, Leopoldo Alas's *La Regenta*, set in the fictional town of Vetusta (the Asturian capital, Oviedo), rowdy young gentlemen of the upper classes, eager to show off at the theatre, 'disperse themselves in various boxes where, making little pretence of keeping the proprieties, they smoke, laugh, talk in loud voices, and interrupt the performance – all because it is the height of fashion to do so, a faithful imitation of what they have seen in theatres in Madrid'.[26] Most of these young men 'had lived in Madrid, and they still imitated the habits, manners and gestures which they had observed there'.[27] Thus, the old story of the iniquitous city corrupting the innocent rural; the seducer Don Álvaro takes a woman's hand 'following the fashion which was then beginning in Madrid'.[28] Provincialism was not just a matter of aping Madrid in the fustian capitals, but also of absurdly denying its influence: any drama or comedy that had been applauded in Madrid was met with loud interruptions; 'a criterion of unalloyed provincialism prevailed among them, this seeming the most natural line to take in art.'[29] Thus, a dual comedy plays out, whereby Madrid is slavishly followed, all the while pretending its style and preferences will not be imposed.

After a number of districts had been incorporated into the city, and its size more than doubled via the *ensanche* developments, another visionary took the eastern edge of Madrid under his wing and began to plan a remarkable, if ultimately unrealisable, urban experiment.

Arturo Soria, born in one of the quintessential streets of old Madrid, Caballero de Gracia, was one of the first urban planners to incorporate utopian social and political ideals of the late nineteenth century into a twentieth-century vision of how a city might function.

At that time Madrid, as today in the flamboyant twenty-first-century capital, faced a critical shortage of housing, compounded by the unaffordability of its inner districts, a problem in turn exacerbated by property speculation. While Baroja was more focused on a literary denunciation of the appalling living conditions of the outcast population on the southern fringes of the city, Arturo Soria sought solutions through the concept of the garden city, a combination of straight-lined discipline and order, hygiene and fresh air; the construction of new, clean, regulated apartments, houses and sports clubs replacing the overcrowded old *chabolas*, or slums, of the outer districts. Soria attempted to blend the healthy virtues of the rural with the productivity demanded by the modern city. Much of his plan was conceptually based around the rigidity of tram and train lines: transport corridors offered the opportunity to develop optimistic living conditions around their strict horizontality. In this, Soria was absolutely contemporary, even if his plans, like those of Castro and Fernández de los Ríos before him, were not followed faithfully from draft to execution. His original idea was for a linear city of some 43 kilometres in length, the distance that connected the principal districts of Madrid via an outer ring, a looping clockwise semicircle from Fuencarral in the north to Carabanchel in the south, via Hortaleza, Barajas and Vallecas, anticipating by the best part of a century the series of motorways – the M-30, M-40 and M-50 – that now encircle the capital. A central artery, a grand avenue some 40 metres wide, would form a core around which to cluster homes and gardens, an ordered urban environment filled with lakes, parks and public transport. Housing might be simple or luxurious, depending on the client, but in all cases buildings, whatever their function, would be accompanied by orchards and gardens. The plan was insistent: to overcome all the problems associated with working-class overcrowding that blighted nineteenth-century industrial expansion, every family must have its own house and its own parcel of land, no matter how small, its own access to fresh air and sunshine. Below the central avenue would run supply systems of water, gas and electricity, a pneumatic postal service and the new technology of telephone communications.

Soria's conception of the linear city – Ciudad Lineal – confirmed the east as the new axis of metropolitan Madrid. The western edge of the city, around the Royal Palace, had been an aristocratic district for centuries, yet the escarpments that fall away from the palace had limited growth in that direction. The late nineteenth century created bourgeois districts to the north and north-east, at the same time as cementing the south as Madrid's zone of industry, manufacturing and the highest incidence of poverty. The new Ciudad Lineal was not Madrid's only experiment in urban development; in the first decades of the new century, pursuant to popular theories of the 'garden city' with an emphasis on urban hygiene, family space and affordability, a series of 'colonies' was designed and built to improve urban overcrowding. Scattered around Madrid, these unique colonies, such as the modernist Colonia de la Prensa in Carabanchel, Colonia Iturbe in Fuente del Berro or La Regalada in Retiro, have in time become some of the most expensive real estate in the contemporary city.

Soria himself was a fascinating character: a revolutionary on the barricades of the 1860s in his youth, a progressive politician, a republican who refused a royal decoration for services, a visionary urban planner and, in the latter part of his life, a theosophist; he admired ideas from an unusual range of sources, including English philosopher Herbert Spencer and the then ubiquitous Madame Blavatsky. Perhaps most importantly, he was inspired by the work of Ildefons Cerdà, the grand theorist and creator of Barcelona's Eixample district. Cerdà, like Soria, faced great resistance to his plans, but today the Eixample is considered one of the finest urban designs of nineteenth-century Europe. Cerdà has had a greater impact on Barcelona than Soria's work, constantly disrupted, neglected after his death and finally abandoned after the civil war, has had on Madrid. Traces of his grand plan remain, a spine running through the district of Ciudad Lineal and along the major avenue of Arturo Soria named in his honour; however, he must be considered a wasted talent, one of the visionaries who was not permitted, through a range of personal, political and financial circumstances, to contribute as much as he would have wished to the development of Madrid.

The city continued to build vertically even as it made rapid increases in its horizontal spread, a constant state of rebuilding, of burying or simply destroying the past, raising new shapes to meet new standards. Bucolic semi-rural scenes such as those enjoyed by Tristana and her lover Horacio were quickly becoming a thing of the past: 'one day they would follow the road to Fuencarral, the next they would explore the sombre depths of El Pardo, where the ground was covered in prickly, metallic-looking leaves, the ash groves that border the Manzanares, the bare peaks of Amaniel, or the deep ravines of Abroñigal.'[30] The advent of trams, trains and automobiles, and from 1919 the arrival of the Metro system, meant people were able to move through the city in ways that had never been possible. Many stayed anchored in their home *barrios*, but there were now more opportunities to traverse the ever-growing city. The advent and popularity of photography meant that *madrileños* and their city were documented as never before; the first daguerreotype of Madrid had been created in 1839, a scratched and blurry image of the Royal Palace, seen as if through muslin, taken from the far side of the Manzanares. French photographer Jean Laurent established himself in Madrid in 1843, becoming 'royal photographer' – the first time such a title had existed – to Isabel II in 1861 and producing one of the finest group portraits of the period, in 1868, of the provisional government that assumed power after her overthrow (from which time his role as royal photographer became redundant).[31] In addition to the great novelists, photography provides an insight, no matter how distorted or selective, into nineteenth-century life: the buildings under construction, the factory workers, bell ringers, soldiers and assassins; the carts and trams, cafés, street vendors, cyclists, vagrants, priests, dead children, politicians, dancers and the quickly changing fashions proudly worn by men and women.

Just as the Madrid of this era of great novelists has been erased by an intrusive and amnesiac twenty-first century, and the photographic images of that time have all the grey and sepia strangeness of scenes from an unrecognisable past, so the late nineteenth-century urban expansion helped to erase the *manolos* and *chisperas*. This was consistent with the bourgeois shift in the nature of the city: those loveable working-class delinquents were relegated, like the *bandidos* of the mountain roads, to folklore and the vast realms of nostalgia. They exist now as costume pieces for the popular celebrations of *castizo* Madrid, such as the fiestas of San Isidro, La Paloma or San Antonio de la Florida. Liberal, bourgeois and modernist Madrid coexisted with the traditional, all the while taking the stock characters of old Madrid and placing them in the theatre or literature, when not in naphthalene: as the working class organised politically and moved out of the slums, these characters were left behind, dancing the *chotis*[32] in a postcard limbo, populating the repertoire of theatre, taking bit parts in the native operetta form of the *zarzuela*. In the inscrutable way of history, of all the styles worn by the people of Madrid in the twelve centuries of its settled life it is the nineteenth-century carnival dress, its costumes and dances that have come to represent 'traditional' Madrid, to be role-played in the downtime from the hectic schedules of the twenty-first; yet another of the ways the nineteenth century's cultural frameworks continue to survive.

Was the Spanish capital 'a grotesque deformation of European civilization', as writer Ramón del Valle-Inclán suggested?[33] Of course not: even allowing for his exaggeration, his love of the grotesque – the *esperpento* – this only makes sense if one assumes that hoary narrative of Spain being somehow apart from Europe, an appendage that shares little of the common ancestry of the continent. Quite the contrary: in its bourgeois modernisation, its grand avenues dedicated to commerce and pleasure, its political turmoil, its restive working class, its exaggerated difference between rich and poor and the challenges of its slum-dwelling underclass, Madrid was very like other major capitals of the time. As in London or Paris, it was a long way between the grimy and often infected edges of the city, to the café conversations, the opera balcony or the literary salon. The internal politics may have been a hall of mirrors, but the national accounts were boosted by key industries – notably textiles in Catalonia and steel in the Basque region – while Madrid's thriving bankers grew even more prosperous financing national and international trade and the city's boom. In the second half of the nineteenth century, Madrid was a beacon for members of the provincial and overseas business class, in the latter case particularly from Cuba, who came 'to consolidate, grow and diversify their wealthy portfolios' at the same time as 'the children of the provincial bourgeoisie came to Madrid in numbers to study at university and to join the upper ranks of government administration'.[34]

The *fin de siglo* city did not carry everyone with it: the last manifestations of pre-modern Madrid trailed away, lost amid an incoming society of electric lights and luminous shop window displays, of skyscrapers and automobiles, underground transport and assertive young women; a place of bright advertising, boulevards, arcades and cinema palaces. Yet despite all it had come through, Madrid's greatest demographic and physical changes, and its most serious social conflicts, were still to arrive.

New hopes, new conflicts

L ife gathered speed. The opening decades of the twentieth century were marked by excitement, change, renovation and violence. Fundamental to this turbulent period were: the increasing political organisation of the working class; a rise in violent expression and counter-expression as labour and discontent met their diverse opponents head-on; the rapid spread of anticlerical, secular, free thinking and programmes of public education; the consolidation of socialism, anarchism and communism as alternative bodies of political thought and action; a military dictatorship of 1923–31 that advanced conservative nationalism in the face of a crumbled empire, preparing the ground for future such manifestations; the social and cultural impact of modernism in literature, the arts and architecture; and, as a culmination to all of the above, the declaration of the Second Republic from April 1931.

Beyond a number of singular exceptions, the great majority of important political, cultural and financial events of this period were based in, or passed through, Madrid. In 1879 in the Casa Labra tavern, on a narrow street just off the Puerta del Sol, a group of typographers, artisans and medical students, gathered around the authoritarian figure of typographer Pablo Iglesias, founded the Spanish Socialist Workers' Party – the PSOE – which would prove, through all its light and shade, the country's most successful political organisation.[1] The growing proletarian movement remained for the time being a largely male phenomenon. The same occurred in cultural matters where, despite the occasional brilliant writer such as Emilia Pardo Bazán, the so-called Generation of 1898, and after it the so-called Generation of 1914, overflowed with male stars of the literary, scientific and philosophical firmament. Unsurprisingly, the members assigned to these 'generations' usually rejected such categorisation. Nevertheless, the tag has stuck; and the generations of 1898 and 1914 – and of 1927 – have all become reference points from which twentieth-century Spanish cultural politics are measured. All three generations were central to the political, cultural and intellectual course of life in Madrid, and in each of the three, a successively larger number of women played prominent roles.

The success or failure of reform marked the political lives and attitudes of those attached to the Generation of 1898. Despite the stagnation of the 'system of turns', significant change was fomenting in the decades before and after the loss of Cuba, starting with the radical transformation of the countryside from the middle of the nineteenth century that had such an impact on the demographics of Madrid. Arising from the deprivation faced by so many of these internal migrants was an increasing political consciousness, stirred by a combination of education, community and workplace politics and inevitable doses of demagoguery; anarchist and socialist labour movements called for an end to centuries of monarchy, clerical influence and economic oppression. Europe was once again a guiding light; republican leaders saw in political movements north of the Pyrenees a model to follow based on a belief in rational progress, a democratisation of justice and the establishment of social and political equality. For the young Manuel Azaña, fresh out of the provincial environment of Alcalá de Henares, French culture was the light of hope, with Paris embodying the Age of Reason; it was, he wrote, 'a spiritual home for educated men of the so-called Latin race',[2] overwhelmed by his first visit in 1911 and giving in to a combination of self-pity and disdain for his own cultural roots. A decade earlier in 1903, he had summarised the problems facing Spain and its rulers, problems that remained at the time of Primo de Rivera's dictatorship in the mid-1920s: the rooting out of rural political corruption known as *caciquismo*; reform of church–state relations; the suppression of a wide range of privileges; the promotion of freedom of association; the entry of 'the masses' into the political system and the public realm; universal suffrage and the role of the state as a guarantor of equality.[3]

All this was to be taken step by step: Azaña had no time for the nostalgic 'regenerationists' after 1898, with their gloomy heads turned to a lost past, lamenting the venality of modern life and wishing to reinvent a glorious Spain; nor did he have any time for the wild young revolutionaries, ready to burn things down without regard for the ongoing significance of heritage. For one of Spain's most prominent early twentieth-century intellectuals, José Ortega y Gasset, 'Spain was the problem and Europe the solution.' If Spain was the problem, then Madrid either personified that problem or stood as an example of how to find the true path of modernity. Unsurprisingly, this formulation continues to enjoy currency even today: in the eternally divided world of the Spanish body politic, the European Union can be seen as the ultimate arbiter in domestic cultural, economic and political disputes, with the opinion of 'Europe' used as the last word in a political argument. Then and now, Europe was not just a place; it was a concept, a series of beliefs, a way of understanding the world. Others strongly reject this deficit model whereby policy developed externally to Spain is considered always and necessarily more progressive. The obvious point as regards this largely sterile debate is that Spain and Europe are not separate entities: they are both intimately part of each other, and have been for centuries; both teach, and learn from, the other. The very same point can be made for the question of Madrid's role in relation to the broader Spanish nation, notwithstanding all the nuances of regional difference: neither is conceivable without the other.

The republican, socialist and anarchist political projects – socialism grew deeper roots in Madrid, anarchism in Barcelona – faced the task of winning hearts and minds to a vision of the world that, while attractive, was for many deeply unfamiliar; one in which a necrotic monarchy, nobility and clergy would give way to a twentieth-century society of educated and engaged citizens participating in the construction of their own lives. There was a captive audience: Madrid continued to grow rapidly due to internal migration, with the population exploding in districts such as Tetuán, Prosperidad, Chamartín de la Rosa, Vallecas, Vicálvaro or Carabanchel.[4] Sanitation and health facilities improved, and infant mortality dropped sharply. This increase in population exacerbated the need for housing reform and education among the poor, who year by year were being expelled from the old centre of Madrid and out into the still largely unplanned periphery which did not enjoy the rectilinear urban design of the middle- and upper-class districts. Work was to be found among the new industries: food processing, paper, textiles, chemicals, tobacco and large-scale manufacturing,[5] but it was education that was seen as the baseline from which political change might occur.

Since the late 1870s from its headquarters in Madrid, the Institución Libre de Enseñanza – the Free Institution of Education – had conceived and driven a thoroughgoing reform and literacy programme across Spain that opposed the leading role the church and its many affiliate institutions played in education. The programme attracted to it many of the country's leading scientists, philosophers and artists of the time, including José Ortega y Gasset, Santiago Ramón y Cajal, Joaquín Sorolla, Leopoldo Alas and Antonio Machado; hundreds of others lent support to the grassroots activity of community education. The decades either side of the end of the century were prolific in new institutions: 'from laic schools to choirs, masonic lodges, neighbourhood improvement associations, cultural centres, "free thinking" societies, and worker *ateneos*' all with the purpose of relearning the past and present, all in 'the pursuit of human perfection through self-improvement'.[6] Reflecting social change across other parts of Europe, women began to move in from the wings and towards centre stage; their integration into society as equal members in status and opportunity was a principle, albeit one followed irregularly, of the Free Institution of Education.

True to its history as a city of contrasts, while parts of Madrid were restive and increasingly radicalised, others were perfectly comfortable with the changes brought by modern technology, finance and design. Madrid experienced an economic boom, with enormous trade opportunities opening up as a result of Spain's neutrality during the First World War. A new cityscape was about to emerge as a swathe was cut through the old city to create the Gran Vía, a paradise of commerce, luxury apartments, hotels, entertainment and technology. The city was illuminated, not with the precarious torches or gas lamps of the past, but with electricity, an invisible energy that gave a constant source of light, spurring new styles of nightlife and entertainment, and simultaneously creating new forms of concern around hygiene, civics and public morality.[7] For Ramón Gómez de la Serna, to emerge from the underground Metro and into the night-time illumination of the Puerta del Sol was an experience that was new, surreal and dazzling, a passage from one world into another.[8]

Between 1919 and 1925, the northern district of Cuatro Caminos and the southern district of Puente de Vallecas – both resolutely working class – were connected via the Puerta del Sol and the brand new Madrid Metro, opening a thoroughfare across and below the city, helping to ease the chronic congestion of the streets. New tunnels opened up their winding ways; there had not been so much activity beneath the city since Felipe IV was regularly gondoliering along the candle-lit canals between appointments with his lovers. To subterranean Madrid's network of water supplies and secret tunnels, there was now a more substantial city being created below ground, a parallel world that would depend entirely on electricity. As it developed, the Metro system became one of the aesthetic triumphs of Madrid: a cheap, beautifully designed and highly efficient means of navigating the city, with its first stations designed by architect Antonio Palacios, responsible for some of the finest buildings in early twentieth-century Madrid. The Metro network grew its slender arms as the city grew, reaching out in every direction, connecting periphery with heart via slums, middle-class districts, business and government quarters and the most aristocratic of streets. The Metro went everywhere, transporting thousands and then millions daily from task to task, hypnotised by the rocking of carriages, terrified by the high-pitched braking, the fervent prayers of the claustrophobes for whom the next station, an island of light amid the vast dark highway along which the city travels, cannot come soon enough. Commuters daydream, buskers sing and beggars plead amid the marvellous and poetic beauty of the station names – words as contours that follow time and place, track local and national history: Tirso de Molina, Noviciado, El Capricho, Sierra de Guadalupe, Miguel Hernández, Esperanza, Alonso Cano, Eugenia de Montijo, Núñez de Balboa, Arroyofresno, Las Musas, Alfonso XIII, Paco de Lucía. The entire Metro system is a dictionary of national significance.

Particularly in its centre, Madrid remained a city that had been formed between the medieval and the baroque. Its streets struggled to cope with an early twentieth-century traffic of cars, trams, buses, horses and carts, all competing with pedestrians and ambulant vendors. Period photographs show tight and frenzied streets where the new phenomenon of gridlock became common. For a disgruntled Azorín, the hectic confusion of street life and the rapidity of change were the products of 'modern industrialism' and the dominance of 'the all-powerful market', in turn responsible for profiteering, exploitation, excessive noise, the hazard of traffic and for introducing a formerly unknown means of death – accidental electrocution.[9]

The singular decade of the 1920s left a deep impression on Madrid. On the one hand, a flowering of secular architecture and an astonishing concentration of writers, thinkers and artists; on the other, a military dictatorship. Fed up with the failures of Spain's conservative and liberal turns which had overseen not only increasing social violence – the rotten system was entirely unequipped to address the needs of a fast-changing society – but also one of Spain's greatest military disasters, at Annual in the Spanish Protectorate of Morocco, in 1923 General Miguel Primo de Rivera staged a coup and took control of the nation, a move approved by the largely hapless King Alfonso XIII. Madrid thus entered a period of rapid technological change and cultural modernism while politically straddled with the antiquated figure of the strongman. This did not seem to matter unduly, as the economy was buoyant, employment was growing, work conditions were negotiated and improved, and the violent opposition of unions and anarchists in the previous decade gave way to greater social calm, Primo de Rivera even managing for a time to bring the socialists into his tent. The middle class was increasingly estranged from the monarchy, but this did not manifest itself in organised protest. By no means were all republicans politically on the left; the reality was far more complicated. There were not a few republicans in Madrid as the 1930s began who were socially, religiously and politically conservative. They had grown exasperated with the monarchy, but as conservatives never bought into a narrative of social ferment. Intellectuals, meanwhile, divided into different camps, without yet taking up the more defined positions they would have to adopt as war drew near.

Since the 1880s there had been plans to modernise central Madrid, if not in the same manner as the *ensanche* urban reforms – there was simply no room – then at least to endow the cramped inner city with a grand avenue in the style of Paris or New York. Given the morphology of old Madrid, there was only one way to connect the eastern edge with its ancient western side – by carving a path through the often ramshackle, cheek-by-jowl and precarious old buildings. Just as homes were expropriated to shape the Plaza Mayor 300 years earlier, so now sections of the centre were torn down, fourteen streets disappeared altogether and fifty altered as, between 1910 and 1932, in three sections, downtown Madrid was opened up and the Gran Vía constructed. Neighbourhood resistance slowed the start of the project, but municipal eyes were on the higher prize of modernisation and glamour. From its very inauguration, the Gran Vía has been one of the great symbols of the city. It announced spectacle and allure: its buildings were the tallest and grandest in the city, its pavements the broadest; it housed theatres for the hugely popular new art form of cinema, luxury hotels, banking and telco headquarters and department stores. At the same time, the avenue was barely finished when, in 1936, it became a site of resistance to the nationalist shelling of the city in the opening months of the civil war.

One of the most famous and representative images of Madrid, whether captured in its infinite moods in infinite postcards, or now mobile phones, or in the remarkable work of realist painter Antonio López, is the view up the Calle de Alcalá from Cibeles, past the Bank of Spain, the Círculo de Bellas Artes and the Edificio de las Cariátides – now the Instituto Cervantes – to the grand Metrópolis Building.[10] Opposite one of Madrid's finest religious buildings, the eighteenth-century parish church of San José, the avenue bifurcates, with the Gran Vía commencing on the right, following a gentle rise up to the Red de San Luis. Opposite here stands Madrid's first skyscraper, the Telefónica building, made famous by Arturo Barea's accounts of working inside the building, overseeing foreign correspondents during the first months of the civil war; the building was also a sitting target for nationalist shelling, launched from the nearby Casa de Campo, that caused so much havoc on the Gran Vía. From here, the second or middle section of the Gran Vía, the most intensely commercialised, the most standardised by international capital and branding, runs down to the Plaza del Callao to join other buildings of superb weight and style: the Palacio de la Prensa, the Hotel Atlántico and former Hotel Alfonso XIII, the Palacio de la Música, the Cine Avenida, the Cine Callao, the Edificio Carrión with the Cine Capitol and the Edificio La Adriática, all built in the decade between 1925 and 1935. From Callao, the Gran Vía runs downhill to the Plaza de España; parts of this final section were not completed until after the civil war, as the conflict brought conventional life in the capital to a standstill, damaging this brand new symbol of urbane modernity in the heart of Madrid.

Cinemas had recently established themselves not only as enormously popular entertainment, but as a profound break from settled ways of conceiving the world. In the 1920s grand cinema palaces were built along the Gran Vía; among intellectuals, debates arose as to the cultural or political usefulness of this new art form. In seeing the world from unimagined angles and providing an entire new stock of visual metaphors, cinema was a freshly minted alphabet with the capacity to create wholly alternative meanings or, perhaps, no meaning at all other than the rendering of what came before as irrelevant and antiquated. It was also a tremendous platform for comedy. For Valle-Inclán, with its constant shift of images and its capacity for simultaneity, 'the techniques of cinema suggested methods and metaphors for writing the visual force of the city'.[11] In some respects a precursor of our hyper-surveilled cities, cinema was another form of light that was flooding the urban, banishing the murky corners and inky shadows where, for centuries, elements of Madrid life had found their natural habitat. The cinema also defined new versions of those clichéd cultural phenomena of the interwar years and beyond: the sex symbol, the villain, the playboy, the goddess, the war hero and the impossible love story.

Cafés – many with their own distinct *tertulias* – were an essential part of the Gran Vía, as they always had been around the Puerta del Sol. Among those to have staked a place in the legend of the city were the Granja El Henar on the Calle de Alcalá, where at different times one might find Valle-Inclán, Ortega y Gasset, Manuel Azaña or the writer Ramon J. Sender; the Pombo, home to the then ubiquitous Gómez de la Serna; the sumptuous Negresco, frequented by local playwright Jacinto Benavente or painter Julio Romero de Torres, and which hosted one of the first female *tertulias*; the long-standing Levante, or the Suizo. The centrality of the male-dominated *tertulia* cafés is highlighted in *Fortunata y Jacinta*, being a place where men escaped the responsibilities of domestic life, while also providing them a platform from which to brag or pontificate, when not plotting a marital infidelity. As for their importance as sites of political conspiracy, Castillo sums it up: one could leave the *tertulia* and head straight to prison, or straight into government, such was the volatility of the times and the shifting nature of allegiances.[12] Newer establishments, such as Chicote on Gran Vía, while being thoroughly *madrileño*, drew inspiration not from Paris but from New York and the frenetic years of 1920s to 1940s United States;[13] the drawcard was not so much an intellectual discussion, an artistic axe to grind or a political creed to expound, as the opportunity to see and be seen amid the cocktail glamour of Hollywood stars, aristocrats, writers, bullfighters and politicians, most marked by the status of their metaphorical blue blood.

The Gran Vía is rarely empty; Antonio López's painting renders the city at 6.30 a.m., a strange moment of limbo calm for a city such as Madrid. Even today, and despite the overwhelming stand-ardisation of international commerce along its length, it still presents as spectacular: its east–west orientation gifts stunning light effects at dawn and dusk, and its heritage architecture has been carefully protected and reformed. Yet there is another side: given the magnif-icence of its buildings, it is perhaps unfair to suggest the Gran Vía had a touch of the Potemkin village; nevertheless, a few blocks behind the splendid facade of capital and style, narrow streets still crouched in relative darkness. In the late 1980s, spending countless hours in this area, I recall a Gran Vía dotted with wretched, disa-bled beggars and the streets behind the great avenue – Desengaño, Caballero de Gracia – full of equally wretched prostitutes; thieves and drug addicts were also common, the latter representative of a terrible heroin scourge that ruined so many lives in Madrid during the 1980s.[14] Madrid may have been the 'capital of capital', but beyond the finance and entertainment industries, the thousands of service industry workers and the equally ubiquitous thousands of government and municipal employees, it was and is a city with a significant underclass living precarious and damaged lives.

In the first decades of the twentieth century Madrid was either the permanent or temporary home to a remarkable range of writers, artists and intellectuals. Considered 'the Silver Age', this period saw the finest concentration of creative minds since the fabled Golden Age three centuries before. These decades combined gloom at loss of empire with ebullient enthusiasm for the possibilities of a new politics and a new modernity, and forged an aesthetic vision of Spain and its capital which remains influential to this day.

Other cities are rightly proud of their periods of creative intensity – 1920s Paris or Weimar Berlin come to mind. Yet Madrid could boast an equal concentration of artistic talent: the cultural, intel-lectual and political ferment of these years made the Spanish capital one of the most creative and fascinating, if fractious, cities in the world. After a quiet opening decade of the century, Madrid was wide awake; within a generation the city had gone from being an elegant and conservative capital – albeit fringed with slums – full of smug *tertulias* and intellectuals licking the wounds of an empire lost, to a suddenly swarming and expansive city, roaring and bursting for change.

Two revered and elderly writers – Benito Pérez Galdós and Emilia Pardo Bazán – had died at the opening of the 1920s, an older guard passing on the baton. The extraordinary Pardo Bazán had, among a lifetime of achievements, been the first female member of the Athenaeum, a prominent voice of nineteenth-century feminism, and promoted the work of Russian novelists such as Dostoyevsky, Turgenev and Tolstoy into Spain.[15] The Madrid these literary masters left behind flocked with talent, both native and imported. Without classifying them into any schools or movements, their careers overlapping at different points, we can observe in the first decades of the century writers such as Pío Baroja, Ramón del Valle-Inclán, Ramón Gómez de la Serna, Carmen de Burgos, Corpus Barga, Juan Ramón Jiménez, Pedro Salinas, Azorín, Vicente Aleixandre, Jacinto Benavente, Agustín de Foxá, Dionisio Ridruejo, Concha Espina and Elena Fortún; the great street chronicler of Madrid, Pedro de Répide; Clara Campoamor, trailblazing feminist politician and writer; Margarita Nelken, María Zambrano, Arturo Barea and Manuel Chaves Nogales, all active in the decade and a half prior to the outbreak of civil war. Working mostly elsewhere but spending periods in Madrid were Miguel de Unamuno, Antonio and Manuel Machado, Rafael Alberti and María Teresa León, Pablo Neruda, Miguel Hernández and Federico García Lorca. Painters were also thick on the ground; after the romanticism, landscapes and history genre paintings of the nineteenth century, the early decades of the twentieth were another brilliant age for Spanish art. The teenage Picasso had lived in Madrid at the close of the nineteenth century, and the great female Cubist, María Blanchard, spent time studying and exhibiting in the capital in the first decade of the new century. Juan Gris had been born by the Puerta del Sol; masters such as José Gutiérrez-Solana, Maruja Mallo and Joaquín Sorolla worked in Madrid; Remedios Varo, Salvador Dalí and Ignacio Zuloaga came and went from the capital. Then, film-makers Luis Buñuel or Edgar Neville, eminent scientists such as Santiago Ramón y Cajal, scientist, historian and writer Gregorio

Marañón, philosopher José Ortega y Gasset directing the *Revista de Occidente*[16] with its spectacular list of national and international contributors, young political and literary aspirant Manuel Azaña and a host of other writers across the political spectrum, from José Moreno Villa to Ramiro de Maeztu and Eugenio d'Ors. Boom years for magazines, there was no lack of opportunities for writers, intellectuals, graphic artists and photographers: Ortega's *Revista de Occidente* was only one of a host of literary and cultural publications in the Madrid of this era, including *España*, *La Pluma*, *El Sol*, *Estampa*, *Crónica* and *Nueva Revista*, illustrated magazines such as *Nuevo Mundo* and the politically conservative *Blanco y Negro*, or liberal-leaning newspapers such as *El Imparcial*, *El Liberal* or *Heraldo de Madrid*. The city was also thick with international visitors: John Dos Passos, Leon Trotsky, Ernest Hemingway, Arthur Koestler, Gerda Taro, Robert Capa, Martha Gellhorn, Albert Einstein, Errol Flynn, André Malraux, Antoine de Saint-Exupéry and Igor Stravinsky, among others. Like Paris and Berlin, Madrid was a crucible where the European twentieth century was being forged.

A reference point for many of these talents, apart from the Athenaeum, the Prado or the many *tertulias*, was the Residencia de Estudiantes, a beautifully designed complex on a small hill in north-eastern Madrid that opened in 1915. Emerging from the work of the Free Institution of Education, the Residencia came under the directorship of Alberto Jiménez Fraud and was one of the most exciting hubs for learning, creativity and free thought in the European interwar years. The Residencia was undoubtedly elitist, yet the creative record of many of its alumni speaks for itself: famously, the Residencia was where Lorca, Dalí and Buñuel first met.

Of Andalusian and French origins, Jiménez Fraud dedicated much of his life to the theory and practice of education. He was an enthusiastic Anglophile, and is one of the countless personalities thrown up by the history of Madrid that one feels, had Spanish culture not been so neglected, would have deserved an outstanding place among cultural figures in the feverish world of European ideas of the 1930s. The institution he oversaw brought together a who's who of present and future Spanish arts, science and culture; additionally, the

Residencia hosted, in those years of swelling optimism and lurking darkness, a lustrous catalogue of visitors and speakers, ranging from Einstein to Stravinsky, Keynes to Chesterton, Manuel de Falla to Maurice Ravel, H.G. Wells to the young Alexander Calder, to Bauhaus founder Walter Gropius and architect Le Corbusier. Einstein's 1922 visit included a lecture attended by Alfonso XIII, translated into Spanish from the German by Ortega y Gasset.[17]

For all its glittering alumni and stellar cast of visitors, perhaps the director Jiménez Fraud was the noblest of them all. He attempted to remain neutral in the civil war, and was accused of being a fascist for his troubles. His friend, the philosopher Manuel García Morente, wrote to him in 1937 words that rang true for the historic moment and echo today: 'At this particular moment one is required – it is demanded of one – to adhere to a "doctrine", that is to say, a sect, a party; and as for those of us who prefer to offer our kindness, our appreciation, our faith in other people and their works independently of any doctrine, sect or party, we are very much outsiders, even considered enemies by one side and the other.'[18] It could be the epitaph not only for Jiménez Fraud, but also for Manuel Chaves Nogales or Clara Campoamor. A century earlier, the same fate had awaited free-thinking journalist and writer José María Blanco White, another of the great losses to Spanish patrimony.

A passing reference in Elizabeth Nash's work on Madrid[19] provides a clue to a particularly terrible loss of cultural memory: in the early days of the civil war, in fear of the political consequences of the material he held, Jiménez Fraud retreated from threat, possibly to a basement incinerator, a silent and appalled setting, where he set fire to the celluloid archive where many of the visiting lectures given at the Residencia had been filmed. A precious historical documentation was lost: a film record of the conferences and the personalities who had passed through the Residencia, and the ideas they came to express in the Madrid lecture theatres. Should the Republic fall, which in those first days seemed likely, Jiménez Fraud was sitting on what he judged a deeply incriminating body of evidence. A priceless film archive of European intellectuals and artists of the 1920s and 1930s went onto the bonfire of history, as had so many hundreds of artworks in the centuries preceding: Madrid's artistic legacy and heritage damaged irrevocably, and repeatedly, by war.

Experiments in cultural form in Madrid, despite the volatile times, were not uniformly political. Viewed with the benefit of decades, there was ultimately something innocent about the flâneur Gómez de la Serna and his attempts to create 'a new literary cartography of the city', fascinated by modern technology, by triviality, by the ephemeral, by the weightlessness of electricity, by the teeming sensory impressions of the new.[20] As ever, the Puerta del Sol was ground zero for this obsession with multiplicity, with capturing the *everythingness*, the cinematic simultaneity, the social and the sensual, the personal and the anonymous, the flesh and the inanimate, the body electric, all flowing with life: what Jorge Luis Borges, who lived briefly in the Puerta del Sol in the early 1920s, was to call 'an inventory of the world'.[21] Gómez de la Serna's aesthetic mission to render the strangeness of things was uninterested in politics or political theory; his was a contemporary version of a religious attempt to explain the furious multiplicity of the world, a modernist theologian embracing the universe. The dirty grind of politics, of organisation, of community work and action, was a far cry from the lofty aesthetics some pursued; for many an aesthete, the Bolshevik revolution and its consequences were vulgar, an act of rowdy and common hordes. The capitalist world was full of original glimmer and light, the rush of vehicles and traffic, the heady vertigo of skyscrapers: this was the material for a certain art and poetry, rather than idealised factory workers or the victims of rural oppression.

Working-class life, however, was not all grim: the 'common people' contributed to the festive dimension of the city, with its series of *castizo* carnivals and *verbenas*[22] – La Latina, La Paloma – that celebrated tradition. Yet to some extent this was tradition as stage prop, a substitute for political action; if the *verbenas* were part of the life force of an authentic Madrid that stood in opposition to a dully mechanical bourgeoisie,[23] such festivities did not belong to a process of class struggle. In many cases, the traditions of Madrid did not speak to the constant flow of new arrivals from the provinces who came with their own festive calendar and background, and for whom the *verbenas* of Madrid were alien. And there was a new force – communism – staking its claim for the affections of the working class. The Madrid communist magazine *Nosotros* (*We*) expressed its disregard for most artists and intellectuals – who were by no means one and the same, but were often lumped together – on account of their apparently being ignorant of the suffering of the people. Committed to specific action and a strategic assault on power, the communist movement was disdainful of intellectuals whom they saw as useless; they were not *men of action* but were, above all, *thinkers* at a time when history called for *doers*.[24] The communist strategy would not end well.

The battle was on to engage 'the masses' entering the political sphere. The districts of the *extrarradio* were no longer just an appendage; they were increasingly central to the identity of Madrid itself, with all the demographic, cultural and political consequences of such a shift. If the eighteenth century had seen the closing down of the aristocratic grip on society, and the nineteenth had seen the rise of newly prosperous merchants and the bourgeoisie, the opening of the twentieth heralded another change, as the 'great unwashed' swept in from the outlying *arrabales* and *barrios* and demanded both a political and a sociocultural presence within the life of the city. The masses were both fascinating and sinister for intellectuals of the period, some of whom saw them as amorphous, ignorant and passive; for writer Agustín de Foxá, a 'grey and filthy mass' had burst upon the public spaces of the city centre, spaces previously reserved for social elites, their private and urbane zones overtaken by those who rose up 'like wolves from their wretched tin shacks amid the slum districts'.[25]

Such dangerous hordes needed to be educated, and this commitment could be either a pre-emptive defensive move – education to tame the working classes – or an active belief in broadening human experience and opportunity, setting loose an instinct for further liberation through learning. High rates of illiteracy were beginning to fall, albeit Madrid was something of an oasis amid a widespread rural lack of formal learning. Meanwhile, 'the masses' were organising themselves without waiting for the blessing of an intellectual caste, joining trade unions and backing general strikes. Forming part of these swelling ranks was a new generation of students and workers who entered committees, offices and factories, clubs, scientific and literary societies, with a previously unheard-of percentage of female participation, and with female suffrage among the top of their demands.[26]

Much of daily life in Madrid was, as ever, founded on a base of female labour. It was always easy to overlook their invisible but essential work: the scrub and starch hidden by a laundered shirt; the strained back and tired muscles hidden by a crisp billowing sheet; the tales suggested by hints of bleach and caustic soda; the hands gnarled and cracked, the joints bruised, the skin shrivelled and poisoned by chemicals. The washerwomen on the banks of the Manzanares were one of the best documented of these scenes of female drudgery, but others played out everywhere: the army of maids in domestic service, and others doing every task from selling chestnuts to scrubbing floors, running errands, mending clothes, selling fruit, vegetables and poultry, fortune tellers and the full range of prostitutions. If literature at times idealised these professions, adding a veneer of romance or sharp-tongued cheekiness, they had their own rituals and liturgy: their patience, their strength and their shared voices; a connection to the very marrow of life; an indissoluble partnering of work and being.

In Madrid and across the nation, different visions of the present and future faced a deepening rift; modern political ideology had raised its head, with its various ugly calls to arms and bloodshed, its garrulous conviction and its iron certainties. All was to be won: not only hearts, minds and souls, but even more importantly power, money and resources, the ability to determine the course of lives, their material conditions and their political sympathies. This was a battle that was to have dire consequences for Madrid during the 1930s and beyond.

The Puerta del Sol, ever the nerve centre of Madrid for political protest and celebration, was filled to bursting on 14 April 1931, when the Second Republic was declared. Alfonso Sánchez Portela, son of Alfonso Sánchez García, patriarch of a dynasty of photographers and a reference point for the social documentation of the first half of the twentieth century, took one of the enduring images of Spanish history: densely packed and cheering crowds, some of whom have climbed atop newspaper kiosks to wave republican flags like victorious soldiers claiming territory conquered; Sol overflowed with hectic enthusiasm. People surged up Calle de Alcalá from Cibeles, or along the Calle Mayor; thousands poured in from the side streets, filling the backs of trucks, leaning from trams, cheering from windows, all packed tightly, milling around the administrative headquarters of the Casa de Correos. At eight years, the Second Republic would outlast the first by some margin yet, despite the fervour, it had been born into a hostile world; any new political regime would by default be controversial in a polarised society, and the Republic inevitably manifested, or in some cases amplified, social and political fault lines.

The days were jubilant and full of dread. Yet again, it was the best of times and it was the worst of times. The political system of turns that had operated since 1876, and then given way to a first military dictatorship, was in utter discredit. Spain and Madrid were changing too fast; there were too many urgent demands for social, agricultural and political reform to hold back any longer. Another symbol of undemocratic wastefulness, King Alfonso XIII was swept from the throne. Events in Madrid were not divorced from what was happening elsewhere in Europe: following years of potential or actual revolution, war, boom and economic depression, the continent was full of threats and promises. Any number of new worlds were just over the horizon, but they would have to be fought for. Obstacles needed to be removed; universal justice would be preceded by a process of extermination. And so the ambitious utopians, the ideologues, dreamers and murderers sat down together.

Despite this volatile mix of adherents, the new regime drew on all the optimism of the early part of the century, the hope that the world might finally experience a profound change towards equality; a regime whose goals were justice and peace, and whose authority came not from God but from Reason, and whose principal considerations were directly material: land, bread, work, social justice.[27] Here, one of the paradoxes of the Republic emerges, for its mission may have been anticlerical in many respects, but it was also profoundly Christian, with its fight against oppression and cruelty, and its focus on earthly justice and happiness. A meeting, in other words, of secular religiosity and modern reason.[28] However, 'Republican' and 'revolutionary' were not synonymous terms; the social texture of Madrid was too complex for such simplicities, and many supported the Republic simply out of a desire to be rid of the dysfunctional political system that had held sway for the past fifty years, a major stumbling block to true social progress. In a time of institutional crisis, people had voted with both hope and rejection. No one knew what was coming, only that they wanted no further part of the existing system. Many, including conservatives and members of the military, desired change; others were determined to do whatever was necessary to enforce change. Republicanism was only one – and even for some not the most ideal – form of shifting history further along, to move the country beyond the prejudice and hindrance represented by those obscure windmills of inquisitors, ignorant rural priests, lack of education, cruelty, misery, poverty, hunger, suffering and the assorted barbarisms by which a decadent ruling class kept an illiterate populace in its place. Such was the theory and the conviction.

There were two obvious consequences for Madrid. As the seat of government, it was both the driving force behind this period of social ferment, a home to revolutionary ideas and actors, and the target for a panoply of forces, within the city and external to it, for whom Madrid had been converted into a species of abominable city, embodying 'the worst of the French and Soviet revolutions', a city that, on its downward slide from liberalism to republicanism to communism, 'had been overtaken by masons, Jews and assorted scum'.[29] This was not only a matter of politics; Madrid's thriving cultural avant-garde, full of brilliant artists and groundbreaking feminists, was considered deeply suspicious. For nationalist conservatives, revolution was distasteful not merely because of its class elements, but also for how it undermined an essentialist vision of Spain that was hierarchical, Catholic, rural, largely pre-industrial – the Republic was associated above all with the city and the urban world – and obedient to an immutable order of things.

For a city that has long endured a reputation as a bastion of social conservatism, Madrid was also considered in some quarters *too revolutionary*. The capital of the nation, the point of fusion for people from every corner of the peninsula, faced absurd charges of being anti-Spanish, or at least of harbouring such devils in its midst. Since the mid-nineteenth century there had grown up a specifically anti-Madrid genre of thought and letters, where the opposition was not so much to Madrid's centralising of power, but to its modernity, its tolerance for the radically different and its readiness to experiment. Nowhere was this changing of the city's texture and appearance more evident than in the participation of the 'lower classes' from the crowded urban periphery in the politics of the city and the nation.

For every urgent desire for change there was, by corollary, the fear and loathing of those threatened by direct challenges to their beliefs and privileges. The ruling political, military, financial and clerical elites now faced an uppity and increasingly educated servant class, independent and brashly confident women and, once the civil war began, armed workers. This power shift was part of a continuous social progression that had its roots as far back as the rural dislocations of the Industrial Revolution and the free thinking of the 1920s, becoming fully manifest in the eight years from 1931 to 1939 that encompass the Second Republic. Against this turbulence thrown up by a world of free education, technology and suffrage, the nativist and rustic ideal rejected even the industrial world, for it had swapped out the compliant rural peasant – always poor and hungry, yet idealised in this vision of the world as embodying a form of Castilian purity – for the dissatisfied and hungry factory worker, lurking on the edges of Madrid, plotting resistance to exploitation, demanding better work conditions.

A prominent example of opposition to the ills of modernity was in the writing of Ernesto Giménez Caballero, a former student socialist and member of Madrid's avant-garde community, a brilliant mind who had championed futurism and surrealism, yet who soon felt the allure of fascism as a remedy to the sweeping Americanism and, paradoxically, Sovietisation, exemplified by the triumph of the Gran Vía. A native son of the quintessential Madrid quarter of La Latina, Giménez Caballero was fundamental to the intellectual justification of Spanish fascism as a bulwark against foreign influences – both capitalism and communism were equally detested – that, in his opinion, encouraged the citizens of Madrid to turn their backs on their own glorious national history. Spain's natural place was at the right hand of Rome, far from the excesses of the democratic United States or the oriental cruelty of the Soviet. Just as Giménez Caballero had disapprovingly observed trade union and anarchist demonstrations along the spectacular new avenue at the height of the Republic, the opening months of the civil war confirmed the secular treachery of the Gran Vía, hosting parades of Republican soldiers and International Brigades, while its modern hotels accommodated foreign correspondents who, for Giménez Caballero, had no business interfering in domestic affairs. The fast-moving, democratic, neon-lit and show-business Gran Vía represented 'the Five-Year plan, the Bolshevik novel, the Yankee film, the free woman and the dissolution of the family'.[30] Such a response was a desperate desire to return to the more predictable, less socially mobile Madrid of autocratic, pre-industrial times, a Madrid of obedience and order. Not only was such a Madrid never coming back – not even under Franco; notwithstanding the strictures of the old regime, such a Madrid had never really existed, for the city has always been a restless place, a meeting point for those wanting to create new lives. Just as Madrid has never belonged to anybody, it has never been still, or quiet, or fully obedient.

Amid cross-currents of intense political propaganda, new urban thinking, prison reform, divorce law, workers' education, literacy programmes and burgeoning feminism, of telecommunications, the arts of advertising and the blossoming of mass media, a specific vision of the world continued to take shape, and in turn face resistance, in Madrid. Not just for the privileged few, but for the many in all the shacks and hovels and dust- or mud-filled streets that fringed the capital, those camped out on open ground under tin or refashioned wood, those cramped in basements.

The future had never seemed so open to possibility, but the question remained, amid such a fervour of change: who might embody this new world? What type of person would step into the gap left behind by the recently vanished Madrid of Galdós, that suddenly fossilised world of rigid 'upstairs, downstairs' privilege, a world fast being dissolved by the promises of various types of utopian thinking? What type of *madrileño* or *madrileña* might step up to typify the new order of things?

Such a tempestuous period threw up prodigies, none so brief and strange as that of Hildegart Rodríguez, a *madrileña* born in the immediate aftermath of the Great War. Young Hildegart was a phenomenon, a child genius whose mother Aurora, obsessed with eugenicist ideas of regeneration and purity, subjected her to a series of social experiments. Beginning with a carefully selected father – Aurora was otherwise celibate – Hildegart was born 'not of sexual passion but of meticulous planning, carried out with mathematical precision'.[31] With her mother taking exclusive charge of her education, Hildegart mastered multiple languages in childhood and entered university by the age of 14. She also entered politics, at 15 being elected vice-president of the National Federation of Young Socialists and joining the socialist-affiliated UGT trade union (General Union of Workers). She penned regular columns on feminist issues such as sexuality and contraception, despite also being known as the 'Red Virgin' owing to her lack of experience. In 1932 she fell out with her fellow socialists over the question of female suffrage – Hildegart was opposed and believed, along with socialist politician and lawyer Victoria Kent, that women needed to be 'fully educated' in the responsibilities of suffrage before being allowed to vote.

Gaining social profile was fine, but an ever-greater independence of thought and action did not match her mother's iron-clad plans for daughterly obedience. To craft the perfect woman of the future was no easy task; indeed, the utopia to which Aurora had determined she would direct her daughter was positively dystopian. To keep Hildegart close, in 1932 her mother proposed they jointly found a society for 'sexual reform' whose aim would be to purify the Spanish race via, among other means, a wide-scale programme of male vasectomy.[32] Hildegart wanted nothing to do with such unhinged thinking. Mother and daughter began to fall out; Aurora suspected her daughter of having an affair with H.G. Wells, with whom she had an intense correspondence, with whom she worked as a guide and interpreter on one of his visits to Madrid and with whom she shared a wide range of views around socialism and the future construction of society. Wells, highly impressed, was said to have offered to take Hildegart from Madrid to London to be his secretary.

In the early summer of 1933, Hildegart told Aurora she was not prepared to be considered her property or the vehicle for her mother's social experiments. Shortly after, Aurora approached her daughter while she was sleeping in their home on Calle Galileo and shot her four times, killing her immediately. Hildegart was still only 18 years of age. Her mother, who claimed at trial that it is the responsibility of a sculptor to destroy any work in progress should it be found to contain serious flaws, was committed to the psychiatric hospital in Ciempozuelos south of Madrid, where she lived for another two decades.[33]

Those who cheer on revolution often end up threatened or consumed by it. In Madrid, the Second Republic was marred by regular street violence, some provoked by reactionary opponents, some driven by the Republic itself. Much of the early conservative support for the Republic began to turn amid the burning of churches and convents. At times, it was difficult to discern the line between historic claims to justice and redistribution, and simple thuggery and revenge. Zeal was misplaced, or used as a cover for criminal activity. With rumours abounding of land expropriations in the countryside, the distant rumble of revolution was constant. The 'lower orders' were no longer quietly shuffling in through the tradesman's entrance, but were tramping into Madrid through the front door, placing their muddy boots on the carpet and staining immaculately starched linen. For polite middle-class Madrid, one way of facing such defiance was simply to ignore it. 'The whole of Spain, and Madrid above all, lived in an atmosphere of absurd optimism', Baroja had written two decades earlier in his classic novel, *The Tree of Knowledge*.[34] There existed a 'natural tendency to self-deception' and a 'stagnancy of ideas'.[35] Baroja may have been right to reflect on the lazy self-satisfaction of large sectors of the Madrid bourgeoisie, moving languidly between theatre, restaurant, *tertulia* and their latest infidelity, but the stagnancy was not universal; there were members of the middle classes closely engaged in revolutionary thinking and planning.

The city was on the edge between two worlds: 'the old ecological balance had disappeared and a new one had yet to take its place.'[36] Hamstrung by political infighting as the Republic teetered towards civil war, the local government of Madrid was unable to provide adequate facilities for a population that had now reached 1 million. Regardless of the political strife brewing, many people on the urban fringes still lacked basic amenities; planning was haphazard or non-existent, while 'unprotected rubbish dumps, septic tanks and sewage ditches ensured that infection and disease were rife'.[37] The lower middle class were vulnerable as continent-wide unemployment spread and monopolies dominated commerce and business, inhibiting competition and innovation. Small family businesses, a generation or two earlier so central to the novels of Galdós and to the life of Madrid, struggled to survive. In the absence of any established social safety net, these were perfect conditions for agitators from both sides of politics, and in Madrid the divide between 'red' and 'blue' ran as deeply as anywhere. Frenetic activity from trade unions of different stripes – anarchist, socialist, communist – was met by young falangists, surging followers of the new discipline of fascism, an Italian import that enthralled sections of Madrid's intellectual elite, along with many of its upper-class sons and daughters. The newly founded Falange were busy 'raiding union offices, noisily peddling their newspapers and working hard at provoking disorder with constant street clashes, chases and shooting incidents with serious casualties on both sides'.[38]

National governments in Madrid were a merry-go-round of populists from across the political spectrum. In such vexatious times, 'so much had been said about the inevitability of the revolution, victory had been so taken for granted that . . . no one had taken any steps to organize it'.[39] The failure of revolutions in Asturias and Catalonia in late 1934 allowed conservative forces an opportunity to crack down and imprison student leaders, unionists and militants. There was no compassion or long-sightedness; only the desire for immediate revenge. The pendulum had swung again; the Republican left, once a broad and generous collective desirous of moving the country forward, progressively and without the burden of a monarchy, was increasingly radicalised and under communist influence. Much middle-class support was lost: 'The streets no longer belonged to all the people of Madrid, but only to its workers.'[40] There is an interesting comparison to be made with the starry-eyed vision of the apparent workers' paradise of Barcelona offered by George Orwell in 1936, all the more striking for one who had emerged from the class strictures and humourless gloom of pre-war England. In practice, workers' control of the city was often violent and vengeful, as if history had left too many accounts to settle. Brinkmanship on both sides helped bring matters to a head; Madrid fell into a state of lawlessness.

From 1934, only magical thinking could have believed in the success of a full-blown national proletarian revolution, a new social order wrought by strike action and arms with Madrid as its centre. Given everything learned during the bloody twentieth century, such hopes can be seen for the delusions they were; social orders born from coercion or violence never start or end well, and so it was for the latter part of the Second Republic. By 1936 there were simply too many rogue elements beyond the Azaña government's control. Madrid filled with uniformed youths, all seeking to provoke a fight: socialists and communists on the one hand, falangists on the other. These hastily constructed militias marched and sang in central Madrid in displays of strength and bravado; as war drew near, such ambitious preening often turned into thuggery, violence and murder. Madrid contained and exemplified all the tensions and polarisation that led to war; every act was freighted with ideology with all sides on high alert, sensitive to offence, quick to see attacks against what they held most dear in any and every action of those on the other side of the political, and often social, divide. While this type of civil disturbance was also happening on the streets of Paris or Berlin or Munich as different variations of fascism, socialism or communism fought for social and political control, for Madrid this was a new phenomenon. Violence itself was nothing new – the city had seen more than its share over the centuries – but this strife sprang from previously unknown ideologies, battling for hearts and minds on the streets of the capital.

For many sympathetic to it, the Second Republic to which Madrid was so central remains a lost Eden, for it not only represented an attempt to enact wholesale social and political change, but also stood as the international vanguard of the fight against fascism, generally regarded as the noblest struggle of the era. It is tempting to see the nationalist insurrection of 1936 as an imposition that ended a unique cultural flowering; this is true, and yet the cultural boom of those years had occurred equally under the dictatorship of Primo de Rivera. The latter years of the Republic, particularly after late 1934, were accompanied by violence and reaction: a political and cultural transcript that led a city to war. Finer-grained Spanish sources appreciate not only the heroic conception and dream of the Republic, with its attempt to haul much of Spain out of penury and economic injustice, but likewise the clumsy mistakes, the conflict, the steady violence of a regime that, like all human ventures, was deeply flawed, riven by internal jealousies and fighting. Hindsight, given the outcome of the civil war and the subsequent Second World War, has cast an Arcadian light over that period in which Spain was the centre of the global fight against fascism and Madrid its reporting ground zero.

For all its positive achievements, not least in education, much of the violence has been overlooked by those eager to shoehorn the Second Republic into a place of myth. Clearly, the incoming nationalist regime constructed an ex post facto, demonised version of events to whitewash its own crimes, yet at the same time many accounts, not least among foreigners and exiles, refused to be critical of the Republic, as if to do so were bad form, or were conceding an inch in the propaganda battle against national Catholicism. Few attempted to examine why, when war broke out, others might be in the opposite trenches, or ask if they were necessarily all 'fascists' or 'communists'. Some were; many were not. Many were simply wretched soldiers drafted without a choice and without a desire to kill anyone, much less their neighbours. Much of what occurred could not be helped, could not be stopped: it was both the world, with its conspiring ideologies, and bitter circumstance that closed in upon Madrid in 1936. The city, yet again, was entering a time of war.

The city under siege

The heart of the nation and nerve centre of the Second Republic, Madrid was an obvious prize for the parties contending for control of Spain. During the opening months of the war, its defiant role – Madrid as the international front line against fascism – had been an inspiration to thousands around the world: a capital city destined to fall had refused to do so and, as support for the city gathered and its resistance hardened, the effects of its stubborn, courageous first months under siege rippled out across the world. Fighting against traitors within and invaders without, as Antonio Machado put it;[1] Madrid as heroic city of resistance was not a myth but a tradition, dating back to the times of Napoleon. The capital was all things: a fabled city, almost but not quite captured; a distant object of desire, for years within sight but remaining elusively out of reach of the besieging Nationalist forces; a heroic bastion of freedom; the proud stage for unheard-of liberties and equalities; the backdrop to unimagined treasons; a city of cold, hunger and ruin; a cauldron of debased heresy and murder; a heathen city under Soviet control; a proud Castilian town that finally bowed her head and submitted to the march of fascism.

There were as many experiences of the war as there were residents in Madrid. The engagement shifted over three years, citizens came and went, soldiers arrived confidently, and died; fortunes rose and fell; terror mixed with boredom, excitement with profound grief.

The war was utterly transformative, physically and metaphysically, for the capital. There was the obvious destruction of infrastructure, the shelling of homes and offices, the killing of animals, the murder of neighbours and the stripping and felling of trees; there was the psychological damage wrought by fear, not just of bombs, but of whispered gossip and out-of-control militia; there were the demographic changes as those who were able left Madrid for the uncertainties of exile, or conversely came flooding into Madrid from rural villages; there were foreigners who arrived to observe, report and fight; there were the thousands of victims on both sides of politics, or those who had no politics at all, such as the city's children; and there were, eventually, the members of the new regime rising to prominence. Seldom has a city changed so much in three years.

After that first midsummer day in July 1936, the long battle began. What had been meant to be a walk in the park turned out to be anything but: from their secure bases in the north of the country, Nationalist forces attempted but failed to take Madrid with militarised columns descending from the high passes of Guadarrama and Somosierra. Once again, the mountain ranges north of Madrid proved vital to the defence of the city. Other forces moved on Madrid from the south-west; coming up from the direction of Andalusia and Extremadura was the so-called Army of Africa, some of the most violent and bloody of troops. Despite finding easy passage to the gates of Madrid, and taking control of air bases at Getafe and Cuatro Vientos, they were unable to break through the initially chaotic but fiercely determined resistance of those loyal to the Republic. As outlying southern towns such as Móstoles, Fuenlabrada, Getafe, Alcorcón, Villaviciosa de Odón or Carabanchel fell to the Nationalists, the front moved closer; trenches were dug through the Casa de Campo. By November the assault had become bogged down and a front line established around the University City, in Moncloa and Argüelles. The war was breathing down the city's neck; Madrid was a unique battleground in that foreign reporters could leave their hotels on the Gran Vía and, only a short walk away, find themselves at the front. War in the morning and cocktails in the evening: no one, it was said, lived a better war than foreign journalists. There was even a tramline whose last stop was the front;[2] one could travel out to fight in the morning and in the evening catch the tram home from war. In some instances, those attacking the city from the Casa de Campo could see their homes in the distance, tempting but unreachable.

The war passed through distinct phases of activity and stalemate. In terms of explicit street violence and extrajudicial assassination, July 1936 to early 1937 were the cruellest months in Madrid. The initial midsummer shock of finding the city at war was followed by a critical autumn and winter, the most dreadful, chaotic and murder-filled period. The war was being fought outside the city and within: while Germany and Italy supplied arms to the besieging Nationalist forces, the Republic found itself only able to access Soviet support, a victim of the Allied powers' strategic neutrality. Arturo Barea and José Herrera Petere provide vivid portraits of crowds demanding arms in the thronging streets of central Madrid.[3] The move was a gamble: once the Republican government allowed arms to be distributed among the general population – syndicalists, anarchists, socialists and communists all formed their own militias – Madrid stood a better chance of defending itself from occupation by ground forces; however, many with little or no training, and often dubious motives, now brandished weapons in a highly volatile environment. The improvised militias were in some cases little more than armed gangs.

Despite the military in Madrid remaining mostly loyal to the Republic, one of the main bases and weapons stores, the Cuartel de la Montaña, declared itself for the uprising and its troops entrenched themselves to await support from outside the city. The following day, angry crowds stormed the barracks and a massacre of those inside ensued; photographs of the military base strewn with dead bodies were the first of many shocking images to emerge from the civil war, itself the first war in history to be so amply documented with film and photography. The Cuartel de la Montaña was utterly destroyed and in time razed; in a curious inversion of history, in the late 1960s this civil war black site vanished entirely, replaced by the ancient Egyptian Temple of Debod, rescued from the Aswan Dam project and now one of Madrid's more unusual tourist monuments, boasting a beautiful view out over the escarpments on the western edge of the city.

The military rebellion against the Republic, successful in many parts of northern and western Spain, failed inside Madrid, but with the surrounding Nationalist forces cutting off key highways into and out of the capital other than the road to Valencia, the city was soon choked. In such a feverish environment fear and rumour spread, quickening the dramas of a city under siege: hunger, murder, sacrifice, heroism, treason and betrayal, extortion, an intense traffic on the black market of any and every type of goods. Undeterred, theatres and cinemas stayed open, as did Madrid's intense café life, albeit in an atmosphere of heightened tension. 'Despite these bitter times, the people are happy in their fight,' proclaimed President Manuel Azaña, without it being clear whether an armed people were fighting simply to defend democracy, or to enact a more thoroughgoing revolution.[4] With the enemy at the gates, a united front was essential, but this was easier said than done for anarchists, socialists and communists were mostly at each other's throats; the communists, in particular, were brutal in their elimination of those deemed 'non-compliant'. For now, however, these warring factions had to put on hold their planned end to capitalism, private property and conventional social hierarchies in order to face down a more immediate challenge.

In the first few months, while the weather remained hot, Madrid was a twenty-four-hour city of political speeches, marches and campaigns; the streets were full of people commenting on the news, listening to the radio, exchanging gossip and secrets, reading and distributing pamphlets; militias checked identity papers while armed vehicles sped around the city, patrolling, threatening, watching. A vicious campaign was waged by sections of the newly formed militias against any suspected of being traitors, spies or class enemies. Old scores might be settled under the excuse and confusion of war; old foes and fifth columnists[5] hunted down, private property and businesses expropriated. These were the awful months when Madrid, for all its defiant attempts at normality in the face of attack, went to sleep each night fearful of a knock on the door, and awoke each day to the sound or sight of summary executions. In such an environment, many of those opposed to the Republican government and the brash militias of the Popular Front left the city if they were able, or went into hiding. Hundreds sought refuge in embassies.

What might have been a period of delirious, revolutionary happiness had quickly turned dark. One of the ugliest children of this revolutionary moment was the *checa*, an improvised interrogation centre or prison, often installed in the basement of a building, where those suspected of counter-revolutionary activities were taken to be beaten, tortured and subsequently, on many occasions, executed. Up to 300 of these sites were established across Madrid, often but by no means exclusively for the use of the Communist Party and its own war against dissent. Anyone suspected of having the wrong political sympathies might find themselves taken from their home at night: the ongoing purges in the Soviet Union – a political beacon for many communists at the time – had set an appalling example. Victims might be taken to one of the *checas* to be interrogated, or simply to the nearest vacant lot to be shot. The infamous *paseo* – going for a stroll – became the shorthand for this method of 'disappearing others, taken from their homes, their offices, from street corners, and found usually the next day slumped by a wall, or under a tree, shot dead and their personal possessions looted. Cousin to the *paseo* was the equally infamous *saca* – a 'taking out' of prisoners, be they political, religious, class enemies, traitors or altogether innocent, for mass execution, a war crime practised by both contending parties. Such victims numbered in their thousands.

The order of things had been turned entirely on its head. Poet and artist José Moreno Villa, writing in his memoir on the impact on the Residencia de Estudiantes of the first days of the war, commented that 'no sooner had the military rebellion been declared, than there was a change in the attitude of the "servants": certain women began to look at us as if we were the bourgeoisie, in need of being dragged off.' The dreaded *paseo* was a constant threat. 'Every night we would hear the sound of rifles, and in the morning the servant girls would be talking of those who had fallen victim to the latest *paseos*: "Today there was a smart little fascist gentleman with good shoes and wrapped in a monarchist flag . . . yesterday it was some poor fellow with rope sandals."[6] People paid attention to the hands and shoes of the corpses, for they revealed in death close details of life: the types of ring, the worked nails, the fine grain of dirt, or lack thereof; the hands revealed the contours, rugged or gentle, a life may have taken. There were the clues to social origins, which led to other clues or assumptions about class, ideology and sympathies, and perhaps suggested why that person died, and to what extent their killing may have been justified.

Along the road to Extremadura, by the walls of the San Isidro cemetery, in the Casa de Campo, under bridges or by the banks of the Manzanares, among the gentle pines of the Dehesa de la Villa: the abandoned bodies stacked up every morning.[7] They contained horror, and suffered a dreadful indignity; sometimes, the corpses were abused, heckled, smirked at by onlookers such as Moreno Villa's servant girls, who might themselves only be alive for another day, for no one knew how far away was the next betrayal or accusation, a falling bomb or whipping fleck of shrapnel. Photographs were taken in situ of these bodies, and later hung in a macabre gallery where anxious relatives or family members might come to identify them. Given the extreme nature of some of the wounds, this was not always possible. 'In the police-file photos in Madrid the faces of the dead, the murdered, have been so severely disfigured that not even their closest relatives can identify them.'[8] Normal identifying features such as clothes, jewellery or shoes were often stolen, and a gun at close range can ruin the contours of a face.

An enthusiastic young George Orwell had commented approvingly on the proletarian style of clothing in Barcelona, 'a town in which the wealthy classes had practically ceased to exist' and where fashionable style had been dispensed with as an undesirable marker of class distinction.[9] In Madrid, clothing was a matter of politics and survival. There was a radical change in dress codes; as the workers' militias took control of the streets, the bourgeoisie quickly learned to dress down, going ragged and rough to avoid suspicion. 'I used to go about with a torn old coat and a pair of borrowed boots in order not to appear bourgeois,' wrote novelist Juan Eduardo Zúñiga.[10] Dressing down would soon become a necessity born of penury rather than a tactical disguise; people were reduced to wearing whatever they could, including shoes taken from the dead. This was a war with deep roots in class conflict and it was wise, for questions of personal safety, to tone down elegance.[11] Out went symbols of class distinction such as ties, hats or beautifully cut suits; poet Juan Ramón Jiménez was stopped in the street by an anarchist militiaman to have his teeth inspected for gold fillings.[12] He was not, as it turned out, the suspect they were looking for, but the example was served. Distinctive style or obvious wealth became dangerous, potentially giving one away as a class enemy; being well-groomed might indicate one was a priest or a member of some other profession implacably opposed to that class who were, in theory, taking the weight of history and the responsibility for historical change upon their shoulders, while in practice they were all too commonly engaged in the simple thuggery associated with arms and power.

There were exceptions, as the flux of war threw up surprises and grotesques: members of workers' militia and other ungoverned armed groups sacked and looted the homes of departed aristocracy and, as the cold of autumn arrived, could be seen wearing their luxurious furs or other superb garments, demonstrably inverting traditional power relations and, in so doing, adding a carnivalesque atmosphere, a layer of absurdity and comedy over the horror of a city where innocent people were being murdered every day even as others did their best to maintain routines of work, pleasure and entertainment. Such incidents only served to exacerbate the tension between social groups who already eyed each other with suspicion when not open loathing. Far from being a beacon of liberation, for a nationalist propagandist such as Giménez Caballero, Madrid had become 'atrociously plebeian', and for another right-wing contemporary, Agustín de Foxá, Madrid had become estranged from its true self; it was no longer Spain, but a ruinous city controlled by working-class mobs, thugs and foreign mercenaries.[13] For Juan Ramón Jiménez, hopelessly wishing the beauty, truth and poetry of the Spanish language might inspire a path beyond the filth of war, the first year of fighting in Madrid was a 'mad and tragic festival'.[14]

Despite increasing street violence, the people of Madrid stepped up to serve in the defence of their city against the besieging Nationalist forces. Many were happy to see the old class-ridden Madrid disappear, and happy to fight for its Republican vision despite its flaws and dangers. 'The people of Madrid offered themselves up,' wrote Herrera Petere, 'men from Cuatro Caminos answered the call to duty; men from Prosperidad, from Guindalera, Puerta de Atocha and from Carabanchel; they answered the call and came with their hands covered in grease, in flour or lime; they came in their uniforms of tram drivers, Metro workers; printers came, mechanics, students, chauffeurs, bricklayers, bakers, musicians, metal workers ...'[15] Streaming into the city from their outskirts of poverty and industry, to the horror of the upper class and conservative establishment, was the fabled proletariat, ready to fight to the death, its representation in propaganda following the Soviet tropes of *homo laborans*: noble, strong, combative, self-sacrificing, visionary; the iconography of the stance with feet apart, workshop tools or weapons in hand; or the women, beautiful, feminist and brimming with purpose. These proto-types stare off towards that distant horizon that is the future. The fascination with Soviet aesthetics and ideology was confirmed in November 1937 when, to celebrate the twentieth anniversary of the Russian Revolution, the Puerta de Alcalá was adorned with full-length portraits of Voroshilov and Molotov on either side of the inevitable Stalin. A century and a half in his grave, Carlos III would have recognised the absolutist now dominating his most famous monument, while being appalled at the secular ugliness of the image.

A year earlier, fearing the imminent fall of the city, the Republican government under prime minister Largo Caballero had decamped to Valencia to fight a rearguard action from the coast. The people of Madrid, for whom this came as a bitter disappointment, were now more alone than ever. It is not difficult to understand, in this context, the rapturous reception enjoyed by the International Brigades as they arrived, got into uniform, underwent rapid training, and marched up the Gran Vía to join local forces fighting in the defence of Madrid, both at the immediate front line on the western edge of the city and in some of the famous battles that raged around the capital, such as Jarama in February and Brunete in July of 1937.

Events could not continue at the hectic pace of the first six months of the war. Nationalist troops took large swathes of the country, yet around Madrid became bogged down as one battle after another failed to change the status of the enemy forces. Positions hardened into 1937 and 1938 as Franco diverted his attention away from Madrid to other strategic targets. The siege drew longer as life slowed, grew poorer, more ragged and exhausting. Hunger stalked the city; people were ground down; malice, cowardice, heroism and generosity were interwoven. 'I would sooner see Madrid destroyed than in the hands of Marxists,' Franco had boasted;[16] his troops certainly did their best to achieve the former, while the latter, for all the revolutionary fervour of the time, was never more than a political fantasy.

In another unwanted new experience, Madrid began to be bombed from the air. Months before Guernica, Madrid was the first major European city to experience this form of aerial terror with all its random fury. The city had no defence system in place: its citizens were sitting ducks, its buildings target practice. Artillery shells fell constantly from Nationalist positions in the Casa de Campo, bombs from German and Italian planes overhead. To the numbness of war was added the intense winter cold of Madrid, and other miseries: 'The next day it rained again,' wrote foreign correspondent Martha Gellhorn, 'and Madrid picked itself up as it had done before. Streetcars clanked slowly through the streets, collecting the fallen bricks, the broken glass, the odd bits of wood and furniture. People stopped on their way to work, looking at the new shell holes.' Nothing went to waste; everything was repurposed: the people of Madrid 'make plans for a beautiful new city, which they will build in place of what has been destroyed, when the war is over'.[17]

Much of the photographic documentation of the time reveals the physical destruction of the city. In Cuatro Caminos, Argüelles, the University City, the Gran Vía, the Calle Montera or countless other sites, the city looms up like the shattered place it was, full of rupture and the dead. To the physical transformation of buildings ruined, markets bombed, tramlines ripped up, streets cratered, electricity supply disrupted, hospitals overcrowded and sanitation broken – to say nothing of the dead, those who dashed across roads or squares at just the wrong time, or fell asleep in the wrong room, or for whose wounds there was insufficient medical care – was added the environmental disaster of trees cut down for firewood, dead and mutilated animals, parks stripped and waterways polluted. And amid all this chaos thousands drifted, homeless and dislocated by war, rural folk who had wandered into the city from outlying areas now converted into trenches, fronts and bombed fields, bringing with them children, blankets, chickens, piglets, sheep, goats and mules. It was an easy time for the strong, or simply the wicked, to prey upon the weak; in a city of rumour, conspiracy and paranoia, many citizens were killed not by the weapons of a besieging army but by its own roaming gangs, militias drunk on that first frisson of revolution, which always turns to ash and blood and dust.

Soon to go into exile, Chaves Nogales left a range of descriptions of Madrid by night: the deep, broad gash of streets, now black chasms; avenues of nothing and silence. His short story 'And in the distance, a tiny light'[18] contrasts a tiny rooftop light with the epic nature of the darkness that characterised both the blacked-out city and the fratricidal times. The light – so fragile, intermittent, unpredictable – that blinks from rooftops is a signal in Morse set, in all its treacherous subterfuge, against the overwhelming weight of night. In its thick darkness Madrid is a dead star, a vortex from which escapes only the flicker of an enemy's signalling. A fifth columnist, huddled among the washing lines of a rooftop terrace, is attempting to send word as light to fellow collaborators. These traitors against the cause of the Republican government are spread out across the city, a chain of tiny lights from the aristocratic Salamanca quarter, to Chueca, to Gran Vía and across to Pintor Rosales, the elegant avenue overlooking the Parque del Oeste, a line drawn from east to west across the very centre of the pitch-black city. As each secret signaller is uncovered by the night patrol, they are executed in situ, apart from a young woman from a wealthy home who is led out into the fields and shot as she attempts to escape: her arms flailing, her silk gown billowing. As each death is carried out, the city responds with silence: neighbours knew better than to make enquiries or raise a fuss. For in every house there was the humble concierge – the *portero* or *portera* – typically anonymous figures who now found themselves, by virtue of knowing everybody and everything that passed in and out of residential buildings, in an unparalleled position to report, whisper, betray; or to hide, occlude truth, protect. Like household spies under any claustrophobic regime, their actions fell somewhere between politics and self-protection, feeding the innocent, and perhaps sometimes the guilty, into the always hungry machines that crushed so many during the European 1930s.

The city, ragged and bejewelled, carried on. As Zúñiga observed, a city bombed and starved and ruined does not only exist for the observer – journalist, diplomat, passer-by – who records the shattered buildings and lost lives, the smoky boredom of confinement, the corpses along the footpaths. The besieged city exists also for all the thousands of invisible, all those who stay quiet and hidden, whether from fear or prudence; all those who stay well out of sight and wait for the destruction to pass and for the killing to recede; all those waiting for the sound of rifles and mortars and falling brickwork to be replaced by the more conventional sounds of commerce, traffic, conversation without threat, laughter. The great bustle of humanity carried on among the congested streets around the Puerta del Sol, down Mayor and up Montera and Preciados, the soldiers, beggars and rural peasants overwhelmed by the crowds; the uniformed and the elegant, the frocked priests and the dirty children; the street carts selling tobacco and lottery tickets; the fashionable window displays in the department stores. The frenetic pace of life on the street slowed only with the darkness, when the city dispersed and went underground, into taverns, basements and tunnels, into any form of hiding. In the empty streets, gaslights were painted blue to limit the sight of the Italian aviation arriving – a screaming comes across the sky – to litter the city with fire.

Not all was deprivation and debris. Parts of the city, such as the Salamanca quarter, escaped unscathed from the bombing campaign; knowing the high proportion of residents in this area sympathetic to the Nationalist uprising, care was taken to avoid damaging its lovely streets and elegant buildings. The Salamanca district thus attracted a vibrant community of black marketeers, prostitutes, domestic and foreign spies, delinquents, shady dealers in stolen art, contraband medicine and drugs, enforcers and traffickers in every kind of influence.[19] Money and power, despite the strictures of the situation, could always buy an element of relief, if not luxury. For every person spending endless nights in the dank and smoky tunnels of the Metro, listening to the rumble of falling masonry, there were others who, albeit putting their wealth away discreetly, nevertheless spent the years in comparative comfort. For all its heroic legend as a city of resistance, Madrid was also a city divided, and many went into a tactical holding pattern, waiting for the 'Marxist hordes' and their regime to pass so they could once again take their place at the apex of the social pyramid.

While a host of writers in favour of the Republic have had their names inscribed in history – Alberti, Neruda, Hernández, Machado, Barea, Orwell, Hemingway and others – the military insurrection did not lack for intellectual support among writers in Madrid. After a long period of denial, some are having their literary reputations restored. Most have been forgotten, however, either because their work was not up to an enduring literary standard or the changing times have simply relegated them to relics of an undesirable past. Their political positions often ran parallel to a brutal classism in their work; they denounced the proletariat as lazy, illiterate, ill-dressed, resentful, immoral, whoring, drunken and thieving, and proletarian women as the antithesis of the modest, sober, obedient and morally impeccable Catholic model. When the servant class came into the heart of Madrid, they believed, it should be to serve, not to raise fists and brandish weapons; not to shout or demand; not to disturb the neoclassical serenity of Cibeles, the lovely symmetry of the Salamanca quarter, or the birdsong of the Botanic Gardens. One of the strangest, and now altogether forgotten, writers of this period was José María Carretero, known by the pseudonym of 'El Caballero Audaz' ('the Fearless Gentleman'). Having established his name as a journalist specialising in the new genre of the profile interview – at which he excelled – and as a writer of cheap erotica, the Fearless Gentleman later took up his pen against what he perceived were the horrors of a lawless working-class Republic. Improbably wearing dark glasses and a false beard to disguise himself from the revolutionary patrols who sought to capture him, he roved around central Madrid, observing the physical and moral degradation of the city, awash with 'Marxist filth'.[20] His patently biased accounts related how an apparently illiterate and uncultured mob had emerged from the slums in order to terrorise establishment Madrid. They closed on the centre of the city from all the usual points of geographic prejudice: from Vallecas, Carabanchel and Usera, from Cuatro Caminos, from the lower ends of the Calle Toledo, from the squalid banks of the Manzanares. It was as if all the restless characters from the earlier Pío Baroja trilogy had come to life once more, determined to take control of the city, rather than simply exist in its dank corners.

Nor did those writers indulgent towards the military uprising have any admiration for the International Brigades in Madrid, on whom they unleashed their own prejudices, unfairly considering them a bunch of mercenaries, criminals and fanatics, butting into what was none of their business, helping to further spread the 'infection' that was unholy communism through the body of the Spanish nation. Foreign journalists and certain members of the International Brigades were believed to be the source of easy money, the journalists in particular stereotyped as living among an endless flow of fine hotels, cocktails and prostitutes. Sophisticated conservatives and nationalists, however, were by no means anti-foreign; it was only the most reactionary wing of Catholic nationalism that abhorred Madrid's status as a home to liberalism, republicanism, Marxism and a host of associated 'foreign' revolutionary ideas such as feminism and workers' rights. For them and their many followers, the city had drifted badly and was now contra the apparent essence of Castile: agrarian, rural and faith-bound.[21] Upon a longed-for victory over the forces of evil, Madrid would need to be punished, purified and redeemed; upstarts from outlying 'red' districts such as Ventas, Vallecas, Cuatro Caminos or Tetuán put back in their place, servants and women returned to faithful obedience, and the city restored to its rightful owners. The tone of some writers, such as Agustín de Foxá, was unhinged by the strange times: classical ruins were all very well, but were useful only for what he called 'tourist kodaks', witnesses without suffering. Charred beams and shattered walls, on the other hand, spoke of the cleansing flame of fascism: 'we need fresh ruins, new ashes', he wrote, to purify the sins of liberal society.[22] This abhorrent thinking, redolent of deeply reactionary nineteenth-century Carlism, might have inspired a significant number of officials and fascist propagandists, but that genie was long out of the bottle. Madrid was a secular world capital; no amount of nostalgic, wishful thinking would change it back to an obedient Manchegan village, albeit there would be a concerted effort made, especially in the first two decades of the dictatorship, to reverse the anticlerical 'disobedience' of working-class movements.

As for the Fearless Gentleman – worried at one point the game was up for him, he attempted to seek asylum in the British embassy. Having failed, and to escape the prospect of being taken by his enemies, he ended up hiding out in a tomb in one of Madrid's cemeteries, an experience that is said to have left him traumatised. He died in 1951.

Under rainy winter skies and mats of grey cloud, the fields in the Jarama valley outside Madrid take on the look of chewed straw, rough, wearing a pearl shine; its plants bony and begrudging, the low hills crumbling. It can be bitterly cold, an awful and lonely place to fight and die. The change of seasons brings an altogether different face: the valley becomes beautiful in early summer when its inclines wear a gentle green, the river flows calmly and flowers line the fields. Since the days of fierce fighting in early 1937, when the Nationalists launched an offensive attempt to break the defensive lines protecting the capital, time has blurred the steep count of casualties and the collected shrapnel of war – coins, combs, bullet casings, teeth, chipped fragments of bone, tins, knives, grenades, broken equipment and leathery old boots. These are buried forever, or periodically emerge, pushed up by an excavator or rolling plough-share. In other places, where once were surly tracks amid the mud and death of February, the remnants of war have in places been concreted under industry and its necessities: warehouses, parking lots, workshops.

A list of objects left behind by a largely British battalion of the International Brigades, scrambling through olive groves to ascend a strategic hill in the Battle of Jarama, tells its own story: the heaviest, and first to be discarded, were Marxist textbooks – their existence on the battlefield as good an indicator as any of the absurdity of this war – along with poetry, pornography, Nietzsche, Spinoza, Shakespeare.[23] Much has been projected back upon the motives of the international participants in this war but, in intense pain and longing, dying of appalling injuries, many must have wondered at the value placed on a romanticised struggle. Hundreds of international volunteers fell around Madrid without any clue about the country into which they had wandered. Like countless local soldiers and their innocent countrymen and women, they fell without an understanding of how and why this was happening. An utter waste; history simply rolled over them.

Some of the finest observations of war in Madrid come from two women writers, Clara Campoamor – ignored for years, Madrid's main northern train station at Chamartín is now named in her honour – and Elena Fortún. Neither had their work published in Spain for decades.

A native *madrileña*, writer, lawyer, member of parliament and feminist who pioneered the cause of female suffrage, Clara Campoamor is yet another of those figures who, in different circum-stances, would be internationally famous. A committed Republican, she was nevertheless sharply critical of the violent excesses happening in Madrid, 'the disorganisation of the country and the slide into anarchy'. In exile, she left behind a substantial body of literary, political and feminist writings, the most famous being her take on the Spanish revolution seen from a supportive but sceptical Republican point of view.[24] This did not enamour her with the intolerant times or her fellow-travellers; criticism of one's own side of politics is easily dressed as unforgivable heresy.

Over the years, many on the political right have sought to delegitimise the Second Republic for the prevalence of violence yet, in Campoamor's view, this was a product of the times more than a product of the Republic per se. The brutality in Madrid, she argued, was part of a wave of uncontrolled violence going back at least to the failed 1934 workers' revolt in Asturias and, much as she might have sympathised with the frustrations involved, she was very critical of the Popular Front government's inability to stem this tide. In Madrid in the months leading up to the first days of the war, buildings were sacked and burned, churches suffered arson attacks, priests were murdered. This was no basis upon which to build a new society, for a wild mob is a wild mob, regardless of its political leanings. She condemned the way the legitimate tricolour Republican flag was often replaced, with sinister consequences, by the red flag of the communists or the red and black flag of the anarchists. This was symptomatic of a fragmented discipline and lack of control, circumstances under which the innocent were the first to suffer. Campoamor loathed the prevalence of thugs bringing disrepute to the Republic she supported: the gangs happily arresting and executing enemies without due process, and the dozens of corpses they left behind each day. Likewise, she loathed and condemned the treatment of women who were used as prostitutes for Republican soldiers on the front line, and the high incidence of venereal disease among the troops.

It was crucial not to dissent publicly from support for the Republican cause but, for Campoamor, her beloved Madrid had become an ugly place, not only due to the fear and chaos generated by war and aerial bombardment; the city that prided itself on the coquettish style of its beautiful people suddenly seemed to champion the dirty, uncombed and half-dressed; elements of sartorial style were considered bourgeois affectations, and this applied equally to women and men. Underlying all these changes was Campoamor's frustration that people's genuine desire for a different life and a better society was being lost under a wave of moral squalor and misery, perhaps never better exemplified than by the crowd that marched along the streets carrying on the end of a bayonet the head of military general López de Ochoa – himself certainly no saint – who had previously been lynched in a military hospital in Carabanchel.

Notwithstanding her denunciation of violence on her own side of politics, Campoamor was unflinching in her condemnation of the cowardly bombing of civilians by Nationalist forces and their allies, and the reports that reached Madrid of the appalling murders committed by those troops on their march to the capital. She went into exile at the end of 1936, fearful of the behaviour of both warring parties, and would never return to Madrid. Published in French in 1937, her most famous work, *La revolución española vista por una republicana*, was not published in Spain until 2002.

Another native *madrileña*, Encarnación Aragoneses Urquijo had developed a successful career as an educator and children's author using the pseudonym Elena Fortún. Her books followed the fortunes of a young female protagonist, Celia, through the byways of life. A great supporter of the Republic, Fortún went into exile in 1939 where she continued to write the unfolding adventures of Celia, including *Celia en la revolución* in 1943. The book would not be published until 1987, long after her death. Like Campoamor, Fortún was a witness to the best and the worst of life in wartime Madrid, tracking with horror the daily executions in the first months, the bodies piled up in the usual sites; the stench of the city, the destruction of homes and offices. Staying until close to the end of the war, she observed that what most consumed citizens, over and above the fear of death, was a terrible hunger: 'Worrying about food empties one's mind of all other thoughts.'[25] Hunger broke down any qualms about diet, as people ate dogs, cats, rats, donkeys and even grass. Such scenes recall the wretched young boys in Baroja's trilogy who find a dead pig on the Yeserías Avenue, near the banks of the Manzanares, and feed upon it for a week. Another war memoir,[26] written by Tere Medina-Navascués, a 12-year-old girl at the time of the war, returns to the theme: one is paradoxically filled to bursting with an excruciating emptiness; one has to 'close one's eyes so as not to observe others eating their meagre crumbs, so overwhelming is the desire to rob them of that tiny morsel'.[27] Albeit within a context of darkness, the mood is lightened when, as her parents hustle her down into a Metro station to escape a bombing raid, they explain that Madrid would be 'the graveyard of fascism' – a famous refrain then and now – to which the young girl replies, 'Why can't it be somewhere else?'

As was often the case, Pío Baroja, by now in his mid-60s, was pessimistic. He was out of Madrid when the war began and did not return until 1940, but this did not stop him expressing his contempt for those who dragged the populace with them in their yearning for political power. In his 1951 novel *Miserias de la guerra* (*Miseries of War*), censored and not published until 2006, his character Hipólito remarks to a group of victorious Nationalists, 'Having to obey you lot, I would live very badly', while still venting his spleen at the rabble of forces – too often vengeful, murderous, criminal – standing for the Republic.[28] The Second Republic, Baroja remarked, was like a party that starts well but ends in drunkenness and an all-out brawl, an observation that contrasts with the dewy-eyed devotion of a foreign correspondent such as Martha Gellhorn. In his clear-headed but somewhat misanthropic way Baroja, whom Hemingway idolised, believed it an absurd mistake to try and make lasting changes to a society in a very short time. Such a belief foreshadowed the doomed fortunes of radical political formation Podemos in the twenty-first century, a movement born in Madrid that arrived in spectacular fashion, promising to end deeply entrenched political corruption, won an important degree of power and then floundered under its own contradictions. Podemos loved to appeal to *la gente* – the people – but, as Baroja knew, 'the people' can be a sinister and brutal collective.

If the military were unable to lead the people, neither were the intellectual class, a group whose membership and very definition was always up for dispute.[29] Poet Miguel Hernández, who had earlier in his career been ignored by the cultural darlings of Madrid, was convinced many radicalised authors had a tendency to cowardice, more comfortable brandishing a rifle well back from the front line, full of empty rhetoric, than fighting in the mud and dust. His suspicions are reinforced by an anecdote told by Luis Buñuel, who goes to see French art historian Élie Faure, visiting Madrid at the time, in his hotel: Faure, recounts Buñuel, was standing at his window, in his long underwear, 'weeping at the sight of the people in arms'. Such noble sentiments come cheaply when it is not oneself carrying the arms. Buñuel was distant, but still appropriately moved: 'One day we watched a hundred peasants march by, four abreast, some armed with hunting rifles and revolvers, some with sickles and pitchforks. In an obvious effort at discipline, they were trying very hard to march in step. Faure and I both wept.'[30] A deeply committed poet, serious and romantic, Miguel Hernández had no time for such mawkish nonsense. The illiterate – whom Hernández knew so well – were once again on the way to sacrifice themselves for their masters: here, rural workers with unreliable weapons, sickles and pitchforks stumble out to meet an opposition being supported by the latest German technologies of death.

As the end drew into sight, those who still could, and who feared they might be compromised under a new regime, fled Madrid. Others were simply trapped. An internal coup within the Republican ranks and the overthrow of the socialist government of Juan Negrín only added to the exhausted confusion of the final days. The coup leaders, realising the game was up, hoped to negotiate a ceasefire and an equitable end to the war. It was naive of them to imagine Franco would be so benevolent, and the communists who had dug in with Negrín wanted no part of any compromise. Across Madrid, fighting broke out again, an internecine conflict from Ciudad Lineal to the Castellana, Serrano and Ríos Rosas.[31] It was all too late, too hopeless: all that remained was for the victorious Nationalist troops to enter the city. Madrid once again held its breath.

Strange days followed. The war had been lost, but Franco had not yet arrived to claim the final prize. Negotiations for the surrender were ongoing. Nationalist troops were in the city, while some Republican forces still remained. Madrid was in a kind of grey limbo, people unsure of whether to hide or reveal their colours. It had been so dangerous, for so long, to display open hostility to the Republic that all bets remained hedged. The line between hope and fear was fine; the nervousness of the city palpable. On 28 March 1939, amid dread, relief and flag-waving enthusiasm, the first patrols came into Madrid through the ruin of Argüelles, up Princesa and towards the Gran Vía. Any remaining republican, communist or anarchist flags or symbols were torn down, stamped underfoot, along with images of Lenin, Stalin or the infamous Dolores Ibárruri, la Pasionaria. All the propaganda posters that spoke to a resistant Madrid now vanished.

Fifth columnists came out of hiding; girls rushed to kiss young soldiers; allegiances changed in a heartbeat. The war was over.

Ways of healing

A s if the war had not been sufficiently cruel for Madrid, while the city lay in exhausted ruin all eyes turned to the broader European conflict. Any hopes that the coming European war might prove beneficial for the Republic, and that a broad anti-fascist alliance would come to assist Madrid, were dashed as the city and the nation were largely forgotten. The timing was terrible, even tragic. Europe was forced to look the other way: while the whole continent was in flames, little attention could be paid to the traumas of Iberia. Had they looked, in the smoking ruins of Madrid could be seen the fate that lay around the corner for one European city after another. Even after the war, a hope still flickered: given Italy and France had been liberated from Nazi control, could not Madrid too be liberated from the strange talons of Franco?[1]

The answer was no. So much sadness was concentrated in these silent years, years of ongoing hunger, illness and debris; of retribution and still more executions; of penury, food rationing and broken families. No one in Europe was paying any attention. Intent on imposing a new regime and purging all traces of republicanism, secularism or cultural modernism, the victorious general Franco, albeit within the limits imposed by the impoverishment of war, could largely do as he pleased. In the decade and a half between the end of the civil war and the early 1950s, almost every aspect of life in Madrid – educational, cultural, familial, religious, judicial and political – fell under the supervision of the new government. All those who had 'lost' the war faced punishment, incarceration, exclusion from employment, social ostracism and, if they were fortunate enough not to be executed, a very long, slow redemption. Among those who had 'lost' the war was the city of Madrid.

Twenty years were consumed, from the mid-1930s to the mid-1950s, in war, waste and cultural stagnation. Yet sheer human exhaustion can flatten out the demands of ideology. In a recent epic novelisation of the post-war years in Madrid, Cristina, a young woman formerly associated with the Communist Party, one of whose brothers has been murdered by fascists, and whose other brother has fled Madrid to fight in the mountains of Andalusia with the resistance, wants only a semblance of normality. For all the years of struggle, 'I no longer care who is in charge. I just want to live,' she says. 'To be a normal person with a normal life. Is that too much to ask?'[2]

Every person, every family and every institution in Madrid would heal in its own way. The 1940s were the hardest years of the century: a decade of want, incarcerations and score settling, but also of slow and painful rebuilding. The dictator, whose erstwhile allies had by 1945 all gone into the dustbin of history, was scorned by the western powers and his regime boycotted by the United Nations. There were no international plans, however, to overthrow the government in Madrid. In 1947 Britain and France invited representatives of twenty-two European countries to discuss the terms of the Marshall Plan; Spain and the Soviet Union – for different reasons, each at their own end of the continent – were excluded.[3] Given the Allied victories over Mussolini and Hitler, the continuation of the Franco regime makes sense only in the context of the sheer exhaustion of the European continent by 1945 and, very soon, the strategic use to which an anti-communist government could be put. By the early 1950s, the authoritarian regime in Madrid was a convenient presence, especially for the United States, as a southern European bulwark against communism. The underwhelming Franco finally earned the attention of western victors and cosied up, making himself useful to the triumphant allies. The 1953 Pact of Madrid provided recognition of the regime and offered substantial economic aid to an economy crippled by an absurd policy of attempted autarky; in exchange, the establishment of a series of US military bases, including the air force base at Torrejón de Ardoz on the eastern edge of Madrid, operational until 1992.

The post-war years in Madrid began with a purging of any elements that carried the taint of the Republic; Franco displayed a small-minded lack of generosity towards the people he had defeated. Military victory in itself was only the beginning; social change was a project of decades. Any Republican institutions or collectives that might have survived the war and had somehow limped into the 1940s were destroyed by the new regime, for the reconstruction of Spain, in all its dimensions, would commence with the reconstruction of Madrid. What the regime ingenuously described as a 'Catholic and organic democracy' was, in its early stages, a conservative authoritarianism with a strong and punitive mission of national rebirth.[4] Against the festive nature of the capital, the triumphant Nationalists brought, in those first years, a form of puritanism that sought to expel the modern, celebratory elements that had characterised Madrid for much of the previous two decades. The humourless Franco, in his own way as dour as any of the orthodox communists he so loathed, disapproved of the wild secularism, nods to sexual freedom and the playful subversions of religious pieties inherent in the carnivalesque. These were too much for a strict reading of Catholicism that was not a liberating force for human freedom but a partner to militarism, discipline and social order.

It would be wrong to describe Madrid as joyless; after all, many had eagerly awaited the fall of the Republic. Yet it was a deeply wounded city. Always rambunctious, it was punished and shamed for its daring, condemned to a period of sobriety and penance. The dreams of many of its citizens had turned to ash, countless children had been orphaned, families across the political spectrum had buried loved ones who had died violent deaths. 'In what kind of city did I now live?', the young Zúñiga asked himself during the slow years of recovery. Madrid had lost its vital fire. It seemed no longer the home of hundreds of thousands of diverse and often astonishing people; it was now 'a provincial, broken, poor, famished, dry, dusty and empty city'; a cowed and defeated populace where strength and a shameless will to survive were more important than any sense of fraternity.[5] As he tells it, his post-war youth was spent under the politically and culturally isolating effects of the catastrophe, living through critical levels of unemployment, delayed when not ruined industrialisation, poor communications, lack of appropriate education, high levels of illiteracy and a population generally fearful of innovation.[6] This last is hardly surprising given the constant ruptures of the previous decade, but Zúñiga is damning of a Madrid 'overflowing with conservative bureaucrats and pen-pushers, deeply Catholic, jealous of progress and all things foreign and, above all, assiduous clients of cafés and brothels, both of which were to be found in abundance.'[7]

What did not change in Madrid was an undertow of fear and violence; in its first years the new regime was especially vicious. There were personal accounts to be settled, and there were Republican killings – most infamously the massacre of prisoners at Paracuellos[8] – to be avenged. Organised legal repression was enacted; following the so-called Law of Political Responsibilities, and pursuing evidence supplied by agents and countless unreliable witnesses, close to 12,000 people were rounded up in the weeks following the fall of Madrid. Mass incarcerations ensued and, in the years after the war, some 3,000 were executed, including the infamous case of 'Las Trece Rosas'.[9] Many of the incarcerated were put to work on the construction of a monument to 'the fallen', in the process unwittingly creating the ugliest monument in the province of Madrid.[10] The city also hosted more than a dozen of the hundreds of concentration camps the new regime established for political prisoners or the otherwise undesirable. Given politics could be read as a form of unreason and danger, it was not surprising the regime repurposed old asylums for a new class of persons who could not be allowed to wander free; one such was the mental asylum of Alcalá de Henares. Football stadia – Chamartín de la Rosa and Vallecas – were temporary prisons; internment camps sprang up at Leganés, El Pardo, Rivas,

Carabanchel and Guadarrama, among other sites. The new government believed re-education and the contrition of hard labour to be part of healing; in conformity with Franco's expectations, the city had to be deeply 'cleansed', not only morally and spiritually, but also physically and politically. Symbols of a defeated regime were toppled and street names changed, better to reflect regime sympathies and orthodoxies. Within Nationalist ranks, some voices were heard calling for the heretical Madrid to be stripped of its status as capital in favour of loyal Castilian cities such as Burgos, Valladolid or Salamanca. This proved, however, to be nothing more than opportunistic provincialism.

The loss of Madrid represented the failure of those who had dreamed of her alternate future but had unwittingly caused so much damage of their own. As the Spanish refrain goes: *Everyone killed her, but she died alone.* For the defeated, there was everyday survival and, more abstractly, the dispiriting gap to be faced between the Madrid envisioned by its optimistic Republican defenders – a Madrid of class solidarity and egalitarian culture, without want, poverty or hunger – and the hard reality of the Madrid that swung into view in the immediate post-war: a city shrunken by the very extent of its physical and moral ruin. A city where heads disappeared silently into doorways, hoping not to have been noticed; a city without much to celebrate. David Eccles, a member of the British diplomatic corps, wrote in late 1940: 'As we walk to the Embassy in the morning we see an ever-increasing number of men, women and children picking over the dustbins and the slop pails standing on the kerb. As they spy a bit of potato peel among the filth, they eat it, and stuff into sacks garbage too terrible to describe.'[11] Such anecdotes point to the much broader tragedy of mass hunger in post-civil war Madrid and Spain.

It was unlike Madrid to be down for long. Its natural ebullience was stronger than the desire of nationalist ideologues to forge a new – or rather, old – identity, going back to an anachronistic purity, purging the vices of a capricious and liberal city that had been poisoned by excessive cosmopolitanism, had indulged the sarcasm, humour and sexuality of European modernism and the avant-garde, and had embraced the political vices of Marxism and Republicanism. There was nevertheless no return to the nostalgic *costumbrismo* version of Madrid, with its servants who knew their place. Those same servants – many of whom had so recently grown bold, swapped the uniforms of domestic service for the colours of the militia and taken up arms – had been radically suppressed, but what had been seen could not now be unseen. Too much blood had been shed for the city to simply fold back into a world of organ grinders, *churros* and *zarzuela*;[12] this hyper-folkloric Madrid had, in any case, only ever been a fantasy. The political struggle for a greater measure of equality and justice had been flattened and defeated, but only temporarily. For all the new conformity imposed in religion, culture, politics and education, those ideas subversive to the regime had not vanished, but simply gone underground. It was only a matter of time before the post-war twentieth century and its polit-ical and economic alliances imposed itself upon the regime in Madrid, and not the other way around.

As the war began to recede into the past, other possibilities arose for Madrid: models were drawn up – more in fevered heads than practical minds – of a gleaming, fascist capital: broad-avenued, granitic, monumental. These followed pre-war Italian and German ideas of the future city, ideas that had turned to dust. More grounded was the plan, conceived in 1939 and finally begun in 1946, of urban planner and architect Pedro Bidagor, head of the Office for the Reconstruction of Madrid. A range of housing projects had been under way since the early 1940s in popular districts such as Vallecas, but the Bidagor Plan dealt with Madrid in its entirety, as a resi-dential, commercial and industrial capital into which had to be woven the appropriate spaces for transport and communications, greenery and leisure.

The Bidagor Plan confirmed what had been developing of its own accord: that Madrid's suburban areas and outlying villages – soon to be incorporated into Greater Madrid – were the scene of a range of specific activities, from residential to purely industrial. The planned urban zones of the nineteenth century were further broadened, the six radial highways that lead out from Madrid were confirmed as the principal arteries of the nation, and rail tracks ran heavy goods across the city from north to south, with the southern half of Madrid further established as the home of industry and of the majority of the poorer and working-class families. The plan had its failings: for all it conceived of Madrid as a major capital city, it did not anticipate the sheer volume of internal migration in the post-war years that again swelled the population. This was not just a question of work, food or opportunity; for many, Madrid was a place to be lost, to be anonymous. It was the chance to get away from smaller villages where neighbours remembered all too well what had happened during the recent war, on both sides. Disappearing into the mass and swirl of Madrid offered the possibility of escaping retribution.

By the 1950s the periphery had expanded beyond the control of urban planners, and critical infrastructure needs were not being met. As formerly outlying towns were added to the metropolitan footprint, Greater Madrid now incorporated districts such as Fuencarral, Chamartín, Hortaleza, Canillejas, Vicálvaro, Entrevías, Vallecas and Carabanchel. The population pushed towards 2 million. The web of the capital spread out across the plains, embracing old town squares and churches, building over the goat tracks, the riding paths, the blackberry-filled gullies, the mud- and dust-filled ways: 'Canillas Street in Prosperidad was the limit of reality; beyond were rubbish dumps and threatening vacant lots, a kind of dirty nothingness that floated as far as the eye could see,' wrote Juan José Millás in his autobiographical work *El mundo*.[13] As Madrid unfurled, the periphery was pushed further and further out from the centre; the temporary shacks without running water or electricity, the scrap yards, warehouses and, before long, the complex looping motorways occupied field after field, creating a new ring of poverty around the city. Half a century earlier, the principal slums of Madrid had been centred around the banks of the Manzanares, by Las Injurias and Las Cambroneras; now, as the population exploded, the line where the countryside met the slums had both moved outward, and increased in size. For the victorious Nationalist government, the question was whether to ignore the squalor that grew up along the metropolitan fringe – very few supporters of the new regime would be found there – or to keep a close observation upon political and industrial threats that might emerge over time. As it was, it tended to do both.

The evolution of the district of San Blas, once dubbed 'the largest working-class suburb in Spain', is a perfect example of the outer urban transformation of Madrid 'from penury, to promise, to aspiration'.[14] In the decades following the end of the war, many an impoverished rural family dragged their few belongings and their young children to the squalid margins, the only affordable place to live, and from those bare tracts of land emerged another generation. As the economy picked up, they were within sight of employment, improvement, sustenance, education. For years, life was dirt poor, overcrowded, at times even brutal, but the only way was up, into the prosperity of the final third of the twentieth century. For countless thousands, this was Madrid: a first step from centuries of rural hardship towards a more comfortable urban existence. And for countless thousands it worked, if not for the first generation post-war, then certainly for the second, by which time the dictatorship was dying, the global economy was pouring into Spain and employment, by the standards of fifty years earlier, was abundant.

An entire generation would come of age in the 1960s and 1970s, a time of extraordinary political and cultural change, in a Madrid that was, in many of its outlying districts, conventionally ugly, poor, humble and chaotic. The combination of population explosion and a lack of sufficient development resulted in an estimated 50,000 slum dwellings springing up by the mid-1950s to accommodate the influx of workers and their families.[15] Attempts were made to control this growth – everything about these shanty towns, from the overcrowding, to the lack of sanitation and services, to the potential for social unrest, defied the image the regime had established both for itself and for the consumption of the slowly increasing foreign presence in Madrid and Spain – but to no avail. Up to 400,000 residents lived in these sagging, unkempt combinations of sheet metal, blankets, plastic, wire, cardboard and found objects that came, in time, to set down roots, convert tracks to roads, connect electricity and eventually sprout TV antennae like an old man's hair. This was not the Madrid on display for visiting US officials and, needless to say, it was beyond the ken of international tourists who began to flock to Spanish beaches in the 1960s. The very temporality of this type of housing meant it was impossible to eradicate: a shack bulldozed one day could be erected again the next, and eventually the municipal authorities had to settle for an accommodation with this blight on progress, this obvious reminder of the harsh inequalities still intrinsic to life in Madrid.

New social housing developments at Entrevías and Orcasitas in the poorest zones south of the city, or in San Blas to the east, went some way to alleviate the problem, but it was not enough. Its economy still hampered by the war recovery and Franco's earlier, ill-fated attempt to snub the world and create Spain as a self-sufficient autarky, Madrid had been left without sufficient financial resources or the administrative skills to tackle the housing crisis. Over the final decades of the twentieth century, the periphery of Madrid would be transformed and enlarged again and again, housing blocks spilling further and further across the plains. It would take until 2018 before the last recognised *chabola* settlement, El Gallinero, was cleared and its residents resettled. There remain, inevitably, pockets of acute disadvantage, poor housing and poor living conditions – San Cristóbal de los Ángeles, La Cañada Real – but they bear no resemblance to the mud and sewerage and roaming animals of the first two post-war decades.

The process of social healing, like the housing plans, was imperfect. Hope rested with the first generation born beyond the war, growing up in its shadow but outside of its direct animosities. Thousands would be born into families in one way or another mutilated by the experience of the previous decade – that impact was dreadful – but the historic remove of one generation was a first, small, yet important step in stitching up the wounds of conflict. Geographic divisions remained, by which conservative and wealthier Madrid, largely a beneficiary of the new regime, clustered around the established suburbs of the nineteenth-century *ensanche* – Chamberí, Salamanca, Retiro, Argüelles – along with the leafy zones to the north-west of the city, such as Las Rozas, Majadahonda or El Pardo. In time, however, opposition to the Franco regime would come not only from workers and doubting clerics, but also significantly from the children of the middle and upper classes who occupied the most comfortable areas of metropolitan Madrid: well-educated, exposed to (comparatively) radical social and political theory, and envious of the freedoms enjoyed by their peers in other parts of Europe and the United States.

Life gradually settled; a semblance of normality was restored. Much of the city had little option but to be calmer, whether through repression or fatigue, than in previous decades. The 'masses' in the expanding working-class districts to the south and east put on hold the popular Madrid tradition of revolt against oppressive govern-ment. Union activity was tightly controlled. Political repression remained strong – elements of clandestine resistance remained throughout the city – and democracy was nowhere in sight, yet the barbarity of vengeance slowed. Informers were active throughout the capital, their work enhanced by a generally faithful army of concierges and nightwatchmen who saw all comings and goings, noticing anything that might suggest an illegal gathering, a subver-sive plot, an unusual arrival or departure.

Like every authoritarian regime that seeks to justify its presence and dominate the nation from an imperial capital, control of the press, elimination of any remnant opposition, and education of the next generation were all key. Control of the armed forces was taken as given. Both state and church were keen to reverse the secularisa-tion of education that had characterised the first decades of the century and the Republic in particular. Bodies such as the Free Institution of Education, vital to the revolution in Spanish education over the previous sixty years, were an obvious target; considered not merely anti-Catholic, but anti-Spanish, it was dissolved at the end of the war, and education in Madrid, as across the country, became closely tied to the norms and values of the regime. Yet there were always cracks through which dissident literature and ideas might enter, and in the 1960s, particularly on the university campuses and via the parish priests of Madrid, they would find fertile ground.

Not all in the regime were as petty and jealous as its leader; once the grimmest years of the 1940s were over, signs of reform began to appear. The regime was never monolithic, for it combined different conservative groups who, while all opposed to the Republic and socialism, were nevertheless varied in their ideas for the future direction of the country. With the passing of time, it is increasingly clear that cultural life was more vibrant under the dictatorship than has often been allowed, albeit many artists and writers sympathetic to the Republic were either in exile or had been silenced. For philosopher Julián Marías, the war and dictatorship would not and could not erase the brilliance of the culture that had blossomed in Madrid in the first three decades of the century, a cultural heritage that rose above the simplistic idea of two irrevocably opposed and Cainite Spains, radicalised into hatred of each other. This was a brave stance to take, coming out of a period of civil war, but it was also intellectually faithful to tradition. The inability to look beyond two irreconcilable Spains sells the country and its cultural life short; it patronises and infantilises Spaniards. For Marías, the war and its aftermath were not the end but rather the beginning of an opportunity to construct a calm, balanced and responsible nation that drew on its infinite cultural resources.[16] It was no surprise that Madrid was home to one of the most spirited cultural explosions of the late twentieth century: those luxuriant and often uncontrolled wild flowers did not bloom from nowhere. The seeds were planted during the dictatorship, and during the early twentieth century, and during the extravagant nineteenth; for culture is an eternal connecting thread, and while it might go underground, it is never eliminated.

In the immediate aftermath of the war, an entire genre of literature dedicated to denouncing the iniquities of 'red' and 'Bolshevik' Madrid flourished; those who had lived through the three years of siege, and some who hadn't, weighed in with their novelised versions of the menace that had been chased from the streets of the capital. In some respects, this was a way of carrying on the war that had already been won on the battlefield. These potboilers were short-lived; for the most part their literary value was not significant, though they have value as historical documents for understanding contrasting visions of the city. By the 1950s a new generational consciousness had emerged, especially among writers too young to have experienced the war as fighters or political activists. Photographers and film-makers also set about describing the new reality of Madrid as it began to look again towards the modernity it had embraced two and three decades earlier and sought, in their own subtle ways, to challenge the orthodoxy imposed on cultural expression, and the political prescriptions of daily life.

The city and its people were amply documented through novels, film and photography; its life was reflected, distorted, dulcified, reimagined. Baroja died in Madrid in 1956, but there was already a new generation of writers mapping social contours, among them Luis Martín Santos, Juan Benet, Rafael Sánchez Ferlosio, Juan García Hortelano, Camilo José Cela, Carmen Martín Gaite and Ignacio Aldecoa. To cite just three from this rich vein, Cela's *La Colmena* (*The Hive*), Santos's *Tiempo de Silencio* (*Time of Silence*) and Ferlosio's *El Jarama* (*The River*), in their different ways and styles, all celebrate Madrid life during these decades with its subtle forms of resistance and pleasure. Unlike the post-war 'red Madrid' genre, these works did not abhor the city. It was a flawed environment, full of frustration and at times cruelty, but it was home. Artistic works of the highest quality and integrity emerged in the post-war process of assuming, analysing and confronting the more restrictive Spain that had emerged.

Madrid was a perfect stage for film-makers and photographers. Artists charted a path between the imposed virtues of national Catholicism and the clandestine desires of those who kept one eye on French, Italian and North American visual culture. Madrid and its surrounds played host to a range of Hollywood epics and glamorous artists poured in, Ava Gardner, Orson Welles, Grace Kelly and Cary Grant among them. The local industry was divided between the regime-friendly production, much of which fell back on comfortable stereotypes, and neorealist social criticism. The city is either the convenient background for conservative light-hearted escapades, costume dramas and living-room capers or a sinister landscape, such as in Carlos Saura's *Los golfos* (*The Delinquents*) of 1960, filmed among the lowlands of Legazpi and Vista Alegre. In long, slow panning, the shrouded city, almost medieval in its twilight or its dawn, appears, if not hostile, then threatening to outsiders. The blind tobacconist with her lottery tickets, the young bullfighter, the unpaved streets, the sharply delineated, black-and-white simplicity of the poor, the chaotic children, the discontented and thuggish youth, the tenebrous streets and vacant lots of outer Madrid: if these elements appear clichéd now, it is because they have been relentlessly copied as shortcut symbols of Francoist Spain, and because viewers now recognise that city as unrecognisable. Representations of a deprived Madrid that encircled the lovely comforts of its established inner neighbourhoods continued across the years, emerging in full colour to feature in the early films of Pedro Almodóvar where the M-30 motorway served as a clear demarcating line between Madrid and its outlying, poorer *barrios*. Meanwhile, prolific director Pedro Lazaga was churning out film after film, inoffensive, light, drawing-room comedies that did nothing to challenge the regime. In classics such as the 1966 *La ciudad no es para mí* (*The city is not for me*) or the 1969 *Abuelo Made in Spain*, Madrid is interpreted as a bewildering place through the eyes of the walking cliché that was actor Paco Martínez Soria, the apparently stupid but ultimately wise country bumpkin, the embodiment of the wisdom of rural Spain, pilloried but ultimately triumphant; a role the actor would specialise in for years.

Photography was arguably Spain's leading art form in the postwar years, and from the late 1950s neorealism dominated the most important collectives based in Madrid, such as La Palangana and the loosely defined 'Madrid School'. Including some of the finest Spanish artists of the mid-twentieth century – Ramón Masats, Gabriel Cualladó, Francisco Gómez, Francisco Ontañón – most members were not *madrileños*, but the magazines and institutions from which they developed their art were in the capital; one of the finest photographic documenters of the social reality of Madrid at the time was Francesc Català-Roca, who hailed originally from rural

Catalonia. The aesthetic – bleak and often grainy black and white, stark images of social observation, social injustice or simple contradiction seen through hard-edged symmetries of light – influences a contemporary reading of Spain and Madrid in those years, tending to the fierce, unjust and brutal, against which survives a dedication to form and beauty that is its own denunciation of the conditions in which the work was produced.

Two decades after the end of the war Madrid embodied, however imperfectly, a modernity many desired and sought urgently. The city was no longer that caricatured ogre under the control of murderous communists, but a thriving metropolis – the population of the greater metropolitan area rose from 2 million to over 3 million from 1955 to 1965 – that had abandoned autarky and was embracing the benefits of capitalism; even many erstwhile conservatives, and in particular their children, looked to Madrid with fresh eyes and without animosity.

This was the perfect scenario for a wave of political ferment emerging from the universities. The proposed creation of a National Congress of Students in 1956, in opposition to the regime, and a series of protests that were met with falangist violence, marked a parting of the ways: from this point on, the university was the 'new epicentre' of opposition to Franco,[17] and two decades of student unrest, driven largely by the children of a middle class mostly loyal to the regime, marked a significant cultural and intellectual shift in Madrid. Many of those who received an education characterised by a strong adherence to religion, class difference, inequality between men and women, and steeped in the values of conservative Spanish nationalism[18] – an education imparted by a profession that, like so many others, had seen its 'undesirable' members purged in the years following the war – would now be the leaders of a student movement that demanded greater freedoms, greater representation and an end to political repression.

The end of the regime was still two decades away, but life in Madrid was now changing significantly. There was even a slow wave of returns by those who had gone into exile in the late 1930s. Not all: those who had been, and remained, implacably opposed to the regime were not welcome back. There were some, such as the extraordinary historian and philologist Ramón Menéndez Pidal, who returned immediately the war was over; in response to criticism that he had returned to a Madrid subjugated by Franco, he replied pragmatically: 'If I were to exile myself every time Spain had a government I disliked, I would have lived virtually forever in exile.'[19] For others, wounds would never be forgotten but had begun to heal; there is always today to be lived, in preference to yesterday. Childhood memories burned brightly, no matter what the country had been through: Jorge Semprún, a Madrid-born, Paris-based communist, many years later the Minister of Culture under a socialist government, spent some years living in clandestine caution in the Madrid of the 1950s, where he helped to organise the activities of the Communist Party: 'The city of my childhood had not yet become the sprawling industrial metropolis, so savagely magnificent and dilapidated, that it is today. There one still breathed the dry, pure air of the neighbouring hills, the sky was still a deep blue, the water was still deliciously cool and clear.'[20] He finds the neighbourhood around the Retiro, where he had grown up, to be unchanged – a testament to the fact that the civil war bombing campaigns had indeed protected the 'better' districts of Madrid. Coming from the opposite end of the political spectrum were those who had fled the Republican violence, such as the now elderly writer Azorín, who nevertheless sang from the same hymn sheet upon his return: 'In Madrid everything is the same. Spain is as it always was. Under the high and bright blue sky . . .'[21]

Madrid may have displayed eternal verities – the blue-skied city on the high plains, hugged by mountains, swept by pure air – but the idea that in Madrid everything was the same, or that Spain was as it always had been, was dewy-eyed nonsense. A deep trench had opened up between the experience of the 1930s and the Madrid of the 1950s and 1960s. This was both generational and a result of the dividing line marked by the war; the world burnt away in the furnace of war was gone forever. The decade of the 1940s stands as a profound separation between before and after as would, in the near future, the decade from 1975 to 1985. Life in Madrid may still have been restricted by the limitations of the dictatorship, but economics and technology had their way, as did student movements, new understandings of feminism, art and literature, increasing trade union activism, and new possibilities for people and their children to aspire to move from the working to the middle class. As Kamen argues, cultural patterns on both sides of the Atlantic had undergone a tectonic shift, and more were to come. Exiles returning to Spain found a country that was not interested in them; Ortega y Gasset found his public role hugely diminished after his return in 1945. Nor was the public interested in the exiles' narratives of the furious past, for it was now a distant and foreign place. Daily life took priority, and with it the previously unsuspected material comforts of a capitalist system into which Spain gained entry as the 1950s gave way to the vibrancy of the coming decade.

'Very quickly one realised that the arch-conservative State had little interest in conserving Madrid, but rather in selling it off, ruining it by leaving it in the hands of speculators and a series of mayors with appalling bad taste.'[22] Thus Francisco Umbral, a young journalist and writer born in Madrid, raised in Valladolid and who came, as did thousands of others like him, to the capital city in the 1960s to fashion a life beyond the stifling restrictions of his provincial home. Umbral was complaining that some of the great boulevards of Madrid had been asphalted over to make way for rivers of traffic or, as he called it, 'the empire of the automobile'. Nothing would so exemplify this change as the construction of Madrid's first motorway. Conceived in the Bidagor Plan as far back as the 1940s, when construction finally began in 1970 the M-30 orbital buried the historic Abroñigal, along whose banks sat squalid clusters of housing. The Abroñigal had been a part of Madrid for a thousand years, critical to its early medieval water supply; all that remains is the name, and yet another of the spectral channels that runs under the modern city, unseen and unremarked.

By the 1960s, technocrats in Madrid, closely aligned with the Catholic institution of the Opus Dei, had taken control of the national economy and were attempting to steer Spain towards a future reintegration with the broader European and world economy. It was not easy, for they attempted to take advantage of the European economic boom without allowing access to political or cultural liberalisation.[23] Naively, it was hoped economic growth would further entrench the regime, that relative abundance would be rewarded with happy compliance. While huge public investment went into the traditional industrial centres of Catalonia and the Basque region, Madrid continued – notwithstanding the massive inflow of migrants from Andalusia and Extremadura into Catalonia – to shoulder an enormous part of the seemingly endless wave of exiles from rural Spain into the centre of the peninsula. There was now a counter-vailing impact on the population via the hundreds of thousands who left Spain not for political but economic reasons, streaming into Germany, France and Switzerland to provide cheap labour for those rapidly expanding economies, and at the same time boosting the national economy through the remittances sent home. The future was not in agriculture – that ancient version of Spain was fast disappearing, and much of its control would later come under European Union directives – but in the factories of the world and the new service industries. In the capital, however, the housing problems of the 1950s continued, even as more and more of Madrid's outlying zones were opened up for residential development. Between 1960 and the death of the dictator in 1975, Greater Madrid's population rose sharply to 4 million. Indeed, in its waves of internal migration, its rapid growth of cities, its cultural rebirth, its mobilisation of student and union activists, its expansion of a professional middle class and its increasing secularisation of daily life, the 1960s had much in common with the 1920s, where the flowering of an alternative Spain had begun, only to be shut down by a reactionary wave of military-backed conservatism.[24] What could not now be stopped might at least be channelled, and the regime sought a new legitimacy through economic development and 'peaceful' social progress. Progress, albeit often far from peaceful, was undeniable, with both Spain and Madrid booming in the 1960s; legitimacy, however, would remain elusive, both then and subsequently.

Upper-class Madrid retained its dependence on domestic servants, and they arrived in their thousands, especially young women, from smaller towns and villages. Carmen Martín Gaite's deceptively gentle novel, *Fragmentos de interior*, portrays with a quiet lament this social and demographic transition: 'The milk from the village is what you will miss the most when you move to Madrid, everyone had told her.'[25] The 20-year-old, wide-eyed Luisa is warned by Pura, an older servant, that 'these large cities are full of vice, young lady; all this business of going out into the street and doing whatever you want without having anyone recognise you'.[26] As if freedom were a threat; perfectly encapsulating conservative fears of change, the anonymity of the city is interpreted as a cover for possible iniquity. There is no iniquity, but everyday pain: Luisa suffers a broken heart, and the estranged mother of the house where she has gone to serve commits suicide. In a literary trope thousands of years old, the city is that cruel wheel on which all hearts – and especially those of a rural innocence – are broken.

Yet for every rural migrant experiencing a quiet moment of despair, there was another keenly embracing the city and all it offered. The spectacular metropolis that Madrid has become took off not after the death of the dictator, as is often popularly assumed, but a good decade or more beforehand. The bourgeoisie, comfortable in their government posts, enjoyed a safe and splendid city even as their growing children began to itch for more; the housing estates, meanwhile, lined up row after row of new arrivals in a large-scale stacking of families and ordering of dreams. Entire new districts were built from scratch. The first generation who would live the majority of their lives not under a dictatorship but in a democracy were now filling the playgrounds, schools, streets and vacant lots around the edges of the capital. They might have occupied functional and ugly new residential areas, devoid of trees and many municipal services, but this was home, and it was the future. In a country and city desperately in need of new housing, aesthetic considerations were secondary; 'Urgency', wrote Sergio del Molino, 'was the enemy of beauty,' and it was often in the humble kitchens and living rooms of these very ordinary homes where dreams of freedom and democracy took hold.[27]

Given so much of the modern city has been built by internal migrants from all over Spain, and immigrants from the rest of the world with their diverse cultural backgrounds, Madrid often boasts of being a city where no one cares for, or asks after, the origin of others. This is not to deny that in Madrid, as much as anywhere else, being from the right family brings considerable social advantages. Not everyone has been deracinated; the layers of native *madrileños* grow generationally deeper and deeper. In the 1960s and 1970s, the children of then outer districts such as Barrio del Pilar, Hortaleza, La Elipa or San Blas faced a complicated heritage: was this a place to be proud of, these half-built, sometimes forlorn, rough-edged, weed-filled acres, with their dispersed tower blocks, their basic schools and amenities? The parents, who had arrived in the 1950s and 1960s, could look back fondly on their roots in ancient towns such as Soria, Badajoz, Segovia or Ávila, could refer with enormous pride to their place of origin, celebrate the saints' and feast days of those ancestral places. What did it mean for this first generation, who grew up in the *extrarradio* in the late 1960s and 1970s, to say they were from Madrid? The old and sometimes arthritic inner city, with all the monuments and institutions by which people commonly recognised the identity of Madrid – including all that was photogenic – was a foreign place beyond a broad belt of motorway. Their horizons, until they reached university or working age, were mostly prescribed by the local *barrio*, a world unto itself, and almost all who went on to university were the first in their families to do so.

There came a point, in the great transition to the city, where the village – ground zero for a sometimes Edenic and sometimes hellish family story – became lost. A number of generations on, no one was nostalgic for a pile of stones in some harsh valley, a whitewashed house on a burning plain or claustrophobic mountainside. Home was now Madrid and not that other place that ran in the grandparents' blood. There were still the annual visits, where distant cousins shyly went about their rudimentary daily lives, while the capital with all its attractions laid claim to the heart and those who had grown up there gave thanks for the broader horizons it provided.

Generations of new *madrileños* married with others from families likewise new to the city, and so the next generations grew up, fully immersed in the environment, adding depth to this modern heritage, liberated from the strictures of village or small-town life. It was only in the twenty-first century, with spiralling house prices, difficult access to employment – and then a pandemic – that the empty or near-empty ancestral village once again became a site of interest, and the urbane grandchildren and great-grandchildren took a closer look at their forgotten heritage. Some moved back, some sought alternative lifestyles; some believed in the regeneration of the village. In Daniel Gascón's series of comic novels, those returning from the city are keen to impart the political and cultural orthodoxies of the age: sustainable agriculture, gentle masculinities, veganism – a majestic parody of the bizarre progress of hipster culture amid the eternal verities of the Spanish village.[28]

In the cafés, in the streets and avenues, in the factories, in middle-class living rooms, in churches and on university campuses, Madrid continued its political and cultural expansion. Increasingly, conversations turned on the question of who and what might succeed Franco. The past of course clung on; also did the dictator. The war and its long aftermath was still there, crouching and present. Umbral paints the famous Café Gijón on Recoletos as a type of redoubt for those who had lost out: even twenty or thirty years later, there was 'a lot of pain, tiredness, refuge and death' amid the lives of those gathered, such as a Latin professor and sonnet writer who had invested his faith in the Republic. The café was 'a pavilion for those convalescing from the defeat, a smoke-filled sanatorium for the incurable wounds of war and culture, a still-warm amputated stub of exile . . . the trough or hollow where ended up all the frustrated, the unclassified, the defeated, the humiliated.'[29]

University protests had started as early as 1956, when the regime began to lock up the children of those who had been a part of the victory some twenty years earlier.[30] Just as importantly, the regime began to lose the unequivocal support of the church, especially after Vatican II had laid out a path for a confluence between Catholicism and democracy. Historian Santos Juliá sums up the situation in one sentence: 'the clergy went to bed as national Catholics, and woke up as democrats and even socialists.'[31] Parish priests in Madrid, particularly in the poorer areas, offered their churches and meeting rooms as a safe site for clandestine meetings.

In March 1965, and despite the warnings of the DGS – the feared state security apparatus headquartered in the Puerta del Sol – some 5,000 students and professors participated, in the heart of Madrid, in the largest demonstration since the collapse of the Republic. It was the first time since the civil war that 'shouts in favour of freedom had been heard in the capital'.[32] In hindsight, the years 1966 to 1969 might have seen the end of the regime: the economic boom was well under way; the middle class were sending their children to university in increasing numbers; the church hierarchy was more and more accommodating of those sectors that were resistant to the regime, such as students and trade unions; and democracy was afoot. There was a serious flowering of resistance at this point, and real changes should have come a decade before they did. Most of society was ready for it; the social revolution of the late seventies could have occurred in the mid- to late sixties. So strong were the protests becoming by 1969, in the wake of the infamous police murder of young student activist Enrique Ruano, that, as Javier Marías fictionalised, 'during the demonstrations that followed, even students like Berta Isla took part, students who had previously been either apolitical or unwilling to take risks' and such an unlikely student ends up running before the mounted, baton-wielding police around the Plaza de Manuel Becerra.[33] Instead, Madrid witnessed yet another harsh crackdown by an increasingly senile regime: the intense dark before the dawn. The regime would only go out kicking – not the dictator, who would die calmly in bed – and jealously kept a grip on the levers of power.

These social changes and student protests were, in some respects, a way of Madrid regaining some of the affection of the broader national population. Given that, in many parts of Spain, 'Madrid' was a metonym for the regime, for years to be anti-Madrid in any dimension was synonymous with being anti-Franco and thus contra everything the regime stood for, a feeling most strongly expressed in Catalonia and the Basque region. It was in the interests of independence movements – or at least their intellectual and political authors – to downplay the diversity of Madrid and the points of political resistance within the city. It was easier to emphasise its authoritarian nature, and to continue the nineteenth-century grievance that the centrality of Madrid to the national economy was a hindrance to the full development of their regions. Thus, Madrid faced the hostility not only of the Castilian purists who abhorred its modernising tendencies, but too of regional nationalists who found fault in the opposite direction: Madrid was not liberal enough, if by liberal one understands the devolution of political and economic control to regional parliaments. This would eventually happen, but not until the 1978 Constitution enshrined such powers in law.

Yet 1960s Madrid, as much as anywhere in Spain, was aware of the counter-cultural breezes sweeping across the continent. The regime's censorship apparatus that reached into so many private corners could not stop the diffusion of the cultural dissent embodied in external influences. They filtered in, became adopted and merged with local patterns of cultural expression. Artists in Madrid were not merely copying popular forms from elsewhere in music, fashion, art and literature – this is the nature of cultural transmission in any time or place – but were translating and adapting, adding new layers onto an already rich, deep bedrock of local cultural resources.

Madrid paid a high price for its political prominence by being a regular target for domestic terrorism. This was a tragic corollary of national leadership, and too often its citizens had to suffer for no other reason than being citizens of Madrid, an innocence in common with all victims of random atrocities. The assassination in 1973 of Franco's appointed successor, Luis Carrero Blanco, in a spectacular and minutely planned explosion as he was on his way home one morning from church in the Salamanca district, was widely applauded at the time given the political context, the high profile of the victim and the daring execution of the attack. It was a case, however, of being careful what you wish for: when Basque terrorist group ETA claimed responsibility for the murder of this somewhat antediluvian figure – a henchman to the dictatorship, an anti-Semite and fervent anti-communist – it was not the closing of a mission but rather the start, for the capital, of three decades of sporadic terrorist attacks that in theory targeted 'state oppression', but in practice often murdered innocent civilians.

ETA formed part of the catalogue of terrorist groups that plagued Europe in the 1970s and 1980s. Yet while others such as the Baader–Meinhof or the Red Brigades fell, ETA, like the IRA who were their sometime nationalist comrades-in-arms, continued their campaign of murder and extortion until the twenty-first century. Had ETA abandoned their brutality once the dictator died in 1975, or once the new democratic constitution was in place in 1978, or even once the first Socialist majority was achieved in 1982, worlds of suffering might have been avoided. They may have been consigned to history as a curio – deadly yet evanescent – much like those other groups. ETA garlanded their 'struggle' with anti-colonial rhetoric – residents of one of the wealthiest regions in Spain insultingly compared themselves with the oppressed of the Global South – and localist revanchism. Once the dictatorship was buried and Spanish democracy was on its feet, ETA had no excuses; they were simply a band of low-rent assassins who plagued the nation with particularly ugly forms of violence. Many residents in Madrid in the first decades of democracy experienced, if not the terrible chaos and agony at close quarters, then the thump and rumble of a distant explosion, the aftermath of blocked traffic, shattered windows, smoke, rubble, grieving families. The list of bombings grew: after the Basque region, Madrid was the most targeted site during the long years of their terrorist campaign. Some 123 victims, from Carrero Blanco to the inexplicable cruelty of a car bomb at the international Barajas Airport that killed two Ecuadorian immigrant workers in 2006. Car bombs, kidnappings, extortion and executions in broad daylight; from the city centre to military buildings, from Barajas to Vallecas to the Autonomous University of Madrid: a desperate, mostly random pattern of atrocities.

Yet even in the midst of ETA's cowardly bombing campaigns Madrid lived, as it always does, as if there were no time to be lost.

Having seen off Napoleon, and held a Nationalist army at bay for three years, the people of Madrid were not about to bow to a bunch of armed thugs obsessed with a deadly ideology that preached armed conflict and scarcely paused before the prospect of the loss of innocent lives. With the country making its way to full and effective democracy, the continued activity of ETA across the final decades of the century and into the first years of the twenty-first was an act of enormous, deadly and inexcusable treachery committed upon the Spanish people.

At last the dictator died. The ogre – loved, admired, feared, loathed – having become frail, withered and papery with time, was extinguished.

Despite having claimed to have left everything 'all tied up' for the continuance of his political legacy, once the military processions through the Plaza de Oriente were over, once the long queues of citizens had trailed past the body lying in state in the Hall of Columns in the Royal Palace – many, as the old cliché goes, to make sure he was dead – and the requisite rituals performed, including an elaborate military funeral attended by the likes of Augusto Pinochet and Imelda Marcos, Franco was buried under a 1,500-kilogram slab of granite in the Basilica of the Holy Cross in the Valley of the Fallen, since renamed Cuelgamuros Valley. Under that giant slab, in the cold dark, the dictator was filed away for decades, an obscure archive best forgotten. Yet often in Spain corpses have exceedingly long lives, and there on the outskirts of Madrid, amid that granite landscape, Franco would spring back to life in the twenty-first century. The country had left much unsaid and much undone in terms of reconciling the long-term effects of its brutal civil war; while civil society went about the quiet and painful task of uncovering the thousands of forgotten dead, the political class found Franco a convenient football, when not an ongoing scapegoat. Now some fifty years dead, at some point the dictator will no longer serve as a means by which to account for the practical ills of the present; for the time being, even when lifted out of his tomb in 2019 and reburied at the Mingorrubio Cemetery in El Pardo, he continued to serve an array of political purposes.

IV

WORLD

Into the twenty-first century

The world turned upside down

Tony Judt's *Postwar* opens with the author in Vienna as the iron curtain falls and communist control of Eastern Europe collapses; the city had 're-entered history', Judt writes, after 'nearly half a century of quiescence'.[1] Many have been tempted to read the immediate post-Franco Madrid in much the same way: a thaw at the end of a long freeze, a time mired in political, cultural and intellectual stasis. Such a reading gives little credit to the people of Madrid; throughout the dictatorship, for better or worse, the city had been saturated with history and had, for some time, been preparing for this new era.

There was a difference between the political apparatus – creaking, hidebound, authoritarian – and the (particularly urban) society that had been evolving beyond the constraints of the dictatorship since the late 1950s,[2] exemplified by student movements, labour strikes, an increasingly progressive middle class and reform within the church, judiciary and business. The idea of a deep sleep, from which the country emerged blinking into the light of the late 1970s, is condescending. There remained elements of cruelty and repression that were inherent to the regime, yet the latter two decades of the dictatorship were years characterised, albeit within limits, by a progressive economic and social opening. The relative smoothness of the democratic transition and explosion of experimental cultural forms in the years immediately following the dictator's death was

383

a tribute to how much preparation had been done: 'society had, for some time, begun to behave as if he had already gone.'[3] Subcultures had been busily active for years and expectations were high. Madrid had been waiting, some of its residents for a very long time. For a younger generation coming into adulthood, there was a whole world to be gained.

History was not about to restart; it was simply moving onto another phase. The capital served as the engine room of the new Spain, where the blueprint for the change of regime – known as 'the Transition' – was drafted. A new country, its divisions and historic grievances temporarily on hold, emerged from the funeral rites of the dictator. The path would be crooked and at times deadly, but there was an abundance of energy, colour and optimism to push aside the marmoreal face of the old regime.

'We all accepted our status as second- or third-class Europeans,' Francisco Umbral had written of the writers gathered in the Café Gijón.[4] There was no need for such self-abasement: Spain was coming home to the continent whose destiny it had shared and helped shape since the Greeks and Romans, the invasion of the Visigoths, the transmission of translated classical knowledge that helped feed the Renaissance; the growth of the pilgrimage route to Santiago, the Spanish popes; the wars in Holland, Flanders and Italy, the influence of the Jesuits, the diplomacy of Juan de Austria and Rubens; the Venetian and Neapolitan artists, the French designers and Italian architects; the relationships with Napoleon, with nineteenth-century revolutionaries, with the modernists and avant-garde; with Hitler, Mussolini and Stalin, with Paris and London, Vienna and Moscow. Europe, struck down with grief and ruin in 1945 and occupied with its own reconstruction, had turned its back on Spain. Three decades later it was a path out of the shadow; it was freedom – sexual, political and artistic – and a guarantor of democracy. Europe was, simply, everything the dictatorship was not. For all the reservations around its international politics – and not forgetting its role in providing a lifeline to the Franco regime – the United States also represented a cultural promise through its literature, film and music.

In Madrid there was time to make up; a world to turn upside down. There was a rush to fill the void, to take advantage of gaps left between two systems, to forge the very new, to cover any potentially embarrassing tracks. Pasts were quickly reinvented; many who had tacked closely to the regime turned out to have immaculate credentials as lifelong democrats.

The Amnesty Law of 1977 and the Constitution of 1978 were twin acts of enormous generosity from a generation determined not to revert to old and predictable divisions. The new Constitution was an act of immense statecraft with its foundations built on democracy, liberty, justice, security, welfare and the rule of law. Albeit in practical terms the new era concentrated further power and protagonism in the hands of Madrid, the Constitution nevertheless attempted to compass the linguistic and cultural diversity that is inherent to the Spanish nation. As time has shown, a number of territorial bear traps had been laid for future governments, and it would be from Madrid they had to be negotiated. Over the following two generations of prosperity, the nation continued to change, develop and expand, subject to contradictory forces: integrated into a pan-European and pan-global network of commercial and cultural influences – standardising and conforming – while at the same time regions and peripheries, not content with the high degree of financial, administrative and linguistic autonomy accorded them, rekindled their feudal claims against the centre, threatening the territorial integrity of the nation.

In early 1986 my parents briefly visited Madrid. Years later, going through forgotten papers of my mother's after her death, I found a diary entry written in January of that year, describing a visit to the city centre; she had found it choked with mourners. Unwittingly, my parents had stumbled across the public paying their last respects to Enrique Tierno Galván, to this day the most famous and beloved of all the mayors to have served Madrid post-dictatorship. ('An important mayor has died,' my mother wrote.) The grey-suited, straight-laced old academic had found a new lease of life in his final years, and led Madrid from 1979 to 1986 towards an alternative vision of the world. As he lay in state, the 'old Professor', as the socialist Galván was popularly known, was remembered fondly for overseeing profound political and legal changes: he had assisted in the drafting of the Constitution and written its preamble. The cultural changes he enthusiastically promoted were exemplified above all in the rise of the *movida madrileña*.

Over the previous 100 years, Madrid had witnessed the artists and philosophers of the turn of the century; the writers and artists of the Silver Age; lesser-known but culturally vital movements such as the School of Vallecas, whose maximum exponent was painter Benjamín Palencia; the abstract artists and realist novelists of the 1950s and 1960s, the film-makers and photographers of the 1960s and 1970s. Now came *la movida*, the most striking – and mythologised – cultural movement of the Spanish late twentieth century, inseparable from the contemporary history of Madrid.

Time has been indulgent with this cultural explosion, whose broadest parameters encompass the decade from 1977 to 1988. A spontaneous flowering of youth culture has, with time, been reduced to a limited number of key players, elevated to the status of High Culture and consecrated as part of the official narrative of the transition to democracy. An aesthetic unity has been applied ex post facto to music, art, fashion and media that followed no manifesto or formed part of any vanguard. There were to be no limits, no dogma, no theory: this was a new and, for the time being, apolitical generation who had not been forged in intellectual opposition to the regime; they rejected the older generation, caricatured as bearded, po-faced Marxists, as much as they rejected the puritanical and authoritarian remnants of the regime itself. Though contemporaneous with the punk and new wave explosions in the UK and US, which were major aesthetic and stylistic influences, it was really a matter of choose your own adventure, including with Spain's own long artistic traditions which might be repurposed and plundered, often with heavy doses of irony. Not pertaining to any school, there was a blending of punk, dope, acid, speed, pop art, long hair, spiked hair, metal, blasphemy, nihilism, goth, sleeplessness, androgyny and sexual 'deviance'; among the social responses to the new freedoms were dope-driven pleasure, speed-driven energy and heroin-driven despair. Anyone who wanted could experiment with cultural forms, borrowing liberally from contemporary pop, rock and visual culture and coming up with their own wild inventions; Warhol, who visited Madrid in 1983, was a major influence. The *madrileños* did not take themselves as seriously as many of their British or American counterparts: the point was not so much to be cool, or gothic, or rebellious, but simply to *have fun* and party. This did not mean the best were any less talented as musicians, artists and film-makers, for the *movida* threw up some superb practitioners; simply that, for all the music of the time was influenced by the UK and US new wave, it was never morose, for it was beyond grey skies and was based on excitement rather than anger, able to blend those Anglo influences with styles drawn from the deep well of their own cultural resources.

Currents that had run underground in Madrid came bursting to the surface, no longer fearing repression or prosecution. The capital became an essential proving ground for hundreds of young artists from provincial or rural Spain: 'From the very first moment, Madrid was the city I had been looking for,' wrote Julio Llamazares, a young writer from the northern province of Leon, fictionalising his arrival in the city.[5] And so it was for thousands. The *movida* was founded on spontaneous experimentation in music, art and film, on the transmission of comics, fanzines and cassettes, on glam meeting anarchy and the ethic of punk. Madrid's youth took over the night and made it their platform for entertainment, for queer sexualities, for new forms of slang. It was thrilling, and it was short-lived. It was also, critically, given the tick of approval by the new political masters, for whom the *movida* represented the cosmopolitan, democratic modernity they wished Spain to project to the world, in this case through the vehicle of Madrid.[6] The *movida* was never dangerous or threatening; it was always celebratory rather than revolutionary, a celebration that the principal threat to liberty was now in his grave. Much of the cultural production of the *movida* was deliberately ephemeral and so has been lost, or was juvenilia that has not stood the test of time. This tremendous moment quickly vanished, yet left deep traces throughout contemporary cultural practice. Some of those involved have gone on to considerable fame, setting cultural parameters: Pedro Almodóvar the most renowned internationally, along with Rossy de Palma and Carmen Maura. Others have become anointed with honour in Madrid and Spain's recent cultural history: the music of Alaska, Los Secretos, Radio Futura or Gabinete Caligari; photographers Alberto García-Alix and Miguel Trillo, who documented the social milieu of the *movida*; the late photographer Pablo Pérez-Mínguez; the late graphic artists El Hortelano, Ouka Leele or Ceesepe. Others such as comedian El Gran Wyoming or singer Ramoncín have long been embedded as part of the national establishment. Former outliers who over time assumed positions of cultural or political power have played a major part in constructing the framework through which their own generation, and themselves as actors in it, has come to be understood. A small group of people has come to mark an entire generation;[7] hundreds of other names simply disappeared.

La movida had much of the 'art school' about it; apart from the occasional outlier in *barrios* such as Prosperidad or Tetuán, it was a movement centred on the inner city, particularly Malasaña and the Rastro. Despite some porosity, for the most part the periphery beyond the M-30 was excluded, as were whole swathes of Madrid oblivious to this particular fashion, pursuing lives unrepresented in the early films of Almodóvar or the various extravagances of the *movida*. Other musical subcultures – harder, heavier, less inclined to glamour – found fertile ground in the peripheral districts of Madrid. Nor were all major cultural players in Madrid of the time associated with the *movida*. The great hard rock poet of outer-urban Madrid, Rosendo Mercado, and perhaps the finest of all the artists of that period, Camarón de la Isla – working in Madrid since the mid-1960s – prospered through the *movida* years without being associated with the movement.

There can be no denying his cultural importance as an artist and film-maker, and his centrality to the *movida*, but Almodóvar's was a very specific framing of modern Spain and Madrid. Given the international success of his films from the late 1980s – Almodóvar

served up a city and a country with all the eccentricity foreign audiences loved to see – that framing of Madrid became for some time
a dominant narrative; a cultural version of the winners writing
history. Brash, feminist, heretical, naive, queer, juvenile, hysterical,
kitsch, erotic, perverse, crass and eccentric; brightly coloured camp
tomfoolery. Here were the wild, the beautiful and the damned; a
glamourised and absurdist reinterpretation of Zuloaga or Gutiérrez-
Solana with techno-pop soundtrack. These were indulgent rather
than dissident works; by the 1990s Almodóvar's register had
changed, as had his status from Madrid film-maker to internationally recognised director; as had the city that had launched him on
his career.

For suddenly, *la movida* had gone as quickly as it arrived, and
Madrid carried on towards the twenty-first century. As ever, overlapping cities existed side by side; other Madrids beyond the
hyperbole of the inner city. Places both poorer and darker; places
that were very real, rather than fictive or cinematographic representations. Districts where heroin was not a gauche entertainment or
middle-class transgression, but symptomatic of deprivation and
crime. The parish priests and social workers in districts such as
Vallecas had noticed this new drug arriving on the streets, settling
its ruin among a generation with newfound freedom but without
viable employment or security, their days filling with boredom.[8]
Barrios in the south, such as El Pozo del Tío Raimundo in Vallecas,
or in the north, La Ventilla in Tetuán, entered a cycle of addiction,
crime and associated illnesses such as hepatitis as heroin bulldozed
its way through the poorer peripheral districts.

Conspiracy theories have maintained that the heroin plague that
devastated so many in working-class areas of Madrid was a government tactic to reduce social unrest – *barrios* such as el Pozo del Tío
Raimundo, Orcasitas or Palomeras had a tradition as sites of clandestine neighbourhood organisations in opposition to the abuses of
power.[9] A blind eye was mostly turned to the widespread anaesthe-
tising of the potentially most rebellious of a generation, removing
them from active participation in the social movements than ran
concurrently with the first years of democracy.[10] The extent to which

agents of law enforcement – civil guards, local and national police – implicitly or explicitly aided and abetted, and thus profited from, the drug trade and its miseries is open to debate; drug trafficking has long been a lucrative industry in Spain with its tight connections to North Africa, Central and South America, and the reach of corruption is long indeed. Despite the trafficking and damage, there was community resistance, not least from mothers who refused to see their children lost as pawns to larger power plays. They organised at street level, educating the *barrio*, and took their protests to the media, to prisons, to the Puerta del Sol.[11] Their resistance was humble, desperate and improvised; ultimately, it was also effective. The outlying *barrios* may have been beyond the tourist routes, off the cultural map of the city and outside the line of sight of the political class, yet they have always been fundamental to the identity of Madrid. In the 1980s, under a series of socialist mayors, the state at last arrived to do what it had always neglected: provide services beyond the centre. Focus turned to the infrastructure of the periphery as, one by one, the outlying *barrios* received improved public transport, medical centres, parks, upgraded street lighting and paving, cultural and leisure facilities. Former villages, now high-density suburbs where housing developments sprang up to meet demand, were locked into the transport and labour networks of the city. With their natural tendency to distrust conservative parties, the southern, industrial half of Madrid was a 'red belt', a power base that for decades assured votes for the Socialist Party at municipal, regional and national elections. In a fascinating inversion, the twenty-first century, with its fluctuating social and demographic profiles, has seen the next generation swing much of the region to a conservative blue.

After the tide of the dictatorship receded, those who had to be convinced of the enchantment of Madrid were, first and foremost, *madrileños* themselves. Many had grown accustomed to thinking of their city as a blighted place: other cities were worthier and, in all ways, more sophisticated; Madrid was a beloved home, but it was plain and ugly and recovering from two generations of repression.

Much as it spoke to a limited audience, *la movida* was part of the reinvention of Madrid as a dynamic and expansive capital, one the thousands of children of migrants from other parts of Spain could proudly call their home. Madrid was no longer the remedy to their parents' lives, but the starting point for their own. Various campaigns were launched from the town hall to promote pride in the city as its cultural offerings grew exponentially under the mayoralty of Tierno Galván and his successor, Juan Barranco.

Meanwhile, another of the many Madrids – the intellectually sophisticated upper middle class and its environments – was captured by Javier Marías, as brilliant a chronicler of life in the capital as any other, as he delineated the troubled shoals below a calm of affluence and achievement. The interior monologues of his characters and ornate personal digressions of the author combine with exteriors that are plain yet quintessentially Madrid: a drinks kiosk under shady trees in El Viso, in *The Infatuations*; the glamorous, if deeply melancholic, views of the Plaza de Oriente in *Berta Isla* or, in the same novel, the wealthy, leafy streets of the Almagro district, with its stylish embassies and magnificently serene museum dedicated to the art of Joaquín Sorolla. Or the anonymous streets, familiar only to residents of the city, in *Tomorrow in the Battle Think on Me*: Conde de la Cimera, General Oraá, Hermanos Bécquer. These otherwise anodyne places contain sinister undertones, for below the lovely sophistication of districts such as Almagro or El Viso, amid their beautiful and successful professionals who triumph both in Spain and internationally, there always lurk hints of danger, of death, of malfeasance. So apt to riff on Shakespearean motifs, in the comfortable Madrid of Marías the past steals quietly, ambition embitters, love sours. History lies in wait; falsehood is everywhere. Marías delicately unravels the careful and, in some ways, almost perfect lives of his protagonists, revealing the deceptions, misunderstandings and disjunctures that emerge to throw established narratives of life off track and break comfortable lives apart.

For some, this vision of upper-class Madrid is equally true of contemporary Spain: a miracle of sorts that was nevertheless constructed on falsehoods, even if with the best of intentions; a success that was only ever partial and superficial, and below which stirred long-held desires of vengeance. The social calm and relative prosperity enjoyed by one generation meant little to following generations, with their acute need for meaning and belonging in a much-transformed city and nation. The political manifestation of this sense of grievance, of unfinished business, would emerge with full force in the second decade of the twenty-first century.

The new behemoth

The Quinta de los Molinos at the eastern end of Calle de Alcalá is one of the loveliest sites in Madrid. It contains all the elements of a city park – picnickers, quiet readers, couples falling in or out of love, parents strolling with their children – without the intense display of jugglers, mime artists, fire eaters, puppeteers, magicians or buskers typical to the Retiro. It forms a twin with the nearby Quinta de Torre Arias, magnificent historic properties of the Canillejas district bequeathed to the city by their former owners, parks replete with almond and olive trees, pines and eucalypts, heritage architecture, statues, fountains, lakes, paths and extensive flower beds. Like the Quinta del Fuente del Berro these parks, located beyond tourist itineraries, are mostly enjoyed by locals, beautiful examples of the range of green spaces the city provides.

'The people of Madrid are urban animals ... they regard the conquest of nature, not the celebration of it, as the mark of civilized living,' wrote Elizabeth Nash.[1] On the contrary, the people of Madrid love to be outdoors, and not only at terrace bars and cafés; over recent decades there has been an upsurge in environmental awareness parallel to a concerted programme of greening the capital, to say nothing of the popularity of the mountain landscapes of the Guadarrama and Somosierra ranges. The most spectacular of many urban regeneration projects has been the Madrid Río complex, burying large sections of the M-30 orbital, converting former industrial wastelands and traffic black spots into cultural centres, parks, playgrounds, sports fields and water features that bring birdlife back to the centre of the city. In exchange for years of disruption, the river and its surrounds have been returned to citizens, pollution levels have drastically reduced in surrounding suburbs, and the extensive park system provides relief during extreme heat events. Across Madrid, piece by piece a series of green corridors continues to take shape; when Madrid made a bid for the 2012 Olympic Games, this programme of regeneration towards cultural and leisure facilities and selected reforestation was already central to the proposal. The *bosque metropolitano* – a metropolitan forest plan for Madrid, conceived in 2021 – proposes a restorative 75-kilometre green belt around the entire metropolis, sections of which are already in place; an altered and updated version of the original dream of Arturo Soria, to encircle Madrid in ways that make the city more convenient, more liveable and more sustainable. The old idea of green spaces and landscapes as a matter of class privilege has long gone; nature is neither a threat, nor an inconvenience, nor an exclusive possession of the wealthy, but part of the enormously valuable heritage of the city and province of Madrid.

Greenery and green spaces – specifically tree cover – traffic control and environmental policy are all at the heart of considerable contemporary political disagreement. Many residents feel concrete and asphalt retain their priority over trees, shade and lawn, especially within the M-30 beltway. It can seem that shade and greenery are the last considerations in urban redevelopments; every tree cut down to facilitate a new infrastructure project is met with protest, regardless of how extensive is the replacement planting. There is a longer and broader objective: the reimagining of Madrid as a successfully sustainable, digital, twenty-first-century capital driven by the combined motors of culture, tourism, innovation and finance. It is a matter of sometimes heated debate whether this will prove viable, or to what extent Madrid as a global financial hub might entrench, or help alleviate, the centuries-old divisions of north and south, rich and poor, haves and have-nots. Meanwhile, the city's ancient fluvial character is re-emerging; long damaged by industry, overcrowding or neglect, waterways such as the Butarque and the Manzanares are better protected and slowly regenerating as part of a closer marriage between the built and natural environments. Such changes do not happen quickly; the ambitious plans for the regreening of the city are a matter of decades, requiring sustained political commitment. Tight emission controls mean the highly polluted air of the late twentieth century is mostly a thing of the past, and the toxicity of the Manzanares has been significantly reduced.

Despite the post-dictatorship social upheaval, the *barrio* remained central to Madrid life, the focus of social, commercial and communal activity. The array of small, local businesses were staples; as Madrid took on the status of major international city it preserved its essential nature, being a collection of villages built around squares and parish churches. Yet this too is changing. Relentlessly expanding with new business parks, residential and recreation zones, twenty-first-century Madrid is less and less the *castizo* town, and more and more the metropolis whose streets reflect seismic demographic and consumer shifts across the globe. The *castizo* town remains magnificent, but it now carries a world city on its back; increasingly, residents of new urban zones, dependent on sprawling mall complexes, are left without the crux of small businesses around which *barrios* grow, points of community from which emerge identity and belonging.

The intense industrialisation of the urban periphery is inseparable from the emergence of Madrid as a new behemoth. So too are the extraordinarily high rates of internal migration and foreign immigration; notwithstanding a somewhat folkloric Chinatown in the southern district of Usera, this immigration has come mostly from Eastern Europe, North Africa, Central and South America. The city has grown over recent decades at double the national average as the greater metropolitan population approaches 7 million. These numbers point to a serious question of sustainability in an increasingly dry environment, further underlining the importance of the greening projects across the city.

The 'deep ravines of the Abroñigal', mentioned by Galdós in *Tristana*, long gave way to the ceaseless rush of the M-30 motorway, just as the motorway itself has given way to further orbitals, the M-40 and M-50, Madrid encircled in an intense and at times bewildering road transport network catering to a vast logistics and manufacturing industry. In the 1970s and 1980s the M-30 became part of the folklore of Madrid, loved for its centrality to so many lives, for its multiple faces, a river of human ingenuity, ambition and despair; it was integral to an urban landscape full of dreams and desires and childhood memories. The M-40 and M-50 have not captured the imagination in the same way, belonging to a more objective, less tangible world of business and finance, much of it foreign-owned and -controlled. Where the M-30 had roped in the old city from Argüelles, Arganzuela and Lavapiés, to Prosperidad, Chamartín and El Pilar, the new orbitals embrace a different type of city, compassing low forests of warehousing and industry, different functions of landscape and dormitory zone. New office complexes, huge malls and thickets of apartments have grown up around the latest corridors in frenzied succession. The M-40 and M-50 are twin rivers along which flow merchandise and capital, but fewer dreams. Other motorways that spring from these major orbitals are identikit and mostly soulless connectors; as yet they have no one to sing their praises or film their dawn and sunset moods.

Nearby, dormitory towns rear from the plain in regimented brick, broken here and there by a remnant church or electricity pylon thick with nesting storks; beyond rises a close geometry of windows, walls and beating human hearts, full of moods and vices, anguish and delight, for every seemingly anonymous apartment is someone's intimate landscape: the swings and slides, the shadowed entrance halls, the banging glass; a dry wind in winter; the green blinds on the balconies where life's overflow builds up with thirsty plants, abandoned objects, mops and buckets, a bicycle, perhaps a restless dog; a place for smokers, the chastised, the contemplative or the grumpy; a place to sit on stiflingly hot summer nights. All around lies Madrid with its thrumming urban mass; without pause, the container terminals and cranes are busy, while endless trucks work through dawn's grey light towards the midday and the darker blue of evening.

During the opening decades of democracy the Paseo de la Castellana, Madrid's finest boulevard, reverted from the ugly name of Avenida del Generalísimo and consolidated as the financial and business spine of the city, a spine that commenced with the Bank of Spain at Cibeles. In the 1980s new towers such as the Torre Picasso and Torre Europa highlighted the AZCA finance and business district north of the Nuevos Ministerios, a dinosaurian government administration complex dating back to the Republic in 1933. These business towers hinted at a new age of architecture as stellar signature, part of a city's aesthetic boast. By the mid-1990s, the Castellana hosted the twin, leaning Torres KIO as part of the redevelopment of northern Madrid; the city no longer ended at a morose and ugly water tower by the Plaza de Castilla. The redevelopment is far from over: the Cuatro Torres (Four Towers) business area where, paradoxically, five towers have already shaped new visual representations of the city is but the beginning of the altogether more ambitious Madrid New North project joining Chamartín with Las Tablas and Fuencarral, the city clearly positioning itself as a sustainable hub for the digital and financial services of global capital. The most closely integrated of all Europe's financial markets with Central and South America, Madrid has added this strategic business advantage to its already long reputation as a centre for art, museums, fashion, literature, entertainment and gastronomy.

The often-profligate expense of signature architecture has also seen a complete remodelling of the downtown stadium of Real Madrid – arguably the world's most successful sporting club – and cross-town rivals Atlético de Madrid, the latter abandoning the old Vicente Calderón stadium on the Manzanares, with its working-class surroundings, and moving into the twenty-first century at the Metropolitano stadium in the San Blas-Canillejas district. Both arenas are spectacular, at the same time as they are oddly normal, fitting perfectly within the contemporary global blueprint for extravagantly designed football stadia. Both major clubs, along with the smaller and humbler Rayo Vallecano, Getafe and Leganés, are a deeply embedded part of the sociocultural identity of the metropolis, albeit no brand reaches the global influence of Real Madrid, consonant with its ongoing sporting and business success over decades.

For centuries, one popular theory regarding Spain's development posited that an economically weak Castile held back the development of the richer peripheries. At the base of this misconception was the jaundiced view that Madrid produced nothing beyond bureaucracy, swindlers and all the artifice that attends a court. The capital has often been treated as vampiric, sucking the life from the smaller towns and economies that surround it, 'bleeding dry the surrounding countryside without stimulating any productive activity in return'.[2] For two centuries after the Bourbon centralisation under Felipe V, economic and political power were perpetually divorced, claimed Elliott; the 'centre and circumference thus remained mutually antagonistic, and the old regional conflicts stubbornly refused to die away'.[3] The twenty-first century, however, is a different animal: the age of digital capital has seen national, European and intercontinental business in Madrid grow exponentially. If not politically, given the resurgence of regional nationalisms, then certainly financially, the centre can indeed now hold.

This financial power is to some degree a corollary of those same peripheral independence ambitions. Madrid's unquestioned place at the head of the Spanish business world comes at a time of sharp decline for Barcelona, a city that has suffered the mismanagement of local and regional governments sympathetic to separatist causes. Preferring stability, international finance has little time for such ambitions. Madrid is proudly autonomous, while also proudly Castilian, Spanish and European, and proudly of the cross-Atlantic world of the Americas. And as it has expanded this century, the city has absorbed substantial immigrant populations from Africa, the Middle East and subcontinental Asia: as always throughout its history, Madrid has welcomed any and all into its daily swirl.

Parallel to high rates of immigration, the explosion of infrastructure spending and outer metropolitan urban development, the old, inner city has been gentrified in a pattern observed in many cities across the Global North. Facilitated by digital technologies, international tourism has swamped the apartments along the Instagrammable streets of old Madrid; precious little housing remains for the anachronistic inner city *madrileños* who lived through the dictatorship and its aftermath. They too have become victims of enormous social and urban change. For some, mass tourism has made the old centre unliveable, converting parts of Madrid into alien, hostile spaces.

All over central Madrid this transformation has been under way. The deeper layers are resistant, but along the surface the Spanish morphs into the global. The Gran Vía and the streets around Sol have been branded – here, literally – with the signatures and logos of international capital; the sameness, the repetition, the triumph of the ubiquitous. Anywhere the tourist industry might enter, it does, for Madrid has become hugely popular, its secrets finally being uncovered at the same time as its smoky, grimy old charm has mostly vanished. Mass tourism imposes a normality; gone are many of the old taverns, *fondas*[4] and *pensiones*, the cheap restaurants with an aerial photo of the owner's ancestral home – Sahagún, Jadraque, Zamora – on the wall; the antiquarians or haberdashers, the booksellers and philatelists with their oddities of empire past, their curious medals coined for now-forgotten awards, their serried ribbons, stacked idols and dusty virgins; perhaps, under the counter or camouflaged among unsuspecting display cases, a stash of fascist memorabilia.

The San Miguel market close by the Plaza Mayor is indicative of these changes. In the recent past this market, along with the nearby La Cebada, was a hub for locals doing their daily or weekly shopping; it was a vital resource during my first two years in Madrid. Since 2009 the market has been refashioned, thoroughly cleansed of any hint of its humble origins. Like any inner-city site of value in the world of modern tourism, the market has upscaled, transformed into a polished wood, iron and glass menagerie of creative gastronomy and spectacle. The market is superb, the food among the finest in the world, yet all such pleasures are built on those who came before: here the poor gave up their place and their traditions. The best of these, such as their cooking, were seized on; the ancient ways varnished and resold to a new class of tourists and professionals. Refashioned peasant foods now grace the smartest social media accounts. This progress was inevitable: the San Miguel market could no longer exist as a social and commercial hub for unassuming *madrileños* for the simple reason they no longer exist in the area, pushed out by old age, finance and tourism. In the end, the most *castizo* barrios are too valuable and too attractive to be left to their original purposes.

In a world where everyone is beautiful, Madrid can be no less; social media platforms have allowed a virtual restyling of the streets, quarters, vistas and classic buildings; on smartphones, the city at times resembles a carefully curated tourist village. Madrid now glows: the stone, iron and woodwork of the Habsburg quarter, the rediscovered Moorish Madrid, the haughty French and Italian architecture, the lovely and abundant squares with their terrace cafés, the concentrated sites of *castizo* Madrid, painted up and prettied for tourists, extensively gentrified. Instagrammable Madrid combines the best of the Castilian and Manchegan village with all the elements of a classically European capital – avenues, statues, plazas, palaces – along with touches of the Mediterranean – a splash of flower, a stone staircase, a dusty pine against a deep blue sky – and the strut of the global.

Madrid's many celebrated layers of genius include the old literary quarter between Plaza de Santa Ana and the Prado. The giants of the Golden Age lived here, battling their rivals and their own demons; literary history speaks from embedded brass-metal quotes in the street paving, providing a species of lucid commentary as one wanders the quarter, packed with bars and people of an evening, full of ghosts and shadows at dawn as cafés and bakeries ready for the traffic of the day, and the chattering satirists, poets and dramaturgs retreat once more below the paving stones into their golden tombs. Elsewhere, parallel to the Madrid Río regeneration project, insalubrious old districts have been reimagined to include arts and culture complexes such as the Matadero – the former abattoir – and the Arganzuela crystal palace, and in the centre of the city, the huge eighteenth-century military quarters of Conde Duque – another masterpiece of Pedro de Ribera – has been repurposed as a series of arts and exhibition spaces. Not only has the old centre and the inner south been gentrified; with the inevitability of urban change, sites for 'alternative' cultural expression follow where affordability and space allow, and *barrios* across the river, such as Puerta del Ángel, have been part of a major reinvention of the historic districts of Latina and Carabanchel as arts collectives move in to avoid the inaccessible costs and cramped spaces of the old centre, yet at the same time, in centrifugal fashion, making these traditional *barrios* less accessible. The profound cultural changes taking place in Madrid have also included a strong wave of feminist literature from both Spanish and South American writers, restoring forgotten female voices while thematically swerving away from a canon long dominated by male authors.

On the fringes of the city, meanwhile, new residential and business zones combine the typical rectangular, orange and brown brick apartment blocks with plentiful examples of more adventurous architecture and design. The twenty-first-century *barrios* are the latest in the deep stratigraphy of Madrid: in Arroyo del Fresno, Valdebebas, Montecarmelo, Valdebernardo and the *ensanche* extensions to Vallecas and Carabanchel, children are growing up who will live to be residents in the twenty-second-century city.

In the constant renovation of Madrid, layers of the city become invisible. In 2015, shortly after his premature death, one of the many celebrated plazas of central Madrid was named in honour of the socialist lawyer, city councillor and prominent LGBTQ rights activist Pedro Zerolo. For years I had known this plaza, on the edge of the legendary gay district of Chueca, as Vásquez de Mella, never enquiring into the nineteenth-century traditionalist after whom the plaza was named. Even earlier, with the arrival of the Second Republic, it had been Plaza Ruiz Zorrilla, yet another nineteenth-century political figure; before that, Plaza Bilbao, home to city chronicler Mesonero Romanos. Prior again, the site had been home to the Cristo de la Paciencia Convent, a Capuchin establishment that had stood for more than 200 years – it appears on Teixeira's 1656 map of Madrid – until, damaged during the Napoleonic invasion, it was demolished as part of the broader shake-down of church property in the 1830s. Before the convent was built, the area had been tightly packed with houses, including that of a Jewish family denounced to the Inquisition in 1630 for the alleged desecration of a cross. On the orders of Felipe IV, the offenders were led to the Plaza Mayor where they were burned at the stake. Prior to the ill-fated Jewish family, the trail is lost, fading into one of the numberless blank stretches of history.

Longing for a lost Madrid is a tradition in itself; perhaps there never was a golden past. Working a poorly paid English teaching job out of a dimly-lit institute on Calle Arenal, run in the late 1980s by a Galdosian couple, I had been sent out to provide classes in companies across the city. Thus, I learned early the peripheric skin of the capital – Aluche, Coslada, Alcobendas – and from those outskirts homed in on the inner city, its noisy teeming glory, the wild and dark seduction of its nightlife. The specific city, rowdy and beautiful, I fell in love with as a young man no longer exists, albeit the urban framework of that formative experience remains. All but a few of the people are gone, or lost; the music, the fashion, the bars, all replaced again and again in a constant update and renewal. The city and its art, however, abide. The character of its people abides. Elements of the city are perceived differently now: the view up Calle Serrano from the Puerta de Alcalá; a painting in the Sorolla Museum; a shopfront on Ponzano; the Plaza del Conde de Casal; the hypnotic stations of the Metro; the lean pines at the bottom end of the Retiro; the radically altered walks along the Manzanares. Change has been a constant for over a thousand years and every generation lives their own version of the city, observes a steady morphing while clinging to elements that constitute solid ground. The institutions stand, weighty in their architecture and civilian authority; the streets have their faces scrubbed; the heritage that remains is carefully guarded and repurposed. Exiles from the civil war who were willing or able to return found a Madrid transformed from that of their heady days; the revolutionary fervour of their youth had vanished. Many idealised Madrid while in exile, remembering the flavours and scents of childhood, the excitement of social revolution, perhaps the embrace of a lover long since dead. The previous generation had pined for the sureties of the *fin de siglo*, the sturdy routine of *tertulia, zarzuela*, mistress, *cocido*[5]; the dependable comfort of obedient servants. Later there were some, albeit few, who pined for the days of Franco: a political rally of the National Front, with hundreds giving the fascist salute and whipped up by the redoubtable figure of politician Blas Piñar, was an unforgettable memory of my first year in Madrid. My childhood had not prepared me for such scenes.

Not everything old can or should be saved, but Madrid has too often been criminally negligent with its heritage. A matter of historic representation, aesthetic importance and simple self-esteem, the city has been slow to find the balance between its constant push to modernity and the need to protect cultural heritage; too slow for many fine buildings that should never have been lost. Of some 140 named buildings on Teixeira's 1656 map – royal, civil, religious, fountains and hospitals – only 27 survive.[6] At its height, baroque Madrid would have boasted one of the most spectacular collections of architecture in the realm, but 80 per cent of that heritage has disappeared. It has not helped that Madrid has repeatedly been ground zero for armed struggles that seek to define the path of the nation, struggles that have left great physical damage in their wake. Sites such as the monasteries of Las Descalzas Reales and La Encarnación, the churches of San Jerónimo, San Nicolás and San Pedro, or civil constructions such as the Plaza Mayor and the Casa de la Panadería, the Plaza de la Villa, the Torre de los Lujanes and the Posada de la Villa, sites that take us back from 500 to 800 years, are of extraordinary value not simply because of their age, though that attests to their staying power – or luck – but because of the glimpse they provide of a town that has almost completely disappeared. Likewise, Madrid's neglect of its Islamic heritage, snaking here and there through the subterranean stretches of the inner city, surfacing shyly as if unwanted and without permission, has finally begun to shift towards a deeper appreciation.

Many have become rich and famous in these decades of the reinvention of Madrid; others paid with their lives. The capital has always been a target for attack; ETA's three decades of terrorist violence are a contemporary version of what Napoleon, Carlists, anarchists, communists, falangists and nationalists had all, with their diverse agendas, sought to achieve: to disrupt life in Madrid, killing if necessary, in pursuit of a specific political goal. In reach, impact and number of victims, ETA was the deadliest terror group, but the far right was active too: in Atocha in 1977 a group of communist labour lawyers were gunned down in their office by extremists, and in 1981 a delirious lieutenant colonel attempted an armed coup in the Congress of Deputies that, after some tense hours, was snuffed out.

These were domestic matters, no matter how crude or tragic. International terrorism – the dark back of the global village – arrived in Madrid in March 2004 with an atrocious series of jihadist bombings along the railway line leading into Atocha station from Alcalá de Henares. It was at Alcalá, 30 kilometres to the east, that thirteen bombs – explosives packed around with metal shrapnel and nails to maximise impact – were placed on four different trains. In the event, ten exploded in ten awful minutes between 7.39 and 7.49 a.m., tearing apart the morning commute along the Henares corridor: at Santa Eugenia, at El Pozo, alongside Calle de Téllez on the final approach to Atocha, and inside Atocha station itself. It was the worst peacetime attack in Spanish history and the first foreign attack on Madrid since the German and Italian aerial bombardment of the civil war. Within the grim devastation of 193 killed and around 2,000 injured, there was a small miracle: dozens are alive today due to the timers on a number of the bombs not working correctly, allowing these materials to be deactivated.

The four trains had between them been carrying up to 5,000 commuters. As they were identified amid the carnage, the list of victims told its own truth about the changing demographics of the city, of its peripheral labour force, of immigrants getting their feet on the first rung of the ladder, just as hundreds of thousands of internal migrants had done for centuries, just as millions of native-born *madrileños* continued to do that day and every day. It was a tragic snapshot of a working city: beyond Spaniards, who made up some 80 per cent of the victims, were Romanians and Bulgarians, and a net cast wide across the countries of Latin and South America, of sub-Saharan Africa, Poland and Morocco. The dead had been going about the banal tasks of the everyday: commuting to work, school or university, listening to music, reading, calling friends and lovers, bosses, siblings, parents. As often happens, the depth of the tragedy is found in minor details: the hundreds of phones, ringing in the wake of the attacks, that would not be answered.

The place of the March 2004 atrocity in the history of the city and the nation is ambiguous. Over and above the tragedy itself remains the bitter reality that this attack, so inseparable from the political dynamics of the time – Spain was just three days out from a national election – has been a point of division and contention ever since, mired in accusation, counter-accusation and conspiracy theory. The extent to which the jihadist attack was a response to the then conservative government's embrace of the 'Coalition of the Willing' in the Iraq War – a position held against the vast majority of public opinion – will probably never be known, but this is a common assumption, despite evidence later emerging that the attacks had been conceived well before the Spanish government adopted its geopolitical position with regard to Iraq. The immediate political response to the Atocha bombings – the attempt to focus blame on ETA and divert attention from growing evidence of radical Islamic responsibility – played an important part in an unexpected election win for an anti-war, socialist candidate. The deep wounds and grievances opened up by this singular tragedy and its aftermath have in many respects still not been healed, while the victims of terrorist atrocities, neither for the first nor last time in Madrid, are either forgotten or used as instruments for sordid political point-scoring by both sides.

The transition years had long passed. A generation with no living memory of the dictatorship had grown into adulthood; those forty years survived only in older minds, or reportage, books, films, slogans. To a context of high unemployment, cost of living pressure, difficulty of housing access and increasing political corruption was added the devastating financial crisis that began in 2008. Democratic Spain and its political system were failing many of its youth; the streets were full of discontent, and Madrid became the centre of a national protest movement that would become known across the world.

Launching between the Arab Spring and Occupy Wall Street, the 2011 *Indignados* or 15-M movement,[7] with its base at Madrid's Puerta del Sol, laid the foundations for a generational shift in national politics. Sol was important as it remained the symbolic centre of popular protest in Madrid, in contrast to de-centred alternatives such as Cibeles, the Plaza de Colón[8] or, more recently, the Plaza de Felipe II. Initially amorphous, always combative, 15-M challenged the widespread and bipartisan corruption of the body politic and the insecurity experienced by a generation facing stark austerity measures as it came into adulthood. If the first post-dictatorship generation had thrown itself into hedonism, the second generation faced sterner challenges. After thirty years, the democracy in which so much hope had been placed was displaying the tendency to institutional corruption and nepotism that had been part of politics in Madrid since the Restoration years of the late nineteenth century. There were positives, however: the military, at least, was no longer an important player in determining national leadership. It was time to 'reinvigorate the public sphere',[9] repoliticise an apolitical generation – many of those involved in the *movida* thirty years earlier had deliberately eschewed politics – to emphasise collective solidarity over individualism, place dissent at the forefront of political action in the fight against the privatisation of public services such as health care, challenge the privileges of the banking sector and the increasing unaffordability of housing. These problems, relevant in Madrid and globally, could be theorised across countries, platforms and social movements. In the case of Madrid, there was an additional, republican dimension to collective grievance: the stumbling final years of monarch Juan Carlos I only added to the perception of a system that had reached the end of its useful life.

After an initial day of protest, 15 May 2011, thousands made the decision to camp out in the Puerta del Sol and remained there for up to a month. An improvised mini-city of protest gave voice to anger and frustration with politics as usual, seeking to demolish the two-party dominance of national institutions. For the new politics, red and blue were indistinguishable; they argued against the 'illusory binary of ideological taxonomies' which likewise supposed an intense dissatisfaction with traditional parties of the left and trade unions.[10] For the protestors, the transition to democracy had been a fraud, an institutionalised delinquency, and the way forward was through a revolution in, among other things, public ethics.

Late 1960s Madrid, wrote Javier Padilla, 'was the last moment in history when one could be a revolutionary poet without, at the same time, being ridiculous'.[11] One of the many deleterious effects of the long mid-century dictatorship was that many in Spain, unlike other European countries, had not had the practical opportunity to fall out of love with communism. What had become an anachronism in the rest of the continent, and even more so after 1989, still found fertile ground in Spain among those for whom political action meant following ideals and praxis abandoned in 1939, and to which was added a veneer of anti-capitalist and anti-globalist rhetoric. The principal party to emerge from these protests and take advantage of their traction was Podemos – essentially a Madrid phenomenon – many of whose leaders came from the faculties of the Complutense University with the aim of, according to an early manifesto, 'transform[ing] indignation into political change'. In this, they were, at least initially, very successful. Romanticised by sections of the Madrid media, there was nevertheless little by way of poetry to accompany their ascent to power. Young and charismatic, many celebrated this new force in politics, while others recognised undercurrents they had seen elsewhere. This new left, enamoured of a generation of Latin American autocrats such as Hugo Chávez, maintained a winking complicity with violence; fundamental to their agenda was a radical decentralisation of political and cultural control from Madrid to regional bases. Here were strange bedfellows: the extreme left found common cause with the nationalist right, their mutual enemy the centralised Spanish state and its arch-representative, Madrid.

It is in the nature of fervent promises that they are often not delivered on; in politics in Madrid, the realities of power and its capillaries are adamantine. In the end, the rise and fall of 15-M and its most famous representatives, Podemos, had all the hallmarks of reality TV; a political version of a survival show, replete with fatal allegiances, grievous mistakes and unforgivable infidelities. The politics that had come to the heart of Madrid to renovate ethics and institutional practice was, in short, politics as usual, highly mediatised and, to the disappointment if not surprise of many, besmirched with human frailty.

Hermosa Babilonia

The frenetic activity that is typical of daily life in Madrid came to a halt in the spring of 2020. For months the city emptied before the expansive embrace of the virus; the streets, always so brash, fell vacant. The suburban parks, used to the traffic of children and grandparents, of teenagers scheming loves and rivalries and vague futures, were silent. The slides were not slid and the monkey bars not climbed. Footpaths emptied and cinemas closed. Buses and taxis mostly vanished. The streets changed their complexion entirely and gave themselves over to a silence that was strange and unfriendly. Not a calm silence, soothing and restorative, but one of smothering and restriction, of death and the mortuary; a silence that accompanied police controls and jealous neighbours patrolling the movements of their fellow citizens. These were nervous and uncertain times.

Into that silence swept new sounds: birds could be heard as they had not been since before modernity with its noise of industry and traffic; along the edges of some dormitory towns animals snuffled back. These incidental creatures were not weighted with symbolism like the tiny beings inserted into medieval and Renaissance paintings; were not standing in to represent some shame, or lust, or furtive sentiment, but simply being themselves, participants in the loose fringes of the metropolis. As if the earth had held these quiet beings within invisible fissures, a wholescale camouflage from which, given a rare opportunity of an extended lockdown, they were able to pour forth.

The wind had not run as freely along the avenues for decades. Carlos III would have been proud of the cleansing air that blew down the urban corridors, many of which had been opened up during his absolutist and monumental reign. Central arteries such as Calle de Alcalá, Gran Vía, Princesa, Paseo del Prado or Paseo de la Castellana could not remember such quiet; the complex of motorways that twist around the fringes of the metropolis breathed softly. The cityscape glittered with empty office windows; shopfronts reflected back nobody bar the occasional emergency worker. In all the famous galleries, the portraits – faces moody, resplendent, terrified – stared out at empty salons. No one came to polish wood or marble; no cleaners, leaning on their mops, stared back at long-dead queens and kings and bishops. The cultural and political greats of centuries past, bronzed and marbled, looked down on empty plazas, hushed roundabouts. If not for the life played out on balconies – oscillating between vibrant and celebratory to resigned and angry – the city might have been preparing for a long sleep to ward off the plague. Scrubbed clean of traffic pollution, the sunsets turned coppery and brilliant orange; social media filled with spectacular versions of the Madrid horizon. By day, as if in mockery of an isolated and house-bound populace, the skies became an even brighter blue. Perhaps they had not shimmered so cleanly since the days of Diego Velázquez: those skies with which the artist, released from the interiors of Seville, washed the backdrop to many a royal portrait: a seventeenth-century blue with prince and hunting dog; a prince atop a rearing, barrel-chested horse.

Elsewhere, out of view, desperate medical professionals were overwhelmed; military personnel transported cadavers to an ice rink; coffins lined up, multiplying in chains and stacks of cheap timber. In Madrid, as in cities and towns around the world, many of the aged – those who had lived the bleak years of post-war hunger and helped rebuild the country – died alone, confused, not having seen the virus approach nor understood the lethal way it separated human being from human being. A city largely dedicated to life in the street, to conversation and contact with others, paused at an existential crossroads: from baroque palaces to dormitory sprawl, from lovely attic apartments to dark, unheated boarding rooms, from the polished technology of modern medicine to random shacks thrown up against the intemperance of night, the city slowed its breathing.

In the second year of the pandemic, a sudden form of grace fell from the sky: the wondrous beauty of Cyclone Filomena, for days draping the city in drifts of snow. It was the most astonishing snowstorm in memory, leaving Madrid both paralysed and unimaginably beautiful. Another type of silence blanketed the city: gentler, of forgiveness rather than punishment, of joy rather than anger. The wonderment was hedged with problems of urban practicality: fallen trees and damaged cars, broken drains and frozen pipes, the disrupted service of hospitals; a region of 7 million under sudden ice. Routines of work and transport slowed to nothing as residents emerged onto miraculously transformed streets to ski, sled, snowboard, walk their restless dogs through the crunch of snowbank. Children enjoyed a week off school. The lions pulling Cibeles wore a thick snowy mane; the Visigoth kings of the Royal Palace were crowned with white. After a plague year, everywhere now received a brief gift of mercy and remittal: down the long sweep of the Campo de Moro, through the winter trees of the Retiro, along the verges of the motorways and the banks of the Manzanares, on church towers and office complexes, on campuses and vacant lots, basketball courts, parks and playgrounds, railway lines, ponds and cemeteries – a thousand streets paused. Snow lay in Sol and the Plaza Mayor, in Ópera, Las Ventas, Chamartín, and alongside all the radial highways. In Barajas, the seventeenth-century hermitage of Nuestra Señora de la Soledad was surrounded by a deep moat of snow; by the Plaza de San Juan de la Cruz, the minimalist marble cube that honours the 1978 Constitution vanished in white-on-white. Outside Atocha station snowdrifts mounted, partly concealing the cylindrical monument to the victims of the 2004 atrocities. Days of snow placed a protective blanket around their memory; everywhere submitted to the slide and crunch, the blind white veil, the darling embrace: Filomena offered a wholly new cartography of Madrid.

Individually absent for large swathes of the city's long history, the people of Madrid weave together to constitute the metropolis regardless of the governing regime. The texture of the city builds through passing contemporary tableaux: a young mother pushing triplets through Alcampo on Pío XII; basketball players just off Marqués de Corbera; on a shaded park bench in Torre Arias, a young woman dries the tears from her face while her partner assures her, in tones both serious and anxious, that *he has changed*; on a side street in Ascao, an old Maghrebi wearing a motorcycle helmet stands on the footpath outside a mechanic's garage, incongruously preaching the love of Jesus; identical twin sisters in their sixties sit in a side chapel in the Convent of Las Carboneras, gazing with veneration upon an image of the afflicted Christ; in San Blas, a dozen teenage girls, under a blazing sun, take turns carrying an enormous birthday cake covered in bright blue icing; a nurse emerges from the Begoña Metro station, looking upwards to the Hospital of La Paz, struggling to light her cigarette while carrying two armfuls of shopping; inside the Hermitage of La Virgen del Puerto, a priest shoos a playful white labrador with a ragged cloth toy in its mouth, off the tombstone of the Marquis de Vadillo; a yoga group stretches out in the Parque Atenas; a dark rain falls on the black marble pantheon of Dominican dictator Rafael Trujillo at the cemetery of Mingorrubio; a cluster of children sets off fireworks in a vacant lot in Pinto; weary retail workers bring down the shutters with a loud metallic screech on Preciados, on Fuencarral, on Bravo Murillo, on Amaniel; in polished homes, domestic servants from Ecuador, Gambia, El Salvador or Senegal collect their personal belongings before taking the long commute back to their children, who are already *madrileños* and *madrileñas*; a Filipino man, modestly dressed, slips into the Great Awakening Church in Tetuán, while in nearby Parque Barón, a group of left-wing activists sets up a stall; in Carabanchel, a grandfather buys a tub of ice cream and sits at a bus stop with his grandchild; an immaculate young man pulls a royal blue handkerchief from his pocket as he marches down the Paseo Imperial. The day and night tick over: the strolling, shopping, chatting, complaining, flirting, fighting, the ceaseless wave of activity across the city, in its elegant stores and cheap bars, by appointment or by chance, the constant colliding, the milling, the thronging of

Madrid and its streets, its pavements, its parks and avenues, everywhere alive.

Art, theatre, history, architecture, sport, music, nightlife, gastronomy and endless conversation: Madrid has put on its very finest suit of lights to become one of the most popular and outstanding tourist destinations in the world. A sophisticated industry caters to those who come to enjoy this magnificent and thriving capital, and silent thousands facilitate the twenty-four-hour experience: drivers, escorts, chefs, guides, cleaners, entertainers, bar staff. It is the people of Madrid, as in the seventeenth century under Felipe IV, who make the spectacle happen. To paraphrase Brecht, the vastness of a population: those who quietly and anonymously place brick upon brick, dig trenches and foundations, pour concrete, tend to the public gardens and mourn their dead; who keep the cogs of the city turning; who serve, maintain, transport, lug, carry, exchange, sweep, polish and sell. Beyond its tourists, Madrid hosts thousands of temporary residents: refugees, international students, foreign business executives, diplomats, regional politicians elected to the Congress of Deputies or the Senate, visiting entertainers and inevitably a floating criminal class. For the overwhelming majority, however, Madrid is home: the place where life begins, takes daily shape and ends; a place of work, business, education and family.

The tour guide, come evening, might make their way home not through classical streets or across polished floors, nor down the weighty and historic avenues, but along the bus route and the Metro tunnels, through the ordinary everyday, across the square where children, teenagers and pigeons gather, into the post-war apartment blocks, or the fresher homes thrown up in the mad abandon of the real estate boom; along the road with sculpted trees, through a dense forest of pale orange brick, green awnings over balconies, satellite dishes, Spanish flags, air-conditioning units, pot plants and the eternal washing hung to dry; past the park, the shrubs, the shuffling men and dogs, past the bar with its lottery tickets and cheap meals, the dollar store, nail salons and fast food outlets; the ubiquitous posters advertising rappers, crooners, superannuated metal bands and touring circuses. Unlike at work, walking fields of palace carpet or galleries hushed and sumptuous, her image here is not reflected back from gilded mirrors in the rooms of the magnificent. But she is home; she is part of the community, with its limitless present breadth and vanishing historical depth, that is Madrid.

In the 1580s, young poet and playwright Lope de Vega found himself in the grip of a demonic jealousy. He had fallen in love with Elena Osorio, the highly talented and strong-willed only daughter of a famous theatre director, Jerónimo Velázquez, for whom Lope occasionally wrote plays. The sixteenth-century equivalent of a tabloid scandal ensued: the pair were both young, gorgeous and well-known. Elena, however, was already married, though her husband was away in the Americas. When the none-too-private affair ended – Elena was drawn to another lover, a man of greater wealth and 'better breeding' – an embittered Lope wrote a series of scathing and libellous poems. He was arrested in one of the *corrales* of central Madrid, sued in court by the Velázquez family and sent to jail in Segovia. He soon reoffended and found himself ostracised, expelled for two years from Castile and for eight years from Madrid, on pain of death in the case of disobedience. In his famous sonnet 'Hermosa Babilonia' he not only chides Elena, but rails against Madrid as a nest of vipers and flatterers, a place of insults, rumours, ignorance, rage and deception. He carried this grudge with him for the best part of his life, yet none of this stopped the writer returning to the 'beautiful Babylon' as soon as he could. Nor did it stop him, fifty years later, celebrating the bold *madrileña* Elena Osorio as the principal muse of his life. Whether exiled first in Valencia or later in Toledo, for Lope Madrid lived on as a city remembered and a city imagined; a city that offered an intensity of life that equalled the teeming imagination and the insatiable heart, that welcomed the wretched and the ambitious, the shy and the haughty; the aristocrat, the actor, the merchant, the poet and the scoundrel; a city full of love and cruelty and genius. By 1595 Lope was back from exile and where he always belonged: early seventeenth-century Madrid was not even the half of what the city was destined to become, yet its defiant and infinitely generous character had already taken shape.

Notes

A city remembered, a city imagined

1. Published in four parts during 1887, *Fortunata y Jacinta* is set principally in the old centre of Madrid. It is widely considered the major work of Benito Pérez Galdós (1843–1920), a brilliant and prolific novelist in turn considered the finest exponent of late nineteenth- and early twentieth-century literary realism in Spain.
2. One of legion Spanish artists who went into exile during the civil war, poet Antonio Machado (1875–1939) barely survived the crossing of the Pyrenees, dying only one month after his distressed and distressing arrival in southern France.
3. In 2020, in a stylish confluence of urban design, nineteenth-century literary realism and commuter practicality, the walkways and platforms of the Metro station of Ríos Rosas were papered from floor to ceiling with an illustrated version of the novel. To pass through Ríos Rosas is to be submerged in the world of *Fortunata y Jacinta*.
4. Constructed in 1968 over the Emperor Carlos V roundabout and located near the city's cluster of major art museums, the overpass lasted only until 1986 when it was torn down and replaced by the more pragmatic and aesthetic solution of an underpass.
5. *Elucidario*, quoted in Trapiello, *Madrid*, p. 168.
6. Parsons, *A Cultural History of Madrid: Modernity and the Urban Spectacle*, p. 1.
7. The adjective *castizo/castiza* refers to the quality of being local, born-and-bred, and thus possessed of a guaranteed cultural authenticity.
8. García Ortega, 'Amor por Madrid', in *Fantasmas del escritor*, p. 104.
9. Quoted in Thomas, *Madrid: A Traveller's Reader*, p. 60.
10. The decades immediately following the 1898 loss of Spain's last overseas colonial possessions – Cuba, the Philippines, Puerto Rico and Guam – were marked by a certain intellectual angst and national self-doubt.
11. Nash, *Madrid: A Cultural History*, p. xi.

12. Trapiello, *Madrid*, p. 168.
13. Ugarte, *Madrid 1900: The Capital as Cradle of Literature and Culture*, p. x.
14. Hemingway, *Death in the Afternoon*, p. 44.
15. Ibid.
16. Per square metre, Barcelona is more densely populated.
17. The royal monastery of San Lorenzo de El Escorial, commonly a contender for the 'eighth wonder of the world', was constructed at the western base of the Guadarrama mountain range, some 45 kilometres north-west of Madrid, between 1563 and 1584.
18. Quoted in Elliott, *Imperial Spain 1469–1716*, p. 254.
19. Cervantes, *Don Quixote* (J. Rutherford, trans.), p. 446.
20. Alcobendas to the north and Canillejas and Coslada to the east are districts of Madrid that combine extensive light industry with concentrated residential complexes. Since the 1980s they have become increasingly subsumed into the larger metropolis.
21. From the text of a speech delivered in Caracas, Venezuela, in 1995, upon Marías being awarded the International Rómulo Gallegos Prize.

In Carpetania

1. Marías, *Understanding Spain* (F. M. López-Morillas, trans.), p. 49.
2. Cervantes, *Don Quixote* (J. Rutherford, trans.), p. 15; the quote is part of a suggested fictional annotation relating to the Tagus, by which the prospective author might show himself to be 'erudite in the humanities and a cosmographer'.
3. Marías, *Understanding Spain*, p. 48.
4. Martínez Ruiz ('Azorín'), *Castilla*, p. 33.
5. García de Cortázar & González Vesga, *Breve historia de España*, p. 56.
6. The Oretani region overlapped parts of present-day Ciudad Real and Jaén provinces.
7. Livy, *The War with Hannibal* (A. de Sélincourt, trans.), p. 35.
8. Ibid., p. 45.

Hispania

1. Marías, *Understanding Spain*, p. 56.
2. Álvarez Junco, *Mater Dolorosa: la idea de España en el siglo XIX*, p. 31.
3. Kulikowski, *Late Roman Spain and its Cities*, p. 5.
4. Ibid., p. 8.
5. García de Cortázar & González Vesga, *Breve historia de España*, p. 94.

The first heretics

1. The Sueves continued to hold power in the north-west of the peninsula, in Galicia, until absorbed into the Visigoth kingdom in 585.
2. García de Cortázar & González Vesga, *Breve historia de España*, pp. 119–20.
3. Collins, *Early Medieval Spain: Unity in Diversity, 400–1000*, p. 109.
4. Ibid., p. 263.
5. Carr (ed.), *Spain: A History*, p. 8.

6. Elliott, *Imperial Spain 1469–1716*, p. 256.
7. García de Cortázar & González Vesga, *Breve historia de España*, pp. 137–8.

Heaven and earth

1. Castellanos Oñate, https://madrid-medieval.blogspot.com/p/sociedadviixi. html.
2. The emirate of Córdoba (756–929) and the subsequent caliphate of Córdoba (929–1031) were ruled by the Umayyad dynasty whose roots were in Damascus.
3. Muhammad I of Córdoba ruled 852–86; Abd al-Rahman III ruled 929–61, placing construction of the great defensive wall across the Madrid region in the century from roughly 860 to 960.
4. Christians who lived under Islamic rule in Al-Andalus.
5. González Zymla, 'Los orígenes de Madrid a la luz de la documentación del archivo de la Real Academia de la Historia', p. 20.
6. Bahamonde Magro & Otero Carvajal, 'Madrid, de territorio fronterizo a región metropolitana', p. 7.
7. Arroyo Ilera, 'La imagen del agua: ideas y nociones hidrográficas en las relaciones topográficas de Felipe II', pp. 156–7.
8. Reilly, *The Contest of Christian and Muslim Spain, 1031–1157*, pp. 7–8.
9. Izquierdo Benito, 'Población y sociedad en época omeya', pp. 95–6.
10. Ibid., p. 93.
11. On the trades and occupations of Mayrit, see Reilly, *The Contest of Christian and Muslim Spain, 1031–1157*, p. 11; Castellanos Oñate, madrid-medieval. blogspot.com.
12. López Carcelén, *Atlas ilustrado de la historia de Madrid*, p. 16.
13. Segura, 'Madrid en la Edad Media. Génesis de una capital', in Juliá, Ringrose & Segura, *Madrid: Historia de una capital*, chapter 3.
14. Real Academia de la Historia: https://dbe.rah.es/biografias/7778/maslama-al-mayriti.
15. In contemporary Spain, the term *taifa* continues to be used pejoratively to refer to political provincialism characterised by squabbling with neighbours and prioritising the local ahead of the national interest.
16. Segura, 'Madrid en la Edad Media', chapter 3.
17. Ibid.
18. Asenjo González, 'Los cambios territoriales de la provincia de Madrid', p. 74.
19. The term refers to those Muslims who continued to live under Christian rule, and who developed a striking architectural style seen in many smaller churches in Spain, particularly in Aragon.

Butcher, soldier, pastor, lord

1. Tarrero Alcón, 'Raíces cristianas de Madrid: Santa María La Real de la Almudena', p. 5.
2. Ibid., p. 14.
3. Ruiz, *Medina Mayrit: The Origins of Madrid*, p. 56.

4. Segura, 'Madrid en la Edad Media. Génesis de una capital', in Juliá, Ringrose & Segura, *Madrid: Historia de una capital*, chapter 1.
5. Andreu Mediero, 'El Madrid medieval', p. 691.
6. Stewart, *Madrid: The History*, p. 12.
7. Kamen, *Philip of Spain*, pp. 4–5.
8. Fletcher, 'The Early Middle Ages, 700–1250'.
9. Kamen, *Philip of Spain*, p. 5.
10. Puñal Fernández, 'Mercado y producción en el Madrid de los siglos XI y XII: una economía de frontera', pp. 5–6.
11. This and all subsequent descriptions are from Alvarado Planas & Oliva Manso, *El fuero de Madrid*.
12. Puñal Fernández, 'Mercado y producción en el Madrid de los siglos XI y XII', p. 7.
13. Segura, 'Madrid en la Edad Media', chapter 8.
14. Ibid.
15. Cited in Carr (ed.), *Spain: A History*, p. 2.
16. *Huerta* – vegetable garden.
17. *Vega* – field, meadow, fertile plain.
18. For an excellent portrait of medieval markets in Madrid, see Puñal Fernández, 'Mercado y producción en el Madrid de los siglos XI y XII'.
19. The three faiths conducted their own, separate slaughter of animals.
20. Segura, 'Madrid en la Edad Media', chapter 5.
21. There is a large volume of work on the origins and evolution of the name of Madrid. Here I have drawn variously on Juan Antonio Pellicer, Ramón de Mesonero Romanos, José Manuel Castellanos Oñate, Herbert González Zymla, Federico Corriente and Federico Carlos Sainz de Robles, the more contemporary of whom draw on the work of Arabist and historian Jaime Oliver Asín, along with linguist Joan Coromines.
22. Castellanos Oñate, https://madrid-medieval.blogspot.com/p/nombre.html.

Work and prayer

1. In other versions, the river is the Manzanares. Like all accounts of miracles, those surrounding San Isidro and Santa María de la Cabeza exist in multiple versions.

The emergence of Castile

1. Bahamonde Magro & Otero Carvajal, 'Madrid, de territorio fronterizo a región metropolitana', p. 5.
2. Ibid., p. 4.
3. From the eleventh until the late fifteenth century, all royalty mentioned here, unless otherwise indicated, pertains to Castile and Leon.
4. Morena Bartolomé, 'Arte y patrimonio en la sierra norte de Madrid', p. 379.
5. A fourteenth-century hunting manuscript, the *Libro de la Montería de Alfonso XI*, shows a richly adorned landscape, an abundance of forest and animals for hunting; see Fernández García, *Madrid, de la Prehistoria a la Comunidad Autónoma*, p. 70.

6. Despite the intermarrying of European royal bloodlines so typical of the time, Spain was only indirectly implicated in this conflict.
7. Puñal Fernández, 'Espacios madrileños de producción documental: el cuaderno de las primeras Cortes de Madrid de 1329', p. 23.
8. Stewart, *Madrid: The History*, p. 15.
9. Castellanos Oñate, https://madrid-medieval.blogspot.com/p/sectores.html.
10. Two of Pedro I's daughters married into English nobility: Constance of Castile (d. 1394) was the Duchess of Lancaster, and her younger sister Isabel of Castile (d. 1392) was the Duchess of York.
11. Bahamonde Magro & Otero Carvajal, 'Madrid, de territorio fronterizo a región metropolitana', p. 15.
12. Andreu, 'El Madrid medieval', p. 692.
13. García de Cortázar & González Vesga, *Breve historia de España*, p. 217.
14. A common form of medieval Spanish currency, whose name derives from 'Almoravid coin'.
15. Here and subsequent references are from Markham's Preface to the 1849 edition of the *Narrative of the Embassy of Ruy González de Clavijo to the Court of Timour, at Samarcand, AD. 1403–6.*
16. Belief in this geographic oddity dated from the time of Pliny, and was held to be true until disproven in the nineteenth century.

The great turn

1. Lynch, *Spain under the Habsburgs*, p. 12.
2. A late medieval property register.
3. López Carcelén, *Atlas ilustrado de la historia de Madrid*, p. 25.
4. Puñal Fernández, 'El comercio madrileño en el entorno territorial y urbano de la baja edad media', p. 116.
5. Ibid.
6. Kamen, *Spain 1469–1714: A Society of Conflict*, p. 1.
7. Ibid., p. 14.
8. Ibid.
9. Quoted in ibid., p. 31.
10. Oviedo (1478–1557) had a distinguished career in the Spanish Caribbean, and as a historian authored the *Natural History of the Indies*, self-published in Toledo in 1526, which gave the first description for European audiences of such curiosities as tobacco, the pineapple and the hammock.
11. Stewart, *Madrid: The History*, p. 20.
12. López Carcelén, *Atlas ilustrado de la historia de Madrid*, p. 28.
13. From the Spanish word for a pack of mules; a rubbish heap, or place for animal excrement.
14. Segura, 'Madrid en la Edad Media. Génesis de una capital', in Juliá, Ringrose & Segura, *Madrid: Historia de una capital*, chapter 7.
15. Including Isabel de Josa from Lérida and the Latinist Luisa de Medrano in Salamanca, among others.
16. La Latina is the popular name for the inner-city suburb, distinct from the district of Latina, part of Carabanchel on the far side of the Manzanares River.

17. Concejo de Madrid, 1481.
18. Kamen, *The Disinherited: The Exiles Who Created Spanish Culture*, p. 9.
19. Contreras et al., *La expulsión de los judíos*, p. 5.
20. Kamen, *The Disinherited*, p. 9.
21. Montero Vallejo, 'Los primeros núcleos urbanos: Madrid antiguo y medieval', p. 130.

Gold trimmed with lead

1. A somewhat grandiose title for what was in reality rule over Germany, Austria and Bohemia.
2. Rizzuto, 'Conversos, judíos y conspiración diabólica en la revuelta de las Comunidades de Castilla', p. 66.
3. See, for example, Álvarez Junco, *Mater Dolorosa: la idea de España en el siglo XIX*, p. 78.
4. Alvar Ezquerra, 'La elección de la Corte: La política en los siglos XVI y XVII', p. 140.
5. Kamen, *Spain 1469–1714: A Society of Conflict*, p. 31.
6. García de Cortázar & González Vesga, *Breve historia de España*, p. 269.
7. Elliott, *Imperial Spain 1469–1716*, p. 255.
8. 'Introducción', in Juliá, Ringrose & Segura, *Madrid: Historia de una capital*.
9. Elliott, *Imperial Spain 1469–1716*, p. 253.
10. Cabrera de Córdoba, *Filipe Segundo, Rey de España*, quoted in ibid., p. 254, and in Cepeda Adán, 'El Madrid cultural en la España de Felipe II', p. 24.
11. Kamen, *Philip of Spain*, p. 180.
12. Cepeda Adán, 'El Madrid cultural en la España de Felipe II', p. 24.
13. Brown, *Velázquez: Painter and Courtier*, p. 36.
14. Blasco Esquivias, 'Madrid, utopía y realidad de una ciudad capital', p. 50.
15. Mesonero Romanos, *El antiguo Madrid: Paseos históricos-anecdóticos por las calles y casas de esta villa*, p. 40 (emphasis added).
16. Ringrose, 'The Impact of a New Capital City: Madrid, Toledo, and New Castile, 1560–1660', p. 765.
17. Quevedo, *The Swindler* (M. Alpert, trans.), p. 130; also Cepeda Adán, 'El Madrid cultural en la España de Felipe II', p. 29.
18. Sainz de Robles, *Breve Historia de Madrid*, p. 78.
19. Ibid.
20. Álvarez Junco, *Mater Dolorosa*, p. 57.
21. Ibid., p. 43.

Strange universe

1. Kamen, *Spain 1469–1714: A Society of Conflict*, pp. 32–3.
2. María barely survived the birth, and died four days later.
3. These included placing the mummified remains of Diego de Alcalá, a former Franciscan friar, next to his body in the hope it would work a miracle.
4. Kamen, *The Disinherited: The Exiles Who Created Spanish Culture*, p. 117.
5. Álvarez Junco and Shubert, *Spanish History since 1808*, p. 3.
6. Stendhal, *The Charterhouse of Parma* (M. Shaw, trans.), p. 19.

7. Fuentes, 'Introduction' to Cervantes, *Don Quixote* (T. Smollett, trans.), p. xviii.
8. Stewart, *Madrid: The History*, p. 37.
9. Álvarez Junco and Shubert, *Spanish History since 1808*, p. 3.
10. Quoted in Kamen, *The Escorial: Art and Power in the Renaissance*, pp. 239–40.
11. Ibid.
12. Ibid., p. 240.
13. Stewart, *Madrid*, p. 38.
14. Ibid.
15. Ibid.
16. For example, Geoffrey Parker's balanced and rigorous *Imprudent King: A New Life of Philip II.*
17. Fernández-González, *Philip II of Spain and the Architecture of Empire*, p. 9.
18. Giralt Torrente, *The End of Love* (K. Silver, trans.), p. 93.
19. Ibid., p. 115.
20. Quoted in Kamen, *The Escorial*, p. 246.
21. John Eliot in 1593, quoted in ibid., p. 226.
22. Fernández-González, *Philip II of Spain*, p. 8.
23. Kamen, *The Disinherited*, p. 97.
24. Quoted in Fuentes, 'Introduction'.
25. Ibid.

Carnival and Lent

1. *Vista de Madrid desde el oeste, frente de la Puerta de la Vega*, 1562, National Library of Austria, Vienna.
2. Fernández-González, *Philip II of Spain and the Architecture of Empire*, p. 7.
3. Azorín, *Leyendas e historias del barrio de las Letras*, p. 13.
4. Elliott, *Imperial Spain 1469–1716*, p. 243; Sainz de Robles, *Breve Historia de Madrid*, pp. 79–80, provides a complete list.
5. Virgilio Cepari, quoted in Friedrich, *The Jesuits: A History* (J. N. Dillon, trans.), p. 88.
6. Friedrich, op. cit., p. 94.
7. Mendoza, *Riña de gatos: Madrid, 1936*, p. 22. The novel was translated into English as *An Englishman in Madrid*, thus rather missing the nuance of the title; '*gatos*' is a common nickname for the people of Madrid; '*riña de gatos*' can be translated as 'catfight' or 'brawl' and is, additionally, the title of a memorable work by Goya.
8. Barón, *El Greco y la pintura moderna*, p. 15.

Sic transit gloria mundi

1. 1571; the most famous participant in this naval battle was Miguel de Cervantes, who was badly injured and lost the use of his left hand.
2. Marañón's two-volume biography of Antonio Pérez is quoted in Thomas, *Madrid: A Traveller's Reader*, pp. 96–8.
3. Lynch, *The Hispanic World in Crisis and Change, 1598–1700*, p. 17, draws on nineteenth-century historian Modesto Lafuente to suggest Felipe also remarked: 'God, who has given me so many kingdoms, has denied me a son capable of ruling them.'

4. In colloquial Spanish, a business operation, usually of dubious legality, which earns an extraordinary financial return in a very short time. The word is often used in association with the real-estate industry.

5. Cited by Défourneaux; quoted in McDonald, *Renaissance to Goya: Prints and Drawings from Spain*, p. 82.

6. Sainz de Robles, *Breve Historia de Madrid*, p. 96.

7. Rubens, *Retrato ecuestre del duque de Lerma* (Equestrian Portrait of the Duke of Lerma), 1603, Museo del Prado, Madrid.

8. Sainz de Robles, *Breve Historia de Madrid*, p. 97.

9. Pinelo, *Anales de Madrid hasta el año 1658*, quoted in Lozón Urueña, *Madrid. Capital y Corte: Usos, costumbres y mentalidades en el siglo XVII*, p. 13.

10. See Castillo Cáceres, *Los años de Madridgrado*, pp. 222–7.

11. Ringrose, 'The Impact of a New Capital City: Madrid, Toledo, and New Castile, 1560–1660', p. 765.

12. Domínguez Ortiz, 'Velázquez y su tiempo', p. 8.

13. Ibid., p. 7; parts of rural Castile have never fully recovered from the long social and economic decline that began in this period.

14. Fernández Hoyos, 'El Madrid de los Austrias', p. 10.

15. Ibid.

16. Pérez Galdós, *Misericordia*, p. 21.

17. *Actas de las Cortes de Castilla, 1563–1632*, quoted in Lynch, *The Hispanic World in Crisis and Change, 1598–1700*, p. 4.

18. Ibid.; González de Cellorigo, quoted in ibid., p. 5.

19. Quoted in Kamen, *Spain 1469–1714: A Society of Conflict*, p. 254.

20. Lozón Urueña, *Madrid*, p. 31.

21. Fernández Talaya, 'La vivienda madrileña en tiempos de Cervantes', p. 45.

22. Bravo Lozano, 'Economía y sociedad bajo los Austrias', p. 193.

23. Fernández Talaya, 'La vivienda madrileña', p. 46.

24. Ibid., p. 51.

25. Blasco Esquivias, 'Madrid, utopía y realidad de una ciudad capital', pp. 61–2.

26. Ibid., p. 62.

27. An account of the healing waters of Corpa and Loeches is given in Leralta, *Madrid: Cuentos, leyendas y anécdotas*, vol. 1, pp. 127–9.

28. Elliott, *Spain, Europe and the Wider World, 1500–1800*, p. 280.

29. Bravo Lozano, 'Economía y sociedad bajo los Austrias'.

30. Kamen, *Spain 1469–1714*, p. 248.

31. Lynch, *Bourbon Spain, 1700–1808*, p. 242; see also Elliott, *Spain and its World, 1500–1700*, pp. 277–8.

32. Just as, in the eighth century, the surviving son of the overthrown Umayyad dynasty of Damascus had fled to Córdoba and subsequently founded the new Umayyad emirate which would dominate Al-Andalus for centuries.

33. López de Hoyos, *Declaración de las armas de Madrid y algunas antigüedades*.

34. Mesonero Romanos, *El antiguo Madrid*, vol. 1.

35. Among others, Mesonero was critical of the inaccuracies – when not simple inventions – of historian and priest Jerónimo de la Quintana, whose history of the 'ancient, noble and mighty' city of Madrid first appeared in 1629.

36. Blasco Esquivias, 'Madrid, utopía y realidad de una ciudad capital', p. 58.

37. Ibid.

38. Montero Reguera, 'Miguel de Cervantes: Un poeta en el final de sus días', p. 14.
39. Fuentes, 'Introduction' to Cervantes, *Don Quixote* (T. Smollett, trans.), p. xv.
40. Lope de Vega, *Rimas sacras*, 1614.
41. Quevedo, *The Swindler* (M. Alpert, trans.).
42. Ibid., p. 128.
43. Ibid., p. 132.
44. Juan van der Hamen, *Retrato de Francisco de Quevedo*, Instituto Valencia de Don Juan, Madrid.
45. Hernández (ed.), *Cuadernillos de poesía: Luis de Góngora*, p. 8.
46. Micó (ed.), *El oro de los siglos*, pp. 24–6.
47. The *mentideros* of Madrid were much loved by Arturo Pérez-Reverte's most famous literary creation, Capitán Alatriste.
48. Cepeda Adán, 'El Madrid cultural en la España de Felipe II', p. 32.

The court of the Planet King

1. Mateos, *Origen y dignidad de la caça*, 1634, National Library of Spain, Madrid.
2. Velázquez, *La tela real*, 1632–7, National Gallery, London; a copy, entitled *Cacería de jabalíes en el Hoyo*, is held in the Museo del Prado, Madrid.
3. Mendoza, *Riña de gatos: Madrid, 1936*, p. 73.
4. Carrascal Antón, quoted in Diallo, 'La figura de Don Rodrigo Calderón a través de la literatura, s.XVII–XXI', p. 33.
5. Felipe's wife Margarita of Austria was the maternal grandmother of Louis XIV of France.
6. The details of the procession to the scaffold and the responses of the crowd are adapted from Diallo, 'La figura de Don Rodrigo Calderón a través de la literatura, s.XVII–XXI', pp. 39–45.
7. Gómez de Mora was also responsible for the Casa de la Villa, one of the finest extant seventeenth-century buildings in Madrid, used by the Town Council to this day.
8. Fernández Talaya, 'La vivienda madrileña en tiempos de Cervantes', pp. 55–9.
9. Cumming, *The Vanishing Man: In Search of Velázquez*, p. 44.
10. Ibid.
11. The quest to unlock the riddle of what happened to this portrait is the subject of Cumming's excellent book.
12. Ibid.
13. Elliott, *Spain and its World, 1500–1700*, p. 142.
14. Fernández Hoyos, 'El Madrid de los Austrias', p. 4.
15. Álvarez Junco, *Mater Dolorosa: la idea de España en el siglo XIX*, p. 68.
16. 1808–14; the invading French troops used the Retiro as their main barracks, looting and trashing the complex.
17. Barbeito Díez, 'El Palacio del Buen Retiro: ideas para una arquitectura', p. 16.
18. Brown and Elliott, *A Palace for a King: The Buen Retiro and the Court of Philip IV*, p. 118.
19. Elliott, *Spain and its World, 1500–1700*, p. 280.

20. Ibid., p. 282.
21. McDonald, *Renaissance to Goya: Prints and Drawings from Spain*, p. 81.
22. Brown and Elliott, *A Palace for a King*, p. 68.
23. Ibid., p. 47.
24. López Carcelén, *Atlas ilustrado de la historia de Madrid*, pp. 32–3.
25. Nash, *Madrid: A Cultural History*, p. 71.
26. Umbral, *La noche que llegué al Café Gijón*, p. 24.
27. Brown and Elliott, *A Palace for a King*, p. 42.
28. Ibid., p. 31.
29. Ibid., p. 38.
30. Negredo, 'El Madrid de Velázquez: Mercado y propiedad inmobiliaria entre 1623 y 1650', p. 31.

Velázquez and Teixeira

1. Velázquez, *El aguador de Sevilla*, 1623, Wellington House, London; *Vieja friendo huevos*, 1618, National Gallery of Scotland, Edinburgh; *Cristo en casa de Marta y María*, 1618, National Gallery, London.
2. Elliott, *Spain, Europe and the Wider World, 1500–1800*, p. 278.
3. Velázquez, *El triunfo de Baco*, 1628–9; *La fragua de Vulcano*, 1630; Museo del Prado, Madrid.
4. Velázquez, *Pablo de Valladolid*, 1635, Museo del Prado, Madrid. The actor represented was in fact from Vallecas, whereas his father was originally from Valladolid.
5. Cumming, *The Vanishing Man: In Search of Velázquez*, p. 9.
6. An exceptional preparatory drawing on this theme survives: Vicente Carducho, *La expulsión de los moriscos*, 1627, Museo del Prado, Madrid.
7. Blasco Ibáñez, *La maja desnuda*, p. 182.
8. Velázquez, *La venerable madre Jerónima de la Fuente*, 1620; *Don Diego del Corral y Arellano*, 1624; Museo del Prado, Madrid.
9. Escobar, 'Map as Tapestry: Science and Art in Pedro Teixeira's 1656 Representation of Madrid', p. 50.
10. Ibid., pp. 50–1.
11. Fernández Hoyos, 'El Madrid de los Austrias', p. 14.

Regime change

1. Velázquez, *El príncipe Baltasar Carlos, cazador*, 1635–6, Museo del Prado, Madrid.
2. Descriptions of Carlos II taken from Trapiello, *Madrid*; García de Cortázar & González Vesga, *Breve historia de España*; Mesonero Romanos, *El antiguo Madrid*; Elliott, *Spain and its World, 1500–1700*; Lynch, *The Hispanic World in Crisis and Change, 1598–1700*; Thomas, *Madrid: A Traveller's Reader*; Stewart, *Madrid: The History*; Kamen, *Spain 1469–1714: A Society of Conflict*; Macaulay, *Critical & Historical Essays, Volume Two*.
3. Trapiello, *Madrid*, p. 377.
4. Pepys, 1683; quoted in Elliott, *Spain and its World, 1500–1700*, p. 263.
5. Juan Carreño de Miranda, *Carlos II*, 1675; *Carlos II*, 1680; *Carlos II, con armadura*, 1681; Luca Giordano, *Carlos II*, 1693; Museo del Prado, Madrid.

6. Kamen, *Spain 1469–1714: A Society of Conflict*, pp. 281–5.
7. Kamen, *The Disinherited: The Exiles Who Created Spanish Culture*, p. 151.
8. Quoted in Lynch, *Bourbon Spain, 1700–1808*, p. 201.
9. Defoe, *Robinson Crusoe*, p. 178.
10. Kamen, *Philip V of Spain: The King Who Reigned Twice*, p. 3.
11. Elliott, *Imperial Spain 1469–1716*, p. 373.
12. Stanhope, *Correspondence*, 11 June 1698.
13. Elliott, *Imperial Spain 1469–1716*, p. 373.
14. Stanhope, *Correspondence*, 8 October 1694.
15. This detail is drawn from an account given by Henri Harcourt, Louis XIV's ambassador to Madrid.
16. Stanhope, *Correspondence*, 29 April 1699.
17. Ibid., 21 May 1699.
18. Ibid., 27 May 1699.
19. Ibid., 23 May 1696.
20. Ibid., 21 October 1699.
21. Macaulay, 'War of the Succession in Spain', p. 87.

New absolutisms

1. Kamen, *Philip V of Spain: The King Who Reigned Twice*, p. 7.
2. For this discussion, see Kamen, *The Disinherited: The Exiles Who Created Spanish Culture*, chapter 4.
3. See Jiménez Torres, *La palabra ambigua: Los intelectuales en España (1889–2019)*.
4. Mesonero Romanos, *El antiguo Madrid*, p. 76.
5. Macaulay, 'War of the Succession in Spain', p. 93.
6. Kamen, *Philip V of Spain*, p. 8.
7. Stradling, *Europe and the Decline of Spain*, p. 190.
8. Sainz de Robles, *Breve Historia de Madrid*, p. 119.
9. Phillips, 'The Allied Occupation of Madrid in 1710: A Turning Point in the War of the Spanish Succession', p. 18.
10. Ibid., p. 25.
11. Bacallar, *Comentarios*, quoted in ibid., p. 26.
12. Kamen, *Philip V of Spain*, p. 30.
13. Quoted in Thomas, *Madrid: A Traveller's Reader*, p. 231.
14. Stradling, *Europe and the Decline of Spain*, p. 201.
15. Álvarez Junco, *Mater Dolorosa: la idea de España en el siglo XIX*, p. 64.
16. Ibid., p. 72.
17. Ibid., p. 62.
18. On the broader question of the relation between 'reform' and 'patriotism', see ibid., pp. 85–105.
19. Tovar Martín, 'El desarrollo espacial y monumental de la ciudad hasta 1800', p. 181.
20. Roca Barea, *Fracasología*, p. 150; the point is made more generally about French customs of the era, without specifically referring to the Bourbon court in Madrid.
21. Sainz de Robles, *Breve Historia de Madrid*, p. 125.

22. Ringrose, 'Madrid, capital imperial' in Juliá, Ringrose & Segura, *Madrid: Historia de una capital*, chapter 15.
23. Kamen, *Philip V of Spain*, p. 220.
24. Ibid., pp. 235–6.
25. Sainz de Robles, *Breve Historia de Madrid*, p. 126.
26. Described as a 'small, discreet and somewhat unfrequented museum' in Marías, *Thus Bad Begins* (M. Jull Costa, trans.), p. 112.
27. Sainz de Robles, *Breve Historia de Madrid*, p. 130.

The spring of hope

1. Goya, *La merienda*, 1776; *Baile a orillas del Manzanares*, 1776–7; *El bebedor*, 1777; *El quitasol*, 1777; *La riña en el Mesón del Gallo*, 1777; *La riña en la Venta Nueva*, 1777; *La cometa*, 1777–8; *El ciego de la guitarra*, 1778; *El cacharrero*, 1778–9; *La feria de Madrid*, 1779; *El columpio*, 1779; *Las lavanderas*, 1780; Museo del Prado, Madrid.
2. Luis Paret y Alcázar, *Carlos III comiendo ante su corte*, 1771–2, Museo del Prado, Madrid.
3. Hughes, *Goya*, p. 64.
4. Ibid.
5. Ibid.
6. Carrasco Martínez, 'Ciudad y sociedad en el Madrid del siglo XVIII', p. 168.
7. Ibid., p. 171.
8. Ibid., p. 172.
9. Parsons, *A Cultural History of Madrid: Modernity and the Urban Spectacle*, p. 1.
10. Marín Perellón, 'Madrid: ¿Una ciudad para un rey?', p. 127.
11. Ibid., p. 126.
12. Fraguas de Pablo, 'Expulsión de la Compañía de Jesús bajo el reinado de Carlos III', p. 298.
13. Carrasco Martínez, 'Ciudad y sociedad en el Madrid del siglo XVIII', p. 175.
14. Ibid., p. 178.
15. Galán Cabilla, 'Madrid y los cementerios en el siglo XVIII: el fracaso de una reforma', p. 257.
16. Ibid.
17. Ibid., p. 260.
18. Ibid.
19. Ibid., p. 282.
20. Ibid., p. 283.
21. Ibid., p. 284.
22. Luis Egidio Meléndez, *Bodegón con servicio de chocolate*, 1770; *Bodegón con un trozo de salmón, un limón y tres vasijas*, 1772; Museo del Prado, Madrid.

The winter of despair

1. Goya, *Gaspar Melchor de Jovellanos*, 1798, Museo del Prado, Madrid.
2. Count of Floridablanca, correspondence quoted in Lynch, *Bourbon Spain 1700–1808*, p. 378.
3. De Diego García, 'El significado del dos de mayo', p. 16.

4. Napoleon in correspondence to his brother Joseph, quoted in Thomas, *Madrid: A Traveller's Reader*, p. 52.

5. Quoted in ibid., p. 81.

6. De Diego García, 'El significado del dos de mayo', p. 21.

7. Sorolla, *Dos de Mayo*, 1884, Museo del Prado, Madrid.

8. Félix Lorrio, 'Jóvenes ácratas encaramados a las estatuas de la madrileña plaza del Dos de Mayo en plenas fiestas del barrio de Malasaña, 2 May 1976', private collection, Madrid.

9. Goya, *El 3 de mayo en Madrid o 'Los fusilamientos'*, 1814, Museo del Prado, Madrid.

10. De Diego García, 'El significado del dos de mayo', p. 20.

11. Bolufer, 'Reasonable Sentiments: Sensibility and Balance in Eighteenth-Century Spain', pp. 34–5.

12. Lopezosa Aparicio, 'Sobre los planes de intervención de José I en Madrid', p. 50.

13. Ibid., pp. 51–3.

14. Fernández de los Ríos, *El futuro Madrid*, 1868; quoted in ibid., p. 47.

15. Cumming, *The Vanishing Man: In Search of Velázquez*, p. 9.

16. Vicente López Portaña, *El Pintor Francisco de Goya*, 1826, Museo del Prado, Madrid.

17. Calvo Serraller, *Del futuro al pasado. Vanguardia y tradición en el arte español contemporáneo*, pp. 24–5.

18. Sainz de Robles, *Breve Historia de Madrid*, pp. 144–5.

19. Goya, *No llegan a tiempo* (*Desastres de la guerra*, 52), 1812–14, Museo del Prado, Madrid.

20. The Cortes, gathered in Cádiz during the rule of José I, had written and passed a constitution for the Spanish nation in 1812 that, while confirming the singular role of the Catholic Church, nevertheless codified a series of revolutionary articles, including freedom of the press, separation of powers and universal male suffrage. The constitution was overturned by Fernando VII in 1814. Despite its brief life, it is considered one of the founding documents of the modern Spanish nation.

Stasis and discovery

1. Galdós, *El terror de 1824*, quoted in Trapiello, *Madrid*, p. 206.

2. DeLillo, *The Names*.

3. The story of the artworks and their journey is recounted in Calvo Poyato, *El milagro del Prado*.

4. Álvarez Junco, *Mater Dolorosa: la idea de España en el siglo XIX*, p. 97.

5. Ibid., p. 99.

6. Mesonero Romanos, *Escenas matritenses*, p. 30.

7. Richard Ford, *A Handbook for Travellers to Spain*, 1845; *Gatherings from Spain*, 1846.

8. Inglis, 1830, quoted in Thomas, *Madrid: A Traveller's Reader*, p. 70.

9. Ibid., p. 71.

10. Kamen, *The Disinherited: The Exiles Who Created Spanish Culture*, p. 78.

11. Dumas, 1846, quoted in Thomas, *Madrid*, p. 74.

12. Luengo & Dalmau, 'Writing Spanish History in the Global Age: Connections and Entanglements in the Nineteenth Century', p. 427.
13. Ibid., pp. 426–7.
14. Ibid., p. 428.
15. Stradling, *Europe and the Decline of Spain*, p. 192.
16. Borrow, *The Bible in Spain*, p. 69.
17. Ibid., p. 67.
18. Ibid.
19. Ibid., p. 70.
20. Ibid., p. 67.
21. Ibid., p. 69.
22. Ibid.
23. Lynch, *Bourbon Spain 1700–1808*, p. 241.
24. Ibid., p. 201.

The emerging metropolis

1. Bahamonde Magro & Otero Carvajal, 'Madrid, de territorio fronterizo a región metropolitana', p. 41.
2. Caro Baroja, quoted in Trapiello, *Madrid*, p. 204.
3. Madrid's status as an autonomous community would be not formalised until 1983.
4. Among his most famous works are *Manual de Madrid*, 1831; *Escenas matritenses*, 1851; *El antiguo Madrid*, 1861; and *Memorias de un setentón, natural y vecino de Madrid*, 1880.
5. Parsons, *A Cultural History of Madrid: Modernity and the Urban Spectacle*, p. 19.
6. Cayetano Martín, 'Lo municipal en la obra de Galdós', p. 62.
7. Haidt, 'Emotional Contagion in a Time of Cholera: Sympathy, Humanity and Hygiene in Mid-Nineteenth Century Spain', p. 88.
8. Parsons, *A Cultural History of Madrid*, p. 18.
9. Like the *majos* and *majas* who are amply represented in Goya's splendid cartoons of the late eighteenth century, *manolos* and *manolas*, along with *chisperos* and *chisperas*, were other slang terms used to describe working-class archetypes of Madrid.
10. Ibid., p. 23.
11. This anecdote is recounted in multiple sources and in multiple languages.
12. Espadas Burgos, *La España de Isabel II*, p. 6.
13. A type of musical theatre especially popular in Madrid.
14. Carr (ed.), *Spain: A History*, p. 211.
15. Ibid., p. 207.
16. Quoted in Thomas, *Madrid: A Traveller's Reader*, p. 127.
17. Ibid.; no nineteenth-century account of Spain is without its blind beggar.
18. Parsons, *A Cultural History of Madrid*, p. 49.
19. Gautier, quoted in Thomas, *Madrid*, p. 109.
20. It would be impossible to list all the significant cafés in nineteenth-century Madrid; they were especially prolific in the second half of the century.
21. The reference is to the first Carlist War, 1833–9.
22. Martínez Ruiz ('Azorín'), *Castilla*, p. 10.

23. Ibid., p. 12.
24. M. Fiter, 'Asaltos, secuestros y leyendas: cuando Madrid era un nido de bandoleros', *El Independiente*, 28 February 2021.
25. Navascués Palacio, 'Madrid y su transformación urbana en el siglo XIX', pp. 412–13.
26. Juliá, *Transición: Historia de una política española (1937–2017)*, p. 15.
27. Galdós, quoted in Thomas, *Madrid*, p. 126.

Pleasures and anxieties

1. Juliá, 'Introducción: La frustración histórica de una capital' in Juliá, Ringrose & Segura, *Madrid: Historia de una capital*.
2. Parsons, *A Cultural History of Madrid: Modernity and the Urban Spectacle*, p. 34.
3. Galdós, *La de Bringas*, p. 303.
4. Galdós, *Fortunata y Jacinta*, quotation from Galdós, *Fortunata and Jacinta* (A.M. Gullón, trans.), p. 351.
5. Ibid., quotation from Galdós, *Fortunata and Jacinta*, p. 350.
6. Galdós, *Tristana* (M. Jull Costa, trans.), p. 3.
7. Ibid., p. 5.
8. Galdós, *Miau*, p. 16.
9. Galdós, *Misericordia*, p. 91.
10. Galdós, *Miau*, pp. 268–9.
11. Ibid., p. 271.
12. Beruete, *Vista de Madrid desde la Pradera de San Isidro*, 1909, Museo del Prado, Madrid.
13. Baroja, *La busca*, p. 8.
14. Ugarte, *Madrid 1900: The Capital as Cradle of Literature and Culture*, p. 57.
15. Baroja, 'Crónica: Hampa', *El Pueblo Vasco*, 1903; quoted in Parsons, *A Cultural History of Madrid*, p. 59.
16. Galdós, *Tristana*, p. 78.
17. Baroja, *La busca*, p. 51.
18. Parsons, *A Cultural History of Madrid*, p. 65.
19. Carmen del Moral, *La sociedad madrileña fin de siglo y Baroja*; quoted in Ugarte, *Madrid 1900*, p. 58.
20. Baroja, *Mala hierba*, p. 13.
21. Parsons, *A Cultural History of Madrid*, p. 34.
22. Ibid., p. 39.
23. Galdós, *Tristana*, p. 31.
24. Ibid., p. 32.
25. Ibid., p. 49.
26. Alas, *La Regenta* (J. Rutherford, trans.), p. 366.
27. Ibid., p. 370.
28. Ibid., p. 377.
29. Ibid., p. 372.
30. Galdós, *Tristana*, p. 53.
31. Laurent, 'Gobierno provisional tras la revolución de septiembre de 1868', Biblioteca Nacional de España, Madrid, 1869.

32. A type of dance, believed to have originated in Bohemia, that is associated with the traditional customs of Madrid.
33. Parsons, *A Cultural History of Madrid*, p. 5.
34. Otero Carvajal, in Pallol Trigueros, *El Ensanche Norte. Chamberí 1860–1931: Un Madrid moderno*, p. 11.

New hopes, new conflicts

1. The two oldest labour organisations, the socialist UGT (General Union of Workers) and anarchist CNT (National Confederation of Labour), were founded in Barcelona in 1888 and 1910, respectively.
2. Juliá, *Vida y tiempo de Manuel Azaña, 1880–1940*, p. 75.
3. Ibid., p. 51.
4. Otero Carvajal, in Pallol Trigueros, *El Ensanche Norte. Chamberí 1860–1931: Un Madrid moderno*, p. 12.
5. Juliá, *Demasiados retrocesos: España 1898–2018*, p. 25.
6. Álvarez Junco and Shubert, *Spanish History since 1808*, p. 145.
7. Pallol Trigueros, 'Conquistar, democratizar y domesticar la noche en la ciudad moderna', p. 150.
8. Gómez de la Serna, quoted in Parsons, *A Cultural History of Madrid: Modernity and the Urban Spectacle*, p. 78.
9. Azorín, in José María Díez Borque, *Vistas literarias de Madrid entre siglos (XIX–XX)*.
10. López, *Gran Vía de Madrid, 1974–1981*, private collection.
11. Parsons, *A Cultural History of Madrid*, p. 88.
12. Castillo Cáceres, *Los años de Madridgrado*, pp. 186–7.
13. Parsons, *A Cultural History of Madrid*, p. 85.
14. Heroin addiction struck particularly hard in the poorer neighbourhoods south of Madrid; for a detailed account of this crisis, see Lezcano, *Madrid, 1983: Cuando todo se acelera*.
15. Burdiel, 'Emilia Pardo Bazán', in Álvarez Junco & Shubert (eds), *Nueva historia de la España contemporánea (1808–2018)*, p. 656.
16. Founded in Madrid in 1923 and one of the most intellectually cosmopolitan journals in the world at that time, the first phase of the *Revista de Occidente* lasted until 1936.
17. Nash, *Madrid: A Cultural History*, p. 156.
18. García Morente, quoted in Trapiello, *Las armas y las letras*, p. 576.
19. Nash, *Madrid*, p. 162.
20. Parsons, *A Cultural History of Madrid*, p. 99.
21. Borges, quoted in ibid., p. 103.
22. A popular celebration of open-air music and dancing, usually held to coincide with a traditional festival.
23. Ibid., p. 93.
24. Jiménez Torres, *La palabra ambigua: Los intelectuales en España (1889–2019)*, p. 67.
25. Foxá, *De corte a checa*, quoted in Sánchez Zapatero, *Arde Madrid: Narrativa y Guerra Civil*, pp. 145–6.
26. Juliá, *Vida y tiempo de Manuel Azaña, 1880–1940*, p. 108.
27. Juliá, *Demasiados retrocesos*, p. 118.

28. Ibid., p. 119.
29. Castillo Cáceres, *Los años de Madridgrado*, p. 188.
30. Ibid., p. 144.
31. Rámila, 'Hildegart Rodríguez: la historia que conmocionó a la II república española', p. 10.
32. Ibid., p. 13.
33. The story of Aurora Rodríguez is the subject of the 2020 Almudena Grandes novel, *La madre de Frankenstein*.
34. Baroja, *El árbol de la ciencia*, p. 18.
35. Ibid.
36. Juliá, 'Economic Crisis, Social Conflict and the Popular Front: Madrid 1931–6', p. 140.
37. Ibid., p. 141.
38. Ibid., p. 146.
39. Ibid., p. 148.
40. Ibid., p. 151.

The city under siege

1. Machado, quoted in Pérez Segura, 'La ciudad se despierta. Madrid y la cultura de lo nuevo', p. 29.
2. Chaves Nogales, *La defensa de Madrid*, quoted in ibid., p. 30.
3. Barea, *The Clash* (I. Barea, trans.), pp. 107–10; Herrera Petere, *Acero de Madrid*, pp. 58–60.
4. Juliá, Ringrose & Segura, *Madrid: Historia de una capital*, chapter 31.
5. The term 'fifth columnist' (*quinta columnista*), to describe sympathisers embedded among an enemy population, originated with the siege of Madrid in 1936. It is often ascribed to General Emilio Mola, referring to four Nationalist columns approaching Madrid, with a 'fifth column' of sympathisers already in the city.
6. Moreno Villa, quoted in Trapiello, *Las armas y las letras*, pp. 119–20; Sánchez Zapatero, *Arde Madrid: Narrativa y Guerra Civil*, p. 204.
7. Juan Iturralde, *Días de llamas*, quoted in Sánchez Zapatero, *Arde Madrid*, p. 415.
8. Muñoz Molina, *In the Night of Time* (E. Grossman, trans.), p. 3.
9. Orwell, *Homage to Catalonia*, p. 9.
10. Zúñiga, *Recuerdos de vida*, p. 32.
11. Castillo Cáceres, *Los años de Madridgrado*, p. 162.
12. Trapiello, *Las armas y las letras*, p. 109.
13. Castillo Cáceres, *Los años de Madridgrado*, p. 155.
14. Trapiello, *Las armas y las letras*, p. 110.
15. Herrera Petere, *Acero de Madrid*, p. 112.
16. Sánchez Pérez, 'Política y sociedad en el Madrid del siglo XX', p. 555.
17. Gellhorn, *The Face of War: Writings from the Frontline, 1937–85*, pp. 24–5.
18. Chaves Nogales, 'Y a lo lejos, una lucecita', in *A sangre y fuego: Héroes, bestias y mártires de España*, pp. 75–103.
19. Castillo Cáceres, *Los años de Madridgrado*, p. 260.
20. Sánchez Zapatero, *Arde Madrid*, p. 161.
21. It goes without saying this is an extraordinarily reductive vision of Castile.
22. Castillo Cáceres, *Los años de Madridgrado*, p. 270.

23. Tremlett, *The International Brigades: Fascism, Freedom and the Spanish Civil War*, p. 215.
24. Campoamor, *La revolución española vista por una republicana*.
25. Fortún, quoted in Sánchez Zapatero, *Arde Madrid*, p. 241.
26. Medina-Navascués, *Sobre mis escombros*.
27. Medina-Navascués, quoted in Sánchez Zapatero, *Arde Madrid*, p. 260.
28. Baroja, quoted in ibid., p. 382.
29. See Jiménez Torres, *La palabra ambigua: Los intelectuales en España (1889–2019)*.
30. Nash, *Madrid: A Cultural History*, p. 165.
31. Sánchez Zapatero, *Arde Madrid*, p. 318.

Ways of healing

1. For this argument see also Martínez de Pisón, 'El año decisivo'.
2. Martínez de Pisón, *Castillos de fuego*, p. 378.
3. Judt, *Postwar: A History of Europe since 1945*, p. 91.
4. Balfour, in Carr (ed.), *Spain: A History*, pp. 268–9.
5. Zúñiga, *Recuerdos de vida*, p. 54.
6. Ibid., pp. 58–9.
7. Ibid., p. 59.
8. In November 1936, thousands of prisoners of the Republic were taken from their cells in Madrid and driven to the surrounds of Paracuellos de Jarama to the east of the city, where they were systematically murdered.
9. The 'Thirteen Roses' were a group of young socialist women, aged between 18 and 29, collectively executed by the incoming regime in August 1939.
10. El Valle de los Caídos (The Valley of the Fallen) at Cuelgamuros, some 50 kilometres north-west of Madrid.
11. Preston, *Franco*, p. 409.
12. Castillo Cáceres, *Los años de Madridgrado*, p. 252.
13. Millás, *El mundo*, p. 24.
14. Lezcano, *Madrid 1983: Cuando todo se acelera*, p. 14.
15. Bahamonde Magro & Otero Carvajal, 'Madrid, de territorio fronterizo a región metropolitana', p. 98.
16. Fusi, 'Pensar España'.
17. Jiménez Torres, *La palabra ambigua: Los intelectuales en España (1889–2019)*, p. 124.
18. Padilla, *A finales de enero: La historia de amor más trágica de la Transición*, p. 27.
19. Pidal, quoted in Kamen, *The Disinherited: The Exiles Who Created Spanish Culture*, p. 424.
20. Semprún, quoted in ibid., p. 422.
21. Azorín, quoted in ibid., p. 425.
22. Umbral, *La noche que llegué al Café Gijón*, p. 254.
23. Balfour, in Carr, *Spain*, p. 269.
24. This argument is developed by many authors, including Juliá in *Demasiados retrocesos: España 1898–2018*, who sees a repeating historic cycle of promise and failure.
25. Martín Gaite, *Fragmentos de interior*, p. 24.

26. Ibid., p. 28.
27. Del Molino, *Contra la España vacía*, p. 173.
28. Gascón, *Un hípster en la España vacía* (2020); *La muerte del hípster* (2021).
29. Umbral, *La noche que llegué al Café Gijón*, pp. 141–2.
30. Juliá, *Demasiados retrocesos*, p. 204.
31. Ibid., p. 214.
32. Padilla, *A finales de enero*, p. 59.
33. Marías, *Berta Isla* (M. Jull Costa, trans.), pp. 20–1.

The world turned upside down

1. Judt, *Postwar: A History of Europe since 1945*, p. 3.
2. Ibid., p. 523.
3. Marías, *Thus Bad Begins*, p. 33
4. Umbral, *La noche que llegué al Café Gijón*, p. 84.
5. Llamazares, *El cielo de Madrid*, p. 67.
6. Algaba Pérez, 'A propósito de la Movida madrileña: un acercamiento a la cultura juvenil desde la Historia', p. 324.
7. Del Molino, *Contra la España vacía*.
8. Lezcano, 'Maldito Caballo', in *Madrid, 1983: Cuando todo se acelera*, pp. 41–58.
9. Ibid.
10. Ibid., pp. 46–9; despite being discredited, these theories are still often postulated.
11. Ibid., p. 51.

The new behemoth

1. Nash, *Madrid: A Cultural History*, p. 5.
2. Ibid., p. 147.
3. Elliott, *Imperial Spain 1469–1716*, p. 378.
4. A cheap inn, usually more affordable than a *pensión*.
5. A traditional Madrid stew.
6. López Carcelén, *Atlas ilustrado de la historia de Madrid*, p. 31.
7. 15 May: as is the custom in Spain, key events are marked by reference to their date and month.
8. Castillo Cáceres, *Los años de Madridgrado*, p. 255.
9. See Jiménez Torres & Villamediana González, *The Configuration of the Spanish Public Sphere*.
10. Cameron, 'Spain in Crisis: 15-M and the Culture of Indignation', p. 3.
11. Padilla, *A finales de enero: La historia de amor más trágica de la Transición*, p. 90.

Bibliography

Alas, L. *La Regenta* (J. Rutherford, trans.), Penguin Books, London, 2005

Aldecoa, I. *Neutral Corner* (photographs by Ramón Masats), Editorial Lumen, Barcelona, 1962; Penguin Random House, Barcelona, 2015

Aldecoa, I. *Cuentos completos*, Alianza Editorial, Madrid, 1973

Algaba Pérez, B. 'A propósito de la Movida madrileña: un acercamiento a la cultura juvenil desde la Historia', *Pasado y memoria*, 21: 319–29, 2020

Almagro-Gorbea, M. 'Las primeras huellas humanas. La prehistoria y sus yacimientos en las tierras madrileñas', in Fernández García, 2008, pp. 99–115

Alvar Ezquerra, A. 'La elección de la Corte: La política en los siglos XVI y XVII', in Fernández García, 2008, pp. 139–65

Alvarado Planas, J. & Oliva Manso, G. *El fuero de Madrid*, Agencia Estatal Boletín Oficial del Estado, Madrid, 2009

Álvarez Junco, J. *Mater Dolorosa: la idea de España en el siglo XIX*, Taurus, Madrid, 2001 (ebook)

Álvarez Junco, J. & Shubert, A. *Spanish History since 1808*, Arnold, London, 2000

Álvarez Junco, J. & Shubert, A. (eds). *Nueva historia de la España contemporánea (1808–2018)*, Galaxia Gutenberg, Barcelona, 2018

Andreu Mediero, E. 'El Madrid medieval', *Caesaraugusta*, 78: 687–98, Institución Fernando el Católico, Zaragoza, 2007

Anon. *La vida de Lazarillo de Tormes*, Biblioteca EDAF, Madrid, 1987

Aparisi Laporta, L.-M. 'Legado madrileño de Carlos III'; Instituto de Estudios Madrileños, *Ciclo de Conferencias: III Centenario del nacimiento de Carlos III*, 169–99, Consejo Superior de Investigaciones Científicas, Madrid, 2017

Aponte, A. 'Las santas pascuas', *The Objective*, 25 December 2021, https://theobjective.com/elsubjetivo/zibaldone/2021-12-25/las-santas-pascuas/

Ara, J. *El Bosco*, Aldeasa, Madrid, 2000

Arroyo Ilera, F. 'La imagen del agua: ideas y nociones hidrográficas en las relaciones topográficas de Felipe II', *Madrid: Revista de arte, geografía e historia*, 1: 155–94, Consejería de Educación de la Comunidad de Madrid, Madrid, 1998

Asenjo González, M. 'Los cambios territoriales de la provincia de Madrid', in Fernández García, 2008, pp. 71–97

Aub, M. *La Calle de Valverde*, Cátedra, Madrid, 1985

Ayuntamiento de Madrid. *Las villas romanas de Madrid. Madrid en época romana*, exh. cat., Madrid, 1995

Azorín, F. *Leyendas e historias del barrio de las Letras*, Ediciones La Librería, Madrid, 2015

Bahamonde Magro, Á. & Otero Carvajal, L.-E. 'Madrid, de territorio fronterizo a región metropolitana', in Fusi, J. (ed.), *España. Autonomías*, Espasa-Calpe, Madrid, 1989

—— (eds). *La sociedad madrileña durante la Restauración 1876–1931*, 2 vols, Consejería de Cultura de la Comunidad de Madrid, Madrid, 1989

Barbeito Díez, J.-M. 'El Palacio del Buen Retiro: ideas para una arquitectura', *El Paseo del Prado y el Buen Retiro, paisaje de las artes y las ciencias: Ciclo de conferencias*, 15–60, Escuela Técnica Superior de Arquitectura, Madrid, 2020

Barea, A. *The Clash* (I. Barea, trans.), Fontana, London, 1972

Baroja, P. *La busca*, Biblioteca El Mundo, Madrid, 2001

—— *Mala hierba*, Biblioteca El Mundo, Madrid, 2001

—— *Aurora roja*, Biblioteca El Mundo, Madrid, 2001

—— *El árbol de la ciencia*, Alianza Editorial, Madrid, 2015

Barón, J. (ed.). *El Greco y la pintura moderna*, Museo Nacional del Prado, Madrid, 2014

Blasco Esquivias, B. 'Madrid, utopía y realidad de una ciudad capital', *Madrid: Revista de arte, geografía e historia*, 1: 47–72, Consejería de Educación de la Comunidad de Madrid, Madrid, 1998

Blasco Ibáñez, V. *La maja desnuda*, Cátedra, Madrid, 1998

Bolufer, M. 'Reasonable Sentiments: Sensibility and Balance in Eighteenth-Century Spain', in Delgado et al., 2016

Borrow, G. *The Bible in Spain*, Cassell and Company, London, 1908 (transcribed to Project Gutenberg e-book edition)

Bravo Lozano, J. 'Economía y sociedad bajo los Austrias', in Fernández García, 2008, pp. 189–215

Brown, J. *Velázquez: Painter and Courtier*, Yale University Press, New Haven and London, 1986

Brown, J. & Elliott, J. *A Palace for a King: The Buen Retiro and the Court of Philip IV*, Yale University Press, New Haven and London, 1980

Calvo Poyato, J. *El milagro del Prado: La polémica evacuación de sus obras maestras durante la guerra civil por el Gobierno de la República*, Arzalia Ediciones, Madrid, 2018

Calvo Serraller, F. *Del futuro al pasado. Vanguardia y tradición en el arte español contemporáneo*, Alianza Editorial, Madrid, 1990

Calvo-Sotelo, P. *Leopoldo Calvo-Sotelo: Un retrato intelectual*, Marcial Pons, Madrid, 2010

Cameron, B. 'Spain in Crisis: 15-M and the Culture of Indignation', *Journal of Spanish Cultural Studies*, 15: 1–2: 1–11, February 2015

Carbajo Isla, M. 'La inmigración a Madrid (1600–1850)', *Reis*, 32: 67–100, Centro de Investigaciones Sociológicas, Madrid, 1985

Carr, R. (ed.). *Spain: A History*, Oxford University Press, Oxford, 2000

Carrasco Martínez, A. 'Ciudad y sociedad en el Madrid del siglo XVIII', *Cuadernos de investigación histórica*, 27: 157–82, 2010

Castellanos Oñate, J.-M. *El Madrid medieval*, madrid-medieval.blogspot.com

Castellote, A. & Canals, J. *España a través de la fotografía 1839–2010*, Fundación MAPFRE, Madrid, 2013

Castillo Cáceres, F. *Los años de Madridgrado*, Fórcola Ediciones, Madrid, 2016 (ebook)

Castillo Oreja, M.-Á. 'Al este de la corte: los valles del Jarama y del Henares. Alcalá y su entorno', in Fernández García, 2008, pp. 322–45

Castillo Solórzano, A. *Las harpías en Madrid y coche de las estafas* (1631), http://www.cervantesvirtual.com/nd/ark:/59851/bmcsb408

Cayetano Martín, C. 'Lo municipal en la obra de Galdós', Instituto de Estudios Madrileños, *Ciclo de Conferencias: 2020: Año Galdosiano, madrileño y novelesco*, 59–76, Consejo Superior de Investigaciones Científicas, Madrid, 2020

Cebrián, M. *Tres Madrides literarios*, Letras Libres, 1 March 2021, https://www.letraslibres.com/espana-mexico/revista/tres-madrides-literarios

Cela, C.-J. *La Colmena*, Editorial Noguer, Barcelona, 1982

Cepeda Adán, J. 'El Madrid cultural en la España de Felipe II', *Madrid: Revista de arte, geografía e historia*, 1: 21–46, Consejería de Educación de la Comunidad de Madrid, Madrid, 1998

Cervantes, M. *Don Quixote* (T. Smollett, trans.) André Deutsch, London, 1986
——— *Don Quixote* (J. Rutherford, trans.) Penguin Books, London, 2003

Chacel, R. *Barrio de Maravillas*, Círculo de Lectores, Barcelona, 1976

Chaves Nogales, M. *A sangre y fuego: Héroes, bestias y mártires de España*, Libros del Asteroide, Barcelona, 2013

Checa Cremades, J.L. (ed.). *Madrid en la prosa de viaje*, 2 vols, Consejería de Educación y Cultura, Comunidad de Madrid, 1992, 1993

Clavijo, R. *Narrative of the Embassy of Ruy Gonzalez de Clavijo to the Court of Timour, at Samarcand, AD 1403–6* (C.R. Markham, trans.), Hakluyt Society, London, 1859

Collins, R. *Early Medieval Spain: Unity in Diversity, 400–1000*, Palgrave Macmillan, London, 1995
——— *Visigothic Spain, 409–711*, Blackwell Publishers, Oxford, 2006

Contreras, J., Ladero, M. & Romano, D. *La expulsión de los judíos*, Cuadernos Historia 16, no. 99, Madrid, 1997

Corriente, F. 'El nombre de Madrid', in *Madrid del siglo IX al XI*, exh. cat., Consejería de Cultura, Dirección General de Patrimonio Cultural, Comunidad de Madrid, 1990

Cumming, L. *The Vanishing Man: In Search of Velázquez*, Vintage, London, 2017

De Diego García, E. 'El significado del dos de mayo', *Madrid: Revista de arte, geografía e historia*, 9: 13–26, Consejería de Educación de la Comunidad de Madrid, Madrid, 2007

Defoe, D. *Robinson Crusoe*, Penguin Books, Harmondsworth, 1977

Delgado, L.-E., Fernández, P. & Labanyi, J. (eds). *Engaging the Emotions in Spanish Culture and History*, Vanderbilt University Press, Nashville, 2016

Delibes, M. *El camino*, Destino, Barcelona, 1950
——— *El disputado voto del señor Cayo*, Editorial Planeta, Barcelona, 2017

Del Molino, S. *La España vacía*, Turner Publicaciones, Madrid, 2016
——— *Contra la España vacía*, Alfaguara, Madrid, 2021 (ebook)
——— *Un tal González*, Alfaguara, Barcelona, 2022

Del Río, M.-J. 'Represión y control de fiestas y diversiones en el Madrid de Carlos III'; Equipo Madrid de Estudios Históricos, *Carlos III, Madrid y la Ilustración: contradicciones de un proyecto reformista*, Siglo XXI Editores, Madrid, 1988

Del Río López, Á. *Errores en la historia de Madrid: Tópicos, mitos, bulos y mentiras*, Ediciones La Librería, Madrid, 2021

DeLillo, D. *The Names*, Picador, London, 1987

Diallo, K. 'La figura de Don Rodrigo Calderón a través de la literatura, s. XVII–XXI', doctoral thesis, Universidad Complutense, Madrid, 2009

Díez Borque, J.M. *Vistas literarias de Madrid entre siglos (XIX–XX)*, Comunidad de Madrid, Consejería de Educación y Cultura, Madrid, 1998

Dodds, J., Menocal, M.R. & Krasner Balbale, A. *The Arts of Intimacy: Christians, Jews and Muslims in the Making of Castilian Culture*, Yale University Press, New Haven and London, 2008

Domínguez Ortiz, A. 'Velázquez y su tiempo', in Museo del Prado, *Velázquez*, Ministerio de Cultura, Madrid, 1990

Elliott, J. *Imperial Spain 1469–1716*, Edward Arnold, London, 1963

——— *The Count-Duke of Olivares*, Yale University Press, New Haven and London, 1986

——— *Spain and its World, 1500–1700*, Yale University Press, New Haven and London, 1989

——— *Spain, Europe and the Wider World, 1500–1800*, Yale University Press, New Haven and London, 2009

Ena Bordonada, Á. 'La literatura y la sociedad madrileña en la Restauración', in Bahamonde Magro & Otero Carvajal, 1989, vol. 2, pp. 163–80

Equipo Madrid de Estudios Históricos. *Carlos III, Madrid y la Ilustración: contradicciones de un proyecto reformista*, Siglo XXI Editores, Madrid, 1988

Escobar, J. 'Map as Tapestry: Science and Art in Pedro Teixeira's 1656 Representation of Madrid', *Art Bulletin*, 96:1: 50–69, 2014

Espadas Burgos, M. *La España de Isabel II*, Cuadernos Historia 16, no. 54, Madrid, 1985

——— 'La vida política de Madrid durante el siglo XIX', in Fernández García, 2008, pp. 421–45

Fernández García, A. (ed.). *Madrid, de la Prehistoria a la Comunidad Autónoma*, Consejería de Educación de la Comunidad de Madrid, Madrid, 2008

Fernández-González, L. *Philip II of Spain and the Architecture of Empire*, Pennsylvania State University Press, University Park, 2021

Fernández Hoyos, M.-A. 'El Madrid de los Austrias', Cuadernos Historia 16, no. 4, Madrid, 1985

Fernández Talaya, M.-T. 'La vivienda madrileña en tiempos de Cervantes', Instituto de Estudios Madrileños, *Ciclo de Conferencias: Miguel de Cervantes Saavedra y Madrid*, 45–68, Consejo Superior de Investigaciones Científicas, Madrid, 2017

Fernández y González, M. *La leyenda de Madrid: orígenes, historia, tradiciones y costumbres de esta villa y corte*, Librería de León P. Villaverde, Madrid, 1882

Fletcher, R. 'The Early Middle Ages, 700–1250', in Carr, 2000

Ford, R. *Gatherings from Spain*, 1846, at https://www.gutenberg.org/files/41611/41611-h/41611-h.htm

Fradera, J.-M. 'La materia de todos los sueños', *Revista de Libros*, 1 March 2002

Fraguas de Pablo, R. 'Expulsión de la Compañía de Jesús bajo el reinado de Carlos III', Instituto de Estudios Madrileños, *Ciclo de Conferencias: III Centenario del nacimiento de Carlos III*, 295–308, Consejo Superior de Investigaciones Científicas, Madrid, 2017

Friedrich, M. *The Jesuits: A History* (J.N. Dillon, trans.), Princeton University Press, Princeton, 2022

Fuente, M.-J. *La ciudad castellana medieval*, Cuadernos Historia 16, no. 204, Madrid, 1985

Fuentes, C. 'Introduction' to Cervantes, *Don Quixote* (T. Smollett, trans.), André Deutsch, London, 1986

Fusi, J.-P. 'Pensar España', *Ethic*, 20 July 2023

Galán Cabilla, J.-L. 'Madrid y los cementerios en el siglo XVIII: el fracaso de una reforma', in Equipo Madrid de Estudios Históricos, *Carlos III*, 1988, pp. 255–98

Gallarda Romero, V. *Fuimos indómitas: los oficios desaparecidos de las mujeres de Madrid*, Ediciones La Librería, Madrid, 2021

García Alcalá, J.-A. 'Los pueblos del sur en la edad moderna', in Fernández García, 2008, pp. 347–63

García Ballesteros, J.-Á. & Revilla González, F. 'El Madrid de la posguerra', *Cuadernos de UMER* 41, Madrid, 2006

García de Cortázar, F. *Biografía de España*, DeBolsillo, Barcelona, 2001
—— *Los perdedores de la historia de España*, Planeta, Barcelona, 2009

García de Cortázar, F. & González Vesga, J.M. *Breve historia de España*, Alianza Editorial, Madrid, 2012

García Ortega, A. *El mapa de la vida*, Seix Barral, Barcelona, 2009
—— *Fantasmas del escritor*, Galaxia Gutenberg, Barcelona, 2017

Gascón, D. *Un hípster en la España vacía*, Random House, Barcelona, 2020
—— *La muerte del hípster*, Random House, Barcelona, 2021

Gellhorn, M. *The Face of War: Writings from the Frontline, 1937–85*, Eland, London, 2016

Gil-Benumeya, D. *Madrid islámico. La historia recuperada*, Madrid Destino Cultura Turismo y Negocio SA, Madrid, 2018

Giralt Torrente, M. *Tiempo de vida*, Anagrama, Barcelona, 2010
—— *The End of Love* (K. Silver, trans.), McSweeney's, San Francisco, 2013

González Yanci, M. 'Evolución urbana de Madrid en torno a El Retiro', Instituto de Estudios Madrileños, *Ciclo de Conferencias: El parque del Buen Retiro*, 117–51, Consejo Superior de Investigaciones Científicas, Madrid, 2004

González Zymla, H. 'Los orígenes de Madrid a la luz de la documentación del archivo de la Real Academia de la Historia', *Madrid: Revista de arte, geografía e historia*, 5: 13–44, Consejería de Educación de la Comunidad de Madrid, Madrid, 2002.

Grandes, A. *The Frozen Heart* (F. Wynne, trans.), Phoenix, London, 2011
—— *Los pacientes del Doctor García*, Tusquets, Barcelona, 2017
—— *La madre de Frankenstein*, Tusquets, Barcelona, 2020

Haidt, R. 'Emotional Contagion in a Time of Cholera: Sympathy, Humanity and Hygiene in Mid-Nineteenth Century Spain', in Delgado, L.-E., Fernández, P. & Labanyi, J., 2016, pp. 77–94

Hemingway, E. *Death in the Afternoon*, Vintage Books, London, 2000

Hernández, C.N. (ed.). *Cuadernillos de poesía: Luis de Góngora*, Panamericana Editorial, Bogotá, 2000

Hernández de Miguel, C. *Los campos de concentración de Franco*, Penguin Random House, Barcelona, 2019

Herrera Petere, J. *Acero de Madrid* (1938), Biblioteca Libre, Omegalfa, 2019

Huertas Vázquez, E. 'La política de los ilustrados ante los espectáculos y las diversiones publicas', Instituto de Estudios Madrileños, *Ciclo de Conferencias: III Centenario del nacimiento de Carlos III*, 453–83, Consejo Superior de Investigaciones Científicas, Madrid, 2017

Hughes, R. *Goya*, Vintage, London, 2003

Instituto de Estudios Madrileños. *Ciclo de Conferencias: San Isidro y Madrid*, Consejo Superior de Investigaciones Científicas, Madrid, 2012

—— *Ciclo de Conferencias: El Cardenal Cisneros en Madrid*, Consejo Superior de Investigaciones Científicas, Madrid, 2017

—— *Ciclo de Conferencias: La Huella de Santa Teresa de Jesús en Madrid*, Consejo Superior de Investigaciones Científicas, Madrid, 2017

—— *Ciclo de Conferencias: IV Centenario de la Plaza Mayor*, Consejo Superior de Investigaciones Científicas, Madrid, 2018

—— *Ciclo de Conferencias: El Paseo del Prado y el Buen Retiro, Paisaje de las Artes y las* Ciencias, Consejo Superior de Investigaciones Científicas, Madrid, 2020

Izquierdo Benito, R. 'Población y sociedad en época omeya', in *Madrid del siglo IX al XI*, exh. cat., Consejería de Cultura, Dirección General de Patrimonio Cultural, Comunidad de Madrid, 1990

Jiménez, P., Castellote, A. & Descalzo, A. *España contemporánea: Fotografía, pintura y moda*, Fundación MAPFRE, Madrid, 2013

Jiménez Barca, A. *Deudas Pendientes*, El tercer nombre SA, Madrid, 2006

—— *La botella del náufrago*, RBA Libros, Barcelona, 2011

Jiménez Torres, D. *La palabra ambigua: Los intelectuales en España (1889–2019)*, Taurus, Barcelona, 2023

Jiménez Torres, D. & Villamediana González, L. *The Configuration of the Spanish Public Sphere*, Berghahn Books, New York, 2019

Judt, T. *Postwar: A History of Europe since 1945*, Vintage Books, London, 2010

Juliá, S. 'Economic Crisis, Social Conflict and the Popular Front: Madrid 1931–6', in Preston, P., 1984

—— *Historia de las dos Españas*, Penguin Random House, Barcelona, 2014

—— *Vida y tiempo de Manuel Azaña, 1880–1940*, DeBolsillo, Barcelona, 2015

—— *Transición: Historia de una política española (1937–2017)*, Galaxia Gutenberg, Barcelona, 2017 (ebook)

—— *Demasiados retrocesos: España 1898–2018*, Galaxia Gutenberg, Barcelona, 2019 (ebook)

Juliá, S., Ringrose, D. & Segura, C. *Madrid: Historia de una capital*, Alianza, Madrid, 1994 (ebook)

Kamen, H. *Philip of Spain*, Yale University Press, New Haven and London, 1997

—— *Philip V of Spain: The King Who Reigned Twice*, Yale University Press, New Haven and London, 2001

—— *Spain's Road to Empire*, Allen Lane, London, 2002

—— *Spain 1469–1714: A Society of Conflict*, Pearson, Harlow, 2005

—— *The Disinherited: The Exiles Who Created Spanish Culture*, Penguin Books, London, 2008

——— *The Escorial: Art and Power in the Renaissance*, Yale University Press, New Haven and London, 2010

Kulikowski, M. *Late Roman Spain and its Cities*, Johns Hopkins University Press, Baltimore, 2004

Larra, M.-J. *Artículos de costumbres* (1835), Editorial EDAF, Madrid, 1997

Leralta, J. *Madrid: Cuentos, leyendas y anécdotas*, vol. 1, Sílex, Madrid, 2001

Lezcano, A. *Madrid 1983: Cuando todo se acelera*, Libros del K.O., Madrid, 2021

Livy. *The War with Hannibal* (A. de Sélincourt, trans.), Penguin Books, London, 1977

Llamazares, J. *El cielo de Madrid*, Alfaguara, Madrid, 2005

López Carcelén, P. *Atlas ilustrado de la historia de Madrid*, Ediciones La Librería, Madrid, 2022

López García, J.-M. 'Protesta popular en el Madrid moderno: las lógicas del motín', Proceedings, III International Conference: *Strikes and Social Conflicts: Combined Historical Approaches to Conflict*, pp. 41–54, Bellaterra, Barcelona, 2016

Lopezosa Aparicio, C. 'Sobre los planes de intervención de José I en Madrid', *Cuadernos de Historia Moderna*, suppl. edn IX: 47–61, 2010

Loriga, R. *Sábado, domingo*, Alfaguara, Madrid, 2019

Lozano, I.R. 'El pueblo en armas. Vicálvaro y el golpe de 1936', *Espiral*, 22:64, September–December 2015

Lozón Urueña, I. *Madrid. Capital y Corte: Usos, costumbres y mentalidades en el siglo XVII*, Consejería de Cultura de la Comunidad de Madrid, Madrid, 2004

Luengo, J. & Dalmau, P. 'Writing Spanish History in the Global Age: Connections and Entanglements in the Nineteenth Century', *Journal of Global History*, 13:3, 2018

Lynch, J. *Spain under the Habsburgs*, vol. 1, Basil Blackwell, Oxford, 1981

——— *Bourbon Spain 1700–1808*, Basil Blackwell, Oxford, 1989

——— *The Hispanic World in Crisis and Change, 1598–1700*, Blackwell Publishers, Oxford, 1992

Macaulay, T. 'War of the Succession in Spain' (1833) in *Critical & Historical Essays, Volume Two*, J.M. Dent & Sons, London, 1907

Machado, A. *Campos de Castilla*, Editorial Biblioteca Nueva, Madrid, 2010

Maqueda Abreu, C. 'La corte española del barroco vista por los extranjeros', *Madrid: Revista de arte, geografía e historia*, 8: 11–34, Consejería de Educación de la Comunidad de Madrid, Madrid, 2006

Marías, Javier. *Corazón tan blanco*, DeBolsillo, Barcelona, 2006

——— *Mañana en la batalla piensa en mí*, DeBolsillo, Barcelona, 2006

——— *The Infatuations* (M. Jull Costa, trans.), Penguin Books, London, 2013

——— *Thus Bad Begins* (M. Jull Costa, trans.), Penguin Books, London, 2017

——— *Berta Isla* (M. Jull Costa, trans.), Hamish Hamilton, London, 2018

——— *Tomás Nevinson*, DeBolsillo, Barcelona, 2020

Marías, Julián. *Understanding Spain* (F.M. López-Morillas, trans.), University of Michigan Press, Ann Arbor, 1990

Marín Perellón, F.-J. 'Madrid: ¿Una ciudad para un rey?' in Equipo Madrid de Estudios Históricos, *Carlos III*, 1988, pp. 125–51

Martín-Santos, L. *Tiempo de silencio*, Seix Barral, Barcelona, 1961

Martín Gaite, C. *Fragmentos de interior*, Destino, Barcelona, 1976

——— *La búsqueda de interlocutor y otras búsquedas*, Destino, Barcelona, 1982

——— *Nubosidad variable*, Anagrama, Barcelona, 1992

Martínez, R. *Sobre el Madrid árabe, islámico y andalusí*, madridarabe.es

Martínez de Pisón, E. 'La formación de los suburbios madrileños en el paso del siglo XIX al XX', *Boletín informativo del seminario de derecho político de la Universidad de Salamanca*, 1: 251–7, 1964

Martínez de Pisón, I. *Enterrar a los muertos*, Seix Barral, Barcelona, 2005

———— 'El año decisivo', *Letras Libres*, October 2022, https://letraslibres.com/revista/el-ano-decisivo/

———— *Castillos de fuego*, Seix Barral, Barcelona, 2023

Martínez Ruiz, E. 'Un Rey, un aniversario, un recuerdo: Felipe II y el cuarto aniversario de su muerte', *Madrid: Revista de arte, geografía e historia*, 1: 15–20, Consejería de Educación de la Comunidad de Madrid, Madrid, 1998

Martínez Ruiz, J. ('Azorín'). *Castilla* (1912), Alianza Editorial, Madrid, 2013

McDonald, M. *Renaissance to Goya: Prints and Drawings from Spain*, British Museum Press, London, 2012

Mendoza, E. *Riña de gatos: Madrid 1936*, Planeta, Barcelona, 2010

Mesonero Romanos, R. *Escenas matritenses* (1851), Editorial Bruguera, Barcelona, 1967

———— *El antiguo Madrid: Paseos históricos-anecdóticos por las calles y casas de esta villa*, Madrid (1881), Biblioteca Virtual Miguel de Cervantes, Alicante, 1999, https://www.cervantesvirtual.com/

Micó, J.-M. *El oro de los siglos: Antología*, Austral, Barcelona, 2017

Millás, J.-J. *El mundo*, Planeta, Barcelona, 2007

Montero Díaz, J. & Cervera Gil, J. 'Madrid en los años treinta. Ambiente social, político, cultural y religioso', *Studia et Documenta*, 3: 13–39, 2009

Montero Reguera, J. 'Miguel de Cervantes: Un poeta en el final de sus días', Instituto de Estudios Madrileños, *Ciclo de Conferencias: Miguel de Cervantes Saavedra y Madrid*, 13–24, Consejo Superior de Investigaciones Científicas, Madrid, 2017

Montero Vallejo, M. 'Los primeros núcleos urbanos. Madrid antiguo y medieval', in Fernández García, 2008, pp. 117–36

Montoliú, P. *Madrid, Villa y Corte: Calles y Plazas*, Sílex, Madrid, 2002

Mora Palazón, A. 'El Madrid de Carlos III, al siglo XXI. El plano de Madrid de Tomás López de 1785', Instituto de Estudios Madrileños, *Ciclo de Conferencias: III Centenario del nacimiento de Carlos III*, 25–53, Consejo Superior de Investigaciones Científicas, Madrid, 2017

Moral, C. *El Madrid de Baroja*, Sílex, Madrid, 2001

Morena Bartolomé, Á. 'Arte y patrimonio en la sierra norte de Madrid', in Fernández García, 2008, pp. 365–86

Muñoz Fernández, Á. 'Franciscanos, cultura religiosa e identidad urbana en la villa de Madrid (Siglos XIII–XVI)', *Madrid: Revista de arte, geografía e historia*, 1: 555–72, Consejería de Educación de la Comunidad de Madrid, Madrid, 1998

Muñoz Molina, A. *In the Night of Time* (E. Grossman, trans.), Tuskar Rock Press, London, 2015

Museo Español de Arte Contemporáneo. *Fotógrafos de la escuela de Madrid: Obra 1950 / 1975*, Ministerio de Cultura, Madrid, 1988

Museo Nacional del Prado. *Velázquez*, Ministerio de Cultura, Madrid, 1990

Museo de San Isidro. *M-30: Un viaje al pasado*, exh. cat., Madrid, 2007

Nash, E. *Madrid: A Cultural History*, Interlink Books, Northampton, MA, 2017

National Gallery of Victoria, *Italian Masterpieces from Spain's Royal Court*, exh. cat., Melbourne, 2014

Navascués Palacio, P. 'Madrid, ciudad y arquitectura (1808–1898)', *Historia de Madrid*, Editorial Complutense, Madrid, 1994

—— 'Madrid y su transformación urbana en el siglo XIX', in Fernández García, 2008, pp. 389–419

Negredo, F. 'El Madrid de Velázquez: Mercado y propiedad inmobiliaria entre 1623 y 1650', *Madrid: Revista de arte, geografía e historia*, 2: 15–56, Consejería de Educación de la Comunidad de Madrid, Madrid, 1999

Ordaz, P. & Jiménez Barca, A. *Así fue la dictadura: Diez historias de la represión franquista*, Penguin Random House, Barcelona, 2018

Orwell, G. *Homage to Catalonia*, Penguin Books, Harmondsworth, Middlesex, 1974

Padilla, J. *A finales de enero: La historia de amor más trágica de la Transición*, Tusquets, Barcelona, 2019

Pallol Trigueros, R. *El Ensanche Norte. Chamberí 1860–1931: Un Madrid moderno*, La Catarata, Madrid, 2015

—— 'Conquistar, democratizar y domesticar la noche en la ciudad moderna. Modernización, desigualdad y conflicto en Madrid a comienzos del siglo XX', *Registros. Revista de Investigación Histórica*, 13:1: 149–65, 2017

—— 'La lucha por la calle. Conflictos en la redefinición del espacio público en las ciudades de comienzo de siglo XX', *Crisol*, 5: 1–34, 2019

Parker, G. *Imprudent King: A New Life of Philip II*, Yale University Press, New Haven and London, 2015

Parsons, D. *A Cultural History of Madrid: Modernity and the Urban Spectacle*, Berg, Oxford, 2003

Pellicer, J.-A. *Disertación histórico-geográfica sobre el origen, nombre y población de Madrid*, Imprenta de la Administración del Real Arbitrio de Beneficencia, Madrid, 1803

Pérez Galdós, B. *La de Bringas* (1884), Catedra, Madrid, 1983

—— *Miau* (1888), Alianza, Madrid, 1985

—— *Fortunata and Jacinta* (A. M. Gullón, trans.), Penguin Books, London, 1988

—— *Misericordia* (1897), PML Ediciones, Barcelona, 1994

—— *Tristana* (1892) (M. Jull Costa, trans.), New York Review of Books, New York, 2014

—— *Fortunata y Jacinta* (1887), Reino de Cordelia, Madrid, 2019

Pérez Sánchez, A.-E. 'Velázquez y su arte', in Museo del Prado, *Velázquez*, Ministerio de Cultura, Madrid, 1990

Pérez Segura, J. 'La ciudad se despierta. Madrid y la cultura de lo nuevo', in Various, 2018, pp. 19–33

Peyró, I. *Ya sentarás cabeza*, Libros de Asteroide, Barcelona, 2020

Phillips, C. 'The Allied Occupation of Madrid in 1710: A Turning Point in the War of the Spanish Succession', *Bulletin for Spanish and Portuguese Historical Studies*, 35:1, 2011

Preston, P. (ed.). *Revolution and War in Spain, 1931–1939*, Methuen, London, 1984

—— *Franco*, HarperCollins, London, 1993

—— *The Spanish Holocaust*, Harper Press, London, 2012

Puñal Fernández, T. 'Espacios madrileños de producción documental: el cuaderno de las primeras Cortes de Madrid de 1329', *Anales del Instituto de Estudios Madrileños*, 46: 21–49, 2006

———— 'Mercado y producción en el Madrid de los siglos XI y XII: una economía de frontera'; Instituto de Estudios Madrileños, *Ciclo de Conferencias: El Madrid de Alfonso VI*, Consejo Superior de Investigaciones Científicas, Madrid, 2012

———— 'El comercio madrileño en el entorno territorial y urbano de la baja edad media', *Edad Media*, 15: 115–33, Universidad de Valladolid, 2014

Quevedo, F. *Cuadernillos de poesía: selección*, Panamericana Editorial, Bogotá, 1997

———— *The Swindler* (M. Alpert, trans.), Penguin Books, London, 2003

Rámila, J. 'Hildegart Rodríguez: la historia que conmocionó a la II república española', *Quadernos de criminología: revista de criminología y ciencias forenses*, 18: 8–19, 2012

Ramos, R. & Revilla, F. *Historia de Madrid*, Ediciones La Librería, Madrid, 2007

Reilly, B. *The Contest of Christian and Muslim Spain, 1031–1157*, Blackwell Publishers, Oxford, 1992

———— *The Medieval Spains*, Cambridge University Press, Cambridge, 1993

Richardson, J. *The Romans in Spain*, Blackwell Publishers, Oxford, 1996

Ringrose, D. 'The Impact of a New Capital City: Madrid, Toledo, and New Castile, 1560–1660', *Journal of Economic History*, 33:4: 761–91, 1973

———— 'Historia urbana y urbanización en la España moderna', *Hispania*, 58: 489–512, Consejo Superior de Investigaciones Científicas, Instituto de Historia, Madrid, 2019

Rizzuto, C. 'Conversos, judíos y conspiración diabólica en la revuelta de las Comunidades de Castilla, 1520–1521', *Cuadernos de Historia Moderna*, 43:1: 65–84, 2018

Roca Barea, M.E. *Fracasología*, Espasa, Barcelona, 2019

Ruiz, A. *Medina Mayrit: The Origins of Madrid*, Algora Publishing, New York, 2011

Sainz de Robles, F.-C. *Breve Historia de Madrid*, Espasa-Calpe, Madrid, 1970

Sánchez Ferlosio, R. *El Jarama*, Destino, Barcelona, 2004

Sánchez Pérez, F. 'Política y sociedad en el Madrid del siglo XX', in Fernández García, 2008, pp. 541–63

Sánchez Zapatero, J. *Arde Madrid: Narrativa y Guerra Civil*, Espuela de Plata, Sevilla, 2020

Santos, F. *Día y Noche de Madrid* (1663), Cátedra, Madrid, 2017

Santos, J.A. (ed.). *Madrid en la prosa de viaje,* vols 3 & 4, Consejería de Educación y Cultura, Comunidad de Madrid, 1994, 1997

Serrano Rubio, R. 'La Quinta de Los Molinos', Instituto de Estudios Madrileños, *Ciclo de Conferencias: Parques y jardines madrileños*, 273–89, Consejo Superior de Investigaciones Científicas, Madrid, 2011

Simón Díaz, J. 'Madrid en la literatura durante la Restauración (1870–1931)', in Bahamonde Magro & Otero Carvajal 1989, vol. 2, pp. 139–62

Soto Carrasco, D. *La conquista del estado liberal: Ramiro Ledesma Ramos*, Kyrios, Valencia, 2013

Stanhope, A. *Extracts from the Correspondence of the Hon. Alexander Stanhope, British Minister at Madrid, 1690–1699*, John Murray, London, 1840; available online at the Wellcome Collection

Stendhal, *The Charterhouse of Parma* (M. Shaw, trans.), Penguin Books, London, 1958

Stewart, J. *Madrid: The History*, I.B. Tauris, London, 2015

Stradling, R.A. *Europe and the Decline of Spain*, Allen & Unwin, London, 1981

Swinburne, H. *Travels through Spain, in the Years 1775 and 1776*, P. Elmsly, London, 1789

Tarrero Alcón, M. 'Raíces cristianas de Madrid: Santa María La Real de la Almudena', Instituto de Estudios Madrileños, *Ciclo de Conferencias: El Madrid de Alfonso VI*, Consejo Superior de Investigaciones Científicas, Madrid, 2012

Thomas, H. (ed.). *Madrid: A Traveller's Reader*, Robinson, London, 2018

Tovar Martín, V. 'El desarrollo espacial y monumental de la ciudad hasta 1800', in Fernández García, 2008, pp. 167–87

Trapiello, A. *El rastro*, Destino, Barcelona, 2018

——— *Las armas y las letras*, Destino, Barcelona, 2019

——— *Madrid*, Destino, Barcelona, 2020

——— *Madrid 1945: La noche de los Cuatro Caminos*, Destino, Barcelona, 2022

Tremlett, G. *The International Brigades: Fascism, Freedom and the Spanish Civil War*, Bloomsbury, London, 2020

Ugarte, M. *Madrid 1900: The Capital as Cradle of Literature and Culture*, Pennsylvania State University Press, University Park, 1996

Umbral, F. *Diario de un español cansado*, Ediciones Destino, Barcelona, 1975

——— *La noche que llegué al Café Gijón*, Austral, Barcelona, 2012

Valdeleón, J., Pérez, J. & Juliá, S. *Historia de España*, Espasa, Barcelona, 2015

Valle-Inclán, R. *Luces de Bohemia* (1924), Austral, Barcelona, 2010

Various, *Madrid del siglo IX al XI*, exh. cat., Consejería de Cultura, Dirección General de Patrimonio Cultural, Comunidad de Madrid, 1990.

——— *Madrid 1830. La maqueta de León Gil de Palacio y su época*, exh. cat., Museo Municipal de Madrid, Madrid, 2006

——— (Ernesto Mallo, ed.), *Madrid negro*, Siruela, Madrid, 2016

——— *Letras liberadas. Propaganda cultura y artes gráficas en el Madrid de la Transición, 1975–1982*, exh. cat., Ayuntamiento de Madrid, 2017

——— *Pongamos que hablo de Madrid*, exh. cat., Ayuntamiento de Madrid, 2017

——— *Madrid. Musa de las artes*, exh. cat., Museo de Arte Contemporáneo, Ayuntamiento de Madrid, 2018

Zúñiga, J.E. *Recuerdos de vida*, Galaxia Gutenberg, Barcelona, 2019 (ebook)

Index